CHRISTIAN THEOLOGIES OF SALVATION

Christian Theologies of Salvation

A Comparative Introduction

Edited by
Justin S. Holcomb

NEW YORK UNIVERSITY PRESS
New York

NEW YORK UNIVERSITY PRESS
New York
www.nyupress.org

© 2017 by New York University
All rights reserved

Chapter 13 adapts material previously published in *International Journal of Systematic Theology* 11:4 (October 2009): 428–47; copyright 2009; reprinted by permission; and in "Union with Christ and the Double Grace: Calvin's Theology and Its Early Reception," 49–71 in *Calvin's Theology and Its Reception: Disputes, Developments, and New Possibilities*, ed. J. Todd Billings and I. John Hesselink; copyright 2012, Westminster John Knox Press; reprinted by permission.

References to Internet websites (URLs) were accurate at the time of writing. Neither the author nor New York University Press is responsible for URLs that may have expired or changed since the manuscript was prepared.

Library of Congress Cataloging-in-Publication Data
Names: Holcomb, Justin S., 1973– editor.
Title: Christian theologies of salvation : a comparative introduction / edited by Justin S. Holcomb.
Description: New York : NYU Press, 2017. | Includes bibliographical references and index.
Identifiers: LCCN 2017008037| ISBN 9780814724439 (cl : alk. paper) | ISBN 9780814762943 (pb : alk. paper)
Subjects: LCSH: Salvation—Christianity—History of doctrines.
Classification: LCC BT751.3 .C48 2017 | DDC 234.09—dc23
LC record available at https://lccn.loc.gov/2017008037

New York University Press books are printed on acid-free paper, and their binding materials are chosen for strength and durability. We strive to use environmentally responsible suppliers and materials to the greatest extent possible in publishing our books.

Manufactured in the United States of America

10 9 8 7 6 5 4 3 2 1

CONTENTS

Introduction: Mapping Theologies of Salvation   1
Justin S. Holcomb

PART I. PATRISTIC

1. Patristic Theologies of Salvation: An Introduction   11
D. H. Williams

2. Origen of Alexandria   22
Thomas P. Scheck

3. Irenaeus of Lyons   41
John Behr

4. Saint Augustine   59
David Vincent Meconi, SJ

5. Athanasius   76
John Yocum

6. The Cappadocians   95
Andrew Radde-Gallwitz

PART II. MIDDLE AGES

7. Theologies of Salvation in the Middle Ages: An Introduction   115
David Hogg

8. Anselm of Canterbury   124
Giles E. M. Gasper

9. Saint Thomas Aquinas   143
R. Jared Staudt

10. Julian of Norwich   160
Kerrie Hide

PART III. REFORMATION AND CATHOLIC COUNTER-REFORMATION

11. Theologies of Salvation in the Reformation and Counter-Reformation: An Introduction 181
    Frank A. James III

12. Martin Luther 191
    Carl R. Trueman

13. John Calvin 208
    J. Todd Billings

14. The Catholic Reform 225
    Donald S. Prudlo

PART IV. EIGHTEENTH TO TWENTY-FIRST CENTURIES

15. Theologies of Salvation from the Eighteenth to Twenty-First Centuries: An Introduction 251
    Ryan M. Reeves

16. John Wesley 261
    Thomas H. McCall

17. Friedrich Schleiermacher's Theology of Salvation 281
    James R. Gordon

18. Karl Barth 300
    Tom Greggs

19. Hans Urs von Balthasar and Karl Rahner 318
    W. T. Dickens

20. Gustavo Gutiérrez 344
    Michael Edward Lee

About the Contributors 363
Index 369

Introduction

Mapping Theologies of Salvation

JUSTIN S. HOLCOMB

For us and for our salvation. . . .
—Nicene Creed

For many Christians, the Nicene Creed wonderfully encapsulates the fundamental teachings of historic Christianity and the entire good news of the gospel into a short and rich summary.[1] It describes the Triune God, who turns toward humanity in the person of Jesus, the God-man who suffered, died, rose again, and ascended. Additionally, the Creed goes on to express our future hope, which is a motivating factor in the Christian life.

As a creed recited in numerous churches every Sunday, many are very familiar with its contents. While significant as an historical document, the Nicene Creed reflects the Christian teaching that salvation is closely related to the person and work of Jesus Christ. Throughout the history of the Christian tradition, theologians have written, preached, and debated the doctrine of salvation. What is salvation? How is one saved? From what is one saved? The theologies of salvation in the Christian tradition encompass a wide variety of beliefs and practices.

Christian theology is reflection on the one whom Christians confess as Lord and Savior. This reflection has been informed by the interest in salvation. The role of soteriology is to show why and how Jesus is significant. All Christian theologians would agree that Jesus Christ is the one through whom salvation comes, but explaining what that means has been the subject of debate throughout the tradition.

What are we to make of it? This book provides a map through the maze of options and implications of the various theologies of salvation. It is an introduction to the theologies of salvation of the major theologians and an investigation of these views, primarily their similarities and differences and how they are employed.

The topic of salvation is complex and multilayered, with numerous implications for both the corporate church and the individual believer, a discipline that generates a myriad of questions.

How do you define "salvation"? How and why is one saved? From what is one saved? Is a particular theory of salvation primary, such as moral transformation, *Christus victor*, ransom, satisfaction, penal substitution, deification, or moral example? How is salvation accomplished? By what means is it applied? Faith? Baptism? Obedience? What is Jesus's role in salvation? What is the scope of salvation? Individual? Collective? Cosmic? What about the afterlife: heaven, hell, purgatory, soul sleep, and annihilation?

To ask these questions about salvation is to set forth on a dark and winding path—there seems no end to the list of questions. But we are not the first to ask them; in fact, two thousand years of Christian tradition provide guideposts to mark our way and lampposts to illuminate our path. This book traces what the prominent Christian theologians have said about salvation. The goal of this volume is to map the terrain of the Christian tradition on salvation and let the contours speak for themselves. This is not a work of dogmatic or systematic theology that posits a specific doctrine of salvation that must be rigidly followed. Rather, this book investigates the history of Christian thought by looking at major figures in the tradition and describing their unique contributions to the lingering and over-arching questions about salvation.

The phrase "theologies of salvation" is used herein to refer to these expressions of salvation throughout church history. A wide range of theologies of salvation have emerged throughout church history, new theologies of salvation continue to emerge today, and even more theologies of salvation will likely emerge in the years to come.

Our investigation will find that different theologies of salvation exist, not because the Christian tradition is inherently contentious and cannot reach a consensus, but because each moment, era, and epoch raises different questions about the nature, means, methods, purpose, and effects of salvation. This volume's contributors address various theologies of salvation, each bringing his or her own expertise to bear on theologies of the salvation as expressed in specific theologians and historical periods of church history.

This book has four parts, each of which presents particular theologies of salvation in four different historical eras. Each part begins with an introductory chapter that provides an overview of the theologies of salvation in that era. The goal of the overview chapters is to provide readers with a broader context for understanding the more specialized studies of individual theologians that follow, and also to identify the concerns that bind their work together.

Part I, on patristic theologies of salvation, covers Origen, Irenaeus, Augustine, Athanasius, and the Cappadocians. D. H. Williams begins part I by demonstrating that, although the patristic era of the church never produced a unified or systematic theory of salvation, the ancient writers were diligent to articulate pastoral and practical doctrine helpful to their congregations, which certainly included teaching about salvation. Williams reviews the differing approaches regarding salvation that the early theologians constructed, while explaining how the early church writings focused primarily on the giver of salvation through Christ rather than on the receiver of salvation in the individual.

In Thomas P. Scheck's chapter on Origen, he notes that though Origen lived through a period with little to no doctrinal consensus, he produced a rather organized and consistent theology (for his time) in the face of strong opposition from the Gnostics. Scheck explains that Origen's beliefs regarding salvation lie in the outcome of the believer's fight in the struggle to choose virtue or vice once the divine Word has been introduced to the soul.

John Behr continues part I with a recounting of the theology of Irenaeus of Lyons, an early church father who understood salvation in the gospel to be a recapitulation of all that God had done before Christ. For Irenaeus, salvation coincides with God's creation as the perfect purpose and will of God, fulfilled in the perfect image of God in Christ.

David Vincent Meconi in his chapter on Augustine shows how Augustine's theology of salvation is rooted in conformity to the incarnate Christ. Augustine believed that when one becomes conformed to God in Christ, he or she is cut off from this world and transformed into a lover of God.

John Yocum outlines the theology of salvation of Athanasius in his chapter, noting that Athanasius believed that though man is fully dependent on grace, this grace is received by directing the mind toward God. As Yocum explains, Athanasius believed that the primary purpose of God becoming man in Christ was to do away with death and give way to life through the resurrection for those who are in Christ.

In the final chapter of part I, Andrew Radde-Gallwitz writes about the Cappadocian Fathers—Basil of Caesarea, his younger brother Gregory of Nyssa, and their friend Gregory of Nazianzus. The theology of the Cappadocians, though with disagreements among the members at points, is relatively unified in the idea that the believer's salvation is collective, that it is our nature that is saved.

Part II covers the Middle Ages and includes chapters on Anselm, Thomas Aquinas, and Julian of Norwich. In the overview chapter, David Hogg recounts the development of the theology of salvation through this period, where the life of Christ as the payment to the devil for the souls under his authority became an increasingly popular notion. Over the course of the Middle Ages, this doctrine became known as the harrowing of hell, due to the belief that when Jesus rose from the grave, the righteous were let out of hell itself.

Giles Gasper's chapter discusses Anselm of Canterbury, one of the most important thinkers in Christian history. In contrast to many who came before him, Anselm's view of salvation did not consider the devil to be a major figure, but instead focused on humanity's culpability and the atoning work of Christ in salvation.

R. Jared Staudt continues part II, covering the theology of Thomas Aquinas. Staudt demonstrates that Aquinas's views on salvation are primarily rooted in the internal liberation from sin whereby the soul is renewed and justified by grace, and in the cause of said justification, which is participation in the justice of the soul of Jesus Christ himself.

Kerrie Hide completes this section, examining the life and thoughts of the English mystic Julian of Norwich. Julian's unique life of suffering shaped her understanding of theology, in which salvation is part of the journey of the individual, in which salvation occurs not as a result of humanity running from God, but a great "*oneing*" between Divinity and humanity.

Part III, on theologies of salvation during the Reformation and Catholic Counter-Reformation, covers Martin Luther, John Calvin, and the "Catholic Reform." The overview chapter by Frank A. James III covers both the theology of the Reformers, in which God's declaration of righteousness is based solely upon the righteousness of Jesus Christ, and the ensuing Catholic Counter-Reformation, in which salvation had happened, is happening, and is yet to come.

Carl Trueman writes about Martin Luther, the most important figure in the Protestant theology of salvation. Trueman explains Martin Luther's understanding of salvation as the justification by grace through faith in Christ so fundamental to Protestant and Reformed theology, as well as the implications involved in such a theology, including the sacraments, church authority, and the split from Roman Catholicism.

J. Todd Billings's chapter follows on John Calvin, who, with earlier Catholic theologians, champions the work of the Spirit's indwelling, transforming, and glorifying human beings in Christ, as well as his understanding of the gospel as the double grace of justification and sanctification accessed through union with Christ, received through faith.

Donald Prudlo closes out part III with the ensuing Catholic Reform, in which the Catholic Church, through the Council of Trent, speaks of justification as both an event and a process through which all believers must go. The Council of Trent argues that one can never be certain of one's salvation and that believers grow in holiness through the performance of good works, perfected by grace.

Part IV, on theologies of salvation from the eighteenth to the twenty-first century, covers John Wesley, Friedrich Schleiermacher, Karl Barth, Hans Urs von Balthasar, Karl Rahner, and Gustavo Gutiérrez. In the overview chapter, Ryan Reeves explains that the unique context of this period provides an intriguing backdrop for competing theologies of salvation. The dawn and subsequent growth of modernity and the rise in rational, empirical thinking in this time period reveal the need for theologians to reexamine both the nature and effects of salvation.

Thomas McCall begins this section with an examination of the teachings of John Wesley, one of the most influential men of the eighteenth century. McCall writes of Wesley's theology of salvation, though not unique in Christian history, as an important and unmistakably Protestant view, rooted in the theology of the early church, though with an emphasis on God's universal salvific will together with unlimited atonement.

James Gordon follows with an account of Friedrich Schleiermacher's theology of salvation. Schleiermacher's theology of salvation was unique, directly confronting the challenges posed by modernity, positing that the solution to the sin problem in man is found in the reality of the removal of sin and the incorporation of the believer into the corporate life of "blessedness" in Jesus Christ.

Tom Greggs continues part IV with his chapter on Karl Barth, one of the most important theologians of the twentieth century. For Barth, Christ is both the electing God and the elected man, where the active and passive election of the Son provides the basis for the election of individual men and women. Salvation is primarily the gift of the God of salvation who has chosen to be God in a particular way: in Christ.

W. T. Dickens provides an account of the theology of salvation for both Balthasar and Rahner, eminent Roman Catholic, Jesuit theologians of the twentieth century. Dickens explores both the similarities between these two theologians, such as their disdain for the neoscholastic theological method, and their differences, which primarily exist in their conception of the person, distinctive views of sin, and the scope of the reconciliation of God in Christ.

In the final chapter, Michal Edward Lee seeks to explain the soteriology of Gustavo Gutiérrez, one of the founders of liberation theology. Gutiérrez's theology of salvation is centered on the communion of humans with one another and with God, found not necessarily in a forensic declaration, meritorious works, or exclusive claim to an economic transaction, but in relationship with God the Father who produces human flourishing.

In mapping the theologies of salvation, this book serves as a guide to the variety of views about salvation found throughout the Christian tradition and can also assist us in developing theologies of salvation for our present and future contexts.

Certainly there are many different perspectives regarding theologies of salvation, and yet the recurring unifying theme is the role of the Trinity and the focus on the person and work of Jesus Christ. While this book does not advocate one theology of salvation above any other, the aim is for the reader to gain further knowledge about doctrines of salvation with which they are familiar, and also become further informed about other theologies of salvation, which in turn may foster a deeper sense of humility and respect that leads to fruitful dialogue among Christians of different perspectives.

NOTE

1. The Nicene Creed should be called the Nicene-Constantinopolitan Creed, since later debates led to an expansion of Nicaea's formula at the Council in Constantinople (381). Justin S. Holcomb, *Know the Heretics* (Grand Rapids, MI: Zondervan, 2014), 159–160; Justin S. Holcomb, *Know the Creeds and Councils* (Grand Rapids, MI: Zondervan, 2014), 33–40.

PART I

Patristic

1

Patristic Theologies of Salvation

An Introduction

D. H. WILLIAMS

> Captain of our salvation, take
> The souls we here present to thee.
> And fit for thy great service make
> These heirs of immortality;
> And let them in thine image rise
> And then transplant to paradise.

Charles Wesley first wrote these lines in 1763 for his *Hymns for Children*. Like much of Wesley's material, he was indebted to the images and expressions of early Christianity, and this hymn was no exception. In these few words Wesley grasps certain fundamental concepts that appear within the patristic idea of salvation.[1]

But it was a long and historical bridge to cross, not merely in time; whereas eighteenth-century Methodism and most of Protestantism identified itself most prominently with a theology of soteriology, early Christian thinkers did not.

Doctrinally speaking, the era of ancient Christianity never produced a theory of salvation. One is hard-pressed to find any patristic work that even bears a title having solely to do with salvation. This is not to say that the ancients had little interest in the dynamics of salvation. Far from it. The patristic theological mind was usually very practical and pastoral, revealing that there was no value in doctrine that failed to show how God's revelation of Himself was ultimately the basis of our redemption. Nevertheless, a reader will not find systematic and uniform teaching about salvation among patristic theologians. Like all theologies there were always new needs that required new definitions, which were no less true when it came to propounding soteriological expressions. More specifically, as a doctrine about Christ as the Son within the Trinity developed, so did ideas about what salvation must entail. But the latter was always subservient to the former. The validity of this remark will become clearer in the chapters below, which present conceptions of soteriology from different writers in different times.

If a generalization can be put forward despite the hazards of inherent limitations, it is that the early church was more dedicated to understanding the Savior as the Divine Giver of salvation than it was to salvation for the human receiver. The general idea was that if you rightly grasp the first, the other will certainly be effective. This seems to have been the major idea behind many anti-"Arian" theologies of the fourth and fifth centuries. Certain ancient writers might spell out the implications more clearly than others, as does Athanasius for example, in his *De incarnatione verbi*. But no one was arguing over the doctrine of the Trinity for the mere sake of perpetuating theological discourse. Patristic scholars were reminded of this obvious fact when a book published in 1981[2] on the Nicene-"Arian" conflicts attempted to argue that the beginnings of the Trinitarian controversies in the fourth century were not driven by a search for orthodox Trinitarian or Christology theology; rather, the theological ideas on both sides were motivated by an understanding of salvation. And thus the purpose of the conflict that began between Arius and Alexander, and later, between "Arians" and Nicenes, was about soteriological matters. As ingenious as this study was, its thesis was not generally accepted on the grounds that no one was as interested in hammering out a doctrine of salvation as they were in capturing the proper language for articulating the relation between the Father and Son. While important, the redemption of creation and humanity was not the center of the debates.

And so it seems Yocum is correct to say in chapter 5 herein that if a doctrine of atonement implies a "worked-out theory" of the utility of Christ's work centering on a single scheme, then the early church lacked such a theory. This is not to say there was an absence of stressing the saving person and work of Christ. All used the same gospels and (for the most part) the same New Testament. There was no doubt at all that the foundational articulation was to be found here, as well as prophetically in the Old Testament. In order to understand Christ and Logos and Savior, the Bible was consulted and perceived within the church as the supreme authority for all doctrinal construction. But the need for some clarification of the way God's gift of salvific grace came into the world was necessary.

In the chapters for part I, major figures from the patristic era are considered for the way their theologies impended on the Christian promise of salvation. Ranging from the mid-third century to the early fifth, it will become clear that certain emphases appeared and acquiesced over the years without losing track of the essential purposes of the Gospel. The differences we see in these select writers has largely to do with whom or what they were opposing; the Gnosticizing cosmogonies that occupied Irenaeus and (to a lesser extent) Origen were not an issue for Athanasius, nor were earlier writers consumed by the question of the proper relation between Christ's divine and human natures as were Basil of Caesarea and Augustine.

While we must beware of depicting the thought of the ancients in monolithic terms, it is possible to indicate some of the broad parameters when it comes to grasping characteristics of the early Church's approach to salvation. In doing so, we are better enabled to see the patristic age in its own light instead of one that we might create in our desire to re-appropriate their witness for today.

A very general observation can be made that God's salvation for humanity was less important than the God who was the ground of that salvation. Obviously, it is impossible to isolate the divine work of salvation on our behalf apart from affirming the identity of who does the saving. But the point here is that there was a priority between the two in patristic theology.

A very early, anonymous document from the second century, *II Clement*, opens with the mandate, "Brothers, we ought to think of Jesus Christ as we do of God—as the "judge of the living and the dead." And we ought not to belittle our salvation. For when we belittle him, we hope to get but little." Likewise, Irenaeus (*Adv. Haer.* III.1) argues that all Christians learned the plan of our salvation from no others than from those through whom the gospel came to us. "They first preached it abroad, and then later by the will of God handed it down to us in Writings, to be the foundation and pillar of our faith." His point is simple: The security of salvation was only as good as the means by which it was delivered to us.

The emphasis on the work of salvation is not the believer who accepts this gift, but the God who gives it. Despite the fact that we are hard-pressed to find a "doctrine" of soteriology, there is no question that the hundreds of references to salvation are far more theocentric than they are anthropocentric. No sin or evil scheme can thwart divine grace because nothing is greater than God's purposes and power to save. Even if a whole people sins, as in the case of Israel in the desert, this does not overwhelm the loving-kindness of God. Gregory of Nazianzus states, "The people made a calf, yet God did not cease from His loving-kindness. *Men denied God, but God could not deny Himself*."[3]

Turning to Origen in the mid-third century, we are told that a profession of the Son's divinity was part of God's saving action. While Origen claims that he must examine how fallen human are regenerated,

> nevertheless, it seems proper to inquire what is the reason why he who is regenerated by God unto salvation has to do both with Father and Son and Holy Spirit, and does not obtain salvation unless with the co-operation of the entire Trinity.[4]

It is first necessary to describe the Father's will, the sacrifice of the Son, and the special working of the Holy Spirit, as the beginning of describing our salvation. By the later fourth and fifth centuries, it is an essential postulate of soteriology that the Son's salvific efforts on our behalf had become the operation of the whole Trinity. Given the Son's sufferings and submission to death, it was critical that the Son's passion did not mean his divinity as the Son: "The same Triune God who originally formed humanity through the work of Christ in the beginning now renews humanity through his Passion at the end."[5]

Salvation Is Foremost a Demonstration of God's Omnipotence

A close subsidiary element to the theocentric understanding of salvation above is an emphasis on the power of God which cannot be thwarted or overcome by the power of sin or the will of any creature. In no way can the rulers, the authorities, the cosmic powers of this present darkness, and spiritual forces of evil in the heavenly places (Eph 6:12) effect a change in God's purposes or ability to enact his will. John Behr mentions this feature in Irenaeus, in whose soteriology death accomplished by human will is swallowed by the Divine life in Christ. Another way to say this is that the image of God can never be entirely obscured or dissolved by any agent of the created order. This was a lesson Augustine had to learn when he embraced the Manichaean cosmogony. In this system, there was no question the Kingdom of Light was good and exhibited the virtues of goodness. However, when the Realm of Darkness (or evil) threatened to invade the light, the "God" was incapable of defending itself against the powers of evil. In order to survive, the light had to release some of its particles into the darkness such that the darkness would be satisfied. The Manichaean "God" was good but weak and had to make a change in its original plans because of the aggressiveness of darkness.[6] For the rest of his life, Augustine never propounded a theology wherein God Almighty was less than that. The point in these examples is that the dynamics of salvation was first about God demonstrating through Christ such that the divine image and life cannot be annulled by the aegis of anything that is not God (viz., created beings or powers). Because of this, we know the world will not be completely disposed of because it is unredeemable.

Salvation Requires Faith through Repentance

In his justly famous book, *Conversion: The Old and New in Religion from Alexander the Great to Augustine of Hippo*, A. D. Nock observed that when it came to seeking salvation, "the real novelty in Christianity was the motive which it supplied for good conduct and the abhorrence of past bad conduct."[7] Of course pagan religions demanded purification and a changed life for those who enter a temple. Rather like a quarantine, a kind of ritual disinfection was required, usually for a period of time; i.e., one could not approach the god or the oracle for forty days if an abortion was done, ten days for touching a corpse, etc. But there was little concept of sin within paganism, popular and philosophical, that one should have sorrow for past sins.[8] And as a result, conversion to Christianity required an inner repentance motivated by love of God and devotion to Jesus who had suffered in order that a freedom from sin could be in humanity's reach. Not surprisingly, we hear in catechetical instruction the words of assurance from Cyril to his catechumens that "there is no sin too great or deep that can stifle God's power of forgiveness, as long as one is truly repentant."

> O the greatness of God's loving-kindness, making mention even of harlots in the Scriptures [Rahab and Babylon]. There is then in the case both of men and of women alike the salvation which is ushered in by repentance.[9]

It is only by repentance that one can be purified and made fit to enter the Kingdom: "make heartily confession unto the Lord, that you may both receive the forgiveness of your former sins, and be counted worthy of the heavenly gift, and inherit the heavenly kingdom with all the saints in Christ Jesus."[10]

Salvation Fulfilled through Baptism

This is undeniably a concept that holds true for every era of the patristic age. It is plain in Irenaeus. In contest with gnostic concepts of baptism which deny baptism is necessary for regeneration, since water is a mere physical and "fallen" element of creation, Irenaeus insists that baptism is the "seal of eternal life and rebirth unto God."[11] There is no need to elaborate on this conception at any length. Again we hear Cyril of Jerusalem teach his catechumens about going down into the water, "think not of the bare element, but look for salvation by the power of the Holy Ghost: for without both you cannot possibly be made perfect."[12] Likewise, Gregory of Nazianzus tells of the illumination of baptism which "contains a great and marvelous sacrament of our salvation."[13]

Salvation Is More of a Line than a Point

Salvation in Christ is understood not merely by the immediate belief of the sinner. There was instead a process involved that pertained to the perceived ecclesiology of the day. One moved from commitment to baptism in the Church to holiness of life and perseverance in resisting the world until death. In this way, salvation was regarded as more of a line than a point. For Origen, therefore, it was from the beginning to the end of the Christian life that salvation could be assured. As Thomas

Scheck shows in Origen's *Commentary on Romans*, no one is saved by their own righteousness but on the basis of God's mercy. This was an "open and shut" proposition. And yet Christ's atoning death does not stand in opposition to the need for one called to faith in order to manifest works of righteousness. This is not to deny that redemption and the gift of divine grace precedes any cooperative response on our part. But our faith (belief) and efforts to do what is just and holy contribute to a "line" of salvation in that the fruits of repentance are the proper effects of God's salvific initiative. And this is but the beginning of a process upon which we build upon our salvation for the rest of our lives. As Scheck puts it, "we attain salvation by stages and progressively."

Another way in which salvation is a line is that there is no viable conception among patristic writers that faith without righteousness or obedience could exist. The Protestant insistence on a division between faith and works would not have been understood. Hilary of Poitiers (c. 360) was thoroughly familiar with Paul's "we are justified by faith"[14] and gave this tenet a centrality that is not found in other ancient writers. However, with this justification it was a fundamental axiom that salvation is assured for those who persevere to the end (Mt 24:13). The ancients had little interest in the individual's experience of salvation. Obviously, the authenticity of one's experience of faith was important, but it served as a confirmation of more significant matters such as the ways one's salvation is manifested. Cyril (of Jerusalem) also makes this plain to his catechetical class. Baptism is more of a beginning than a completion of salvation. In that process of catechesis the new believer is being prepared: "God's grace has always been at work, but the believer must remain steadfast unto baptism and beyond."

Alongside of this discussion is the nature of faith as a noun, something that has a specific content: "The true Faith recognizes Him as God; and this belief is necessary to salvation" (Gregory of Nazianzus, *Or.* 41. praef) and such a faith is not only a complete trust in God's provision, but also a faith that is doctrinally true. One must believe in the true God and receive the grace of the Christ who is fully God and fully man.

In his farewell to the bishops who had met in Constantinople in 381, Gregory wanted to make this latter point about faith crystal clear: "For nothing is so magnificent in God's sight as pure doctrine, and a soul perfect in all the dogmas of the truth" (*Or.* 42.8). While the "Arian" may bear the name of Christ, it was a false Christ. To obey such a Christ was ungodly, and to suffer for this Christ was inglorious, "seeing that the truth was in this case perverted, for while they suffered as Christians, they should have been punished as heretics" (*Or.* 42.3). In contrast to pagan religions, *doctrina* was valued as indispensable to the practice of faith. We would be overstating the issue to say there is no belief in Graeco-Roman religions.[15] As one scholar puts it, there is no such thing as orthodoxy or heresy in paganism.

When one turns to Athanasius it is easy to see how most of theological edifice is constructed on the total divinity of the Son, and this divinity needed to be distinguished from the incarnate nature or humanity of the same Son. For the promise of salvation to be realized, there could not be (in Yocum's words) "any leveling of humanity and divinity in the union of Christ. God remains God and humanity remains humanity." The same was true for Basil of Caesarea, that is, our regeneration in baptism is not in itself fully efficacious because salvation is not (per Radde-Gallwitz) "a once-for-all matter." Instead, baptism instills in us the life of desire or longing for God. Here is a marvelous picture of how justification and sanctification are not two separate stages, as the believer grows in grace toward the contemplation of God.

Salvation as Divinization

The idea of what happens to the sinner in the event of salvation has been best captured by a theme that often appears through the patristic ages: "God became man, so that man could become God." In effect, salvation is the divinization of the believer, that is, the human nature being changed by assuming God's character or nature; a progressive transformation into the true image of God. 1 Peter 1:4 was understood to be one of the scriptural warrants: "partakers of the divine nature." There is no single definition of what is later called deification or theosis, but its roots can be located in Irenaeus.

> For it was for this end that the Word of God was made man, and He who was the Son of God became the Son of man, that man, having been taken into the Word, and receiving the adoption, might become the son of God. For by no other means could we have attained to incorruptibility and im-

mortality, unless we had been united to incorruptibility and immortality. But how could we be joined to incorruptibility and immortality, unless, first, incorruptibility and immortality had become that which we also are, so that the corruptible might be swallowed up by incorruptibility, and the mortal by immortality, that we might receive the adoption of sons?[16]

Only by means of the incarnation, nothing less than God's own Word in the assumption of our human nature, can such an exchange be made possible. This is not confined to a Greek eastern theology, though it has been more widely integrated in Greek theology. The wording of this salvific notion alters slightly with different writers, but its point is well-intact. We find a principle of *theosis* from Athanasius to Gregory of Nyssa, from Hilary of Poitiers[17] to Augustine,[18] though the term for it is not coined till Gregory of Nazianzus.[19] For Gregory, theosis was a virtual equivalent for salvation and was, therefore, at the very center of the theological enterprise.

Radde-Gallwitz has noted the importance of theosis for the Cappadocians generally and Christology, in particular, was indissolubly linked to soteriology. Again we see how right doctrine is necessarily connected to the efficaciousness of one's salvation. The fundamental issue here not only is that Christ's death and resurrection brought forgiveness of sins, but it is how the very life of God, transforming our sinful nature and exchanging death for the Divine life, is exhibited and offered in Christ. This process implies a continuity between Christ's humanity and our own. Our salvation becomes a mirror of what took place in Christ for us. In other words, the incarnation amounted to the way Christ's own humanity is so utterly unified with the divine nature that it is not improper to speak of Christ's humanity as first deified so that it could likewise happen to us. This is salvation of exchange—"God takes our life to replace it with his own" in Christ (Radde-Gallwitz).

A similar principle of exchange or *deificatio* is at work in Augustine's explanation of the human reception of salvation. The way in which God fully identifies himself with fallen humanity is through unification via the incarnation. Using a Pauline language of adoption, the person is by grace adopted into the same sonship as the Son before the Father. And yet, in Augustine's mind, the fallen human will resists being drawn to God because the idolatry of the self is so strong. It may be that the person is deified or incorporated into Christ, but "we must also be given the grace to be deified," as Meconi states it, in order to regain our true image of God. Obviously the human will for Augustine has become wholly foreign to its original creation and does not seek the good, even when it is placed in front of it. Because we are first justified, we are able to be deified.

However, the patristic writers sought to understand salvation as a Christian doctrine with varying emphases, and there was no doubt that it was a salvation meant in all things to glorify God. Only the Divine purpose was the initiator and finisher of creation's "last best hope." While it may be an unlikely source for appreciating ancient exegesis, a sermon on Hebrews 2:10 by C. H. Spurgeon captures an essential purpose of the writers described below:[20]

> We start, then, with this as a sort of keynote—that the great Father, who has purposed our salvation, is able to fully carry out what He has planned, for by Him are all things. But, since there is nothing about this work but what will bring Him honor and glory, we rest assured that, having put His hand to it, He will not withdraw His arm until He has fully accomplished His eternal purpose to the praise of the glory of His Grace![21]

NOTES

1. Cyril of Jerusalem (c. 350) speaks of Christ in his catechetical addresses as "the Captain of your salvation." *Catechetical Orations* (*Cat. Or.*) 21.7 (*Cyril of Jerusalem*, trans. Edward Yarnold, The Early Church Fathers [London: Routledge, 2000], 178), though I keep the phrase "captain" in allusion to the KJV translation and Rowan Greer's book, *The Captain of Your Salvation: Patristic Exegesis of Hebrews* (Tübingen: Mohr, 1973).
2. R. Gregg and D. Groh, *Early Arianism: A View of Salvation* (Philadelphia: Fortress Press, 1981), x: "We contend that early Arianism is most intelligible when viewed as a scheme of salvation."
3. Cyril of Jerusalem, *Cat. Or.* 2.10 (trans. Leo McCauley and Anthony Stephenson, FC 61: 101) (FC = *Fathers of the Church* [Washington, DC: Catholic University of America Press, 2000]).
4. Origen, *De principiis* 1.3,5 (*Origen: On First Principles*, trans. G.W. Butterworth (Gloucester, MA: Peter Smith, 1973), 33.
5. Peter Chrysologus, *Sermon* 72A.4 (trans. William B. Palardy, FC 110: 4). Cf. Ambrose, *On the Faith* 1.17.108 (NPNF II/10: 219 4 [Edinburgh, Scotland: T&T Clark, 1886–1900]) (NPNF = Nicene and Post-Nicene Fathers): "That He is God's own

Son declares His Godhead; that He is very God shows that He is God's own Son; His pitifulness is the earnest of His submission, His sacrifice, of our salvation."
6. See, e.g., Augustine, *On the Nature of the Good* 41 (trans. Roland J. Teske, WSA I/19: 340) (WSA = Works of Saint Augustine for the 21st Century [Hyde Park, NY: New City Press, 1997).
7. A. D. Nock, *Conversion: The Old and New in Religion from Alexander the Great to Augustine of Hippo* (Oxford: Oxford University Press, 1933), 218–19.
8. Ibid., 219.
9. Cyril of Jerusalem, *Cat. Or.* 2.9 (FC 61: 101).
10. Ibid., 2.20 (FC 61: 107).
11. Irenaeus, *Demonstration of the Apostolic Preaching* 3 (trans. John Behr [Crestwood, NY: St. Vladimir's Seminary Press, 1997], 42).
12. Cyril of Jerusalem, *Cat. Or.* 3.4 (Yarnold, 90). See also *Cat. Or.* 3.10 (Yarnold, 93): "The unbaptized do not receive salvation, with the single exception of martyrs who receive the kingdom without the water."
13. Gregory of Nazianzus, *Oration* (Hereafter cited as *Or.*) 40.6 (trans. C. G. Browne, NPNF II/7: 361 [Edinburgh, Scotland: T&T Clark, 1886–1900]).
14. D. H. Williams, "Justification by Faith: A Patristic Doctrine," *Journal of Ecclesiastical History* 56 (2006), 649–67.
15. Charles King, "The Organization of Roman Beliefs," *Classical Antiquity* 22 (2003), 275–312.
16. Irenaeus, *Adv. Haer.* 3.19.1 (ACW 64: 93; emphasis original). (ACW = *Ancient Christian Writers* [New York: Paulist Press, 1992]) See also *Demonstration* 31 (trans. Joseph Smith, ACW 16: 67): "So He united man with God and brought about a communion of God and man."
17. Hilary of Poitiers, *Commentarium in Mattheaum* 5.15 (trans. D. H. Williams, FC 125: 84): "A sin against the Spirit is to deny the fullness of power to God and to abrogate the eternal substance in Christ, by which God came into man, so man will become as God."
18. Athanasius, *De Incarnatione Verbi* 54.3 (trans. John Behr [Yonkers, NY: St. Vladimir's Seminary Press, 2011], 105): "For he was incarnate that we might be made God." See also 13.7 (Behr, 63): "So the Word of God came himself, in order that the being the image of the Father (cf. Col. 1:15), the human being 'in the image' might be recreated." See also 16.1; 43.7.
19. Not to be confused with the pagan precept of apotheosis (can also be deification) which glorified an emperor or any human figure with divine qualities.
20. "For it became him, for whom are all things, and by whom are all things, in bringing many sons unto glory, to make the captain of their salvation perfect through sufferings" (KJV).
21. Charles H. Spurgeon, "The Captain of our Salvation" (Sermon no. 2619) in vol. 45 of *The Metropolitan Tabernacle Pulpit* (Pasadena, TX: Pilgrim Publications, 1977), 194.

2

Origen of Alexandria

THOMAS P. SCHECK

Origen of Alexandria (c. 185–c. 254) lived through a turbulent period of the Christian Church, when persecution was widespread and little or no doctrinal consensus existed among the various regional churches. In this environment, Gnosticism flourished, and Origen was the first not only to turn his hand to a refutation of Gnosticism, but also to offer an alternative Christian system that was more rigorous and philosophically respectable than the mythological speculations of the various Gnostic sects. He was also an astute critic of the pagan philosophy of his era, yet Origen also learned much from it, and adapted its most useful and edifying teachings to a grand elucidation of the Christian faith.

Origen was the most prolific of the Christian writers of his time and his six-column arrangement of the Hebrew Old Testament text (known as the Hexapla) was not surpassed for more than a thousand years. He also composed numerous biblical commentaries and sermons. His importance for the history of theology and philosophy rests mainly on two works, his treatise *On First Principles*, and his response to the pagan philosopher Celsus' attack on Christianity, the treatise *Against Celsus*. *On First Principles* is Origen's most monumental work and is the best expression of his theology. It is a comprehensive investigation of Christian doctrine on a scale never before attempted.

Introduction

Origen's soteriology or doctrine of salvation should be interpreted in accordance with his basic understanding of the Christian life. One of Origen's best modern interpreters writes of him: "He conceived the Christian life above all as a combat initiated at baptism, and it is to this combat that he did not cease to exhort his listeners."[1] Especially in his homilies, Origen endeavored to equip his hearers for spiritual warfare against Satan's demons and the vices they incite. Origen believed that from the day when the divine Word is introduced into a soul, the Christian must engage in a struggle of virtues against vices. One's salvation or condemnation is contingent upon the outcome of this struggle. Before the Word came to attack them, the vices remained in peace, but as soon as it undertook to judge them one by one, a great disturbance arose and a relentless war was initiated.[2] Twentieth-century theologian, Henri de Lubac, expands on the significance of this:

> If there is a traditional theme in Christian morality and asceticism, that is it. Now it is to Origen that we owe its name: "spiritual combat." It is also to him that we owe its symbolism. A wholly biblical symbolism. Through his spiritual interpretation, Origen transposes the history of Israel's wars, its captivities, its deliverances, its victories, in order to apply them to the Christian life. All of Scripture is for him the book of the Lord's combats.[3]

How does Satan snatch away souls to destruction in this warfare? One way is by seducing them away from the Church into heretical sects. In his third homily on Joshua, Origen discusses Rahab, the harlot from Jericho who hid two of Joshua's spies at the time of the conquest of Canaan and who recognized the Lord's power and demanded from the spies the promise that she and her family would be spared when the Israelites conquered (cf. Josh. 1:10–2:24). Joshua (Greek: *Jesus*) was faithful to the pledge, and only Rahab and her family were spared after the city's capture (Josh. 6:22–23). Like his predecessor, Clement of Rome (cf. *1 Clement* 12), Origen interprets the scarlet thread let down from Rahab's window as a prefiguration of redemption by the blood of Christ; her house represents the Church.[4] Origen then gives the following striking warning concerning the believer's obligation not to depart from the Catholic Church: "Let no one deceive himself. Outside this house, that is, outside the Church, no one is saved (*Extra ecclesiam, nemo salvatur*). If anyone goes outside, he is responsible for his own death."[5] Thus Origen, not Cyprian,[6] is apparently the oldest source of the theological axiom, "Outside the church there is no salvation," a dogma that has a long and venerable history.[7] In the context of Origen's homily, the claim comprises a warning addressed to believers concerning heretics and schismatics of the perilous consequences of leaving the Catholic Church.

Therefore, on the subject of salvation, whatever philosophical speculations Origen may have put forward about the possibility of a future restoration of rational creatures in the ages to come, a speculation that traces to his excessive Platonism and to his purgatorial understanding of hell; and whatever emphasis he may have given to the necessity of progressive education and moral transformation as constitutive to salvation; these themes should not be interpreted as negating his fundamental ecclesiological principle that salvation is solely by the blood of Christ and is accessible only through the instrumentality of the Catholic Church.

Reclaiming Origen from His Critics

Older German Protestant scholarship was suspicious of the pedagogical emphasis in Origen's soteriology. It is true that in the footsteps of Clement of Alexandria (d. ca. 215), Origen describes the work of the incarnate Word as that of the divine Teacher who brings us perfect truth and reopens for us the way to immortality. H. Koch reproached Origen for this and said that, for Origen, God is above all "the great teacher, who guides and educates souls back to their heavenly place of origin."[8] Origen's Christianity, allegedly, "knows no forgiveness, only education; no eschatology, only idealism."[9] But the pedagogical role of the Divine Logos is not the only side of Origen's doctrine (as Ritschl also seemed to think). Origen's understanding of the atoning work of the Logos is complex, but he gives an all-important position to the death of Christ on the cross, the salutary results of which Origen describes with an abundance of detail lacking in any previous theologian.[10]

This chapter will focus on Origen's neglected *Commentary on Romans* (*CRm*).[11] Origen's theory of original sin may not be identical with Augustine's, but there is no doubt that according to Origen all human beings are sinners and are unable to save themselves.[12] Salvation comes only through God's mercy. In his comment on Romans 3:9–18 he says: "But if all are under sin, consequently there shall be no grounds for the self-exaltation of one group against the other since both come to salvation not on the basis of their own righteousness but on the basis of God's mercy."[13] Neither Jews nor Gentiles can be saved by their own justice but only through God's mercy. Human boasting is excluded. Yet Origen does not view salvation by Christ's death as something that denies the participant the opportunity to be meritoriously justified by faith and works of justice done in free cooperation with divine grace. Faith does not justify us apart from the blood of Christ, but neither does the blood of Christ justify us apart from our faith. There is collaboration. Of the two, however, the blood of Christ justifies us much more than our faith.

> And for this reason, it seems to me that . . . he adds, "how much more then, now, having been justified by his blood"; in order to teach that even if our faith saves us from the coming wrath, and even if our works of justice (*opera iustitiae*) save us, nevertheless beyond all these things it is much more the blood of Christ that will save us from the coming wrath.[14]

Thus, the redemptive work of Christ has its own proper and unique value as the meritorious cause of our salvation. It is anterior to any cooperation on our part and is the original source of the acceptability of our good works. Moreover, it remains constantly the ground for human salvation. Yet our faith and our works of justice also contribute to our salvation in the sense that the fruits of repentance are the objective effect of the entirely gratuitous initiative of God's goodness. They "save us," not in the sense that they are the original cause of our approval before God, or that they cause our sins to be washed away. Rather, the gift of the Holy Spirit is operative and visible in our works of obedience and love. We actualize and effect our divine sonship by our outward deeds (cf. Matt. 5:44–45).

Paul and the Gospels

In a vivid illustration of his conception that both the grace of Christ and also human faith and good works are indispensable for final salvation, Origen borrows language from the Gospels to help explain Romans 5:18:

> By means of Adam's transgression a certain access, as it were, was given by which sin, or the death of sin, or condemnation, spread to all men. Thus, in contrast Christ opened up an access to justification, through which life enters to men. This is why he said about himself, "I am the door. If anyone enters through me he will be saved."[15]

Christ is the door to salvation, the door to life, to a person's being justified. Origen explains this by referring back to his earlier discussion of this theme where he had investigated what sort of door Christ is in order for us to apprehend what sort of people we ought to be who would enter through it and have access to grace. To explain Paul, Origen consults the teachings of Jesus in the Gospels. Origen writes that the door is truth (cf. John 14:6), "and through the door of truth liars cannot enter." Moreover, the door is justice (cf. Luke 23:47), and through such a door the unjust may not pass. The door is gentle and humble (cf. Matt. 11:29), and neither the wrathful nor the arrogant may enter through the door of humility and gentleness.

> Consequently, if there is someone who, in accordance with the Apostle's word, wants to have access through our Lord Jesus Christ to the grace of the Lord in which Paul and those who are like him claim to stand, he must be purged from all these things we have recorded above. Otherwise this door will not allow those who are doing things alien to it to enter through it. Instead it closes at once and does not allow those who are dissimilar to it to pass through.[16]

For Origen, the doctrine that Paul proclaims in his epistles cannot be severed from the teaching of Jesus of the Gospels, since they are harmonious.[17] In light of our contemporary exegetical climate, which tends to minimize or even deny the influence of the Jesus tradition upon the apostle Paul, it seems noteworthy that Origen thinks that St. Paul's meaning can be best and most authentically expounded by shedding light upon it from the Gospel traditions in which Origen believes Paul was immersed and fully conversant.[18] This approach to interpreting Paul via Jesus is programmatic for Origen and other Church Fathers such as St. Jerome;[19] but it plainly sets Origen apart from Rudolph Bultmann, for example, and his school of interpretation, which claims that "Jesus' teaching is—to all intents and purposes—irrelevant for Paul."[20] Bultmann has influenced J. Fitzmyer, who claims that Paul "is not interested in the historical Jesus as a teacher, a prophet, or as the chronological source and the first link in the chain of such transmission."[21] Fitzmyer asserts that precisely because of his lack of interest in Jesus of Nazareth, Paul's writings "create an anomaly for Christians of later generations."[22]

In response to this very recent (Bultmannian) approach of interpreting Paul in radical isolation from the Gospel traditions, the Hungarian New Testament scholar and Cistercian abbot, D. Farkasfalvy, counters, in direct response to Fitzmyer, that the "anomaly" would come about if we were to assume that Paul would have spoken about Christ without providing for his congregations information about Jesus's teaching and deeds.[23] Moreover, the British exegete D. Wenham concludes an impressive study of the echoes of the Gospel traditions in Paul's writings (which Wenham shows Paul received through oral not written tradition) by saying: "If the primary text that Paul is expounding in his writings is the text of Jesus, then instead of reading Paul's letters in isolation from the Gospels, it will be important to read them in the light of the Gospels—not falling into naïve harmonization, but recognizing that Paul was above all motivated by a desire to follow Jesus."[24] Origen would certainly concur with Wenham on this point.

In this particular context, Origen claims that Christ has opened up an access to justification through which human beings can be saved. By faith in his redemptive act and by the reception of baptism, they enter through this door; but at the same time, since other texts in the Gospels show that access to the Lord's grace demands interior cleansing and holiness, then union with Christ requires resemblance to him in the virtues. Those who are alienated from Christ's likeness are still threatened with the possibility of exclusion. The Church's scripturally grounded doctrine of a future judgment according to works contributes to Origen's explanation. In the immediate context Origen illustrates the necessity of being purged from sin in order to attain final salvation by citing the parable of the foolish virgins (Matt. 25:1-12) who, "since they did not bring the oil of good works in their vessels, found the door closed when they came too late."[25] Again Origen clarifies Paul by means of Jesus.

A comparison of these parallel passages shows that Origen equates "access to grace" with "access to justification," a single gift that is ultimately gained by means of both faith and good works. For the same God warns us that we cannot have access to grace if we lack one of these two conditions.[26] Elsewhere, Origen explains Paul's meaning by referring to Ezekiel 44:9: "Therefore thus says the Lord God: No foreigner, uncircumcised in heart and flesh, of all the foreigners who are among the people of Israel, shall enter my sanctuary" (RSV). Origen says that those who show themselves to be uncircumcised either in faith (by holding base and unworthy opinions concerning the faith), or in works (by committing unclean and defiled actions), will be excluded from entering the sanctuary of God.[27]

Faith and Works

Origen repeatedly affirms that faith anticipates good works, which are the necessary fruit of salvation. One without the other is condemned, "seeing that faith without works is called dead (Jas. 2:17, 26); and no one is justified before God by works without faith." Origen cites Matthew 7:24 and Luke 6:46 to show that "everywhere faith is joined with works and works are united with faith."[28] Faith and works cleave (*adhaerens*) to one another and are consummated. The patristic scholar (and German translator of Origen's *Commentary on Romans*), T. Heither, seems to express Origen's meaning well when she says that for Origen faith and works are not opposites but fundamentally related to one another.[29] This synthesis and collaboration between faith and good works explains for Origen why Paul insists in Romans 3:31 that Christians do not make void the law but establish it.[30] In the immediate context Origen supports Paul's thought by citing Jesus's words in Matthew 5:17: "I have not come to destroy the law but to fulfill it."

In a recent monograph, the Protestant New Testament scholar, C. VanLandingham, argues that in Paul's thought, as well as in the whole Bible and early Judaism, behavior determines one's eternal salvation, and not faith alone. Relying on texts such as Romans 2:6–10; 14:12; 1 Corinthians 5:9–11; 2 Corinthians 5:10; Galatians 6:7–9; 1 Thessalonians 4:1–8; VanLandingham claims that Paul's doctrine consistently is that those who are morally just receive the reward of eternal life, whereas the wicked receive the recompense of damnation.[31] The same exegete shows that the concept of a forensic justification according to which one's faith in Jesus in the present time is understood to anticipate and guarantee the believer's acquittal in the eschatological divine judgment is completely foreign to biblical and Pauline thought. Such a resoundingly Catholic thesis, argued as it is by a Protestant scholar in the wake of the "New Perspective" revolution in New Testament studies, is strikingly consonant with Origen's understanding of the soteriological meaningfulness of the future judgment according to works for believers.

Origen's doctrine of salvation is characterized by an emphasis on unity and synthesis. He stresses the consonance of the Old Testament with the New Testament, of St. Paul with the Gospels, the harmony between the law and the prophets and the apostles, and the complementarity of faith and good works. Elsewhere Origen speaks of two kinds of faith, a human and a divine. The addition of the latter makes perfect justifying faith. The one is of reason, the other of grace, the special gift of God, and both must coexist.[32] There are also two justifications, one by faith, one by works.[33] The former makes one just in the sight of God; it is forgiveness, known to God alone; the latter makes one just also in the sight of saints and angels. The former is strictly only the *initium iustificari* (the beginning of justification); it is imperfect faith. The faith that was reckoned to Abraham for justice was perfect faith, which had already manifested itself in obedience.[34] This is what it means to be "justified by God": the person is made really and truly just. Then one's faith is no longer "imputed to him for justice," for he *is* just.

Heither finds in Origen's words no contradiction of his previous statements, but rather completion. Origen is faithfully expounding Paul's very Jewish view according to which any polarity of faith and works is incomprehensible.[35] Clearly Origen understands faith and good works as an organic and synthetic unity. This distances him from Lutheran categories of Pauline interpretation, which usually interpret these terms antithetically. Indeed, Luther and Melanchthon recognized the alienation of their interpretations from Origen's.[36] Yet Origen's synthesis endeared him to Catholic theologians as well as to some Protestants of the sixteenth and seventeenth centuries, including the Anabaptists.[37]

Based on Psalm 32:1–2, which is cited by Paul in Romans 4:7–8, Origen sees the soul's conversion as a three-stage progression: remission, covering, and non-imputation of sins. First, the soul leaves its evil and obtains pardon. Next, by good deeds it covers its sins. Finally it reaches perfection, so that every root of evil is completely cut off from it to the point that no trace of evil can be found in it. "At that point the summit of blessedness is promised to the one to whom the Lord is able to impute no sin."[38] At *CRm* 4.6 Origen will apply the terms faith, hope, and love to these three stages of conversion. The emphasis here is on salvation as a process subsequent to the grace of faith and baptism. Believers are progressively transformed into the image of Christ through faith, hope, and love. The French theologian and student of J. Rivière, C. Verfaillie, comments on Origen's text: "Origen speaks as a moralist here, but his psychology leads to a theology."[39] Origen's soteriology is oriented toward morality and does not dispense with it; but when we consider that many texts in Paul's writings and in the Gospels appear to have a similar moral orientation (cf. Matt. 5:20; 1 Cor. 10), this long-standing Protestant reproach of Origen (of moralism) may one day turn out to be his badge of honor. As de Lubac writes:

> [L]et us not fear to affirm that Origen is in fact a moralist, whose exegesis is constantly oriented toward morality. For what is important in his eyes is, not to speculate on the profound meaning of the Bible, but to receive it with a living faith and to "adapt one's conduct to the words of truth" it contains. He does not dissociate morality and religion, nor does he believe that the preterition [discontinuance] of the one is necessary for the purity of the other.[40]

While admitting that faith is primary in salvation, Origen insists that it must not be separated from works of love. He sees the same organic link between faith and works as between the root and branches of a tree. In a comment on Romans 4:6–8, Origen says:

> The apostle is saying that it is only on the basis that one believes in him who justifies the ungodly that justice is reckoned to a man, even if he has not yet produced works of justice. For faith that believes in the one who justifies is the beginning of being justified by God (*initium iustificari a Deo*). And this faith, when it has been justified, is embedded in (*haeret*) the soil of the soul like a root that has received rain so that when it begins to be cultivated through God's law, branches arise from it which bring forth the fruit of works. The root of justice, therefore, does not grow out of the works, but the fruit of works grows out of the root of justice, namely out of the root of justice, which God accepts even without works.[41]

Heither accurately summarizes Origen's solution to the problem of the relation between faith and works in this passage by showing that Origen seeks a synthesis between the two: "Faith obtains the justice out of which works emerge; and this relationship is not reversible. Only upon the way of faith does man obtain forgiveness of sins, reconciliation with God."[42] "Works are thus not the ground for grace, but the outworking of grace, because grace must be effective in man."[43]

Origen insists that hope and love cleave inseparably (*inseparabiliter coherere*) to faith, and God's promise of salvation will be fulfilled only if faith, hope, and love abide in those who believe: "I consider faith to be the first beginnings and the very foundations of salvation (*prima salutis initia et ipsa fundamenta*); hope is certainly the progress and increase of the building; however, love is the perfection and culmination of the entire work. That is why love is said to be greater than everything else (cf. 1 Cor. 13:13).[44] This text corresponds well with *CRm* 4.1 cited above. Origen states that being justified by God (*iustificari a Deo*) is identical with salvation (*salus*). He views faith as the beginning (*initium*) and foundation (*fundamentum*) of the process that is nourished by hope and culminates in love. In other words, we attain salvation by stages and progressively. The gift of divine grace within us can increase, and it can also perish. Far from representing a doctrine of salvation *sola fide* (by faith alone) according to which love is excluded from the essence of justifying grace, Origen's teaching can be more accurately described as salvation by faith, hope, and love.

It is noteworthy that Origen speaks of reconciliation and adoption similar to the way he treats justification and salvation. These different ways of describing God's gift of salvation are viewed as a process with a beginning, middle, and end; a past, present, and future. With regard to reconciliation, Origen says that Christ's death on the cross has killed the hostility between God and humanity and marks the beginning of reconciliation (*reconciliationis initium*).[45] This assumes that reconciliation is a past experience. But he goes on to say that only when we actually resist sins to the point of death, in imitation of Christ's example, does he reconcile humanity to God, provided that we keep the covenant of reconciliation inviolate. For those who abide in the works God hates cannot be reconciled.[46] Here the primary emphasis is on reconciliation as a present experience that has implications for the future. Finally he says that whoever turns back to sin restores the hostility and rebuilds the wall of separation, thus destroying the work of Christ and making void the cross of his suffering.[47] Thus the process of reconciliation can be nullified by sin. The threat of loss and renewed enmity abides. He speaks similarly of adoption: By our faith in Christ and baptism we already possess salvation and we already have adoption as sons.[48] Thus salvation and adoption have already taken place as past events. But its future aspect is brought out when he says that salvation is still in hope; we wait for it still, and have it now as in a mirror and in a riddle. When the perfect comes we shall have adoption face to face.[49] Thus for Origen the completion of salvation lies in the future.

Universal Reconciliation

What of Origen's famous speculation about the *apokatastasis* or universal restoration of all rational creatures? Origen's philosophical conjectures, which stand in tension with his exegesis, sometimes appear to resemble the Platonist theory of metempsychosis. There are passages in his writings where Origen seems to say that since created spirits never lose their freedom, they may go on falling and rising and falling again forever.[50] Philosophically he adheres to the idea that only the good can be eternal and that evil must eventually disappear altogether. If that is the case, universal salvation would become a matter of necessity, not negated by the long duration of the process that may be required. Yet since Origen admitted that a creature with free will could always refuse to surrender to God, he drew the inference that it was possible for such creatures to go on falling and rising.

The latter point is contrary to the doctrine that the choice made in this life is decisive in character. Yet this element in Christian dogma to my knowledge was only developed and clarified after Origen's lifetime. In any case, the weak point in Origen's philosophical theory is his idea that the soul will return to the purely spiritual state it was in before it came down into the body. This point in particular was condemned by the Fifth General Council in its first canon under the name of *apokatastasis*. "If anyone says or holds that the punishment of the demons and of impious men is temporary, and that it will have an end at some time, that is to say, there will be a complete restoration of the demons or of impious men, let him be anathema."[51]

Had Origen been taught by the Church in his own lifetime, there seems to be no doubt that he would have accepted its verdict on his speculations and erroneous teachings. In *Hom in Jos* 7.6 he says: "I bear the title of priest and, as you see, I preach the word of God. But if I do anything contrary to the discipline of the Church or the rule laid down in the Gospels—if I give offence to you and to the Church—then I hope the whole Church will unite with one consent and cast me off." Though the Church does rebuke some of his doctrines, or rather speculations, she refuses to cast him off, since she owes so much to him.

"Works of the Law" and Salvation

Origen thinks that the Gospel message proclaimed by St. Paul in Romans is based upon Jesus's teaching in the Gospels. It excludes the possibility of human boasting and self-exaltation, but it is not directed against the necessity of good works nor does it undermine their meritorious value in God's sight. Origen distinguishes post-baptismal works of justice, or the Christian virtues, from the Pauline term "works of the law," which he takes to be equivalent to the works of the Pharisees reproached by Jesus in the Gospels. His comments on Romans 11:6 clarify how strongly Origen repudiates the idea that Paul is a preacher of licentiousness:

> One should know that the works which Paul repudiates and frequently criticizes are not the works of justice (*opera iustitiae*) which are commanded in the law, but those in which they boast who keep the law according to the flesh; that is, the circumcision of the flesh, the sacrificial rituals, the observance of Sabbaths and new moon festivals (cf. Col. 2.18). These and works of a similar nature are the works by which he says no one can be saved, and concerning which he says in the present passage, "not on the basis of works; otherwise, grace would no longer be grace." For if anyone is justified through these, he is not justified gratis. But these works are by no means sought from the one who is justified through grace; but this one should take care that the grace he has received should not be in him "in vain" [cf. 1 Cor. 15.10] . . . So then, one does not make grace become in vain who joins works to it that are worthy and who does not show himself ungrateful for the grace of God. For anyone who sins after having attained grace becomes ungrateful to him who offered the grace.[52]

This passage makes an important clarification. Origen so wishes to safeguard the necessity of the Christian's post-baptismal good works that he explicitly states that the "works of the law" that Paul criticizes in his letters do not refer to the Decalogue or to the moral works of justice. Rather, the term refers to Jewish ceremonial works (such as circumcision, Sabbath-keeping, food laws) apart from faith. Thus, Origen in this passage restricts Paul's οὐκ ἐξ ἔργων, "not from works" (Rom. 3:28), to external ritual law.[53] It is not such ritual works that need to be added to faith for the grace of God not to be received in vain, but the moral works done in obedience to the law of Christ, for the doing of which Christians will most certainly be judged.[54] For Origen then, the interpretation that Christian salvation exists "apart from the law" does not mean that moral works of the Law are not required in baptized persons. Such would be an unholy and inaccurate way of interpreting Paul. Origen admits that neither the Jews nor the Gentiles when they approach the Gospel are required to give an account proving that they have kept the Law. Rather, they need only to repent and believe. But Origen stresses most of all that our being justified "apart from the law" means that no one is required to observe those ritual commands that had been imposed on the Galatians by the pseudo-apostles. Those are the kinds of works Paul is repudiating in his discussions in Romans and Galatians.

The Protestant New Testament scholar, M. Reasoner, observes that Origen's rather delimited understanding of the Pauline term "works of the law" is another instance of an early precedent for the so-called new perspective in Pauline interpretation. In the vocabulary of "new perspective" scholars, Paul's words "apart from works" normally mean: apart from those works of the law that visibly separate the Jewish people from the nations.[55] They do not refer to the good works produced in obedience to the law of the Spirit of life in Christ Jesus (cf. Rom. 8:2). Origen says repeatedly that faith alone is not adequate for salvation, for God requires other theological virtues in addition to faith. Mercy, piety, love, and the other virtues can be reckoned as justice, just as faith can.[56] The Scriptural basis of such an interpretation is Psalm 106:31, which says that Phineas's zeal was reckoned as justice. If we do not produce these other virtues by laying aside the old man with his unjust deeds, faith cannot be reckoned as justice.[57] For Christ justifies only those who have received the new life in the pattern of his resurrection and who reject the old garments of injustice and iniquity.[58] Faith is deservedly (*merito*) reckoned as justice when this mortification occurs and when we hold fast to perfection not only in faith but in all the virtues.[59] The Italian patristic scholar and translator of Origen's *Commentary on Romans*, F. Cocchini, summarizes this emphasis in Origen as follows:

> Origen has already said that the resurrection of Christ constitutes an example for Christians, and such an example is based on the "new life" that really unites the resurrected Christ to as many as believe in him. The difference then between Christ and the Christians consists, according to Origen, in the fact that whereas for Christ one is dealing with a new life in the most complete sense of the term—since it has already been made completely manifest as such—for Christians one is dealing with a life that, as long as they are not resurrected, one can manifest as "new" above all in the moral aspect.[60]

The "new" in the "new creation" is visible primarily in post-baptismal moral transformation. This divine-human cooperation or synergism (to use the Greek term) is how the justified share in the fruit of Christ's redemptive death and his resurrection life. Origen bases this idea on the link made by Paul in Romans 4:24–25: "It will be reckoned to us who believe in him that raised from the dead Jesus our Lord, who was put to death for our trespasses and raised for our justification." Elsewhere Origen says that to be alive to God in Christ Jesus (Rom. 6:11) means to be alive to God in all the virtues, which are identified with Christ.[61]

Interestingly, Origen chooses to exemplify the necessity of mortification by returning to the example of the thief on the cross that he had earlier cited as an (exceptional) example of one justified by faith alone. He again makes use of organic imagery and says that this thief had fulfilled Romans 6:5–6, in that he had been planted together in the likeness of Christ's death and of his resurrection, and for that reason he deserved paradise since he had been joined to the tree of life:

> Christ himself then is the tree of life. . . . His death becomes for us a tree of life as a new and a wonderful gift from God . . . Now I think that one could fittingly say this also about that thief who was hanging together with Jesus on the cross and has appeared to be planted together into the

likeness of his death by his confession in which he said: "Lord, remember me when you come into your kingdom"; and he rebuked the other thief who was blaspheming. But it has appeared that he was also planted together in his resurrection by what is said to him: "Today you will be with me in paradise." For truly he was a plant worthy of paradise which was joined to the tree of life.[62]

Origen points to the good thief as a good commentary on Romans 10:9–10. Earlier in his exegesis Origen had used him as an illustration of one justified by faith alone without works.[63] The current passage seems to make clear, however, that in Origen's view this thief is an example of how faith and works cooperate in an organic way in contributing to salvation. He exemplifies the Pauline text about the necessity of dying and rising with Christ by freely carrying out the just works of publicly confessing the Lordship of Christ and rebuking the other thief who was blaspheming. The result is that ultimately the good thief was deservedly justified by a synthesis of his faith and his virtues. By God's wonderful gift of life to him the thief had not only been declared just with respect to the past, with no antecedent works, but he had also become inherently just and worthy of paradise through his free and active adhesion to the living Christ. Verfaillie synthesizes Origen's theology of grace, merit, and works as follows: "This meritorious character of our acts has its source in the grace of justification and completes the conception of it. Liberated from the death of sin, the Christian soul is united to Christ who gives it new life, by means of which he gives the means of bearing fruit that is pleasing to God."[64] Reasoner noticed that there are three references to the good thief in Origen's commentary, and that the point of the final citation seems to be the following: "The necessity of works alongside faith becomes clearer in the final reference to this thief. When exegeting what it means to be planted with Christ in his death in order to share in his resurrection (6:5), Origen cites the thief's confession to Jesus and rebuke of the blaspheming thief as evidence that he was planted with Christ in a death to sin."[65] It seems remarkable that both the Roman Catholic scholar Verfaillie and the Protestant exegete Reasoner seem to admire the way Origen interprets the good thief's behavior as manifesting both his mortification and the new life into which he had been implanted by the grace of Christ. The good thief exhibits graphically the organic connection between faith and good works.

Finally, this example again shows how Origen's exposition of salvation illumines Pauline texts with passages from the Gospels and elsewhere. Origen strives to achieve a synthesis and harmony between the teaching and doctrine of St. Paul and the words and actions of the Lord Jesus in the Gospels. In Origen, we find a resounding affirmation of a synergistic understanding of salvation according to which divine grace and human freedom are both affirmed. Salvation is by faith and by postbaptismal works of love as complementary aspects of a single transformative process. Paul, James, Jesus, the prophets, and the whole Bible are thus brought into harmony.

NOTES

1. H. de Lubac, *History and Spirit: The Understanding of Scripture according to Origen*, trans. Anne Englund Nash, with Greek and Latin translation by Juvenal Merriell of the Oratory (San Francisco: Ignatius Press, 2007) [French original: *Histoire et esprit: L'Intelligence de l'Ecriture d'après Origène*, Paris, 1950], 212.
2. Cf. *Homilies on Exodus* (3.3), trans. R. Heine, *Fathers of the Church*, vol. 71 (Washington, DC: Catholic University of America Press, 1992).
3. H. de Lubac, *History and Spirit*, 214.
4. For more on the exegesis and hermeneutics of Origen, see R. R. Reno, "Origen," in *Christian Theologies of Scripture: A Comparative Introduction*, ed. Justin S. Holcomb (New York: NYU Press, 2006), 21–38.
5. Cf. Origen, *Homilies on Joshua* (3.5), trans. B. Bruce, *Fathers of the Church*, vol. 105, 50 (Washington, DC: Catholic University of America Press, 2002).
6. Cf. Cyprian, *Epistulae* 73.21, Corpus Christianorum, Series Latina (Turnhout and Paris, 1994), 3.2, 795.
7. Cf. R. Martin, *Will Many Be Saved? What Vatican II Actually Teaches and Its Implications for the New Evangelization* (Grand Rapids, MI: Eerdmans, 2012), 31–40.
8. Cf. H. Koch, *Pronoia und Paideusis: Studien über Origenes und sein Verhältnis zum Platonismus* (Berlin: Walter de Gruyter & Co., 1932), 18.
9. Ibid.
10. This point was studied and documented long ago by J. Rivière, *The Doctrine of the Atonement: A Historical Essay*, trans. Luigi Cappadelta, 2 vols. (St. Louis: Herder, 1909), I:157–67. See also Thomas P. Scheck, *Origen and the History of Justification: The Legacy of Origen's Commentary on Romans* (Notre Dame: University of Notre Dame Press, 2008), 13–62; Scheck, "Origen's Interpretation of Romans," in *A Companion to St. Paul in the Middle Ages*, ed. S. Cartwright (Leiden: Brill, 2013), 15–49. For a treatment of this topic that differs notably from mine in its emphasis, see J. O'Leary, "Atonement," in *The Westminster Handbook to Origen*, ed. J. McGuckin (Louisville, KY: Westminster John Knox Press, 2004), 66–68.

11. All citations from Origen's *CRm* are taken (sometimes with slight modifications) from my translation (FOTC 103 & 104), Origen, *Commentary on the Epistle to the Romans*, 2 volumes (Washington, DC, 2001–02). My English translation is based on the new critical edition by C. P. Hammond Bammel, *Origenes, Der Römerbriefkommentar des Origenes: Kritische Ausgabe der Übersetzung Rufins*, 3 volumes, Aus der Geschichte der Lateinischen Bibel 16, 33, 34 (Freiburg im Breisgau, 1990–98). To facilitate referencing, my English translation integrates the Migne column numbers in square brackets within the body of the text. In this chapter, rather than using page numbers, the Migne (PG 14) column numbers will appear in parentheses for all citations.
12. See: P. Widdicombe, "Origen," in *The Blackwell Companion to Paul*, ed. S. Westerholm (Chichester: Wiley-Blackwell, 2011), 316–29 (323–26).
13. Cf. Scheck/Hammond Bammel, *CRm* 3.2(2–5).22–25 (928). (Hereafter cited as *CRm* followed by book, section in the Hammond Bammel critical condition, and lines. The final number in parentheses refers to the Migne (Patrologia Graeca 14) column numbers which are embedded in my English translation.)
14. *CRm* 4.11.67–75 (1001).
15. *CRm* 5.4.3–8 (1029).
16. *CRm* 4.8.76–89 (990).
17. P. Widdicombe, "Origen," 316, noticed Origen's harmonious approach to Scripture as well: "For Origen, the writers of the New Testament, and the Old for that matter, all told one story about one subject."
18. For more on the exegesis and hermeneutics of Origen, see R. R. Reno, "Origen," in *Christian Theologies of Scripture: A Comparative Introduction*, ed. Justin S. Holcomb (New York: NYU Press, 2006), 21–38.
19. See the Introduction to my translation of *St. Jerome's Commentaries on Galatians, Titus and Philemon* (Notre Dame: University of Notre Dame Press, 2010).
20. R. Bultmann, "The Significance of the Historical Jesus for the Theology of Paul," in *Faith and Understanding: Collected Essays*, 220–46 (London: SCM/New York: Harper & Row, 1969), 22.
21. *Jerome Biblical Commentary*, ed. R. Brown et al. (Englewood Cliffs, NJ: Prentice-Hall, 1968), 79:17.
22. J. Fitzmyer, "Abba and Jesus' Relation to God," in J. Fitzmyer, *According to Paul: Studies in the Theology of the Apostle* (New York/Mawhaw: Paulist Press, 1993), 108.
23. "Jesus Reveals the Father: The Center of New Testament Theology," *Communio* 26 (1999), 235–57, at 247, n. 25.
24. D. Wenham, *Paul, Follower of Jesus or Founder of Christianity?* (Grand Rapids, MI: Eerdmans, 1995), 409–10. See also Wenham, *Paul and Jesus: The True Story* (Grand Rapids, MI: Eerdmans, 2002).
25. *CRm* 4.8.89–91 (990).
26. Cf. C. Verfaillie, *La doctrine de la justification dans Origène d'après son commentaire de l'Épître aux Romains*. Thèse de la Faculté de théologie catholique de

l'Université de Strasbourg (Strasbourg, 1926), 70. (Hereafter cited as *Doctrine* followed by a page number.)
27. *CRm* 2.13.407–14 (908).
28. *CRm* 2.9(12–13).403–8 (908); 2.9(12–13).62–63 (900).
29. Cf. T. Heither, *Translatio Religionis: Die Paulusdeutung des Origenes in seinem Kommentar zum Römerbrief* (Cologne: Bohlau-Verlag Koln Wein, 1990), 238.
30. *CRm* 3.7(10).81–83 (957).
31. C. VanLandingham, *Judgment & Justification in Early Judaism and the Apostle Paul* (Peabody, MA: Hendrickson, 2007), 171.
32. *CRm* 4.5.3 (975).
33. *CRm* 4.1.3 (960).
34. *CRm* 4.1.10 (963).
35. Heither, *Translatio*, 238; citing H. J. Schoeps, *Paulus: Die Theologie des Apostels im Lichte der jüdischen Religionsgeschichte* (Tübingen: Mohr, 1959), 212.
36. See Scheck, *Origen and the History of Justification*, chapter 6.
37. Ibid., chapter 7; M. Horton, "Traditional Reformed View," in *Justification: Five Views*, ed. J. Beilby and P. Eddy (Downers Grove, IL: IVP Academic, 2011), 87: "Though more radical in other ways, Anabaptist views on justification were similar to Rome's."
38. *CRm* 4.1.20 (965–966).
39. C. Verfaillie, *Doctrine*, 110.
40. De Lubac, *History and Spirit*, 211.
41. *CRm* 4.1.216–224 (965).
42. Heither, *Translatio*, 235; Heither, *Origenes, Commentarii in epistulam ad Romanos / Römerbriefkommentar*, 5 volumes (Freiburg im Breisgau: Herder, 1990–96). 2:132, n. 72.
43. Heither, *Translatio*, 236.
44. *CRm* 4.6.46–49 (981).
45. *CRm* 4.12.72–73 (1004). Cf. *initium iustificari a Deo* in 4.1.216–224 (965) above.
46. *CRm* 4.12.67–71 (1004).
47. *CRm* 4.8.41–46 (989).
48. *CRm* 7.3.13–23 (1113).
49. *CRm* 7.3.123–125 (1116).
50. Cf. Com in Mt 13.12; Princ 3.1.23.
51. Cf. Denzinger, *The Sources of Catholic Dogma*. Translated by Roy J. Deferrari from the Thirtieth Edition of Henry Denzinger's *Enchiridion Symbolorum* (Fitzwilliam: Loreto, 1954), 211.
52. *CRm* 8.7(6).111–126 (1178). Cf. also 3.7(10).19–21 (955).
53. Cf. Verfaillie, *Doctrine*, 82.
54. *CRm* 2.6(8).23–29 (890).
55. M. Reasoner, *Romans in Full Circle: A History of Interpretation* (Louisville, KY: Westminster John Knox, 2005), 25.
56. *CRm* 4.6.84–89 (982).

57. *CRm* 4.7.75–83 (986).
58. *CRm* 4.7.109–112 (986).
59. *CRm* 4.7.99–100 (986); 4.6.166–67 (984).
60. F. Cocchini, *Origene: Commento alla Lettera ai Romani. Annuncio Pasquale, Polemica antieretica* (L'Aquila: Japadre Editore, 1979), 56–57.
61. Cf. 1 Cor 1.30; Eph 2.14. Cf. Scheck/Hammond Bammel, *CRm* 5.10.264–266 (1055).
62. *CRm* 5.9.27–30 (1043); 5.9.83–90 (1045).
63. *CRm* 3.6(9).22–24 (952).
64. Verfaillie, *Doctrine*, 117.
65. Reasoner, *Romans in Full Circle*, 25.

3

Irenaeus of Lyons

JOHN BEHR

Irenaeus of Lyons is one of the most important Christian theologians of the early centuries: In his writings we can see all the lineaments of Christian orthodoxy sketched out, for the first time, coherently, consistently, confidently, and self-consciously.[1] Yet, as H. B. Swete lamented a century ago, "No early Christian writer has deserved better of the whole Church than Irenaeus."[2] Later figures, apart from the heresiologists plundering his writings for descriptions of exotic heretics long since departed, rarely look back to Irenaeus, and most of his writings have perished. The two works that survive, *Against the Heresies* and *Demonstration of the Apostolic Preaching*, only survive in translation, the former completely in Latin and the latter only in Armenian.[3] But perhaps the reason his writings have not been better preserved is because what he laid out was simply taken for granted thereafter.

Beginning with Christ, the Savior

What Irenaeus has to say can often sound very jarring to modern theology. And this is probably most true in the case of his understanding of salvation. For instance, Irenaeus argues that the genealogy given in the Gospel of Luke (*Haer.* 3:23–38), which traces the lineage of Christ back to Adam, demonstrates how Christ has recapitulated all generations in himself, connecting the end to the beginning, and that it is for this reason that Paul could describe Adam as "the type of the one to come" (Rom. 5:14). This is, he writes,

> because the Word, the Fashioner of all things, prefigured in him the future economy relating to the Son of God on behalf of the human race, God having predetermined the first, the animated human that is, so that

> he should be saved by the spiritual [one]; for, since the Saviour pre-exists, it was necessary that the one to be saved should also exist, so that the Saviour should not be without purpose.[4]

That we have been brought into existence in order to be saved by a Savior, who pre-exists as Savior, sounds very odd to our modern ears. We have, for various reasons, come to think in a theological framework that works, to put it rather crudely, in terms of a Plan A (creation, with all things being good), followed, after the Fall, by a Plan B (salvation). But once put in such crude terms, it can perhaps be seen that it is our usual framework that is odd: Christ is not Plan B!

Irenaeus's position is in fact coherent and consistent. He takes seriously that it is only after the Passion that the books of Scripture are opened, in heaven, by the slain Lamb, who alone has been given the authority to open the books (Rev. 5), and on earth, on the road to Emmaus, where the Risen Christ shows how Moses and all the prophets spoke of how the Son of Man must suffer to enter into his glory (Luke 24:26–27). This hermeneutic point is also made most clear in the example of the apostle Paul, who, before his conversion, considered himself to be "blameless with respect to righteousness under the Law" (Phil. 3:6), not standing in need of salvation, but desiring rather to eradicate those Christians who thought otherwise; but then, after his encounter with the risen Christ, as the one whom he is in fact persecuting, the "veil" lying over the Scriptures was lifted, so that he could now see the glory of God shining in the face of Christ (2 Cor. 3:12–4:6). To paraphrase E. P. Sanders, the solution comes first, and then the problem is understood.[5] And, moreover, the solution shapes how we understand the problem.

This hermeneutic point is the basis for understanding how Irenaeus relates the Scriptures to the Gospel. For Irenaeus, the Gospel is not simply a narration of the next stage or a new step in God's dealings with the human race, but rather the recapitulation of Scripture through the Cross, in a concise word.[6] With the books of Scripture now "opened," the apostles and evangelists drew from their words, figures, and images to understand and proclaim the work of God in Christ, so setting up a typological relation between these words, figures, and images, and Christ himself. The Scriptures and the Gospel thus, for Irenaeus, have the same content, but what was hidden under the types and prophecies, Christ himself, is now clearly revealed, made visible, in the proclamation of the Gospel (cf. *Haer.* 4.26.1). The word "type" comes from the verb "to strike" (τύπος from τύπτω), and so primarily means "impression," as in the "stamp" left in wax when struck by a seal. Thus, when Paul describes Adam as a "type of the one to come" (Rom. 5:14), this implies the prior existence of the one of whom he is a type. While Christ had not as yet come, in terms of the timeline of our world, he nevertheless pre-exists with God in his timeless eternity, and so Adam, as "type," can also be understood as a "preliminary sketch" of the fullness that was to be revealed in the coming of Christ; or, in other words, Adam is made "in the image" (Gen. 1:26–27), whereas Christ is himself "the image" (Col. 1:15). Despite sounding rather jarring, Irenaeus's position is entirely consequential and coherent, and a position held right through to the end of the Byzantine era.[7]

As such, the death Adam brought into the world through his disobedience, and that disobedience itself, must be placed within the scope of the larger arc that moves from the original formation of Adam to its completion in Christ. The person and work of Christ cannot be understood simply as a response to the death that Adam brought upon himself. To take it as such would be to treat Adam as already sufficient unto himself and Christ's work as merely restoring that condition. Rather, starting instead with the person of Christ, the one whom the type prefigures, Adam is seen to be an initial sketch or a preliminary imprint of the figure of Christ. And the difference between the two, for Irenaeus, is that Christ alone first shows us the life of God in human form, so that the life of Adam, before as well as after subjecting himself to death, is but a foreshadowing of this. The difference between them then is not simply, though it certainly includes, the contrast between the disobedience shown by the human creature, Adam, and the obedience of the Son of God, Christ. Nor does it only turn upon Adam's subjecting himself to death through disobedience, as if it were mortality alone that needs to be overcome, for this would only return Adam to his former life, which is already set in an arc leading to something greater. As it is in the life-giving death of Christ, in obedience to the Father and voluntarily assumed for the sake of others, that the uncreated life of God is revealed and communicated to his creature, the contrasting position of Adam from the very beginning is that he did not live this life, but rather, as created and a preliminary sketch of what is to come, this life of Christ is something that he needs to grow into by learning through experience. The unfolding of the economy cannot therefore be told by beginning with Adam, considered in himself, proceeding to the "Fall," then the "history of salvation," and finally to Christ, but must be told such that the end and the beginning mutually inform each other in one arc, both synchronously, so that the arrangement of the whole is revealed together in its recapitulation, and diachronously, as it is unfolded throughout [our] time.

For Irenaeus, to ask whether this means that God planned the Fall, or, in Irenaeus's terms, our apostasy and our death in that apostasy, would be a mistaken question, or rather one that arises from a mistaken standpoint, imagining ourselves in the position of God before creation. For Irenaeus the task of theology is, as Balthasar put it, "to *see* what *is*,"[8] instead of imagining a different starting point or another first principle. Beginning from what has been revealed in Christ, he sees the work of God as encompassing the whole of creation and its history, *including* our apostasy, and *transforming* it into one movement of salvation. This is in fact a theme that runs throughout Scripture, from Joseph being sold into slavery in Egypt, yet telling his brothers that "God sent me before you to preserve life. . . . So it was not you who sent me here but God" (Gen. 45:5, 8), to Christ himself, who though he "was crucified and killed by the hand of lawless men," yet he was, nevertheless, "delivered up according to the definite plan and foreknowledge of God" (Acts 2:23). If human apostasy, and the death that is its consequence, cannot be turned inside out, as it were, to be utilized by the God, who in Christ destroyed death by his death, so granting not only a restored (yet still mortal) breath of life but the life granted by the Spirit which can no longer be touched by death since it is entered into through death, God would not, in fact, be almighty and all things would not be in his hands. As difficult as Irenaeus' claims might seem to us, they testify to his sense that God's overwhelming omnipotence works through the paradox of strength in weakness and articulates this transforming power consistently and forcefully.

Irenaeus theologizes strictly from within the economy, from what can in fact be known and spoken about, with the right hermeneutic, of God's activity and revelation in Christ. He resists any attempt to seek a higher perspective to speak about God prior to and independent from creation, a standpoint that would have to be supra-human and, indeed, above

God himself; to attempt to speak from such a perspective would, for Irenaeus, not only be presumptuous but also groundless.[9] As the starting point for Christian theology is the work of God in Christ, understood through the opening of the Scriptures, the Christ who is now known to be the one to whom God said "Let us make the human being" is already known to be the Savior, to "pre-exist" as Savior, and so Adam's relation to his maker is always already that of being saved by the Savior. We are here far removed from the debate between Thomas Aquinas and Duns Scotus about whether the Word would have become incarnate had Adam not fallen, a debate that has all too frequently set the parameters for interpreting Irenaeus.[10] Starting with Christ, Irenaeus would rather see creation *and* salvation, with carefully defined nuances, not as two moments within one economy, but rather as coextensive, as the *one* economy: God's continuously creative work throughout the economy, resulting in the end in the one who is in the image and likeness of God, is salvation. And as such, Irenaeus can even say that it was necessary for Adam to come into existence, not implying any lack or need in God himself, but simply as a consequence of the fact that the starting point for all theology is Jesus Christ, the Savior.

Returning, now, to the passage with which we began, we can understand how Irenaeus starts from the perfected and completed work of God in Christ, and then turns to consider the preliminary character of what came before. In Adam, the Word outlined in advance what would be revealed and established in the Son of God, Christ himself. As such, the one who was to come exists before Adam; it was by him and for him that Adam came into existence, and, furthermore, as he exists as the Savior, Adam came into existence to be saved by him. Thus, though only appearing at the end, this one is nevertheless the true beginning.

From Breath to Spirit

The passage that we have been considering (*Haer.* 3.22.3) sets Adam and Christ as the two ends of the arc of the one economy of God. But, it also characterizes these two ends in terms of the different "lives" by which they live: The type, Adam, is an "animated" human being, who is saved by the "spiritual" one. As with the language of "type," Irenaeus is again drawing from Paul, this time from the distinction he makes between the first Adam, who by the "breath of life" became a "living soul" (ψυχὴν ζῶσαν), and "the last Adam," who "became a life-creating spirit."[11] As the context in 1 Corinthians 15 makes clear, the transformation from one to the other is effected by the resurrection from the dead, in which what is sown in dishonor and weakness will be raised in glory and power, and what is sown as an "animated body" (σῶμα ψυχικόν) will be raised as a "spiritual body" (σῶμα πνευματικόν, 1 Cor. 15:44, 46). Unlike the RSV, which renders the first as a "physical body" in contrast to the "spiritual body," with the implication that, when raised, the body is no longer "physical," Irenaeus reads Paul as contrasting two different modes of life: The first is the "animation" effected by the "breath of life," and the second, the "vivification" effected by the Holy Spirit, bestowed in Christ, rendering the same body as "spiritual," with the transition between the two turning upon death, that of Christ himself and then those who die in him to be raised to life in him: "What you sow does not come to life unless it dies" (1 Cor. 15:36). It is worth noting that when Irenaeus cites John 1:3–4, he does so in a manner also witnessed by many other early writers and manuscripts: "All things came to be by him and without him nothing came to be. What came to be in him was life, and the life was the light of human beings."[12] "Life," strictly speaking, is what comes through Christ, and, in turn, those who do not live by this life are, simply, "dead."[13]

This contrast and the transformation from the first to the last is also addressed by Irenaeus in *Against the Heresies* 5.1.3, which presents the contrast between the animated and the living with the same intentionality and within the full scope of the economy. Irenaeus here tackles the "Ebionites" who regard Jesus as a human son of Joseph and Mary, rather than accepting "the union of God and human," and so they remain, he says, in "the old leaven of birth [*generationis*]." They do not want to understand, according to Irenaeus, that the Holy Spirit came upon Mary and the Power of the Most High overshadowed her, so that "what is born [*quod generatum est*] is holy and the Son of the Most High God, the Father, who effected his [the Son's] incarnation and demonstrated a new generation [*novam generationem*], so that as by the former generation we inherited death, so by this generation we might inherit life." Rejecting the "heavenly wine," wanting only the "water of this world," they do not "receive God so as to have communion with him, but remain in

Adam who had been conquered and was expelled from paradise." The mention of Adam is the occasion for Irenaeus to set out the arc of the economy in the terms that we have been considering. His opponents, he says, do not understand that:

> *just as*, at the beginning [*ab initio*] of our formation [*plasmationis*] in Adam, the breath of life from God, having been united [*unita*] to the handiwork [*plasmatio*], animated [*animavit*] the human being and showed him to be a rational being, *so also*, at the end [*in fine*], the Word of the Father and the Spirit of God, having become united [*adunitus*] with the ancient substance of the formation [*plasmationis*] of Adam, rendered [*effecit*] the human being living [*viventem*] and perfect, bearing the perfect Father, *in order that just as* in the animated we all die, *so also* in the spiritual we may all be vivified [*vivificemur*]. For never at any time did Adam escape the Hands of God, to whom the Father speaking, said, "Let us make the human being in our image, after our likeness" [Gen. 1:26]. And for this reason at the end [*fine*], "not by the will of the flesh, nor by the will of man" [John 1:13], but by the good pleasure of the Father, his Hands perfected a living human being [*vivum perfecerunt hominem*], in order that Adam might become in the image and likeness of God. (*Haer.* 5.1.3, emphasis added)

The two "just as–so also" parallels are linked by a statement of intent: The beginning of our formation, in Adam, is animation by a breath of life, whereas its end, in Christ, is vivification of the ancient substance by the Holy Spirit, rendering the handiwork a living and perfect human being, and this has been established with the intention that as we all die in the animated life of Adam we may be vivified in the spiritual life of Christ. That the beginning and the end are united in one intentional economy is further emphasized by the statement that Adam "never escaped the Hands of God," being continuously fashioned and prepared to live the life of God. The perfected living human being does not result, for Irenaeus, from the "old generation," or, borrowing words from John's Prologue, "from the will of the flesh or the will of man," but rather by the good pleasure of the Father in the "new generation," and so the living human being is none other than Christ himself, who enables Adam also to become "in the image and likeness of God."

The Pauline distinction between the breath of life and the life-creating spirit, used by Irenaeus to describe the arc of the economy of God, is treated most fully during the course's assertion that "flesh and blood cannot inherit the kingdom" (1 Cor. 15:50). Irenaeus argues that flesh and blood can indeed *be inherited by* the Spirit when vivified by the Spirit (*Haer.* 5.9–10), that is, when we no longer bear the image of the earthly one by working the deeds of the flesh, but rather bear the image of the heavenly one, having been washed in Christ and "made alive by working the works of the Spirit" (*Haer.* 5.11; 1 Cor. 15:48–9). Irenaeus then further explains the relationship between the breath of life and the life-creating Spirit by turning to the previous verses from the apostle's epistle. Although the flesh is capable of receiving both the breath of life and the life given by the Spirit, and while the difference between these can be put in relative terms (temporal/eternal, weaker/stronger), they cannot co-exist in the same body. Just as death cannot co-exist in the same body with life, so also, Irenaeus asserts apropos a quotation from Isaiah (25:8), "the former life is expelled, because it was not given by the Spirit but by the breath, for the breath of life, which made the human an animated being, is one thing, and the vivifying Spirit, which rendered him spiritual, another" (*Haer.* 5.12.1–2). Citing two more verses from Isaiah (42:5; 57:16), Irenaeus concludes from the first that the "breath" is given in common to all people upon earth, but the Spirit is given only to those who tread down earthly desires, and, following the language of the second—"For the Spirit shall go forth from me, and I have made every breath"—that the Spirit is placed "particularly on the side of God," bestowed upon the human race in the last times through the adoption of sons, while the "breath" is common to all creation and is "created" (ποίημα; *Haer.* 5.12.2). As "the created is other than him who creates," the breath is temporal while the Spirit is eternal; the breath increases in strength, flourishes for a period of time, and then departs, leaving its abode destitute of breath, while the Spirit "embraces the human being inside and out" and remains with him permanently (*Haer.* 5.12.2). And then, returning to 1 Corinthians 15:45–6, Irenaeus reminds us that the animated is first, followed by the spiritual: "It was necessary that, first, the human being should be fashioned, then that what was fashioned should receive the soul; and that afterwards it should thus receive the communion of the Spirit." (That he uses the term "soul" here, rather than "breath," is because he is commenting on 1 Corinthians 15:45–6, and the use it makes of Genesis 2:7, rather than the Genesis text itself.) Irenaeus then concludes his discussion, stating: "Therefore, just as the one who became a living soul, turning to evil, lost life, so again, that same one, turning to what is better and receiving the life-creating Spirit, shall find life" (*Haer.* 5.12.2). Turning to evil, the animated human being lost the life of the breath, but what he or she will receive in Christ is more than this, it will be the life-creating Spirit himself.

The Sign of Jonah

The arc of the economy thus moves from Adam to Christ and from the breath to the Spirit, with Christ and the Spirit being the Hands that fashion and animate the human creature, leading the handiwork from animation to vivification. It was certainly by his disobedience that Adam turned to evil and "lost life," becoming not just capable of death but subject to death. Yet, as told from the end, as it must be, death and disobedience are integral to the movement from one end of the arc to the other: It is by death that the animation by the breath is "expelled," giving way to the vivification of the flesh by the Spirit; and it is also by the effect of disobedience that the human being learns obedience, that is, learns to receive life which God alone can give, and so receive it securely. The ultimately pedagogical, and salvific, role of disobedience and death within the economy is brought out in a passage where Irenaeus again depicts the span of the economy and makes clear that the salvific work of Christ is both the beginning and culmination:

> God, therefore, was long-suffering when the human being defaulted, foreseeing that victory which should be granted to him through the Word. For when strength was made perfect in weakness [cf. 2 Cor. 12:9], [the Word] showed the kindness and transcendent power of God. For *just as* he did bear Jonah to be swallowed up by the whale, not that he should be swallowed up and perish altogether, but *so that*, having been cast out again, he might be more subject to God and might glorify him the more who had conferred upon him such an unhoped-for salvation and brought a firm repentance to the Ninevites, that they might convert to the Lord who delivered them from death when they were struck with

awe by that sign that had been wrought on Jonah . . . *so also*, from the beginning, God did bear the human being to be swallowed up by the great whale, who was the author of the transgression, not that he should perish altogether when so engulfed, but arranging in advance the finding of salvation, which was accomplished by the Word, through the "sign of Jonah" [Matt. 12:39–40], for those who held the same opinion as Jonah regarding the Lord, and who confessed, and said, "I am a servant of the Lord, and I worship the Lord God of heaven, who made the sea and the dry land" [Jonah 1:9], *so that* the human being, receiving an unhoped-for salvation from God, might rise from the dead, and glorify God, and repeat, "I cried to the Lord my God in my affliction, and he heard me from the belly of hell" [Jonah 2:2], and that he might always continue glorifying God, and giving thanks without ceasing for that salvation which he had obtained from him, "that no flesh should glory in the Lord's presence" [1 Cor. 1:29], nor should the human being ever adopt an opposite opinion with regard to God, supposing that the incorruptibility which surrounds him is his own by nature, nor, by not holding the truth, should boast with empty superciliousness, as if he were by nature like to God. (*Haer.* 3.20.1, emphasis added)

From the beginning, God has borne human beings while they were swallowed up by the great whale, that is, death. God, emphatically, did not create human beings *in* this condition. It was the "animated" human being who "turned to evil and lost life" (*Haer.* 5.12.2). And, as he puts it in the preceding passage, there was "an author of the transgression." The lesson Jonah learned through his misadventure, according to Irenaeus, was that he "is a servant of the Lord," which is nothing other than the law given to Adam and Eve at the beginning (cf. *Dem.*15). As such, the "author of the transgression" tempts the human being to think that he or she has life of his own nature, "as if he were like to God," or, as Irenaeus states elsewhere, he beguiled Adam and Eve with "the pretext of immortality," that which is God's alone to give.[14] However, God's forbearance has a purpose, which is that, as with the case of Jonah, the human being might learn to subject herself or himself to God, to glorify him the more, and so be glorified in return. Moreover, God is forbearing in allowing the human race to be swallowed up from the beginning because, although unknown to the human race, he had also "arranged in advance the finding of salvation," a salvation that was nevertheless, from the human perspective, "unhoped-for."

In this way, then, the "finding of salvation" was effected through "the sign of Jonah," who in turn becomes a type both of the perishing human race and the salvation worked by Christ. That Jonah can represent both is because it is in and through his death that Christ brings about salvation, as it is through their death that human beings come to know their own inherent weakness and, simultaneously, the strength of God, just as it is also through death that the human being passes from animation to vivification. So, Irenaeus concludes:

> Such then was the patience of God, that the human being, passing through all things and acquiring knowledge of death,[15] then attaining to the resurrection from the dead, and learning by experience from whence he has been delivered, may thus always gives thanks to the Lord, having received from him the gift of incorruptibility, and may love him the more, for "he to whom more is forgiven, loves more" [cf. Luke 7:42–3], and may himself know how mortal and weak he is, but also understand that God is so immortal and powerful as to bestow immortality on the mortal and eternity on the temporal, and that he may also know the other powers of God made manifest in himself, and, being taught by them, may think of God in accordance with the greatness of God. For the glory of the human being is God, while the vessel of the workings of God, and of all his wisdom and power is the human being. (*Haer.* 3.20.2)

Subjection to death, brought upon human beings by their own disobedience at the instigation of the Devil, is thus turned inside out within the full arc of the economy which, as we have repeatedly seen, can only be understood from the end point, Christ and his Passion.

Behold the Human Being!

Christ himself is, for Irenaeus, the first human being, strictly speaking, of whom Adam was but a foreshadowing. As such, it was not simply because the breath of life is "weaker" than the Spirit, nor because Adam, as a newly created infant, was inexperienced, easily led astray, and required a full pedagogy before maturing to his full potential, though these are both true.[16] Most important is that, even though Adam had been created "in the image," the one who is the image had not yet appeared. As Irenaeus puts it:

> For in times long past it was said the human being was made in the image of God, but it was not shown [to be so]; for the Word was as yet invisible, after whose image the human was created; and because of this he easily lost the likeness. When, however, the Word of God became flesh, he confirmed both of these: for he both showed forth the image truly, himself becoming that which was his image, and he re-established the likeness in a sure manner, by co-assimilating the human being to the invisible Father through the Word become visible. (*Haer.* 5.16.2)

The Word was as yet invisible, or, as we have seen, the crucified Christ was hidden beneath the veil of Scripture, in types and prophecies not yet understood. And so, as Irenaeus puts it in the *Demonstration*, "Christ, by being embodied in the same manner as Adam, became the human being, who was written in the beginning, 'according to the image and likeness of God'" (*Dem.* 32). The "likeness" that the human race lost in Adam is not the Spirit, for, as we have seen, the Spirit, together with Christ, is present throughout the whole economy, as the Hands of God fashioning the human being, preparing the human race to be perfected in Christ and to live the life of the Spirit rather than merely a snatched breath. Nor is it that the human race lost life, for as we have seen the arc of the economy moves from animation to vivification, as two distinct modalities of life. Nor, finally, is it simply that human beings became mortal; for they always were mortal, that is, capable of death, even if they had retained the "strength" of the breath and had not died.[17] What happened to the human race in Adam is, specifically, that it became *subject* to mortality, caught in sin and death, unable to escape from the strong man who had beguiled them under "the pretext of immortality." As the passage cited above suggests, they lost the ability to live like God, for the Word as yet had not shown himself and his life in this world. Yet, when Christ does so, it is by using death to conquer death. "Likeness" to God is thus manifest in the *way* that human creatures live the life given to them, if, that is, they do so in the manner revealed by Christ, by laying down their life, rather than trying to preserve their own life (of the breath) in perpetuity. As this had not yet been clearly shown, though with hindsight, as we have seen, the Law and the Prophets speak of this throughout, Adam, though a model of the one to come, had as yet no one on whom to model himself, and so lost this "likeness."[18]

Yet it is in this very way, by death, that human beings in Adam now enter into the fullness of humanity manifested in Christ: "Do you not know that all of us who have been baptized into Christ Jesus were baptized into his death?" (Rom. 6:3). Although Irenaeus knows of baptism as given "for the remission of sins,"[19] for him the primary function of baptism is the "regeneration" of the human being as an adopted son of God.[20] Thus, Irenaeus defines baptism as "the seal of eternal life and rebirth unto God, that we may no longer be sons of mortal men, but of the eternal and everlasting God" (*Dem.* 3). This "new generation" is intimately connected, for Irenaeus, with the Christ's own formation as "the first born of the Virgin" (*Haer.* 3.18.7). As he asks of the Ebionites:

> How can they be saved unless it was God who wrought their salvation upon earth? Or how shall the human being pass into God [χωρήσει], unless God has passed into the human? And how shall he escape from the generation of death [*mortis generationem*], if not by a new generation [*in novam generationem*], given in a wonderful and unexpected manner by God as a sign of salvation, that which is from the Virgin, they being regenerated through faith [*quae est ex Virgine, per fidem regenerentur*]? Or how shall they receive adoption from God, remaining in that generation which is according to the human being in this world? . . . And for this reason in the last days he exhibited the "likeness," the Son of God being made human, assuming the ancient handiwork into himself, as I have shown in the preceding book.[21]

The new generation from the Virgin is manifested by Christ's own arrival in this world, but it is no less a new birth for all believers regenerated through faith. Similarly, a few paragraphs later, Irenaeus says:

> There are those who say that "He is a man, and who shall know him?" [Jer. 17:9]; and, "I came unto the prophetess, and she bore a son, and his name is called Wonderful Counsellor, the Mighty God" [Isa. 8:3, 9:6]; and those who proclaimed the Immanuel, born of the Virgin [Isa. 7:14]:

> declaring the union of the Word of God with his own handiwork, that the Word would become flesh, and the Son of God the Son of Man, the pure one opening purely that pure womb which regenerates human beings unto God and which he himself made pure, having become that which we are, he is "God Almighty" and has a generation which cannot be declared. (*Haer.* 4.33.1)

Becoming human, Christ opens the pure womb, the womb by which human beings are also regenerated unto God. The background for this idea is a Scriptural verse that Irenaeus set before the theologian in *Against the Heresies* 1.10.3: that "The children of her who was desolate are more than her who is married" [cf. Isa. 54:1; Gal. 4:27]. The "barren woman," who as a result of Christ's Passion (the suffering servant described by Isaiah in the previous chapter, Isa. 52:13–53:12) now has many children, is the Church who now gives birth to those adopted in Christ by themselves being regenerated in the same pure womb.[22]

The arc of economy thus moves, as we have seen, from Adam to Christ, from the human being animated by a breath of life to the spiritual human being vivified by the Holy Spirit, with the beginning and the end being understood in terms of each other. The economy is "for the sake of the human race" (*Haer.* 1.10.3) and leads from the preliminary sketch to the perfect and complete living human being. That this is indeed the work of God is shown, for Irenaeus, by the manner in which Christ healed the man blind from birth (John 9). It was not merely by a word that he was healed, but "by an outward action, doing this not without purpose or by chance, but that he might show forth the Hand of God that had at the beginning moulded the human being" (*Haer.* 5.15.2). Just as "the Lord took mud from the earth and formed the human being" (Gen. 2:7), so Christ spat on the ground and made mud, smeared it upon his eyes, thereby "pointing out the original fashioning, how it was effected, and manifesting the Hand of God to those who can understand by what [Hand] the human being was formed out of the dust" (*Haer.* 5.15.2). As in Christ's words, the man was born blind not because of his own sin or that of his parents, "but that the works of God should be manifest in him" (John 9:3), Irenaeus sets this particular work within the intentionality of the economy as a whole:

> For that which the artificer, the Word, had omitted to form in the womb, he then supplied in public, that the works of God might be manifested in him, in order that we might not seek out another hand by which the human being is fashioned, nor another Father, knowing that this Hand of God which formed us in the beginning, and which does form us in the womb, has in the last times sought us out who were lost, winning back his own, and taking up the lost sheep upon his shoulders, and with joy restoring it to the fold of life. (*Haer.* 5.15.2; cf. Luke 19:10, 15:4–6)

If all of this was done so that "the works of God should be manifest in him," Irenaeus concludes that "the work of God is fashioning the human being" (*Haer.* 5.15.2, *opera autem Dei plasmatio est hominis*).

Irenaeus' exposition of this uniquely Johannine miracle account allows us to see one final link between the two ends of the arc of the economy, which is perhaps distinctively Johannine. The Gospel of John, of course, clearly sets itself in parallel with Genesis: both begin, "In the beginning." However, when we turn to the account of creation given in the first chapter with Irenaeus' words in mind—that "the work of God is fashioning the human being"—a fundamental distinction opens up between every other aspect of creation and that of the human being: Every other part of creation is simply spoken into being with a divine imperative, "Let there be"; but when it comes to the human being, God deliberates about this, as his own particular work or project, and then announces it not with an imperative but a subjunctive: "Let us make . . ." (Gen. 1:26). As we have seen, for Irenaeus, what is made at that point, at the beginning, the male and female *in* the image, the creature taken from the earth and animated by a breath, is but a preliminary sketch of what is, at the end, revealed in Christ. As Pilate says, unwittingly, and only in the Gospel of John, just before Christ goes to the cross, "Behold the human being!" (John 19:5).

Conclusion

For Irenaeus, then, salvation is understood, ultimately, to coincide with God's creation, where this latter is not understood as the initial act of creation, nor as the world around us, but rather as the perfect fulfillment of the will and purpose of God, which is expressly to make the human being in his image. The perfect image of God is none other than Christ himself, who shows us the love and life of God by voluntarily, that is, as one not subject to death, laying down his life for others. The creatures made from earth and animated with a breath of life cannot of course be created already living such a life, but are certainly created as called to enter, voluntarily and out of love, into and share in the life of God. For creatures to enter upon this path is both their salvation, an entry into a life which can no longer be touched by death for it has been entered into through death, taking up the cross; and it is also, in the most profound sense, their creation, for, by giving their own "let it be" to God's own work, they enable his intention, to create a human being, to become a reality. The beginning and the end, creation and salvation, coincide, for Irenaeus, in Christ himself, the beginning who appears at the end.

NOTES

1. For full treatment, see my *Irenaeus of Lyons: Identifying Christianity*, Christian Theology in Context (Oxford: Oxford University Press, 2013); much of this chapter is drawn from that monograph.
2. H. B. Swete, foreword in F.R.M. Hitchcock, *Irenaeus of Lyons: A Study of His Teaching* (Cambridge: Cambridge University Press, 1914).
3. Irenaeus of Lyons, *Against the Heresies* (Hereafter cited as *Haer.* with the volume, page, and section numbers following.), 1–3 ed. and French trans. A. Rousseau and L. Doutreleau, SC 263–4, 293–4, 210–11 (Paris: Cerf, 1979, 1982, 1974); 4 ed. and French trans. A. Rousseau, B. Hemmerdinger, L. Doutreleau, and C. Mercier, SC 100 (Paris: Cerf, 1965); 5 ed. and French trans. A. Rousseau, L. Doutreleau, and C. Mercier SC 152–3 (Paris: Cerf, 1969); English trans. ANF 1 (1885; repr. Grand Rapids, MI: Eerdmans, 1987); Eng. trans. of *Haer.* 3 in D. J. Unger, rev. M. C. Steenberg, ACW 64 (New York: Newman Press, 2012). Irenaeus of Lyons, *Demonstration of the Apostolic Preaching* (hereafter cited as *Dem.*), trans. John Behr (Crestwood, NY: St Vladimir's Seminary Press, 1997).
4. *Haer.* 3.22.3. This is a difficult text; for full discussion see Rousseau (SC 210, pp. 371–2) and Steenberg (ACW 64, 195–8) with reference to prior literature. I have adopted Rousseau's suggestion of "*in eo*" instead of "*in semetipsum,*" which Steenberg retains and renders "with a view to himself," rather than "in him," though he accepts that "if *in semetipsum* is retained, Adam must in any case be implied in the clause." I have adopted Steenberg's reading of *generis humani* "as if it were a dative of advantage."
5. Cf. E. P. Sanders, *Paul and Palestinian Judaism* (Philadelphia: Fortress Press, 1977), 475: "Paul's" logic seems to run like this: in Christ God has acted to save

the world; therefore the world is in need of salvation; but God also gave the law; if Christ is given for salvation, it must follow that the law could not have been; is the law then against the purpose of God which has been revealed in Christ? No, it has the function of consigning everyone to sin *so that* everyone could be saved by God's grace in Christ." For further reflection on the implications of starting with Christ, see John Behr, *Mystery of Christ: Life in Death* (Crestwood, NY: St. Vladimir's Seminary Press, 2006) chapter 3.

6. Cf. Behr, *Irenaeus*, 124–44.
7. See, for instance, the statement of Nicholas Cabasilas: "It was for the new human being that human nature was created at the beginning, and for him mind and desire were prepared . . . It was not the old Adam who was the model for the new, but the new Adam for the old . . . For those who have known him first, the old Adam is the archetype because of our fallen nature. But for him who sees all things before they exist, the first Adam is the imitation of the second. To sum it up: the Savior first and alone showed to us the true human being, who is perfect on account of both character and life and in all other respects." Nicholas Cabasilas, *The Life in Christ*, 6.91–4, ed. and French trans. M.-H. Congourdeau, SC 361 (Paris: Cerf, 1990); Eng. trans. C. J. deCatanzaro (Crestwood, NY: St Vladimir's Seminary Press, 1974), where it is numbered as 6.12.
8. Hans Urs von Balthasar, *The Glory of the Lord: A Theological Aesthetics*, vol. 2, *Studies in Theological Style: Clerical Styles*, trans. A. Louth, F. McDonagh, and B. McNeil (Edinburgh: T & T Clark, 1984), 45.
9. Cf. Behr, *Irenaeus*, 103–20.
10. As Gustav Wingren comments, these debates in Irenaean scholarship "might lead one to ask if the main question is really whether Irenaeus followed Thomas or Duns Scotus!" *Man and the Incarnation: A Study in the Biblical Theology of Irenaeus* (London: Oliver and Boyd, 1959), 92–3, fn 37.
11. 1 Cor. 15:45; Gen. 2:7. Cf. Jacques Fantino, "Le Passage du Premier Adam au Second Adam comme Expression du Salut chez Irénée de Lyon," *Vigiliae Christianae* (= *VC*) 52.4 (1998), 418–29.
12. *Haer.* 3.11.1, cf. 1.8.5.Cf. Origen, *Commentary on John*, 2.132: "Some copies, however, have, and perhaps not without credibility, "what came to be in him was life." Now if life is equivalent to "the light of human beings," no one who is in darkness is alive, and no one who is alive is in darkness, but everyone who is alive is also in light, and everyone who is in light is alive." The Codex Sinaiticus and the Western text have this reading of John 1:3–4.
13. Cf. *Haer.* 5.9.1: "Those, then, not having that which saves and forms into life, shall be, and shall be called, "flesh and blood" [1 Cor. 15:50], not having the Spirit of God in themselves. Wherefore they spoken of by the Lord as "dead," for, he says, "Let the dead bury their dead" [Luke 9:60], because they do not have the Spirit which vivifies the human being."
14. *Haer.* 3.23.5; 4.Pref.4. For the Devil's role in the human apostasy, see also *Haer.* 3.23.1–3; 4.40.3; *Dem.* 16.

15. Following the emendation of "*morum*" to "*mortum*" proposed by Grabe and adopted by Rousseau (SC 210, 349–50), who notes *Haer.* 3.23.1 (referring back to the previous passage) and *Haer.* 4.39.1 as parallels.
16. For this pedagogical dimension of the economy, the "symphony of salvation," see *Haer.* 4.37–39; Behr, *Irenaeus*, 185–98.
17. Cf. *Dem.* 14–15; Behr, *Irenaeus*, 155–8.
18. James Barr (*The Garden of Eden and the Hope of Immortality* [Minneapolis: Fortress Press, 1993], 21) makes a similar point in his reading of the Genesis account of Adam and Eve: "Adam and Eve were not immortal beings who by sin fell into a position where they must die; they were mortal beings who had a remote and momentary chance of eternal life but gained this chance only through an act of their own fault, and who because of that same act were deprived of that same chance." Irenaeus would add, however, that, starting with the work of Christ in his Passion, this disobedience and death is incorporated within the arc of the economy, to become the means by which the creature learns to receive and live the divine life.
19. The connection is made explicit only in *Dem.* 3 and *Haer.* 3.12.7, where he comments on Acts 10:43. In *Haer.* 5.14.3, Irenaeus writes of the "remission of sins" of those who have been reconciled to the Father by being incorporated into the righteous flesh of Adam, but no explicit mention is made of baptism. Cf. A. Houssiau, "Le Baptême selon Irénée de Lyon," *Ephemerides théologiques et religieuses* (= *ETL*) 60 (1984), 45–59.
20. Cf. *Haer.* 1.21.1; 3.17.1; *Dem.* 7.
21. *Haer.* 4.33.4, see also *Haer.* 3.19.1; 5.1.3, cited above.
22. Behr, *The Mystery of Christ*, chapter 4.

4

Saint Augustine

DAVID VINCENT MECONI, SJ

St. Augustine (354–430) was born in Thagaste (today, Souq Ahras, Algeria), in the Roman province of Numidia, North Africa, of a non-Christian father, Patricius, and a Christian mother, Monica. Augustine was not baptized until he was thirty-three, having become an adherent of Manichaeism in his teens. Gradually disillusioned by Manichee teaching, Augustine left Carthage, where he had been teaching rhetoric, sailed for Rome, and shortly thereafter, was appointed rhetor at the imperial court in Milan. There he encountered translated works of Neo-Platonist philosophers, and heard the sermons of Ambrose, the great bishop of Milan, who helped him to overcome his earlier prejudices against the Bible. This paved the way for his conversion in the fall of 386. In the Easter of 387, Monica rejoiced to see her son a "Catholic Christian" at last. After his return to Africa in 388 to begin a kind of monastic experiment in Christian communal living, Augustine was pressed to accept priestly ordination, in 391, by Bishop Valerian of the seaside town of Hippo. In 395, Augustine was consecrated bishop of Hippo, where he died in 430, during the siege of the town by the invading Vandals. He had devoted close to forty years as "minister of word and sacrament" in the church in Africa, but through the influence of his writings, his fame had spread throughout the Latin-speaking Mediterranean world.

The spiritual and intellectual journey of Augustine can be traced through his letters, sermons, and writings that have formed a rich religious and cultural legacy for the Christian Church of the West, and beyond, into the contemporary world. This is evident in his writings against the Manichees, and the schismatic Donatist church of Africa, and against the Pelagians who attacked his theology of grace. It can also be traced in the hundreds of extant sermons and letters, as well as in his great work on the history of salvation, *The City of God*. Augustine's contribution to the interpretation and reception of Scripture is of immense significance in the sixteen centuries since his death. With Jerome, he became the biblical voice of the Latin West. His commentaries on the Psalms and the Gospels, and especially his reading of the Epistle to the Romans, have left their imprint on subsequent Christian thought. The three masterpieces of his early episcopacy, *De doctrina Christiana, Confessions,* and *The Literal Interpretation of Genesis,* bear witness to the range and scope of his understanding of Scriptures, as well as to his extraordinary self-application to the biblical texts as the source of life for the Christian church.

Introduction

Saint Augustine of Hippo understood the fullness of human salvation as becoming conformed to the human Christ. Assisting others to receive Christ as a forgiving lover and a life-giving Lord was the point of every sermon and every page Augustine ever brought forth. Salvation in Augustine's theology is ultimately an analysis of the nature of charity, the very essence of God: "Love, then, will see to it that we are conformed (*conformemur*) to God and, having been conformed and configured (*conformati atque figurati*) by him and cut off this world, that we are not confused with the things that ought to be subject to us."[1] Conformity to Christ means to love as God loves, necessitating a transformation of our loves, and once conformed to Christ, the Christian is inevitably cut off from this world (*circumcisi ab hoc mundo*) as merely human. Now Christ loves in and through the fallen creature, transforming him or her into another Christ: "Let us thus rejoice and give thanks, for we have been made not Christians, but we have been made Christ."[2] This is salvation for Augustine—to be made one with Christ in a collective harmony of saintly praise.

The purpose of this chapter is to show how and where Augustine developed his theology of salvation, dividing our reflections into four main parts. In the first section we discuss why humanity stands in need of redemption. In other words: What exactly do I need saving from? We shall here treat the divided heart and the self-imposed autonomy each fallen soul inevitably embraces. The second part turns to how Augustine envisions the process of healing, focusing primarily on the wholly gratuitous and thus ineffable nature of God's grace. The third section takes up Augustine's thinking on the incarnate Christ and why it is the Lord Jesus comes and saves the way he does. In our fourth and final part we examine what such salvation looks like, taking up two related points: Christ's incorporation of the human sinner into his own body, and the consequent deification of the faithful believer into another Christ.

As with most central theological concerns, Augustine has no one systematic treatise on salvation. He was an occasional writer who took up a topic when asked about it by a concerned interlocutor, or when he saw a tenet of the Church's teaching misunderstood or under attack. Since he has no one work dedicated to Christian redemption, the following analysis will be gleaned from sections of Augustine's broader works on grace and the Christian life.

Salvation from What?

Christian salvation for Augustine begins with the first act of human rebellion, described most often as the misdirected attempt to love a creature apart from God. While the fall of Satan from the *caeleum caeli* receives much attention when Augustine comments on God's good creation, it is not for this irrevocably lost enemy that the Son of God became incarnate. Salvation in Christ begins in the Garden of Eden where man and woman were created mutually for divine intimacy; it is also here where this plan for human flourishing went astray. Humanity's primal revolt occurred when Adam chose to love a creature in the place of his Creator. Adam could of course have loved Eve rightly (and eternally) but in choosing to allow her, and not their God, to be the measure of what he considered to be fidelity and loyalty, Adam inverted the only ordering of loves that allows for human happiness.[3] That is, God has ordered the human heart to love him first and in that precedence love all else God has made. Adam, however, was deceived into thinking he could love Eve rightly without divine assistance. This thirst for autonomy from the God who is perfect and participable love is how Augustine most often explains the fallen condition: the attempt to be sufficient without the Sustainer, to be a god without God.

To understand the logic of human salvation for Augustine, then, is primarily to understand sin as the attempt at self-deification. Adam and Eve are the only creatures made for relationship—made in the divine image and likeness (cf. Gen 1:27). Augustine is the first to notice that the sixth day on which humanity's proto-parents are brought into being does not enjoy its own "and God saw that it was good, the sixth day," but Genesis 1:31 instead concludes with a more universal depiction of God's looking at "*all things* he had made" (*cuncta quae fecit*). The sixth day does not have its own stamp of conclusion, Augustine notes, because Adam and Eve are created incompletely, made with an ongoing drama built into their very being (*Gn. litt.* 3.24).[4]

As such, Adam and Eve are the only creatures partially made, created to allow God to still their "restless heart." So, while the human person is of course good, he or she is not created wholly fulfilled. Augustine is unique among the Church Fathers in recognizing also the cunning of Genesis 3:5 and the fallen angel's enticing humanity to become like gods. An angelic intellect, Satan knew well that Adam and Eve were made for divinization in Christ. The enemy also knew that this was therefore the one promise with which he could tempt humanity. How so?

On the natural level, Eden symbolizes satiety and satisfaction; here humanity was above all seduction, possessing all the created goods they could ever desire. Yet, the one unfulfilled promise that the devil could exploit was thus the human propulsion toward godliness: "Our first parents could not have been persuaded to sin unless they had been told, *You will be like gods.*"[5] As such, evil now entices men and women to become gods reliant upon their own feeble powers instead of "gods" in God: "In a perverse imitation of almighty God, what is the human person after if not to be the only one to whom all the rest [of creation] is subject? If he would have only unhesitatingly imitated God by living by his precepts, all created things would have been his."[6]

Men and women were made to be like God by appropriating him through proper worship and imitation. Wanting to be like God apart from these demands (*praecepta*) is tantamount to a creature's attempting to be eternal without elevation, divine without divinity. Adam fell because he was seeking to fulfill his call "to become God" apart from God. This is the legacy of pride (*superbia*) for Augustine: It originates in our innate thirst for unity and omnipotence, but seeks to realize one's greatness apart from Love, to replace the one true God with one's own attempts at divinity. It is this grasp at self-deification that Augustine sees playing out in every subsequent sinful thought and action.

When examining this depravity from the pulpit, Augustine the preacher often echoes the Psalmist's query, "O God, who is your equal?" (Ps 71:19). We then hear Augustine ask:

> Human beings like God? *O God, who is like you?* Nothing . . . But as for me, says wretched Adam—and Adam is every one of us—look what became of me when I perversely tried to be like you! I am reduced to crying out to you from my captivity . . . And how did I fall away from you? By seeking in a perverted way to be like you.[7]

This perversion to be divine apart from God is how Augustine sees all sin. Seeking to possess divinity through their own souls and not through participating in God's own life, Adam and Eve forfeited the divine sovereignty in which God had originally created them to share: "Craving to be what they were not, they lost what they had received."[8] Accordingly, Genesis 3:5 and our misplaced propulsion for godliness act as the paradigm of every sin for Augustine.

Nowhere is this more obvious than at the famous pear tree scene in Book 2 of the *Confessions*. Reviewing the whole of his life, Augustine uses this one episode of his callow youth to provide a meta-narrative lens through which all sin can be confessed. It was not the matter of the act that bothered him so many years later, but the motive. He stole and squandered some measly fruit not because he was hungry or because it was of superior quality. He did it simply because he was in love with his own ruin, seeking to become something apart from the demands of the divine:

> Close to our vineyard there was a pear tree laden with fruit. This fruit was not enticing, either in appearance or in flavor . . . We took enormous quantities, not to feast on ourselves but perhaps to throw to the pigs; we did eat a few, but that was not our motive: we derived pleasure from the deed simply because it was forbidden . . . The malice was loathsome, and I loved it. I was in love with my own ruin, in love with decay: not with the thing for which I was falling into decay but with decay itself, for I was depraved in soul, and I leapt down from your strong support into destruction, hungering not for some advantage to be gained by the foul deed, but for the foulness of it.[9]

Such sin is different than any crime. At least the adulterer and the murderer have an end in sight that renders their viciousness at least somewhat understandable (why the examples of Catiline and a frenzied paramour appear next at *Conf.* 2.5.11). This is different because Augustine executed the theft *not* for a discernible good, but simply because he was driven to his own decay. His fallen soul ravished its own ruin and, echoing Lucifer's fall from grace, Augustine too "leapt" from communion with God into his own search for autonomy.

That is why, without any discernible good in mind for stealing the pears, the closest Augustine can come to giving a reason for his behavior is: "All those who wander far away and set themselves up against you are imitating you, but in a perverse way ... trying to simulate a crippled sort of freedom, attempting a shady parody of omnipotence."[10] This is what every instance of sin effects: Unwilling to rely on God, we flee the other and the riskiness any relationship demands. We choose rather to set up our own selves as deities, however deformed. Only then am I able to do what I want, as I want, and when I want. Yet this desire for godliness is inevitably undermined by my own desires' inability to be wholly integrated around the good, and this internal conflict leads to a hatred and consequent destruction of self. Self-recrimination inevitably arises in the fallen soul because each "side" of the internal division lashes out against the other. This conflicted self thus struggles against its own agitation: We are drawn to the good but must destroy that which is unwilling to be drawn into transparency and truth.

For Augustine, our desires lead to wholeness only when they are drawn in and united around the good. We need saving from our own divided hearts. Later, in the *Confessions*, when he prays for the Lord "to grant me chastity, but not yet," Augustine reveals the inability of the divided heart to be happy.[11] After the Fall, no sinner can wholly will the good, as the divided heart can never have what it wants. Now all stand in need of divine aid.

Augustine therefore makes it quite clear that, while it is good and right that created persons desire to rule and obtain the desires of their hearts, they must do so only in uniformity with God:

> Whoever wants to be like God so as to stand in his presence, and guard his strength in relation to him, as it is written (cf. Ps. 58:10), let him not recede

from him, let him cling to him as wax is sealed by a signet-ring, let him have God's image affixed to him, realizing what is written, *Adhering to my God is my good*, truly guarding the likeness and image which God made. But if one will have perversely imitated God who is neither formed by nor ruled by anyone else, then this one desires to be like God, desiring to live as if formed by no one, ruled by no one. But what occurs, brothers and sisters, is that in withdrawing from God's warmth this one grows numb, receding from Truth this one vanishes, receding from God who supremely and unchangeably is, this one deteriorates, changed into something inferior.[12]

Augustine is quite adamant that the goal of human living is incessant communion with God, depicted here in very strong terms (clinging, adhering, affixed to, formed by), an intimacy so great he likens it to the indelible impression a ring marks into a seal of wax. Such cohesion is a matter of God's grace, because after the Fall, the sinful soul inevitably distances itself from God. This contrary movement Augustine describes in equally stark terms (receding, withdrawing, vanishing, receding)—hearkening back to Origen's imagery of the soul's "cooling" as it moves further from God's warmth (*ab eius calore*).[13] Once the soul thus turns away (*auertitur*) from its maker, the soul cannot help but confuse creatures with the Creator and thereby render itself a god.

It is from this aversion to God's indwelling presence that the fallen human stands in need of saving, and for this, God imparts his grace. That is, in order to break this self-defeating cycle, God chooses to share his own life with creatures. This is a gift that became one of Augustine's central pastoral concerns. What is grace and why does God share it?

The Healing Begins

The account of how Augustine came to stress the indispensability of divine assistance is well rehearsed. Ordained a priest for only a short time (early 391), Father Augustine quickly realized his inability to assimilate and expound on Scripture intelligently. He now faced a hungry flock that relied on him to explain the Christian mysteries intelligently and accurately. He therefore approached Bishop Valerius with an anxious letter, in which he requests time away, for what amounts to a Lenten retreat in order to further immerse himself in the writings of St. Paul.[14] This concentrated engagement with Pauline theology transforms Augustine's views on grace and divine favor in that he admits later to thinking that "God loved Jacob and hated Esau" (Rom 9:13) because God foresaw the good Jacob would do and the evil Esau would perpetuate. This, he eventually came to understand, is a merit-based approach to God's assistance and against the very sense of grace Paul advances.

The contours of Augustine's intellectual sojourn in these early years of priesthood are spelled out for posterity when his former spiritual father in Milan, Simplician (d. 400/01; Ambrose's predecessor as Archbishop), asked him how to understand the thornier passages from Romans. Augustine asserts that there is technically no such thing as "merit" when it comes to Christian salvation but even the good (and necessary) works of the saints are the result of God's prior grace:

> Before every merit, then, there is grace, since Christ died for the wicked (cf. Rom 5:6). Hence it was not because of any merits of his own, but because of him who called, that the younger received [the grace] to be served by the older. This also explains the phrase, *I loved Jacob*, which was because of God who called and not because of Jacob's works.[15]

This emphasis on the gratuitous nature of God's deigning to elevate human agency remained throughout Augustine's life. He repeatedly highlights the priority of God's goodness to his undeserving creatures: "If any merit got in ahead of grace, then grace isn't given gratis, but is paid back as being due. And if it isn't given free, gratis and for nothing, why should it be called grace?"[16]

In this way Augustine refuses to settle on why God saves some and apparently not others. There is no greater truth than the free goodness of God; therefore there can be no greater light shed upon his desire to save sinners. Augustine accordingly never ventures an answer to "why" not all persons are saved, but seems content to bring his questioning to a close with the answer of God's inscrutable will:

> But as to why he sets free this person rather than that one, *his judgments are inscrutable, and his ways unsearchable* (Rom 11:33). After all, it is better in this case too that we hear or say, *Who are you, a man, to answer back to God?* (Rom 9:20), rather than dare to say, as if we had knowledge

of it, what he willed to be hidden who could not, nonetheless, will anything unjust.[17]

Toward the end of his earthly life (427) Bishop Augustine writes to Abbot Valentine of Hadrumetum and shows posterity the two scriptural passages with which he made sense of such a position: first, God longs to save us (cf. Jn 3:17), and second, God does in fact judge the world (cf. Rom 3:6). This shows the fittingness of divine grace given freely and without merit. For if there were no grace, how could the world ever hope to be saved; yet, if there was no human free will, how could the world ever be judged?[18] As sacred authors, both John and Paul must convey the truth, so the best counsel Augustine has to offer Valentine here is to "pray that you may also wisely understand what you piously believe."[19]

What we must understand is that salvation is wholly free; what we must piously believe is that in Christ, I am a saved sinner. Augustine the preacher, Augustine the pastor, carefully exhorts his flock to account (and atone) for their sins while never despairing over total loss of God's grace. What we must not do is rely on some idea of a "good life" apart from God's unmerited assistance:

> You see, there wasn't any pre-existent good life, which he could look down at from up above and admire and love and say, "Come on, let's go down and help these people, because they are leading good lives." He was displeased with our lives, he was displeased with everything we were making of ourselves, but he was not displeased with what he made in us. So he will condemn what we have made, and what he has made he will save.[20]

An Augustinian constant is that we must always strive to discern that which is God's making and that which is our own. Alone, a creature has nothing but decay and destruction; in union with God a creature flourishes and is fulfilled. Augustine's own confessional logic allowed him to see that if one seeks oneself, one will find only isolating sin and destruction. If one seeks God and "forgets" oneself in God, one will find one's truest self and the eternal life that can come only from divine union.[21]

Augustine himself admits that they have heard him preach about this to the point of their erupting mid-homily, wondering, "What's the point of his saying this so often?"[22] Over and over, obviously, Augustine used his homilies to stress how salvation is a wholly gratuitous gift. Alone we have nothing, and that is why we may boast, but only of our weaknesses. This is the Apostle Paul's example (e.g., 1 Cor 12:5–9) and Augustine uses this paradox to move his flock into the work of the humbled Christ. This is how Christians can dually claim their own disobedience as well as the fidelity that saves them: "If, then, your good merits are God's gifts, God does not crown your merits as your merits, but as his own gifts."[23] By incorporating his own sons and daughters into his Son Jesus, in saving creatures, the Father is ultimately redeeming his own gifts in his elect.

He accomplishes such redemption by matching his greatness to creatures' weakness and inability to save themselves. In the Son's incarnation, God himself chooses to become vulnerable and mortal. Love is drawn not to the perfect, but love draws in order to perfect. This is how Augustine can concurrently preach of God's tenderness alongside our own rejection of God. In Christ, the Lord lowers himself to the lowly and redeems our lowliness by his greatness: "There was no other reason at all why he should come into the world. It wasn't our good merits that brought him down from heaven to earth, but our sins."[24] While God can of course impart his life however he chooses, he sends his Son to embody as well as to impart grace to those humble enough to rely on him. We now turn to the mechanics of Augustine's Christology, for in order to understand his theology of salvation, we must also realize his understanding of the Savior.

The Savior Comes

To achieve this outpouring of grace into persons made of flesh, God takes on human flesh; in the Lord Jesus Christ a new moment of grace begins. Augustine's Christology developed between the great Councils in which the Church's creedal confession of the incarnation was authorized. Throughout Book 7 of his *Confessions*, Augustine admits how his understanding of Christ developed. Between his training from Ambrose and his own appropriation of the Church's tradition, Augustine's mature Christology is in every respect in line with the pro-Nicene claim that Christ is consubstantial with the Father, and even anticipates what Pope Leo's Tome proclaimed at the Council of Chalcedon by envisioning how Jesus is a perfectly "twin-substanced giant" (*geminate gigas substantiae*).²⁵ What shines through most often when Augustine turns to analyze the incarnation is exactly this unification of natures: Christ "joins both divine and human natures in the singularity of his person" (*ep.* 137.9), ". . . just as being human means having a body and a soul and does not make two persons, so the Word by becoming human does not make two persons but one Christ" (*Jo. eu. tr.* 19.15), and so Christ is "homo Deus" (*Against Faustus* 13.8) as well as "Deus homo" (*On the Instruction of Beginners* 4.8), truly God made truly human. Such perfect union is used by Augustine to show how the enfleshed Savior Jesus Christ provides humans communion with a God who is both their pilgrim way and their life's destination.

At the moment of the Annunciation and Mary's "yes," the Son of God enters the human condition not out of judgment or condemnation, but out of a desire to re-create the children of Eve. In this act, as Augustine understands it, fallen persons are not only restored to the natural perfection once realized in Eden, they are renovated into new creatures: "But the only-begotten Son became a participant in our mortality, as I have reminded you, in order that we might be created anew and be made participants in his divinity, being restored to eternal life." After quoting the kenotic hymn of Philippians 2:7, Augustine continues: "In the form of God he is equal to the Father, but he took the form of a servant whereby he is less than the Father."²⁶ This is a consistent pattern. The dual nature of the God-man effects a communion with creatures that elevates them into a nature not their own: "Christ had taken the identity of the first human being to himself . . . for it is by longing for him and imitating his passion that we are made new."²⁷

This amelioration means that in Christ the faithful no longer have to live out of a merely human agency. In the perfect and unique assumption of humanity into his divinity, the Son of God offers humans new access into the divine nature. Whereas we were created with the ability not to sin and not to die, in Christ the elect are unable to sin and unable to die. Unlike the Medievals, who rely upon a clearer demarcation between "nature" and "supernature," Augustine never hesitates to call all of creation a grace, God's first gift *ad extra*. But in Christ comes a new grace, a new level of divine-human intimacy, and in that embrace, all of human operation is elevated and transformed:

> The human will's first liberty was able not to sin (*posse non peccare*), but the final will is something much greater, as it is not able to sin (*non posse peccare*). The first immortality was able not to die (*posse non mori*), but the last will be something much greater, as it is not able to die (*non posse mori*). The first was the power of perseverance, an ability not to relinquish the good; but the last will is the felicity of perseverance, an inability to forego the good.[28]

Whereas in Eden humans were able to live fully as human, in Christ they are now able to live *ultra homines*, to live as immortal beings who enjoy divine virtues—like faith, hope, and charity—that are not otherwise humanly available.[29] This is a life in Christ "changed for the better" (*in melius commutati*) because now humanity is able to participate in God's own immortality and righteousness (*eius inmortalis et iusti participatione*).[30]

For Augustine, then, the Christ is infinitely more than a moral example, a sage, or even an exemplary life. He is clearly God who has entered the human condition in order to infuse the created earthly person with the joy and the perfections of the divine nature. Ironically, this occurs only when sinners avail themselves of the grace they need to appropriate the perfection for which they were originally created. In Christ—and here is where Augustine always proves theologically and rhetorically rich—God goes after not the perfect and the strong, but the weak and the stumbling: "How great he was there, and how little he had made himself! Made little, he was seeking the little ones. What do I mean, he was seeking the little ones? Those who are not proud, not too full of themselves; instead he was gathering together the humble and the meek."[31] Augustine's homilies are packed with such invitation—to go back into one's past experiences to see where and why they were proud and tried to live even a single moment from God's grace. In such isolation the self-deified would know only transgression and failure, but in Christ those wounds become wonders![32]

Christian salvation therefore begins with the Son's descent into and assumption of humanity; but for humanity's part, it begins when the humble come to Christ not in pretentious power or feigned faultlessness, but precisely in their wounds and ways they have turned away:

> First of all, you must find your deformity displeasing, and then you will receive beauty from him whom you hope to please by being beautiful. He who formed you in the beginning will reform you ... Begin by admitting your ugliness, the deformity of soul that results from sins and iniquity. Initiate your confession by accusing yourself of this ugliness, for as you confess you become more seemly. And who grants this to you? Who else but he who is fairer than any of humankind?[33]

Instead of making an unknowable, untouchable deity out of our internal divisions as portrayed above in Augustine's analysis of the pear tree, in Christ all are called not to run away from their deformities but to place them trustfully in Jesus's pierced hands. This is an exchange that can be achieved only through the initiative of divine grace and sustained through our trust that Christ longs to make us one of his own.

The Saved Are Transformed into Christ

For Augustine, we can look at our truest selves only in Christ because each of us is most truly ourselves only in Him. This is the beginning of Christian salvation, when believers begin to see themselves as extensions of God's own perfect humanity as the body of Christ on earth:

> Now, however, I wonder if we shouldn't have a look at ourselves, if we shouldn't think about his body, because he is also us (*quia et nos ipse est*). After all, if we weren't him, this wouldn't be true: *When you did it for one of the least of mine, you did it for me* (Mt 25:40). If we weren't him, this wouldn't be true: *Saul, Saul, why are you persecuting me?* (Acts 9:4). So we too are him, because we are his organs, because we are his body, because he is our head, because the whole Christ is both head and body.[34]

This is Augustine's *totus Christus*—the "whole Christ"—wherein perfect Love identifies himself with his beloved. In his condescension Christ the Head chooses to see his own weal and woe in the condition of his Body.

The central effect salvation in Christ has for creatures is that he now begins to identify himself with those who come to him. Phrases like "we are he" (*nos ipse*) and "we are in him" (*sumus in illo*) signal how intimate such identification is in Augustine's mind: "because in me they are also I" (*quoniam in me etiam ipsi sunt ego*).³⁵ This is the essence of charity, the essence of the Church where the Lover longs to become so one with the beloved that there is no longer separation or division. Tarcisius van Bavel (d. 2007) named this identification the "second emptying" (*seconde pauvreté*) of Christ. God himself elects to identify himself with sinners in a love so strong that he can never turn away or reject them: "Christ must add to poverty a yet deeper poverty and transfigure our lowly body into himself; he must be our head and we his members; let us be the two in one flesh."³⁶ This unity is achieved by the fact of the incarnation. The heavens have been opened but Augustine the pastor realizes all too well our own unwillingness to be drawn entirely up to God.

When that occurs the human person is deified, adopted into the same filiality of the Son before the Father, and made temples of the Holy Spirit. This is why we must not only be incorporated into Christ, we must also be given the grace to be deified and thus become our truest selves as God's images and likenesses.

On this point Augustinian salvation is very insistent that the ultimate reason God became human was to make humans into gods: To make into gods those who were human, he who was God became human.³⁷ In 1990, a French medievalist by the name of François Dolbeau discovered twenty-six lost homilies of Augustine in the *Stadtsbibliothek* in Mainz, Germany. One of these *extrauagantes*, labeled now as *s.* 23B (Dolbeau 6; Mainz 13), offers a wonderful glimpse into how Augustine would preach about this final deifying transformation to his people:

> For God wishes not only to vivify, but also to deify us. When would human infirmity ever have dared to hope for this, unless divine truth had promised it? . . . Still, it was not enough for our God to promise us divinity in himself, unless he also took on our infirmity, as though to say, "Do you want to know how much I love you, how certain you ought to be that I am going to give you my divine reality? I took to myself your mortal reality." We mustn't find it incredible, brothers and sisters, that human beings become gods, that is, that those who were human beings become gods.³⁸

In Augustine's mind, justification, salvation, and deification are all part of what it means to live in Christ: "He who justifies is the same as he who deifies, because by justifying us he made us sons and daughters of God."[39] Deification for Augustine means to become so united with Christ the consubstantial Son by nature, that the Christian life is lived by adopted sons and daughters through grace. It is to realize the love of the Father so as to be transformed evermore into his own, a new life Augustine never fears to call "becoming gods."

Conclusion

Salvation for Augustine is first occasioned by human rebellion, choosing to love creatures apart from God instead of in and by means of God. To remedy and heal this self-imposed isolation, God imparts his grace to sinners in order to heal their divided hearts and to bring them to the perfection for which they were originally created. To do this the Father sends his Son into the world, thereby uniting divinity and humanity perfectly in a person who lives and labors as both perfect God and perfect man. This incarnate Christ is no mere historical figure, but continually comes to his Church through his sacraments as extensions of his deifying body: "So, if it's you that are the body of Christ and its members, it's the mystery meaning you that has been placed on the Lord's table; what you receive is the mystery that means you."[40] Through his Church, Christ continues to call all back to the grace and the consequent new life only he can offer.

This new life in Christ is marked for Augustine by the human ability to now exercise superhuman qualities—to live forever (1 Jn 2:17), to live and love like Christ (1 Jn 4:17), and to be perfect as one's own heavenly Father is perfect (Mt 5:48). In this way Augustine's sense of salvation is less a matter of "religion"—ritual and ceremony—and more a matter of "relationship"—allowing oneself to be appropriated and assumed into Christ's own self. For this new connection between the perfection of God and the waywardness of humanity Augustine spent forty years preaching and composing treatises in order to invite all into the love for which every human person has been created.

NOTES

1. *On the Catholic and Manichean Way of Life* 1.13.23 as in *The Manichean Debate*, trans., Roland Teske, SJ, vol. I/19 (Hyde Park, NY: New City Press, 2006) 42; the

Latin comes from *De Moribus Ecclesiae Catholicae et De Moribus Manichaeorum* as at CSEL 90.27 (see below, this note). Unless otherwise indicated, all English translations come from the New City Press series, indicated by English title, translator, and the volume number and page within the series; the Latin will be taken from the *Corpus Christianorum Latinorum* [hereafter cited as CCL], the *Corpus Scriptorum Ecclesiasticorum Latinorum* [hereafter cited as CSEL], or Migne's older *Patrologia Latina* [hereafter cited as PL].

2. *Tractates on the First Letter of John* [hereafter cited as *ep. Jo.* followed by chapter and verse] 10:3: "Et diligendo fit et ipse membrum, et fit per dilectionem in compage corporis Christi; et erit unus Christus amans seipsum (my translation); PL 35.2056.
3. For a primal instance of this disordering, see *On the Literal Meaning of Genesis* 11.42.59, as in *On Genesis*, trans., Edmund Hill, OP (I/13), 463.
4. *Gn. litt.* is an abbreviation for St. Augustine, *Literal Meaning of Genesis*.
5. *On the Trinity* [hereafter cited as *Trin.* followed by volume, chapter, and page] 11.5.8; Edmund Hill, *The Trinity* (I/5) 310; CCL 50.344.
6. *On True Religion* 45.84; Hill (I/8) 87; CCL 32.243. See also *Expositions of the Psalms* [hereafter cited as *en. Ps.* followed by psalm number], 103, *exp.* 2.11 as well as *City of God* [Hereafter cited as *ciu. Dei*], 12.22.
7. *en. Ps.* 70, *exp.* 2.6; Boulding, *Expositions* (III/17), 442–43.
8. *en. Ps.* 103, *exp.* 2.11; Boulding, *Expositions* (III/19), 138.
9. *Confessions* [hereafter cited as *conf.*] 2.4.9; Boulding (I/1), 41.
10. *conf.* 2.6.14; Boulding (I/1), 71.
11. *conf.* 8.7.17; Boulding, 213.
12. *en. Ps.* 70, *exp.* 2.6; Boulding, *Expositions* (III/17), 444; CCL 39.965.
13. Origen understood the Greek word for soul, *psyche*, to be derived from the verb to cool, *psychesthai*. As the individual "cooled" from its love of God, it became more and more separate from God; cf., *First Principles*, 2.8.3.
14. *Letter* [Hereafter cited as *ep.*] 21; see Peter Brown's chapter "Saluberrima Consilia" (from *ep.* 21.6) in *Augustine of Hippo: A Biography* (Berkeley: University of California Press, 2000), 198–206.
15. *To Simplicianus* 1.2.7; trans. Boniface Ramsey, *Responses to Miscellaneous Questions* (I/12), (Hyde Park, NY: New City Press, 2008), 191.
16. *Sermon* [hereafter cited as *s.*] 26.14; dated 417; Hill, *Sermons* (III/2), 101.
17. *On the Predestination of Saints* 8.16; *Answer to the Pelagians* IV (I/26) 163. In *The Works of Saint Augustine: A Translation for the 21st Century, I/26, Answer to the Pelagians IV*, trans. Roland Teske, SJ (Hyde Park, NY: New City Press, 1999).
18. *ep.* 214.2.
19. *ep.* 214.7; Teske, *Letters* (II/4) 39.
20. *s.* 23A (dated 415); Hill, *Sermons* (II/2) 68.
21. Cf. *s.* 34.7; *s.* 179A.4; *s.* 335B.4; *s.* 368.5
22. *s.* 131.6; Hill, *Sermons* (III/4) 319.
23. *On Grace and Free Will* 6.15; Teske, *Answer to the Pelagians* IV (I/26) 81.

24. *s.* 174.8; Hill, *Sermons* (III/5) 262.
25. This phrase for the incarnation is found originally in Ambrose but is picked up and used by Augustine at his *Against an Arian Sermon* §6 as well as at his *Homilies on the Gospel of John* 59.3.
26. *en. Ps.* 138.3; Boulding, *Expositions* (III/20), 258.
27. *en. Ps.* 37.27; Boulding, *Expositions* (III/16), 16.
28. *On Admonition and Grace* 12.33; my translation [PL 44.936].
29. This becoming "more than human" is the key to understanding the nature of the Trinity: *Trin.* 1.2.11; CCL 50.40.
30. *ciu. Dei* 21.19; CC 48.781.
31. *s.* 370.3.
32. One of Augustine's more beautiful lines is his play on the Latin for "torments" and "ornaments," in that with Christ one's *tormenta* become one's *ornamenta*; see, for example, *s.* 280.5 and *s.* 328.6.
33. *en. Ps.* 103, *exp.* 1.4; Boulding, Expositions (III/19), 10–11; *s.* 301A.2.
34. *s.* 133.8; Hill, *Sermons* (III/4), 338; *s.* 263A.2; *en. Ps.* 21.3, 40.6.
35. *Jo. eu. tr.* 108.5; CC 36.618.
36. *en. Ps.* 101, *exp.* 1.2; Boulding, *Expositions* (III/19), 47.
37. *s.* 192.1: *Deos facturus qui homines erant, homo factus est qui Deus erat*; PL 38.1012. For more on this, see my *The One Christ: St. Augustine's Theology of Deification* (Washington, DC: Catholic University of America Press, 2013).
38. *s.* 23B.1, Hill, *Sermons* (III/11) 37; dated around 404.
39. *en. Ps.* 49.2; Boulding, *Expositions* (III/16), 381.
40. *s.* 272; Hill, *Sermons* (III/7) 300; *Jo. eu. tr.* 26.13–18.

5

Athanasius

JOHN YOCUM

Athanasius of Alexandria (c. 296–373) is, by almost all accounts, the most important theologian of the fourth century. Athanasius is best known for his articulation and defense of the theology behind the Creed of the Council of Nicaea. He attended the Council of Nicaea in 325 as a presbyter assisting his bishop, Alexander of Alexandria, whom he succeeded in that episcopal see in 328. His election as bishop was immediately contested, unsuccessfully, for a variety of reasons, but especially by the Melitians, a group who opposed a lenient posture toward those who had given way under the persecutions of the early fourth century and later repented. Not long after Athanasius's election however, he faced even stiffer opposition from those who opposed the decisions of the Council of Nicaea, a varied group that Athanasius came to style "Arians," after Arius of Alexandria. Arius had by his denial of the full divinity of Jesus Christ sparked the controversy that led to the Council of Nicaea. Over the roughly 45 years of his episcopacy, Athanasius was exiled five times, for a total of 17 years, mainly as a result of the Arians' agitation against him at the imperial court. During these periods of exile, he built support for pro-Nicene theology in the West, and also came into close acquaintance with the nascent monastic movement in the Egyptian desert. His *Life* of the movement's best-known figure, Antony of the Desert, was one of the most popular and influential writings in the early church. Athanasius's earliest work, the two-part *Against the Greeks—On The Incarnation of The Word of God*, usually known by the Latin, *Contra Gentes—De Incarnatione*, is also his best-known. In addition, he penned three *Discourses* against the Arians (*Contra Arianos*), a large collection of letters, mostly defending and elaborating pro-Nicene theology, and a variety of other works related to the Nicene controversy.

Introduction

The *Contra Gentes* and *De Incarnatione* form a two-part apology for the Christian message.¹ In these two companion pieces, Athanasius constructs a vision of reality determined by the fact of the incarnation, cross, and resurrection of the Word of God, aiming to offer a holistic interpretation of the Scripture, which, Athanasius says, is "sufficient for the exposition of the truth."² On one hand, the work functions almost like a catechism, offering a primer in Nicene theology in a form that could inspire people of faith to live and proclaim the gospel.³ At the same time, it constitutes an *apologia crucis*, a response to those who object to the scandal of the cross, showing, on the basis of a whole gospel rationality, that "the cross was not the ruin but the salvation of creation," and that "he who ascended the cross is the Word of God and the Saviour of the universe."⁴ This distinctive Athanasian vision remains consistent from one end of Athanasius's career to the other. This chapter uses the *Contra Gentes—De Incarnatione* as a framework, but freely draws upon the polemical works, which substantiate and develop this vision, a vision of the perfection of the work of the transcendent and transcendently loving God to bring humanity into union with him.

Creation by the Transcendent, Loving God

In speaking of the incarnation of the Word of God for the sake of human salvation, Athanasius insists, in profound continuity with a tradition hearkening back to Irenaeus,⁵ that "It is necessary first to speak about the creation of the universe and its maker, God."⁶

Central to Athanasius's vision is the relation between the one God, who has created all things through his eternal Son and the human race created in his Image, through whom he has given knowledge of himself. That God has brought other things into existence from nothing is the effect of both his goodness and his transcendence. As outside creation, and yet having a Son proper to Himself, God creates out of benevolence, and indeed out of his own eternal fecundity and his delight in his Son.⁷ One of the criticisms that Athanasius would level against those who hold that the Son of God is a created instrument used by God to bring other creatures into existence is that they have made the Son dependent upon the world for his raison d'être.⁸ By contrast, Athanasius sees creation itself as an act of loving divine condescension, parallel to the ultimate divine condescension that occurs in the Incarnation.⁹

God's relation to creation is characterized not simply by general beneficence, but more precisely by his *philanthropia*, his love for the human race. By nature, God is completely inaccessible to creatures; but the gap between himself and human beings is bridged by the love of God for the human race. This occurs, first of all, through the creation of humanity in the image of God's own Word, thereby giving human beings perception and the capacity for relationship with God. As the Father rejoices in the Son, and rejoices in his works as they reflect his Son, so, human beings are given to rejoice in God through the Word.¹⁰

Corresponding to the transcendent and philanthropic God on one hand, is the nature of the human being created for relationship with God on the other. The human race is entirely dependent upon God both for its continued existence and for the knowledge of God. As a creature, the human being shares the condition of all those things brought into being from nothing. "The nature of created things, having come into being from nothing, is unstable, weak and mortal when considered by itself."¹¹ As such, all creatures live under the threat of dissolution, and would return to the nothingness, were it not for the goodness of God. God maintains creation in general in being by his providence.

> A good being would be envious of no one, so he envies nobody existence but rather wishes everyone to exist, in order to exercise his kindness. . . . being good, he governs and establishes the whole world through his Word who is himself God, in order that creation, illuminated by the leadership, providence and ordering of the Word, may be able to remain firm . . . lest it suffer . . . a relapse into non-existence, if it were not protected by the Word.¹²

In speaking of creation in terms of the gift of existence, Athanasius shows the crucial place assumed in his thought by the Christian doctrine of Creation from nothing, over against those who deny providence and ascribe the existence of things to chance, or claim that God fashioned things from pre-existent matter, or sever the Creator from the Father of Jesus Christ.¹³

But though human beings have received their being from God and, like all creatures, continue in dependence upon the Word for their very existence, the manner in which they persist in being is different from that of other creatures. God bestowed on the human race "a further gift, making them not simply like all the irrational animals upon the earth but making them according to his own image, giving them a share in the power of his own Word (λογος) . . . [so that] being made rational (λογικος), they might be able to abide in blessedness."[14]

> [So that] he might rejoice and converse with God, living an idyllic and truly blessed and immortal life. For having no obstacle to the knowledge of the divine, he continuously contemplates by his purity the image of the Father, God the Word, in whose image he was made and is filled with admiration when he grasps his providence towards the universe. He is superior to sensual things and all bodily impressions, and by the power of his mind clings to the divine intelligible realities in heaven. . . . It rejoices in contemplating him and is renewed by its desire for him, just as . . . the first man to be created . . . had his mind fixed on God in unembarrassed frankness.[15]

Human beings, then, are not held in being simply by the divine providential government of all creation, but by the active reception of the power of the Word through rational contemplation of God.[16] They are fully dependent upon grace, but they receive grace by directing their minds to God. This active reception depends in turn on human choice (προαιρησις). For that reason, beyond giving human beings rationality through participation in the Word, God set before them a definite law.

> Knowing that the free choice of human beings could turn either way, he secured beforehand, by a law and a set place, the grace given. For bringing them into his own paradise, he gave them a law, so that if they guarded the grace, and remained good, they might have the life of paradise—without sorrow, pain or care—besides having the promise of their incorruptibility in heaven; but if they were to transgress and turning away become wicked, they would know themselves enduring the corruption of death according to nature, and no longer live in paradise, but thereafter dying outside of it, would remain in death and in corruption.[17]

Sin and Its Consequences

It is in relation to this distinctively Christian anthropology that Athanasius interprets the sin of the race and its consequences.

> Men, contemptuous of better things and shrinking from their apprehension, sought rather what was closer to themselves—and what was closer to them was the body and its sensations. So they turned their minds away from intelligible reality and began to consider themselves. And by considering themselves and cleaving to the body and other senses, deceived as it were in their own interests, they fell into selfish desires and preferred their own good to the contemplation of the divine. . . . They imprisoned in the pleasures of the body their souls which had become disordered and defiled by all kinds of desire, and in the end they forgot the power they had received from God in the beginning.[18]

The body and sensible realities are not, of course, evil, but they are not ultimate. Body, soul, and mind for Athanasius, are ordered hierarchically. The mind (not always distinguished from the soul in Athanasius's writings) is the medium of apprehending and communing with God. The soul, a more general term, is the faculty that directs man's body.[19] The body itself—material, taken from the dust of the earth[20]—is what is "closer" to the human being, good in itself, but not an end in itself because human beings are created for relationship with the transcendent God.[21] The body is the means for doing good and for apprehending God through the sensible. "The body has eyes in order to view creation and through its harmonious order to recognize the Creator, although it also possesses hearing in order to listen to the divine sayings and the laws of God, and has hands too, to do the necessary actions and to stretch them out in prayer."[22]

In the *De Incarnatione*, Athanasius affirms the historical origin of sin, quoting Wisdom of Solomon 2:23–24, "God created the human being for incorruptibility and an image of his own eternity; but by the envy of the devil death entered into the world." In *Contra Gentes*, the sin of the first human beings is educed as an example of the ongoing dynamic of sin, which is characterized by both temptation from without, and weakness and culpability within the human being.[23] It is clear that Athanasius considers ongoing spiritual conflict a key feature of human life. The controversy with those who deny the full divinity of the Word, in his estimation, is not simply a matter of human disagreement, but a spiritual combat.[24] Athanasius's *Life of Antony*, an idealized picture of the man of God, is replete with stories of the conflict with demons and temptations as well.[25] Thus, the race in its sinful condition is both culpable and held in bondage.

Athanasius offers a compelling portrait of the plight of the human race in sin. Created teleologically, with an orientation toward God and self-transcendence through the knowledge of him, in sin, human beings turned away from "the right objective," and "began to do everything in reverse."[26] Their hands worked murder; their ears turned to disobedience; adultery took the place of legitimate procreation; blasphemy, abuse, and perjury replaced kind words.[27] In addition, human beings began to suffer discordant desires. Just as Athanasius depicts harmony in creation as evidence of the Creator, disharmony within the human creature and between human creatures is evidence of sin.[28] As John Behr nicely puts it, "The plurality into which each human being has descended, given over to a multiplicity of desires, reverberates in the plurality of multiple conflicting voices, each asserting itself."[29] In language that echoes a variety of New Testament passages, Athanasius describes the sinful human condition as one of fear, frustration, and futility.[30]

> They gave themselves up to various and separate desires of the body . . . Clinging to each and every desire, they began to adopt such an attitude towards them that they were afraid of losing them. In this way the soul has come to harbor fears and terrors and pleasures and thoughts of mortality. For being unwilling to abandon these desires, it has come to fear death and separation from the body. Furthermore, desiring and not obtaining satisfaction, it learned to murder and commit injustice.[31]

Cut off from the source of their continued existence, human beings now suffer death, and with it a life of spiritual and moral corruption, in bondage to fear of death and the fear of loss, and embroiled in constant strife and social disorder.[32]

The Descent of the Word into the Temple of a Human Body

The best-known Athanasian work is *De Incarnatione*, and the best-known feature of that work is what is known as "the divine dilemma." It actually takes two forms, the first employed as a rationale for the incarnation as a means of dealing with the divine sentence of death that hangs over the human race, the second an explication of the renewal of human knowledge of the divine by the same means. Both are important to Athanasius's understanding of salvation. Underlying both is the motif of divine descent, or condescension, that is ubiquitous in his work.

> With death holding greater sway and corruption remaining fast against human beings, the race of humans was perishing, and the human being, made rational and in the image, was disappearing, and the work God made was being obliterated. . . . By the law death thereafter prevailed against us, and it was impossible to escape the law, since this had been established by God on account of the transgression. And what happened was both truly absurd and improper. It was absurd, on the one hand, that having spoken God should prove to be lying; that is, having legislated that the human being would die by death, if he were to transgress the commandment, yet after the transgression he were not to die but rather this sentence dissolved. For God would not be true if, after saying that we would die, the human being did not die. On the other hand, it was improper that what had once been made rational and partakers of the Word should perish, and once again return to non-being through corruption. It was not worthy of the goodness of God that those created by him should be corrupted through the deceit wrought by the devil upon human beings. And it was supremely improper that the workmanship of God in human beings should disappear either through their own negligence or through the deceit of demons.[33]

Athanasius goes on to ask what good, indeed, to have been created, if human beings would ultimately be neglected and destroyed.[34] That would show God to be weak, not omnipotent and beneficent. The dilemma laid out here is a challenge to God as powerful and good. The issue is how to overcome corruption and death in a manner that vindicates the truth of his word and saves the human race for the accomplishment of its purpose.

Repentance and a decree of forgiveness might seem to have sufficed, but this would not uphold the consistency of the divine word if death were simply abolished, nor would it reinstate human beings in the grace of the image in whom they were created.[35] The solution is the particular Athanasian version of the "marvelous exchange."[36]

> Having mercy upon our race. . . . He takes for himself a body and that not foreign to our own. For he did not wish simply to be in a body, nor did he wish merely to appear . . . But he takes that which is ours . . . Although being himself powerful and the creator of the universe, he prepared for himself in the Virgin a body as a temple, and made it his own, as an instrument, making himself known and dwelling in it. And thus taking from ours that which is like, since all were liable to the corruption of death, delivering it over to death on behalf of all, he offered it to the Father, doing this in his love for human beings, so that, on the one hand, with all dying in him the law concerning corruption in human beings might be undone (its power being fully expended in the lordly body and no longer having any ground against similar human beings), and on the other hand, that as human beings had turned towards corruption he might turn them again to incorruptibility and give them life from death, by making the body his own and by the grace of the resurrection banishing death from them as straw from the fire.[37]

The very object of the coming of the Son of God is that he might take on the body of a human being, in order to die our death and so by his resurrection cause death to disappear from the race and corruption to give way to life through the resurrection. This is the primary cause of the Savior becoming a man. Athanasius goes on to apply the scriptural reasoning of Christ's vicarious death and its applicability to the whole human race, quoting 2 Corinthians 5:14; Hebrews 2:9, 14–15; 1 Corinthians 15:21–22; 1 Timothy 6:15; Titus 1:3.[38] Behind this lies the notion of the Son of God as the Second Adam[39] and our solidarity to him through a common human body,[40] an emphasis that comes out in *De Incarnatione* 8–9 by the use of present-tense verbs for the Word's assumption of a body: he "takes," he "dwells."[41]

Given this, it is difficult to grasp the criticism of the historian of fourth-century theology, R. P. C. Hanson, that Athanasius's "doctrine of the incarnation has swallowed up any doctrine of the atonement, has rendered it unnecessary."[42] The whole point of the Incarnation, or at least its "first cause," according to Athanasius, is to enable the Savior to "blot out the death which had occurred through the offering of his own body."[43] Athanasius explicates this death using the whole range of biblical analogies for it: ransom;[44] payment of a debt;[45] the undoing of a divine sentence and the curse of death;[46] healing.[47] At the same time, if one means by a "doctrine of the atonement" a worked-out "theory" of the utility of Christ's work centering on a single schema, one must admit that the Patristic era as a whole is lacking such a theory, as is the New Testament itself.[48] Instead, what we find in the New Testament, and in Athanasius and his near-contemporaries, is an affirmation of the uniquely effective saving work of Christ, employing a variety of analogical descriptions to speak about such effectiveness.[49] The foundation for all these conceptions is relational, as Athanasius makes clear in his analogy of a king coming to dwell in his city in order to care for, protect, and honor it.[50]

Athanasius gives greatest attention to the understanding of Christ's death as a sacrificial offering, as does the New Testament. Christ suffers in order to intercede before the Father.[51] He does not explicitly analyze the cross as an act of obedience to the Father,[52] but the whole thrust of his argument for the effectiveness of Christ's offering is the reversal of human disobedience, and the corruption that accompanies it.

The second dilemma taken up in the *De Incarnatione*, and strictly following the first, is how to bring human beings back to the knowledge of God. Due to the effects of sin, three ways of knowing God have proven insufficient: observation of the human soul fashioned for God; the evidence of creation; the law and prophets.[53] Human beings, turned from directing their thoughts to the one God, have instead come to the last frontier of irrationality and perversion, which is idolatry, the worship of the creature, instead of the Creator.[54] "What was God to do? . . . except to renew again in the image," so that through it human beings would once again be able to know him?[55]

Athanasius speaks again of the Word "descending,"[56] taking a body and thus revealing himself through the works of the body and allowing human beings to know the Father, engaging human senses in order to teach them of his own true Father. If human beings have turned their attention to the sensible, to what is lower, then a good teacher must begin at the level of his students' understanding, in order to raise their minds to what is higher.[57] As the human race should have known God from his effects in creation itself, now God's works will be manifest in a more direct manner, through his immediate action in and through a creaturely body, so that, "although being unseen and invisible, through his works he appeared and made himself known to be the Word of the Father, the ruler and king of the universe."[58]

Union with God through the Son of God

Athanasius's vision turns, and his whole theological project depends, upon the full divinity of the Son. Because all of creation is bound together by certain interdependence,[59] no creature could escape from the corruption that is consequent upon human sin.[60] Still, one might press the point, and ask why an unfallen angel might not come in human form and effect human salvation in a vicarious manner. Against this, Athanasius asserts that an angel could not accomplish renewal in the image for they were not themselves images.[61] All creatures are dependent upon God for their very existence. "It is not possible that He, who merely possesses from participation, should impart of that partaking to others, since what He has is not His own, but the Giver's; and what He has received, is barely the grace sufficient for Himself."[62] As Athanasian scholar Khaled Anatolios observes, it is not immediately obvious that one cannot give what one has received, and such a position might eliminate the possibility of any kind of secondary mediation, which does not seem to be the point.[63]

Instead, Athanasius is arguing from the perfection of the work that God has actually accomplished, which is the work of joining humanity to himself.[64] The agent of mediation, were it a creature, would suffer from two defects. First, he would himself be contingent, and leave the human race vulnerable again to a fall. All creatures require divine grace for continuing in creation, and all creatures are thus vulnerable to dissolution.[65] Second, however, he would stand between God and the human race. Athanasius argues with regard to creation that the requirement of a non-divine mediator betokens weakness in God, not strength.[66] How much more, then, would this be the case in the accomplishment of salvation? What God has brought about in Christ, however, is not a simple return to a pristine recreated state, but an elevation of the human race to a more stable, intimate, perfect union with God.

Access to God has come about because the Word has joined himself to humanity through the appropriation of what is "closest" to humanity: a human body. Henceforth, no higher or stronger union with God is possible.[67] Through the Son of God, human beings have come to share in the life of God as sons. "Because of our relationship to His Body we too have become God's temple, and in consequence are made God's sons, so that even in us the Lord is now worshipped, and beholders report, as the Apostle says, that God is in them of a truth."[68]

In his incarnation, Athanasius asserts, the Son of God does not cease to be fully divine, nor does he relinquish his rule of the universe. There is no emptying of the divinity of the Son in his humble entry into human form. Nor is there any leveling of humanity and divinity in this union. God remains God and humanity remains humanity, in the order appropriate to the relationship. In his human life, the Word appropriates to himself all that belongs to humanity, body and soul, in order to bring about its healing and transformation. Athanasius affirms this primarily through the use, common to the patristic era, of "partitive exegesis," predicating both divine and human attributes of the single subject of the incarnation, who is the Word.[69]

> They ought, when they hear "I and the Father are one," to see in Him the oneness of the Godhead and the propriety of the Father's Essence; and again when they hear, "He wept" and the like, to say that these are proper to the body; especially since on each side they have an intelligible ground, viz. that this is written as of God and that with reference to His manhood. For in the incorporeal, the properties of body had not been, unless He had taken a body corruptible and mortal for mortal was Holy Mary, from whom was His body. Therefore of necessity when He was in a body suffering, and weeping, and toiling, these things which are proper to the flesh, are ascribed to Him together with the body. If then He wept and was troubled, it was not the Word, *considered as the Word*, who wept and was troubled, but it was proper to the flesh; and if too He besought that the cup might pass away, it was not the Godhead that was in terror, but *this affection too was proper to the manhood*. And . . . these things are

done and said as from a man, that He might Himself lighten these very sufferings of the flesh, and free it from them.[70]

Both the human and the divine acts predicated of Christ are done by a single subject, the Word who has now become human.[71]

Precisely because the Word came for the transformation of the human race as its physician,[72] Athanasius stresses the beginning of this transformation in the earthly life of Christ, who conquered human fears and debilities. This, coupled with the language of the body as an instrument (οργανον), has led some, such as Aloys Grillmeier, to impute to him a Christology in which the Word replaces the human soul, or to claim, as R. P. C. Hanson does, that he dons our humanity like an astronaut putting on a space suit, that is, without an intrinsic relation to it.[73] While Athanasius does stress the assumption of the body, this would seem to be for at least two reasons. First, the New Testament speaks of the Word becoming flesh,[74] and depicts the visible life of the incarnate Word in that flesh more than it analyzes it. Second, the body is what is "closer" to the human being, what belongs to the race of Adam as taken from the dust to which, under the divine sentence upon sin, it must return—the very fate from which the Word came to save humanity.[75] Far from being an extrinsic relation, however, Athanasius insists that the Word and the flesh are inseparable, not to be divided because the body is that of the Word himself.[76]

Athanasius, it is true, gives relatively little attention to Christ's emotional experiences. Nevertheless, not only does he not deny, but affirms that Christ took on the passions that belong to human nature. Christ knew fear, hunger, and so on. But he assumed our passions in order to save the human race, which has suffered bondage to fear of death, not by simply feeling them, but by overcoming them, so as to give his life willingly.[77] The Word, according to Athanasius, saved human beings, as Leo the Great would later say, not by misery but by mercy.[78] This may, in fact, be one of the points at which Athanasius offers a salutary corrective to modern theological tendencies. The Son of God incarnate was indeed like us in all things but sin, but not merely like us.

Athanasius's exegesis of passages in which ignorance is imputed to Christ are perhaps the most awkward with respect to affirming the full humanity of the Son. Nevertheless, even in this case, Athanasius affirms the reality of Christ's humanity. "As, on becoming man, He hungers and thirsts and suffers with men, so with men as man He knows not; though divinely, being in the Father Word and Wisdom, He knows, and there is nothing which He knows not."[79] How does a single subject know and not know at once? Just what *was* it like to be the incarnate Son of God on earth? This may be a realm to which the New Testament simply does not give us access, and indeed, could not because it is a case unique to Jesus Christ.

There may yet be a lacuna in Athanasius's account, in that he so intently stresses the receptivity of the humanity of the incarnate Word that he leaves little space for the active human agency of the divine Word. According to Behr, Maximus fills this gap with his theology of two wills.[80] There is much to be said for that view. But, of course, in order to retain the powerful elements of the Athanasian account of the divine rescue, it is necessary to keep in view the full scope of the statement from Constantinople III, which affirms the Athanasian asymmetry of natures: "His human will follows, and that not as resisting and reluctant, but rather as subject to his divine and omnipotent will. For it was right that the flesh should be moved but subject to the divine will, according to the most wise Athanasius."

While the Holy Spirit is mentioned in the *Contra Gentes—De Incarnatione*,[81] treatment of the role of the Spirit in the salvific plan is entirely absent. In his later works, Athanasius gives substantial attention to the work of the Holy Spirit in the saving economy, and the Spirit's relation to both Father and Son. There is good reason to consider that the earlier works simply have a different focus, as an apology for the incarnation, rather than manifesting a lack of appreciation for the work of the Holy Spirit. Athanasius, after all, charges that those who deny divinity to the Holy Spirit depart from the tradition.[82] Making such a charge might be risky if he could credibly be charged with failure to affirm the Holy Spirit as divine. In these later works, his arguments in favor of the full divinity of the mediating Word are extended to the Holy Spirit, who comes to bring the life and power of Christ into the lives of human beings now joined to him, and thus to the Father, by the life-giving Holy Spirit.

Furthermore, in his anti-Arian works, Athanasius shows a substantial and important development. The incarnate Word receives the Holy Spirit vicariously, in order to impart him to human beings. "By receiving the Spirit derivatively from Christ's human reception of it, we thus become conformed to his divinity. The Spirit is here conceived primarily as the Spirit of adoption, the one 'in whom' we participate the Son, and thus become divinized."[83] This development would come to be highly influential in later tradition, especially in Cyril of Alexandria and his heirs.[84] Salvation, then, is achieved in a fully Trinitarian manner.

> The Father does all things through the Word in the Holy Spirit. Thus the unity of the holy Triad is preserved. Thus one God is preached in the Church, "who is over all, and through all, and in all"—"over all," as Father, as beginning, as fountain; "through all," through the Word; "in all," in the Holy Spirit.[85]

Conclusion: The Perfection of the Divine Work

The work of Jesus Christ reaches its telos in the lives of those joined to Christ in the Holy Spirit. This is particularly evident in the life of Antony of the desert, as Athanasius depicts it in his *Life*. Christ himself works in and through Antony, manifesting his power.[86] It is evident as well, however, in the conquest of idolatry and in the martyrs whose fearless confrontation with death is grounded in the Word who triumphed over death,[87] in order to bring life and immortality to light, and to perfect the work of the utterly transcendent and transcendently loving God.

In his over-arching vision of salvation, Athanasius sees the history of the relationship between God and humanity, from creation to the re-birth of human beings as children of God through the Holy Spirit, in the light of the life, death, and resurrection of the Son of God incarnate. In Jesus Christ, the transcendent God, on his own initiative and by his own power, has brought to lasting fulfillment the union with humanity that issues from the love between the Father, Son, and Holy Spirit. Athanasius's whole theological project constitutes a work of elaboration, defense, and praise of this perfect divine work.

NOTES

1. "That the *c.G.* and *d.I.* are two parts of a single work is clear from the internal evidence. Not only does the thought follow through in a coherent fashion, but specific references are made in the *d.I.* to the *d.I.* Furthermore, they are men-

tioned together by other Patristic authors as early as Jerome." *Contra Gentes and De Incarnatione*, translation, introduction, and notes by Robert W. Thomson (Oxford: Clarendon, 1971), xx. All quotations from the *Contra Gentes* are from Thomson.

2. See *Contra Gentes* 1 (hereafter cited as *CG* followed by chapter number). Learning the knowledge of God through interpretation of the Scriptures appears again at the end of the *De Incarnatione* (hereafter cited as *DI* followed by chapter number), thus forming an inclusio for the whole work (*DI* 56). *On The Incarnation*: Popular Patristics Series, translation and introduction by John Behr (Crestwood, NY: St. Vladimir's Seminary Press, 2011), 22. (All translations of the *De Incarnatione* will be taken from Behr.)

3. John Behr, *The Nicene Faith: The Formation of Christian Theology* Vol. II (Crestwood, NY: St. Vladimir's Seminary Press, 2004), 168. Thomas G. Weinandy, *Athanasius: Great Theologians* (Burlington, VT: Ashgate, 2007), 12.

4. *CG* 1.

5. It is the burden of Khaled Anatolios's important study, *Athanasius: The Coherence of his Thought* (New York: Routledge, 1998; hereafter cited as *Coherence*), to show that the coherence of Athanasius's theology turns on a biblical conception of the relation between God and creation. In contrast to the Hellenistic tendency to conceive of a first principle "in increasingly apophatic terms . . . The biblical witness presents a markedly different perspective, in which divine involvement in the world is in no way seen as detracting from divine transcendence, but rather as the very manifestation of divine greatness and majesty." This emphasis is already found in Irenaeus (*Coherence*, 4–5). Several things are notable about the account offered by Anatolios. First, because the foundation of the Athanasian vision, as Anatolios sees it, is biblical, it should be no surprise that the lineaments of the account are present in the earlier great Greek theologian and later in Basil of Caesarea, heir to Athanasius's vision. On the relation between Athanasius and Basil, see John Behr, *The Nicene Faith: The Formation of Christian Theology* Vol. II (Crestwood, NY: St. Vladimir's Seminary Press, 2004), 263. Second, an account of salvation history is not opposed to, but necessarily includes, an ontology (*Coherence*, 30–31). See also Peter J. Leithart, *Athanasius: Foundations of Theological Exegesis and Christian Spirituality* (Grand Rapids, MI: Baker Academic, 2011), xvii. Anatolios's interpretation of Athanasius has influenced that of Behr and Leithart, as well as Thomas G. Weinandy, *Athanasius: Great Theologians* (Burlington, VT: Ashgate, 2007) and others. It agrees substantially with the earlier work of Alvyn Pettersen, *Athanasius: Outstanding Christian Thinkers* (London: Geoffrey Chapman, 1995); *Athanasius and The Human Body* (Bristol: Bristol Classical Press, 1990).

6. *DI* 1.

7. *Discourses Against the Arians* II.82 in *NPNF* 2.4 (hereafter cited as C. Ar. followed by the discourse number, then the chapter number). This "is an aspect of Athanasius's Trinitarian theology that has received remarkably little attention. But it is not an incidental detail for Athanasius." Anatolios, *Retrieving Nicaea*

(Grand Rapids, MI: Baker Academic, 2011), 118. "In whom does the Father rejoice, except as seeing Himself in His own Image, which is His Word? And though in sons of men also He had delight, on finishing the world, as it is written in these same Proverbs, yet this too has a consistent sense. For even thus He had delight, not because joy was added to Him, but again on seeing the works made after His own Image; so that even this rejoicing of God is on account of His Image." C. Ar. II.82. See Peter Widdicombe, *The Fatherhood Of God From Origen To Athanasius* (Oxford: Clarendon Press, 1994), 206–8.

8. C. Ar. II.29.
9. Creation is characterized as "mercy" in DI 3, 8, 11." Anatolios, *Athanasius*, 249, n. 129.
10. *CG* 2.
11. *CG* 41.
12. *CG* 41.
13. Pettersen claims that Athanasius gives content to a doctrine that up to that point had been held in a somewhat ambiguous form. *Athanasius*, 22–23. Nonetheless, Athanasius is unambiguous about its biblical foundations, citing Genesis 1:1; Hebrews 11:3, and the interpretation offered in *Shepherd of Hermas*, Mandate 1.
14. *DI* 3.
15. *CG* 2.
16. Anatolios, *Coherence*, 59.
17. *DI* 3.
18. *CG* 3.
19. *CG* 5; 32.
20. C. Ar. III.33.
21. For a fine sketch of the basic elements of anthropology in Athanasius, see Anatolios, *Coherence*, 61–65.
22. *CG* 4.
23. *CG* 35, quoting Romans 1, suggests that even now human beings ought to know there is a creator from the evidence of his works.
24. On this see Leithart, *Athanasius*, 53–55.
25. See especially *Life of Antony*, 8–14, 22–42 (hereafter cited as *Ant.* followed by chapter numbers).
26. *CG* 5.
27. *CG* 5.
28. On the harmony of opposites in creation as evidence of the act of the Father through his Word, see *CG* 36–42, where Athanasius repeatedly points to the harmony of creation, especially the harmony of opposites, as evidence of a single Creator.
29. Behr, *On The Incarnation*, 31.
30. See Rom. 1:21–31; Eph. 4:17–19; Heb. 2:15; Jas. 4:1–2; 1 Pet. 1:18; 2 Pet. 2:12–14.
31. *CG* 4.

32. *DI* 5, which is reminiscent of the steep descent of the race into violence and disorder described in Gen. 4–11.
33. *DI* 6.
34. There are echoes from the point of view of the divine glory, of the traditional paschal hymn, the *Exultet* here: "What good would life have been to us, had not Christ come as our Redeemer?"
35. *DI* 7.
36. "If, even before the world was made, the Son had . . . glory, and was Lord of glory and the Highest, and descended from heaven, and is ever to be worshipped, it follows that He had not promotion from His descent, but rather Himself promoted the things which needed promotion; and if He descended to effect their promotion, therefore He did not receive in reward the name of the Son and God, but rather He Himself has made us sons of the Father, and deified men by becoming Himself man." C. Ar. I.38, on Phil. 2:10 See Norman Russell, *The Doctrine of Deification in The Greek Patristic Tradition*: Oxford Early Christian Studies (Oxford: Oxford University Press, 2006).
37. *DI* 8.
38. *DI* 10.
39. C. Ar. I.44.
40. C. Ar. II.74.
41. Behr, *The Nicene Faith*, 197.
42. R. P. C. Hanson, *The Search for the Christian Doctrine of God: The Arian Controversy* (Edinburgh: T&T Clark, 1988), 450.
43. *DI* 10. "It was absolutely necessary to die and for this, in particular, he sojourned among us." *DI* 20.
44. C. Ar. II.7.
45. *DI* 9; C. Ar. II.66.
46. *DI* 25; C. Ar. I.49; II.47; 55; 67; 68; 69.
47. *DI* 44. Nearly all the foregoing analogies are assembled in C. Ar. II.67.
48. See Brian Daley, S.J., "'He Himself is our Peace' (Ephesians 2:14): Early Christian Views of the Redemption in Christ," in Davis et al., eds., *The Redemption: An Interdisciplinary Symposium on Christ as Redeemer* (Oxford: Oxford University Press, 2006), 149–176, 153–154 and references.
49. For the idea of "analogical description" as the best way of conceiving the New Testament employment of such images, see Stephen B. Clark, *Redeemer: Understanding the Meaning of the Life, Death and Resurrection of Jesus Christ* (Ann Arbor, MI: Servant, 1992), 115–118.
50. *DI* 9.
51. *DI* 8, 9, 10, 16, 20, 21, 25; Or. Ar. 1:41, 2:7, 2:14, 2:69; On the Council of Nicaea 14; To Epictetus 4, 5, 6; To Adelphius 6. These references are taken from Anatolios, *Athanasius*, 204, fn. 155. Anatolios claims that "Athanasius's employment of sacrificial language in [*DI* 9] resonates with Eucharistic overtones" (46). This seems an odd way to view the matter. Would it not be the case that the Eucharist as an

offering is derived from and participatory in Christ's offering on the cross and intercession in heaven, itself the fulfillment of Old Testament offerings?
52. Thomas Weinandy observes that "one would have liked Athanasius to have elaborated on the exact nature of the sacrificial offering." *Athanasius*, 34.
53. *CG* 11–12.
54. "Athanasius . . . uses idolatry, especially that of the body, as a kind of barometer, measuring the perversity into which humans have fallen, the degree to which their knowledge of God has been lost." Behr, *The Nicene Faith*, 171.
55. *DI* 13.
56. *DI* 15.
57. *DI* 14.
58. *DI* 16.
59. C. Ar. II.72.
60. C. Ar. II.41.
61. *DI* 13.
62. Athanasius, De Synodis, chapter 51.
63. Anatolios, *Coherence*, 127.
64. C. Ar. III.23: "Whence is this their perfecting, but that I, your Word, having borne their body, and become man, have perfected the work, which you gave Me, O Father? And the work is perfected, because men, redeemed from sin, no longer remain dead; but being deified, have in each other, by looking at Me, the bond of charity."
65. C. Ar. II.41. Divine simplicity plays an important, if implicit, role here. On the importance of the notion for early Christianity, see G. L. Prestige, *God in Patristic Thought* (Eugene, OR: Wipf & Stock, 1964), 9–11.
66. C. Ar. II.28–29.
67. On the newness of grace in Christ, see Anatolios, *Athanasius*, 49–59.
68. C. Ar. I.43.
69. I take the phrase "partitive exegesis" from Behr. In the two volumes of *The Formation of Christian Theology*, he traces this practice, arising from an effort to answer the question "Who do you say that I am?" from Ignatius of Antioch through the Cappadocians.
70. C. Ar. III.56.
71. C. Ar. III.35.
72. *DI* 44.
73. See Aloys Grillmeier, *Christ in Christian Tradition* (New York: Sheed & Ward, 1975), 311ff.; R. P. C. Hanson, *Search*, 318ff.
74. Jn. 1:14; Rm. 1:3; 1Pt. 4:1.
75. *CG* 3.
76. Athanasius, *Ad Adelphium*, 5.
77. C. Ar. III.57.
78. Serm. 68.17.
79. C. Ar. III.46.

80. See *The Nicene Faith*, p. 231.
81. Biblical sayings are twice attributed to the Holy Spirit in the *Contra Gentes*. The *De Incarnatione* concludes with a Trinitarian doxology.
82. *Ad Serapion* I.28. The translation is from *The Letters of St. Athanasius concerning The Holy Spirit*, C. R. B. Shapland, tr. (London: Epworth, 1951). The numbers indicate the letter number followed by the chapter number.
83. Anatolios, *Athanasius*, 61–62.
84. See Daniel A. Keating, *The Appropriation of Divine Life in Cyril of Alexandria* (Oxford: Oxford University Press, 2004).
85. *Ad Serapion* I.28. See also I.30.
86. See, for example, *Antony*, 5; 19; 34.
87. *DI* 28; 47; 48; 52.

6

The Cappadocians

ANDREW RADDE-GALLWITZ

Since the nineteenth century, it has been customary to refer to Saint Basil of Caesarea (ca. 330–378), his younger brother Saint Gregory of Nyssa (ca. 335-ca. 394), and their friend Saint Gregory of Nazianzus (ca. 330–390) as the "Cappadocian Fathers" after the Roman province in which they served as bishops. The three are towering figures in the history of Christian thought. Basil and Nazianzen are two of the three "holy hierarchs" of the Greek tradition. Basil has been remembered since his own day as "the Great" and Nazianzen has been honorifically designated "The Theologian" for his eloquent and powerful defense of the Trinitarian dogma. Nyssen's works also were revered for their dogmatic and mystical insights. Although his reputation was somewhat tainted in later tradition by his advocacy of Origen's doctrine of the *apokatastasis pantôn*, or "restoration of all things" to God, he achieved a comeback in the twentieth century as studies of his works outpaced those of the other two Cappadocians.

The three were among the most gifted writers of their generation. Basil, who along with Nazianzen attended some of the finest rhetorical teachers in Athens, left behind a large corpus comprising many genres. His letter collection contains 366 letters, some of them spurious. There are 49 homilies, including nine *On the Hexaemeron*, 15 *On the Psalms*, as well as others on holy days, and a collection of dogma and ethics passed down under the label "Moral Homilies." He left behind a rich corpus of ascetic works intended to regulate the lives of the monasteries he oversaw. He also wrote two influential treatises on the Trinity, *Against Eunomius* and *On the Holy Spirit*.

Gregory of Nazianzus was the most versatile writer of the three. He is best known today for his five *Theological Orations*, masterpieces of theological dialectic which he delivered in Constantinople in 380, and for his two letters to Cledonius (*epp.* 101 and 102), in which he responds to Apollinarianism[1] and enunciates the principle that "whatever is not assumed [by the Logos] is not saved."[2] He delivered many other important orations for various occasions; of particular interest for Gregory's understanding of salvation are his orations for the major feasts of the Theophany, Pascha, and Pentecost. His letters have been read for centuries as exemplars of the genre. And he was a talented poet, rendering for instance the first principles of Christianity in dactylic hexameter with Homeric vocabulary.

Gregory of Nyssa is often viewed as the most philosophically speculative and apophatic of the three. His large corpus includes numerous pieces of polemic on the dogmatic issues of the day, including works against Eunomius, the Pneumatomachians, and Apollinarius. He also wrote ascetic works, biblical commentaries, philosophical treatises, letters, and homilies on important feast days. His *Catechetical Oration* contains an important account of human salvation in Christ and the mediating role of the sacraments.

Introduction

Given the variety of themes and genres in their corpora, any generalization about the three Cappadocians must be tentative. At times, the usage of the common label has created the impression that they shared a single theology. At other times, scholars have portrayed them as fundamentally at odds with each other. On the topic of salvation, it is useful to begin by asking what we are looking for in their works and whether we are prepared to admit the Cappadocians' perspectives into our own reflections on soteriology. Critical scholarship has long recognized that the Cappadocians' approach to the mystery of salvation differs greatly from what is common in contemporary Christianity. Typically and in its simplest form, the contrast has been drawn like this: For the Cappadocians, salvation is primarily the overcoming of death and the gift of new life, whereas for western Christianity the forgiveness of sin is paramount. In 1875, the German Protestant theologian Wilhelm Herrmann wrote an important dissertation on Gregory of Nyssa's soteriology, faulting Gregory for promoting what Herrmann called a "physical" view of salvation instead of the authentically Christian "moral" view, which centers on the individual's sense of alienation and redemption in Christ and on "faith as the inward experience of pure trust," rather than assent to dogmatic formulae.[3] Following Herrmann, Adolf von Harnack in his monumental *History of Dogma* shows that what is at stake in debates about the soteriology of the Greek fathers is not merely the proper exegesis of late ancient authors. Their ideas had what he believed were disastrous consequences:

> Again and again we have deification as a hyperphysical and therefore physical process, but dogmatics tell us little of the tenet that it is appointed unto man to die and after that the judgment. For this reason also the strict connection with morality was lost ... If we compare West and East in the Middle Ages—the theologians, not the laity—no impression is stronger than that the former knew the fear of the judge to which the latter had become indifferent. It was the restless element in the life of faith in the West; it sustained the thought of forgiveness of sins; it accordingly made the reformation of Catholicism possible.[4]

One might not share the enthusiasm of Herrmann or Harnack for a reformed Christianity stripped of its supernatural and sacramental elements. One might dispute their reading of the Cappadocians or of subsequent Christian history. But they still show us that a decision is necessary and it will affect whether the Cappadocians can continue to be dialogue partners for theology and not merely for the history of ideas. The crux, as Herrmann and Harnack rightly perceive, is the firm link between Christological dogma and soteriology in these authors. If one accepts that the two are inseparably linked, one will find the Cappadocians congenial; if not, one is likely to find them as alien to Christianity's fundamental impulses as did Herrmann and Harnack. What one must not do is to seek to rehabilitate them by translating their thought into the categories of Protestant Christianity. While the Cappadocians have more to say about sin and forgiveness than their German critics acknowledge, the critics are not mistaken in perceiving the importance of the collective salvation of human nature in Christ for our authors. For Basil and the two Gregories, salvation is first of all something that happened to Christ's humanity and second is appropriated by the individual through a mystical and sacramental identification with Christ's humanity. Christ's new life, which is beyond the power of death, is given to the believer by the Holy Spirit in baptism and charts the course for a life of identification with Christ's virtues. This can be seen in select passages of their works.

Basil of Caesarea

In Basil's earliest major work, *Against Eunomius* (AD 364/5), he delineates two ways in which the Scriptural authors talk about Christ. Some biblical texts are meant to teach about Christ "in the mode of theology," whereas others convey "the reasons of the economy."[5] A passage employs the former mode when it speaks of the only begotten Son of God's "subsistence (*hypostasis*) before the ages"; in contrast, a text is "economic" when it refers to the incarnate Son. This distinction is important for all that Basil has to say about salvation, and the same goes for the two Gregories. Salvation, properly speaking, is a work of the incarnate Christ. The distinction Basil draws differs from the post-Hegelian distinction of the "immanent" and "economic" Trinities: Basil is speaking about two perspectives on the Son of God in particular (rather than the entire Trinity) and is specifically drawing a distinction between two sets of biblical descriptions.

While there is a distinction of passages, it would be wrong to think that the two categories are entirely independent. Yet, the dependence is not reciprocal. The "mode of theology" is crucial for understanding the economy, though the reverse is not true. Whereas, according to Karl Rahner, the "economic" and "immanent" Trinities are identical, the same is not true of *theologia* and *oikonomia* in Basil's thought. Truths about the "subsistence of the Only-begotten before the ages" affect what one says about his incarnation, but what one says about the incarnation does not change what one says about the Son's "subsistence before the ages." The divine nature is revealed in the incarnation, but there are things one says about the incarnate Son that one would never say about the Son per se. Only if one understands that God is entirely unchanging—indeed without limitations of any kind, whether spatial, temporal, or otherwise—can one speak intelligibly about what happened in Jesus Christ.

Basil hammers this point home in his *Homily on the Holy Birth of Christ*, which was preached at the Feast of the Theophany (January 6), probably in 376–78:

[God] possesses a humanity connatural and united to himself, and restores all humanity to himself through flesh the same as ours in kind. So then, one might say, "(A) How did the splendor come to all by means of one? (B) How can divinity come to be in flesh?" As fire comes to be in iron: not by a change of place, but by a sharing of itself. For the fire does not go out of itself and into the iron; rather, while remaining in its place, it shares its own power with the iron. It is in no way diminished when it shares itself, and the whole of it fills whatever shares in it. So it is in this way too that God the Word did not move out of himself when he *dwelt among us*. Nor did he undergo change when *the Word become flesh* [Jn 1:14]. Heaven was not deprived of what it contained, and earth received the heavenly one within its own embraces. Do not suppose that the divinity fell. For it did not move from one place to another as bodies do. Do not imagine that the divinity was altered when it was transferred into flesh. For the immortal is immutable.[6]

Basil poses two rhetorical questions, the first (A) about how what happened to Christ affects others, the second (B) about how divinity comes to be in flesh. His response to (A) is brief: Christ shared in flesh that is of the same kind as ours. The answer to (B) works by analogy. Just as fire is neither changed nor harmed by its heating of iron, so too for the Word when it becomes flesh. Naturally, the incarnation would not be salvific if the Word had changed. The only change conceivable for a perfect being would be for the worse, and an imperfect power could not affect salvation.

Though the agency lies with the Word, all the change occurs to the human or the flesh. In this passage, Basil assumes that it was necessary that the Word join itself to human flesh in order to restore it. He uses "humanity" and "flesh" interchangeably here. Basil does not entirely spell out why the Word had to take flesh. Presumably the analogy goes that God the Word is like the fire; his flesh is the iron touched by the flame; and our flesh is iron touched by the original iron. How the heat is transmitted is unclear. Basil merely asserts, "He was born so that you might be cleansed by that which is the same kind as you."[7] Note that the metaphor for salvation moves here from restoration to cleansing. This kind of slippage from purification to healing to mixing to restoring is common in all the Cappadocian authors. However, the variety of metaphors is inconsequential, or put differently, each metaphor is essentially gesturing at the same thing, namely, the transmission to humanity of the divine life, as described in the analogy of heated iron. In other words, one should not think of "healing" as primarily an interpersonal interaction in Basil and the Gregories; it is, instead, the giving of health or life to one who is sick. This gift is what occurred in the incarnation.

Basil contrasts Christ's birth with previous appearances of God to the patriarchs and prophets: In Christ, God's Son does not merely communicate to us, but becomes one of us. The underlying premise is that it is somehow necessary or fitting for this to occur in order to save humanity. Basil's stress in the homily is on the continuity in kind between Christ's flesh and our own. This continuity in kind alone ensures the transmission to us of what happened in Christ. While this account is not satisfactory (by this logic, anything that happened to anyone would affect everyone else with the same kind of flesh), it is clear what Basil is trying to avoid. On the one hand, he is staving off any view in which Christ is a mere prophet in a series of wise and inspired men; the Incarnation is a union of natures, not merely a case of inspiration. On the other hand, the homily contains an oblique reference to Apollinarius, who proclaimed that Christ is the "man from heaven" brought down heavenly flesh; this reference alone enables us to date the homily to 376 or after, when Basil became concerned with Apollinarius's Christology. Basil warns against speculation about the kind of flesh Christ had with a striking rhetorical contrast: "The magi adore him but Christians inquire how God can be in the flesh, what sort of flesh he has, and whether the humanity he assumed was perfect or imperfect!"[8] Though Christ's flesh, born from the stainless Virgin, is special, it is nonetheless exactly akin to our own; beyond this, inquiry is fruitless and impious.

In his other works on the Apollinarian controversy (all of them letters), Basil maintains the same principle that salvation is cleansing of like by like in Christ.[9] But he clarifies his reflections on the human element in Christ; "humanity" is no longer simply "flesh." In *Letter* 261, for instance, Basil argues that it was necessary for Christ to assume both our flesh and our psychological conditions in order for us to be healed from both death and sin. Basil mentions, but does not elaborate on, such conditions as grief and anxiety. One wonders if these are healed in exactly the same way as the flesh is healed: Is the soul passive, as iron in fire, or is its active cooperation required?

In Basil's sermons, we get glimpses of how he perceived the subjective appropriation of Christ's work of salvation. Two examples from the collection known as the "Moral Homilies" will suffice. The first comes from Basil's *Homily on the Beginning of Proverbs*. Here he outlines what he takes to be the purpose of the book—namely, to teach ethics—and proceeds to comment on the book's first five verses. Much of Basil's discussion revolves around the virtues of wisdom, discipline, and justice that the book is meant to inculcate. The reader might be prepared to see here a kind of works-righteousness, until we learn that the life of virtue is a result of the gift of grace, rather than its cause. This becomes apparent when we see what Basil takes the audience of Proverbs to be. Commenting on Proverbs 1:44 ("that [Solomon] might give shrewdness to the innocent, and both perception and insight to the young child"), Basil argues that we must understand the "young child" as a youth inwardly, rather than a literal child:

> Thus here in this passage, by "young child" is meant that person who is reborn *by the washing of regeneration* [Titus 3:5], who turns and becomes like a child, and who by such a state is *fit for the kingdom* of heaven [Lk 9:62]. Therefore, after being trained by the Book of Proverbs, the newborn babe, who longs for rational and guileless milk, is given *perception and insight*.[10]

The life of striving for virtue is a result rather than a precondition of the gift of divine regeneration in baptism (a theme apparent in both Gregories). While Basil does not elaborate on the "efficacy" of the sacrament, baptism clearly performs the work of regeneration. Moreover, it is clear that Basil does not think of salvation as a once-for-all matter. Instead, it involves an ongoing life of desire or longing for God. The new life given inwardly to the neophyte is, like ordinary human life, something that takes time to nurture. This cultivation of the gift of grace follows an order. Here, the child is given a curriculum (identified with Solomon's Proverbs) that trains him in how to have the proper longing for the kind of "milk" that is appropriate to the inner child.

A second example can be taken from Basil's *Homily on Humility*. Basil employs a diatribe directed at one who would boast of his own accomplishments; he even cites what would become Augustine's pet verse on the subject, 1 Corinthians 4:17, "What do you have that you have not received?" Basil chides the proud in a way that connects the individual's experience with the story of the incarnation: "You have not come to know God through your righteousness, but God has come to know you through his kindness. . . . You have not embraced Christ through your virtue, but Christ has embraced you through his advent."[11]

It is true that Basil occasionally speaks as if ascetic purification is a precondition for the gift of the Spirit's grace. But clearly it would be a mistake to accuse him of "Pelagianism" without qualifying the term beyond any recognition. One must recall the highly occasional nature of Basil's writings and the fact that he never pronounced decisively on the relative roles of grace and human agency in the appropriation of salvation.

Gregory of Nazianzus

Gregory of Nazianzus so thoroughly identified with the humanity of Christ that he can be said to have articulated, in Andrew Hofer's phrase, an "autobiographical Christology."[12] A good example of this blending of first- and third-person perspectives can be seen in *Oration 29* (the *Third Theological Oration*). Gregory addresses those who disparage the Son of God, viewing him as lesser than the Father because of his incarnation:

> He whom you presently scorn was once transcendent, even over you. He who is presently human was incomposite. He remained what he was; what he was not, he assumed. No "because" is required for his existence in the beginning, for what could account for the existence of God? But later he came into being because of something, namely, your salvation, yours, who insult him and despite his Godhead for that very reason, because he took on your think corporeality. Through the medium of the mind he had dealings with the flesh, the God below become man. He was mixed with God and became a single whole, the stronger side predominating, in order that I might be made God to the same extent that he was made man.[13]

As in Basil, the incarnation is seen as a change for the one who was "assumed," not for the one who assumed. The incarnation (understood as the Word taking flesh with mind as an intermediary) has an explanation, which is to achieve the divine aim of salvation. Salvation is described as a mixture of divinity and humanity such that the latter becomes the former. In other words, "mixture" is understood here along the lines of Aristotle's complete transformation. This doctrine can be contrasted with the Stoic doctrine of "complete mixture." In cases where a tiny amount of one substance is mixed with a much larger amount of another, the Stoics argued that the smaller ingredient retains its proper identity such that it can be separated from the mixture intact; a small drop of wine, for instance, mixes with the entire sea, but always remains distinct and separable from the sea's water. Not so for Aristotle, who had argued that the predominant element transforms the lesser into itself.[14] This is the sense of Gregory's talk of mixture and deification. It appears that the mixture occurs at the time of the incarnation. In his characteristic boldness, Gregory applies this deification not simply to the generic humanity, but to himself.

The language of exchange—that in Christ, God takes our life to replace it with his own—recurs throughout Gregory's works. In two of Gregory's festal orations, one on the Theophany and the other on Easter, a nearly verbatim summary of the story of the creation, fall, and redemption of the cosmos appears.[15] This story enables us to see more fully the sense behind the divine aim of saving humanity. Gregory speaks of creation as an overflow of the divine goodness: The reason anything besides God exists is that God's goodness could not be contained in self-contemplation. And in order for creation to be complete, there cannot merely be those heavenly and angelic powers which are by nature akin to God; there must also be a material creation that is in a sense foreign to God's nature; moreover, although the intelligible and sensible creations were in harmony without humanity, there had to be in addition a creature that unites the two kinds of creation, and so humanity is created. Humanity is given the task of cultivating a garden, which symbolizes the thoughts about God. Humanity is from the start destined not simply for temporal happiness, but for deification, but this must come in due time. At first, humanity is naïve and immature, and so it is forbidden to "eat" from the Tree of Knowledge, which for Gregory symbolizes contemplation. When humanity transgresses God's commandment (eating contemplation before it is ready to do so), God gives a punishment that affects both the intellectual and the sensible parts of humanity. Though the cutting short of life in death is also a mercy, humanity spins gradually downward in sins, terminating in idolatry. In response, God's sending of law and prophets prepares humanity for God's direct intervention in Christ. Given humanity's twofold constitution, God assumes both parts, "mixing" with human body and mind, so that he might purify "like by like." As in his famous letters on the Apollinarian controversy, in his festal orations, Gregory assumes that salvation requires the assumption by God of that which requires healing; put negatively, what is not assumed is not healed.[16] In the *Third Theological Oration*, Gregory speaks of the saving effects of this mixture in the first person. If all of Adam fell, mind and body, then the new Adam must include both.

Gregory clearly wants those attending the Christian festivals celebrating Christ's birth and his passion to grasp where the events fit into the broader story of God and the cosmos. A proper appreciation of salvation is impossible without a proper theology more broadly. God's goodness is consistent throughout Gregory's story: The incarnation achieves the original divine purpose of deifying humanity. Moreover, humans are constitutionally temporal, and so the process of salvation takes time. Salvation is not something that can be simply given to a subject regardless of its state. Just as humanity was originally meant to progress to contemplation of God, so too did it take time for humanity to be corrected by law and prophets in preparation for the incarnation.

In the sacrament of baptism, the individual is conformed to Christ's death and resurrection and thus the deifying mixture of the divine life with human life comes to the baptized. One of Gregory's strengths is to reflect not only on the role of baptism in this exchange, but also on the responsibility placed in the minister's hands. We find this theme in his *Oration 2*, written almost 20 years prior to the *Theological Orations*, in which Gregory moves directly from talking of Christ's healing of humanity to the need for judicious pastoral care. Like a wise physician, the pastor must know when to apply which remedy. Once again, salvation is not given without consideration of the recipient. As Christopher Beeley has shown, while the gift of deification is God's direct action in the individual, its administration lies in the hands of the church's priests. To use Gregory's description,

> The scope of our therapy is to provide the soul with wings, to rescue it from the world and give it to God . . . to make Christ dwell in the heart by the Spirit, and in short to deify and bestow heavenly bliss upon those who have pledged their allegiance to heaven.[17]

This mediatorial work of the church consists in the administration of the sacraments, the exposition of Scripture, the teaching of orthodox doctrine, and the modeling of Christian virtue. There could not be a closer link between the objective and subjective aspects of salvation, as the experience of the church is the locus for the giving of the grace of the Trinity.

Gregory of Nyssa

Gregory of Nyssa read the story of Paradise and Fall somewhat differently than did Nazianzen. His interpretation appears already in what is generally regarded as his earliest work, *On Virginity* from around 370, and again in broadly similar terms in a work from roughly a decade later, *On the Making of Humanity*.[18] Whereas Nazianzen viewed Adam and Eve as immature and in need of steady progress before attaining to contemplation, Gregory of Nyssa saw humanity's original state as one of perfection. Likewise they differed as to the nature of the forbidden fruit: Nazianzen underscored that it was the tree of *knowledge*, and hence of contemplation, while Nyssen placed the emphasis on its mixed character as the knowledge of good *and* evil. Adam and Eve were to enjoy goodness unmixed with evil, but chose (inexplicably) to dilute the purity of their enjoyment with the suffering of evil, rather like a house builder who could cut windows for sunlight but chooses instead to enclose himself in perpetual darkness. The effects of our first parents' choice are disastrous. Humanity falls from living a life according to the Spirit to one according to the flesh. Physical reproduction, with its attendant passions, inaugurates a succession of life-mixed-with-death. Although Adam did not "know" Eve until after the banishment from Eden, God in his foresight had made provision for sexual intercourse in advance by the creation of bodies marked by biological sex. In our exiled state, birth does not lead merely to life, but also to death. Along with this succession come all the other passions: grief, fear, anger, anxiety, and the like. To be sure, the likeness to God that humanity possessed at the beginning remains and is accessible to those who train their minds on it; moreover, humans retain their gift of freedom. The only secure remedy, however, is a new kind of birth from the Spirit: "That which is born of the flesh is flesh, and that which is born of the Spirit is Spirit" (Jn 3:6). As one can find in Gregory's defense of the Spirit's divinity, *On the Holy Spirit*

Against the Macedonians and elsewhere, he places great weight on the Spirit's "life-giving power" that is active at baptism. Gregory argues that through the work of the minister, the Spirit consecrates the water and uses it to give new life to those who come to the font with faith in the Trinity. This picture of the Spirit's work in salvation appears in various places, including at the very end of one of Gregory's latest works, the *Homilies on the Song of Songs*.

Gregory makes a great deal of the Biblical language of the Spirit as the giver of life. What exactly, then, is the role of Christ in saving humanity? In *Against Eunomius* 3.3, we get a clear statement of the saving union of divinity and humanity in Christ. As in the other two Cappadocians, a non-reciprocal change is effected by the Son of God assuming human nature and imparting his own life to it:

> Our own position is that the Only-begotten God having by himself brought the universe into being, has total control of the universe in himself, and one of the things made by him was human nature, and when this lapsed into evil, and for this reason came into the destruction of death, by himself he brought it back to immortal life, through the man in whom he made his dwelling, assuming to himself all that is human; and that he mingled his own life-giving power with the mortal and perishable nature, and by combination with himself transformed our deadly state into lively grace and power.[19]

In the context, Gregory is attempting to reclaim Acts 2:36 ("He made him both Christ and Lord, this Jesus whom you crucified") from Eunomius. For Eunomius, the verse shows Christ's created status, since it refers to God "making" him Christ. Gregory reads the verse more naturally as pointing to something that occurred after the crucifixion. This something is a complete transformation of the one who had been assumed in the Incarnation. The assumed item is called both "the man" and "human nature," with no comment on how these two relate. He uses the same logic of mixture that Nazianzen uses, whereby the predominant element overcomes the inferior element, but places the time of this mixture after the Passion rather than at the point of the Incarnation.[20]

> It happens also where physical things are combined, when one part is greatly superior in quantity to the other, that the lesser is, naturally, en-

tirely converted into the predominant ... [The flesh] however because of its commingling with the Good in its immensity and infinity, no longer remained within its own limits and characteristics, but was taken and lifted up by the right hand of God and became, instead of a slave, Lord, instead of a subject, Christ the King, instead of lowly, most high, instead of man, God. (3.3.44–46)[21]

In Christ, there was an active element, the divine nature, and a passive element, called alternatively the man, the flesh, and the human nature. The paschal transformation is so thorough that it results in a replacement of the properties of humanity with those of the divinity. Elsewhere in the same treatise, he even argues that the human became invisible at this point.

In the *Catechetical Oration*, Gregory provides a lengthy defense of the reasonableness of the incarnation and passion as means to accomplish the end of salvation. He shows how the divine economy reflects the wisest and most just plan for saving humanity from slavery to death and the devil. In the course of this, Gregory encounters a problem: If God's attributes never change, and God is always omnipresent, in what way did the Incarnation differ from God's universal providence? Why is God's presence now not like it was then? Interestingly, Gregory uses the language of mixture both for the Incarnation and for God's providence here and now. But, the result is different because of the intent: Now, God is mixed with us "in the sense of preserving our nature in being"; then, God was mixed with us, "in order that, by mixing with the divine, what is ours might become divine" in becoming free from death and the adversary.[22] Of course, such freedom is not a fact of experience for humans presently, and all this raises the question of whether one can be divinized without realizing it. As Gregory's discussion proceeds, the answer appears to be affirmative.

Gregory tackles the question of whether the Logos employed deception in the Incarnation. He appeared as a human, one under the devil's tyranny, but as fairer and more perfect than the others, drawing the devil's attention. When the devil thought he had Jesus conquered on the cross, the Word destroyed the power of death and the devil by his resurrection.[23] This position must be distinguished from the idea that Nazianzen ridicules, namely, that the ransom of Christ's blood was paid to the devil.[24] For Gregory of Nyssa, while God respects the devil's ownership over human nature and thus does not snatch us away by compulsion, God does not pay the devil a ransom. Rather, God uses Christ's flesh as "bait" on which to catch him and destroy his stranglehold over humanity.[25] Nyssen reasons that, while the means were deceptive, the intent was to heal those affected by the malady of death, including the devil himself, and therefore the intention justifies the deception. The devil has no grounds for complaint, given the great boon given even to him. Note how Gregory extends the Christological reasoning to speak of the devil's own salvation:

> These and others like them are the gifts given by the great mystery of the divine inhumanization. Through all the ways in which he was mixed with humanity—for he went through everything proper to our nature, being born, being nurtured, and growing, advancing even to the point of death—he achieved all the aforementioned things, freeing the human being from evil and healing the very inventor of evil.[26]

However, if it is necessary to be healed "like by like," which explains Christ's sharing in all our nature's properties, then the devil's healing seems *sui generis*. One can perhaps grant Gregory's account of God's motivation to save the devil, but the means do not seem to line up. Why did not Christ have to assume the devil's nature in order to save him? No one would deny that God is capable of saving the devil, but Gregory has just been insisting that God's sheer power should not be considered independently of God's wisdom and justice. If it is just and fitting for God to save us "like by like," why not the devil?

The devil's salvation is not really accounted for so much as it is necessitated by Gregory's vision of salvation as the restoration of all things to God, which owes much to Origen's reading of 1 Corinthians 15. The notion is absent from Basil, who seems to assume the eternal damnation of some and is only mentioned in passing by Nazianzen.[27] Of course, for "all things" to be subject to God eschatologically, even the devil must be saved. This seems to place a necessity on universal salvation, something that has offended more readers than merely Herrmann and Harnack. To them, it negates the idea of grace. But that is not at all clear. Of course, if one said that from the perspective of the individual person, salvation is necessary ("God must save me!"), that would constitute a denial of grace. But, Gregory is viewing salvation from the perspective of the entire history of the cosmos. Perhaps one might object to such a totalizing project, but if one allows it and one believes in providence, it is hard to see how salvation at this level is anything other than a necessary outworking of the divine goodness and power. Naturally, this does not entail that all rational creatures be saved. For that idea, Gregory relies on his understanding of the Pauline "all in all" (1 Corinthians 15:28; Ephesians 1:23). I have suggested that the weakness of Gregory's universalism has less to do with its motivation than its ill fit with his Christology.

The fruits of Christ's saving work will be borne only in the future age.[28] When speaking of the eschaton, three themes emerge in Gregory.[29] The first is the role of desire in motivating the soul's transformation into the divine likeness: The soul desires the beauty of its divine Archetype and seeks to become like it.[30] The second is the need for purification, including after death, before returning to the divine likeness.[31] Third, growth in likeness will never cease. The purified will never reach a point where they perfectly mirror the infinitely beautiful and good God, and so the capacity for growth will always remain. Therefore, souls will alternate between delight in the good and desire for ever-greater likeness to it. The end is therefore not stasis, but a dynamic, endless process. For Ekkehard Mühlenberg, this idea provides at least a partial rebuttal to those who have accused Gregory of Pelagianism: "According to the concept of infinite progress the notion of works-righteousness is eliminated since man never accomplishes any work with which he could present himself to God: An accomplished work presupposes that perfection has a definite *telos* and limit; that, however, is excluded in principle."[32] The doctrine of perpetual progress or striving, labeled *epektasis* by Jean Daniélou, would go on to influence prominent Greek thinkers including Maximus the Confessor.[33]

Like Basil and Nazianzen, Gregory of Nyssa is noteworthy for his simultaneous insistence that salvation cannot be given to humans apart from their free choices, and, on the other hand, the concrete, collective salvation of human nature as a whole. How the two points fit together remains somewhat murky, though it is clear that Gregory himself found a need to elaborate on the way in which what happens to Christ affects the rest of humanity.[34] As Johannes Zachhuber has shown, it was precisely in order to solve this soteriological puzzle that Gregory developed a realist conception of human nature in which "the whole is at once with each part."[35] It is a marvelous vision of God's solidarity with the human race and not merely with successive individuals. Perhaps such theories can continue to enlighten Christian theology; we can be grateful that the Cappadocians saw the need to explore the central mystery of Christian faith with intellectual creativity and seriousness.

Conclusion

In the writings of the three Cappadocians, we do not see a totally uniform doctrine of salvation but rather a recurrent complex of themes. Where differences occur, they are sometimes outright disagreements—for instance, over whether all are saved—and sometimes matters of style and emphasis, as in the case of Nazianzen's "autobiographical" approach. But we should not overlook the overlapping patterns in all three authors. They all write of the transformation of human nature through its contact with the divine nature in Christ, and they employ a common stock of vivid metaphors for this event, including mixture, heating, illumination, and purification. Given its link with Christ's human nature, the Cappadocians viewed salvation as something that is above all collective: It is our nature that is saved. For all three, baptism and the subsequent moral life enabled by the Holy Spirit are essential in appropriating the change effected in Christ. For all three, doctrinal polemic provoked some of their most extensive and serious reflections on soteriology. Moreover, they held that a coherent picture of God is necessary for understanding the non-reciprocal change that occurs in human salvation, as the human is transformed into God's own life without this affecting any change for God. In addition to working out this vision in treatises over against Eunomius, Apollinarius, and the Pneumatomachians, all three Cappadocians also elaborated their visions in homilies preached for the church's major feasts. The doctrine of salvation was, therefore, something celebrated as well as studied.

NOTES

1. Apollinaris argued that the Logos, which he understood as Jesus's divine nature, replaced the human rational soul in the incarnation. In other words, Jesus' "pure" divine nature replaced the "filthy" mind of a typical human. The implication of this argument is that Jesus was not fully human in that his humanity depended

on his divinity and his mind or will was overruled by the divinity. See Justin S. Holcomb, *Know the Heretics* (Grand Rapids, MI: Zondervan, 2014), 99–107.
2. Gregory of Nazianzus, *ep.* 101.5. St. Gregory of Nazianzus, *On God and Christ*, trans. Lionel Wickham (Crestwood, NY: St. Vladimir's Seminary Press, 2002), 158.
3. Wilhelm Herrmann, *Gregorii Nysseni Sententiae de salute Adipiscenda* (Dissertation. Halle, 1875). The quoted phrase is from Wilhelm Herrmann, *The Communion of the Christian with God*, 2nd ed., trans. J. Sandys Stanton, rev. R. W. Steward (New York: J. P. Putnam's Sons and London: Williams and Norgate, 1906), ix.
4. Adolf von Harnack, *History of Dogma*, translated from the third German edition by Neil Buchanan (Boston: Little, Brown, and Company, 1901), volume 3, 189–90.
5. Basil of Caesarea, *Against Eunomius*, ed. and French trans. Bernard Sesboue, Georges-Matthieu de Durand, and Louis Doutrelau, *Contre Eunome*, 2 vols. (Paris: Les Editions du Cerf, 1982–83), 2.3. The distinction is prompted by a discussion of Acts 2:36 in particular, but Basil's comments presume that verses about Christ generally fit into one of the two categories.
6. Basil, *hom.* 27.2 (hom. = Homily). Trans. Mark DelCogliano in St. Basil the Great, *On Fasting and Feasts*, trans. Susan R. Holman and Mark DelCogliano, introduction by Susan R. Holman (Yonkers, NY: St. Vladimir's Seminary Press, 2013), 29.
7. Basil, *hom.* 27.6 (trans. DelCogliano, *On Fasting and Feasts*, 40).
8. Ibid.
9. Basil, *epp.* 261, 262, 263.4, and 265.2 and the oblique references in *epp.* 236.1 and 260.8.
10. Basil, *Homily on the Beginning of Proverbs* 13. St. Basil the Great, *On Christian Doctrine and Practice*, trans., with introduction and annotations, Mark DelCogliano (Yonkers, NY: St. Vladimir's Seminary Press, 2012), 72.
11. Basil, *Homily on Humility* (*On Christian Doctrine and Practice*, trans. DelCogliano in St. Basil the Great, *On Fasting and Feasts*, trans. Susan R. Holman and Mark DelCogliano, introduction by Susan R. Holman (Yonkers, NY: St. Vladimir's Seminary Press, 2013), 113).
12. Andrew Hofer, *Christ in the Life and Teaching of Gregory of Nazianzus* (Oxford: Oxford University Press, 2013).
13. Gregory of Nazianzus, *Oration* (hereafter cited as *Or.*), 29.19 (St. Gregory of Nazianzus, *On God and Christ: The Five Theological Orations and Two Letters to Cledonius*, trans. Frederick Williams and Lionel Wickham, with introduction by Lionel Wickham (Crestwood, NY: St. Vladimir's Seminary Press, 2002), 86 [this translation alters that of Wickham]).
14. Aristotle, *On Generation and Corruption*, Book I, ed. Frans de Haas and Jaap Mansfeld, (Oxford: Clarendon Press, 2004), 328a26.
15. Gregory of Nazianzus, *Or.* 38.7–13 (*On Theophany*, from December 380 or January 381) and *Or.* 45.3–9 (*Second Oration on Easter*, from Easter 383).
16. Cf. Gregory of Nazianzus, *epp.* 101.5.
17. Gregory of Nazianzus, *Oration* 2.22 (translation in Christopher A. Beeley, *Gregory of Nazianzus on the Trinity and the Knowledge of God: "In Your Light We Shall See Light"* (Oxford and New York: Oxford University Press, 2008), 270).

18. The following paragraph summarizes Gregory of Nyssa, *On Virginity*, 12–13. Compare his *On the Making of Humanity*, 16–20.
19. Gregory of Nyssa, *Against Eunomius* 3.3.51, trans. Stuart G. Hall in, *Gregory of Nyssa: Contra Eunomium III: An English Translation with Commentary and Supporting Studies*, eds. Johann Leemans and Matthieu Cassin. Proceedings of the 12th International Colloquium on Gregory of Nyssa (Leuven, September 14–17, 2010) (Leiden: Brill, forthcoming), modified.
20. Pace A. S. Dunstone, *The Atonement in Gregory of Nyssa* (London: Tyndale Press, 1964), 15.
21. Gregory of Nyssa, *Against Eunomius* 3.3.44–46 (trans. Stuart G. Hall in *Contra Eunomium III*, eds. Leemans and Cassin modified).
22. Gregory of Nyssa, *Catechetical Oration* 25. Edward R. Hardy, ed. *The Christology of the Later Fathers* (Philadelphia: Westminster, 1954), 302.
23. See also Gregory of Nyssa, *Catechetical Oration* 16, with the comments of Harnack, *History of Dogma*, vol. 3, p. 297.
24. Gregory of Nazianzen, *Oration*, 45.22.
25. See Gregory of Nyssa, *Catechetical Oration*, 24.
26. Gregory of Nyssa, *Catechetical Oration*, 26.
27. See Morwenna Ludlow, *Universal Salvation* (Oxford: Oxford University Press, 2000). See Basil, *On the Holy Spirit* 16.40 and Gregory of Nazianzen, see *Oration* 30.6.
28. For the metaphor of "fruit," see Gregory of Nyssa, *On the Dead* [G. Heil et al., ed. *Gregorii Nysseni Opera* IX (Leiden: Brill, 1992), 44–48; trans. Rowan Greer, *One Path for All: Gregory of Nyssa on the Christian Life and Human Destiny*, assisted by J. Warren Smith (Eugene, OR: Cascade, 2014), 103–6].
29. For a thorough study of Gregory's eschatology, see J. Warren Smith, *Passion and Paradise: Human and Divine Emotion in the Thought of Gregory of Nyssa* (New York: Crossroad, 2004), especially 183–227.
30. See especially Gregory's *Homilies on the Song of Songs*. In *Gregory of Nyssa: Homilies on the Song of Songs*, ed. and trans. R. Norris (Atlanta: SBL, 2012).
31. An important theme in Gregory's *On the Soul and the Resurrection*. In *Gregory of Nyssa, On the Soul and the Resurrection*, trans. Catharine P. Roth (Crestwood, NY: St Vladimir's Seminary Press, 1993).
32. Ekkehard Mühlenberg, "Synergism in Gregory of Nyssa," *Zeitschrift für Neutestamentliche Wissenschaft und die Kunde der Älteren Kirche* volume 68 (1977): 93–122, at 103.
33. Jean Daniélou, *Platonisme et theologie mystique: essai sur la doctrine spirituelle de Saint Gregoire de Nysse*, rev. ed. (Paris: Aubier, 1953); Daniélou, "Epektasis," in *L'Être et le temps chez Gregoire de Nysse* (Leiden: Brill, 1970). See Paul Blowers, "Maximus the Confessor, Gregory of Nyssa, and the Concept of 'Perpetual Progress,'" *Vigiliae Christianae* volume 46 (1992): 151–71.
34. See the reflections of Ludlow, *Universal Salvation*, 95ff.
35. Johannes Zachhuber, *Human Nature in Gregory of Nyssa: Philosophical Background and Theological Significance*, Supplements to Vigiliae Christianae XLVI (Leiden, Boston, and Köln: Brill, 2000), 236, commenting on *Catechetical Oration* 32.

PART II

Middle Ages

7

Theologies of Salvation in the Middle Ages

An Introduction

DAVID HOGG

From the time of Origen in the third century until well into the eleventh century, the notion that Jesus's death was a ransom price paid to the devil for sinful humanity was an increasingly popular paradigm for explaining and understanding salvation. The general idea was that humanity was bound under Satan's authority because of our sin and the only way we could be freed was if God paid a price to the devil that would be equal to or greater than the value of all the souls under his authority. Jesus's life was that price. What the devil failed to take into account is that he had no authority over Jesus since Jesus was without sin, and so not only could the grave and Hell not hold Christ, but neither could it now hold all those who tied themselves to Christ through faith. Over the course of the Middle Ages, Christ's victory over Satan came to be known as the harrowing of Hell because when Jesus rose from the grave on the third day, he led the righteous out of Hell itself into Heaven to dwell in God's presence forever more.

Although this conception of the work of Christ on behalf of sinners is no longer the dominant paradigm, it should not be disparaged as completely fanciful. That a ransom was involved in procuring salvation for sinful humanity comes straight from the Bible. In Mark 10:45, for example, Jesus says that he came to give his life as a ransom to many. The same statement is also recorded in Matthew 20:28. Paul, in 1 Timothy 2:6, teaches that Jesus gave his life as a ransom for many. There is, then, a firm foundation on which to make the case that Jesus's life was a ransom. But a ransom paid to whom? Origen believed it was to the devil, as did Irenaeus, an older contemporary.[1] And as for Jesus descending into Hell in order to free the righteous from unjust bondage, the difficult passage in 1 Peter 3:18–20 provides food for thought on where Jesus was between his crucifixion and resurrection.²

No less a figure than Gregory the Great, the self-styled servant of the servants of God who, as bishop of Rome in the late sixth century, sent the monk Augustine on a pioneering missionary journey to England and sought to spread the gospel all over Europe, supported and even further developed this theological perspective on salvation. Given his popularity and the longevity of his legacy, it is not surprising that even as late as the early eleventh century, the towering figure Fulbert of Chartres followed in Gregory's footsteps when he wrote,

> For Judah's lion bursts his chains
> Crushing the serpent's head;
> And cries aloud through death's domain
> To wake the imprisoned dead.
>
> Devouring depths of hell their prey
> At his command restore;
> His ransomed hosts pursue their way
> Where Jesus goes before.³

If this is no longer the reigning perspective on soteriology in either popular imagination or scholarly opinion despite holding sway for a wide swath of Christians for centuries, what happened? What changed? The answer is not so much what as it is who.

Anselm of Canterbury

When Anselm was born in Aosta, Italy in 1033, no one would have predicted that he would one day become the Archbishop of Canterbury, let alone the theologian responsible for turning the tide in theological reflection on soteriology. How Anselm came to doubt and even reject the ransom theory to the devil as the preferred explanation for salvation will likely never be known with certainty. It is instructive, however, to consider Anselm's development as a writer.

While Anselm did not leave his oeuvre in chronological order, it is widely accepted that some of his earliest written work included his prayers and meditations. These short works were written to help guide believers' private devotion by stirring their minds to contemplate the majesty of their God and his work on their behalf.[4] While many of the prayers he wrote are to saints, what comes across most strongly is the powerful redemption accomplished by Christ for all. In this light, Anselm's prayers to saints become conversations between friends, straddling the great divide of the grave, in which both the sinner on earth and the saint in heaven marvel at the Father's grace in Christ.

With such a strong emphasis on individual devotion and the direct connection between suppliants and their Lord, it is not unreasonable to posit that this was the genesis of conceiving of salvation less in cosmic terms and more in personal terms. In other words, Anselm was operating in a theological context where the greatest struggle in creation was not between God and the devil, but between God and sinful humanity. Even a cursory reading of a selection of Anselm's prayers evinces an inordinately strong view of the depth of human depravity. A powerful and repeated message of the prayers is that my sin is my own problem and unless God condescends in mercy, I have no hope. To put it another way, the devil may be alive and well, but the devil is not the great enemy to the sinner. The sinner's greatest enemy is God.

This is the message of the *Cur Deus Homo*. Early on in this work, Anselm's interlocutor asks if Jesus was the ransom paid to the devil.[5] Anselm never answers the question directly; instead, he redirects and refocuses his student's attention to the sinfulness of humanity in light of the righteousness of God. Perhaps Anselm did not provide a direct answer because he did not want to reject the prevailing view directly and thereby run the risk of open confrontation with colleagues standing in a long line of tradition. It is also conceivable, however, that Anselm, living up to his reputation for being wise, was stating his case in a way that suggested that his perspective was a better expression of the doctrine of salvation than the prevailing point of view, and not an outright rejection of it.

The *Cur Deus Homo* is, in its entirety, an implicit argument that Jesus paid a ransom to God, not the devil, on behalf of sinful humanity. The power of sin is not ultimately grounded in the authority of the devil, but in humanity itself. According to Anselm, when we understand this, we understand why God is our greatest enemy because the offense of sin is not merely against one another, but ultimately against God. This being so, what hope is there for the salvation of sinful souls whose offense against God is infinite? None, unless there is one who, as a human without sin, could stand before God as our representative, yet as God, could shoulder the debt incurred by humanity. In short, only a *Deus Homo* could possibly satisfy the debt of sin and accomplish permanent reconciliation.

The evidence of Anselm's attempt to redirect the trajectory of soteriological thought appears not so much in direct commentary on his work as in the trends that developed after him. As cathedral schools turned into burgeoning universities, interest turned toward construing salvation more in terms of the divine-human relationship, even as there continued a distinct emphasis on the necessity and priority of divine activity.

Peter Abelard

It is often argued that Anselm provided the church with an objective view of the atonement, whereas Abelard propagated a subjective view. Anselm focused on God who alone could bring about salvation; Abelard focused on humanity as the central actor in achieving redemption. This interpretation began with Abelard's archenemy, Bernard of Clairvaux, who contended that Abelard had reduced salvation to a mere program of self-improvement.[6] In the modern era, this construal of Abelard's position was resurrected by Hastings Rashdall at the end of the nineteenth century when he scoured the theological landscape for historical precedent and support of his own subjective explanation of the atonement.[7] Surely, Rashdall reasoned, the subjective is in view when Abelard wrote,

> [H]e has more fully bound us to himself by love; with the result that our hearts should be enkindled by such a gift of divine grace, and true charity should not now shrink from enduring anything for him . . . Yet everyone becomes more righteous—by which we mean a greater lover of the Lord—after the Passion of Christ than before, since a realized gift inspires greater love than one which is only hoped for. Wherefore, our redemption through Christ's suffering is that deeper affection in us which not only frees us from slavery to sin, but also wins for us the true liberty of sons of God, so that we do all things out of love rather than fear.[8]

It would appear that Abelard did indeed subscribe to a version of soteriology that privileges self-improvement when he speaks of hearts being "enkindled" by grace. Rather than a divine conferral of grace upon the guilty, the selfless act of crucifixion inspires the believer to endure all for the sake of Christ. Consequently, the one who looks to Christ becomes a "greater lover of the Lord" and "more righteous," potentially rendering the subjective experience of belief to be the operative key in salvation. As reasonable as this may seem, the trouble is that this comment from Abelard is a footnote to a much larger argument he has been tracing through Romans.

As Abelard works his way through Romans he briefly reviews popular explanations of the atonement. First, he rejects the notion that God is paying a ransom to the devil. Second, he expresses disappointment over the satisfaction model (likely drawn from Anselm's *Cur Deus Homo*) insofar as he is concerned that it doesn't say enough. Abelard's overarching concern is, in fact, Anselmian insofar as he wants to make sure people understand the immense weight of sin. As he explains humanity's impossible predicament, Abelard draws from the early chapters of Romans to make it clear that apart from the work of God in Christ applied to sinners through faith, salvation would be untenable. What he is doing in his footnote is not diminishing justification, but connecting justification with the evidence of regeneration and sanctification.

Thomas Aquinas

It is helpful to understand Abelard's soteriology as related to, and an extension of, Anselm's brief outline of the subject in order to appreciate Aquinas's position. Just as Abelard and Anselm believed that God alone can make the unrighteous righteous through the atoning work of his Son on the cross, so did Aquinas. There is no revelation, there is no action to which sinful humanity can turn to achieve salvation apart from what God has revealed and accomplished. To leave the matter, there, however, is, for Aquinas as for Abelard before him, insufficient. What Anselm began and Abelard expanded, Aquinas draws out in fine detail.

According to Aquinas, justification is the removal of sin from the ungodly. But justification is not forgiveness alone.[9] It also affects the "interior disposition" of the believer. How is this affected? It is affected when a sinner becomes the object of divine love, the purpose of which is to bring about reconciliation and peace. This, says Aquinas, is what we commonly call grace, and it is by grace that a person is "made worthy of eternal life." Summarizing his own position, Aquinas goes on to say that it is the infusion of grace that remits the guilt of sin.[10] Where Anselm was reluctant to speak of love, Abelard interjected our love, but Aquinas refocuses our attention on the love of God as the means of his grace not only to forgive sin, but also to orient our "interior disposition" rightly.

The further we examine Aquinas's soteriology, the more explanations we find, but also the more we begin to wonder about some of his theological categories. Abelard, for example, appears to understand justification as something that is applied to us in Christ, the outworking of which is our continual sanctification; whereas Aquinas seems to view justification as "an ongoing process in people."[11] Since we do not find clearly defined, consistently used terminology among many medieval scholars (to say nothing of our contemporaries from time to time!), we should take care in not assigning beliefs where we are not on solid ground. Even so, Brian Davies' comments regarding Aquinas's view of justification are intriguing.

> It has been said that God justifies people by treating them as good even though they are sinful. But this idea does not occur to Aquinas. He thinks it obvious that being holy means being holy and not being *taken* to be holy even if one is *not*.[12]

This is, perhaps, where developments would eventually lead to a sharp disagreement in the Reformation. Sixteenth-century reformers and their theological progeny were as clear in rejecting progressive justification as their opponents were at pressing for it. One is either justified in Christ or not. Sanctification may be progressive, but it can only be progressive, so the argument goes, in the life of the one who already stands justified before God. *Simul justus et peccator*, as Luther would one day famously write.

Julian of Norwich

Julian of Norwich was one of the late medieval English mystics. Compared to Aquinas or Anselm, Julian is not well known. This is due in part to the fact that mysticism as a movement was never a mainline preoccupation in the church, and in part because Julian's writings are considerably less systematic than her theological predecessors. Her *Showings* are far more enigmatic and, for many first-time readers, opaque. Julian was, nevertheless, part of a stream in Christianity (especially in England) that both shaped and was shaped by popular spiritual devotion in the period leading up to the Reformation.[13] What is intriguing about Julian with respect to soteriology is that she returns to and amplifies some of the key elements of this doctrine as exemplified in Aquinas, Abelard, and Anselm.

Although Anselm, for example, wrote in a different genre than Julian, his prayers and her experience are of a kind. Anselm wrote his prayers to help individuals feel what they knew. His concern seems to be that while people understood well that they were sinners, that God was holy and righteous, and that salvation was the result of undeserved divine mercy, they did not always appreciate the emotional response that such knowledge should evoke. Anselm's prayers and meditations were a way of more intimately fusing the immanent and transcendent in the experience of worship. In a provocative way, Julian not only lived this experience, but sought to help her audience appreciate its benefits and truth. The reader must be careful here not to assume that while Anselm drew heavily on theology even as he probed the passions, Julian failed to rely on theology and does little more than feed the passions.

As Julian explains the context of her revelations, she tells us that she became so ill that she believed she would die; consequently, the last rites were applied. Her great desire in wanting to be spared from sickness and death was that she "might have loved God better, and longer time, that I might have the more knowing and loving of God in bliss of heaven."[14] When there was little hope that Julian would linger longer on this earth, her curate brought her an image of Christ and asked her to look upon it as she passed. At first, she did not want to divert her gaze from looking heavenward—the direction she thought best to be looking at the point of death. Eventually she consented, and as she looked upon the image of Christ her vision all but failed as everything went dark except for the image of Christ before her. So began her recovery and spiritual journey. As Denys Turner so succinctly states, the lesson conveyed is simple: "The Cross is all."[15]

The centrality of the cross in soteriologies of the Middle Ages was certainly nothing new, and we should take care lest we allow the *opera ad extra* of religious practice during this period to distract our attention from the centrality of Christ's death and resurrection. What Julian sought to elucidate in her *Showings* was not rooted solely in ecstatic experience, but in centuries of theological development. Not unlike Anselm and Abelard, Julian was wary of espousing a doctrine of salvation that objectified Christ's work so as to make it intellectually interesting, but practically of little account. Julian's revelations were not new revelations in the sense that they added to the Bible; rather, they were new revelations insofar as they drew people afresh to the one in whom they professed faith. What Julian offers her readers is not insight devoid of theology, but a reminder that knowledge should make us greater lovers of our Lord.

Despite any number of dissimilarities to which one could point between Julian and the forebears of her faith, an inescapable similarity is the conviction that faith without love is dead. Anselm inspired his readers to meditate on this truth. Abelard could not bear to ignore this truth. Aquinas dared not expound justification without including this truth. Did not Paul say something similar about the necessity of love for those who count themselves among the faithful? (cf. 1 Cor. 13). James, too, points us in this direction when he places love of neighbor at the center of his exposition on the indivisibility of faith and works (cf. James 2).

Soteriology in the European Middle Ages was neither uniform nor static. The motto *semper reformandum* is all too often assumed to apply to healthy theology since the sixteenth century, but this has been the practice in the Orthodox Church since its earliest days. Just as we recognize the contextual nature of theologies in our own day, so we should remember the occasional character of theological works in past centuries. Anselm wrote a brief work to address a particular question that responded to a prevailing paradigm. Abelard expanded this perspective to remind his students that justification may be the beginning, but it is not the end of salvation. Aquinas developed these ideas as he inherited them, explaining that we must work out our salvation even as it is God's operative grace that saves us. Julian stands in this rich tradition of reflection as one who did not reject the love of learning and the riches it revealed, but wished to guard the union between theology and the desire for God. What binds medieval soteriologies is their unfailing aspiration to know nothing except Jesus Christ and him crucified (1 Cor. 2:2).

NOTES

1. Irenaeus, *Against Heresies* in *The Ante-Nicene Fathers*, vol. 1, ed. Alexander Roberts and James Donaldson (Edinburgh: T&T Clark, 1996), 4.41.2, where the first number refers to the book, followed by chapter and section.
2. "For Christ also suffered once for sins, the righteous for the unrighteous, that he might bring us to God, being put to death in the flesh but made alive in the spirit, 19 in which he went and proclaimed to the spirits in prison, 20 because they formerly did not obey, when God's patience waited in the days of Noah, while the ark was being prepared, in which a few, that is, eight persons, were brought safely through water." (1 Peter 3:18–20 ESV).
3. Alister E. McGrath, *Historical Theology* (Oxford: Blackwell, 1998), 134.
4. Anselm of Canterbury, *The Letters of Anselm of Canterbury*, trans. Walter Frohlich (Kalamazoo, MI: Cistercian Publications, 1994), *Ep.* 325 (Ep = epistle).
5. Anselm of Canterbury, *Cur Deus Homo* in *Anselm of Canterbury, the Major Works*, ed. Brian Davies and G. R. Evans (Oxford: Oxford University Press, 1998), 1.1.
6. Bernard of Clairvaux, *The Letters of Bernard of Clairvaux*, trans. Bruno Scott James (Kalamazoo, MI: Cistercian Publications, 1998), *Ep.* 190.
7. See Hastings Rashdall, *The Idea of the Atonement in Christian Theology* (London: Macmillan, 1925).
8. Peter Abelard, *Epistle to the Romans*, in Eugene Fairweather, ed., *A Scholastic Miscellany, Anselm to Ockham*, trans. Gerald E. Moffatt (Toronto: Macmillan, 1970), 283–4.
9. Thomas Aquinas, *Summa Theologica*, trans. Fathers of the English Dominican Province, 1a2ae. 113. 1 reply 1. For Aquinas's works, the first number represents the part of the book, followed by the question number and his answer.
10. Ibid. 1a2ae. 113. 2.
11. Brian Davies, *Thomas Aquinas's* Summa Theologiae: A Guide and Commentary (Oxford: Oxford University Press, 2014), 227.
12. Ibid.
13. For detailed, well-written, yet somewhat opposing views on the relationship between culture and popular devotion, see Eamon Duffy, *The Stripping of the Altars* (New Haven: Yale University Press, 1992) and G. W. Bernard, *The Late Medieval English Church* (New Haven: Yale University Press, 2013).
14. Julian of Norwich, *Revelations of Divine Love*, trans. Elizabeth Spearing (London: Penguin Books, 1998), 44.
15. Denys Turner, *Julian of Norwich, Theologian* (New Haven: Yale University Press, 2013), 208.

8

Anselm of Canterbury

GILES E. M. GASPER

Anselm of Canterbury (1033–1109) is one of the most celebrated of medieval thinkers. Born in northern Italy, in Aosta, he became a monk at the Benedictine Abbey of Le Bec in Normandy in about 1059. Successively Prior (1063) and Abbot (1076) of Bec, Anselm served as Archbishop of Canterbury from 1093 until his death in 1109.[1] A political leader within Normandy and England, Anselm's commitment to church reform brought him into conflict with his secular rulers, Kings William Rufus and Henry I of England. Periods of exile from England and consultation with the Pope resulted eventually in a compromise over the issue of whether the laity had any right to invest churchmen with their ecclesiastical offices. Anselm is associated strongly with the movement toward affective piety from the later eleventh century. He created in his prayers and meditations an emotionally charged but disciplined linguistic framework focused on a personal encounter with the divine and its saintly mediators. Sometimes referred to as the last of the fathers, and the first of the scholastics, Anselm espoused a rational approach to Christian thinking, although one based firmly on the authority of Scripture, and respectful mediation of the Fathers. From the *Monologion* and *Proslogion*, Anselm's early treatises on the nature of God, Trinity, and human experience of the divine, to his majestic treatment of the atonement in the *Cur Deus homo* [*Why the God-Man*]?, Anselm's theological works explore a wide range of central theological issues. His influence was considerable throughout the subsequent medieval centuries and within modern theology, notably on Karl Barth and Hans Urs von Balthasar.

Introduction

Anselm of Canterbury is a central figure in the way in which Western, Latin Christianity configured the relationship between God and humanity. His particular vision of the economy of salvation, that is to say of the ways in which the redemption of humanity might be thought possible, cast the roles of the principal actors, God, Humankind, and the devil, differently to his Patristic forebears. It was a vision that proved influential, especially during the High Middle Ages, from about 1070 to about 1330, and in modern theology, mostly from the nineteenth century onward. Associated above all with his work *Cur Deus homo* [*Why the God-man?*] composed in 1098, Anselm's thought on the incarnation and redemptive work of Christ became enshrined within the modern period as one of a number of theories of atonement, an honor he would not likely have appreciated. Where modern scholarship has tended to over-categorize Anselm's exposition of the atonement, and especially to take issue with the way in which he expressed the interaction between God and mankind, a closer consideration of his own expressed intentions reveals contexts both larger and more intimate. On the one hand Anselm's thought on the matter formed part of, and flowed from, his monastic life and community. On the other, the subject of the atonement and the economy of salvation emerge across a range of his other works, in different genres and with different emphases.

Anselm's theology of salvation operates with a strong sense of the utter degradation of sin. In a phrase that would puzzle later medieval readers, Anselm once stated that he would prefer to be placed in hell, although innocent, than to be allowed to dwell in heaven, even faintly tainted by sin.[2] The incontinence and incapacity of human nature is compensated only by the activity of divine grace and the incarnation and atoning work of Christ. In this Anselm operates within, and manipulates, an Augustinian frame of reference, with strong resonance to a number of Greek Fathers, notably Athanasius and Gregory Nazianzen. Above all, however, it is Anselm's monastic lifestyle that informs the particular cadence and expression of his thought. Without consideration of that context Anselm's theology of salvation is easily misunderstood.

Background and Context

For most of his adult life, Anselm was a Benedictine monk. He was born in the Alpine town of Aosta, in 1033, and moved from there, through France, during his late teenage years, arriving at the monastery of Bec in Normandy in about 1059. The attractions of Bec were two-fold—first, the fame of the then Prior, Lanfranc, whose expertise in grammar was well-known, and second, the strict regime on which the house of Bec was based. Rapidly promoted to Prior in about 1063, Anselm eventually became Abbot of Bec in 1076, after the death of the founding Abbot, Herluin. In 1903, he left Bec to become Archbishop of Canterbury, in succession to Lafranc who had died in 1089. The appointment came, for Anselm, with regret at the disruption to his monastic life, for, although the Cathedral of Christ Church at Canterbury was also a Benedictine foundation (there were four Benedictine cathedrals in medieval England: Canterbury, Worcester, Winchester, and Durham), his duties and responsibilities were now to a larger church and world. A series of clashes with his kings, William II and Henry I of England, over different visions of the jurisdiction and Anselm's fierce proposition of church reform, dominated his archiepiscopal reign, which lasted until his death in 1109.

Anselm's life is documented to a level of detail unusual amongst his contemporaries. In addition to his corpus of works, a letter collection of some 475 items is preserved, as well as two works by his companion and remembrancer Eadmer, monk of Canterbury: the *Vita Anselmi* (*Life of Anselm*) and the longer *Historia novorum in Anglia* (*History of Recent Events in England*). These were written to defend Anselm's actions against those in the community at Canterbury less convinced of the wisdom of his political actions and to promote his saintly reputation amongst the same community and farther afield.[3]

Anselm was famed within his own lifetime for his teaching of the Christian way of life, and for his writings, which both supported and encapsulated his teaching on particular issues. He was a careful author, reluctant to allow early versions of works to circulate without his permission. The preface to the *Cur Deus homo* singles out (although does not name),

> certain men who without my knowledge copied for themselves the first parts of the enclosed work before it was completed and perfected. Be-

cause of these individuals I have been forced to finish this treatise as best I could and more hastily than suited me, and hence in a more abbreviated form than I had intended. For if I had been permitted to publish it unhurriedly and at a convenient time, I would have added many things which I have left unsaid.[4]

There is little doubt that Anselm was an assiduous and patient editor and collector of his own works. To a greater extent than for other medieval writers, it can be suggested that, based on what survives from the later eleventh- and early twelfth-century collections, modern readers encounter his works in the form close to what he would have wished. In the later Middle Ages, the name of Anselm attracted a significant number of works falsely attributed, especially prayers and meditations (and a series of biblical commentaries). Dom F. S. Schmitt and Dom André Wilmart spearheaded the establishment of the genuine corpus, and its presentation in a modern edition, between the 1920s and early 1950s. The main body of Anselm's works (treatises, letters, prayers, and meditations), despite the accreted texts, was, and remains, established on the basis of manuscripts to which he, or his close associates, had close connections.

Writings

Anselm's writing career began in the less hurried context of the monastery at Bec. The chronology of his early works is not wholly settled; the collection's prayers for noble laywomen, including Adela, daughter of William the Conqueror, probably predate the first of his treatises. The prayers and meditations are often, too often, separated as distinct from the rest of Anselm's oeuvre. Not only were they composed, or revised, throughout his writing career, into the early twelfth century, but they are also an integral element in the way in which he explored the particular themes on which he focused, for example, truth, free will, the incarnation, salvation, grace, and predestination. His most formal account of the consequences of original sin and the incarnation, the *Cur Deus homo*, is partnered with the denser, more emotional *Meditatio de humana redemptione* (*Mediation on Human Redemption*). Occasionally, as in the case of the *Proslogion*, Anselm fused meditative and dialectical expression and mingled poetry and prose. This is done in such a manner to underline the paradoxes of the human condition under sin, which the work explores: despair and hope, sadness and joy, desire for God's presence coupled with the shame and degradation of life in sin.

The *Monologion* (a treatment of how the nature of God is to be described) and *Proslogion* (an odyssey on the names of God and God's existence) can be securely dated to 1075–76 and 1077–78, followed by the three linked treatises, *De veritate* (*On Truth*), *De libertate arbitrii* (*On the Freedom of Will*), and *De casu diabolic* (*On the Fall of the Devil*). All three were composed in the 1080s, but their genesis in teaching to, and discussion within, the community at Bec took place over a number of years prior. The next phase of writing involved the *Epistola de incarnatione verbi dei* (*Letter on the Incarnation of the Word of God*), addressed to Pope Urban II on the subject of the Trinity and the assumption of humanity by the Word. A number of different recensions exist of this work, written in a number of different locations (including a period at the Abbey of Westminster at the end of 1092), under its new Abbot, Anselm's friend and former pupil, Gilbert Crispin. At this time, Gilbert was engaged in a debate with Jewish scholars, especially on Christology and the Christian theology of salvation, which would take written form as the *Disputatio Iudei et Christiani* (*The Dispute between the Jew and the Christian*).[5] Gilbert's Jewish interlocutors appear to have been genuine history actors, rather than a rhetorical device.[6] The fruits of this dialogue and dispute would emerge in Anselm's larger discussion of the same themes in the *Cur Deus homo*.

Started after Anselm's appointment to the archbishopric of Canterbury in 1093, *Cur Deus homo* was completed in 1098 at the Abbey of Telese in southern Italy during Anselm's first period of political exile. The accompanying *Meditatio de humana redemptione* took published form at Lyon between 1099 and 1100 where Anselm, still in exile, also completed the *De concepetu virginali* (*On the Virgin Conception and Original Sin*). These three works, much as with the *De veritate* group of treatises, are designed as three parts of a single discussion. Interpretations of Anselm's theology of salvation that place emphasis on the extent to which he advocates retributive justice, or espouses a contract between God and humankind identified by lovelessness and a repellent legalism, on the whole do so with reference only to *Cur Deus homo*. In this case, the other two parts of Anselm's triptych are ignored and his theological position misrepresented; as suggested above, this was precisely the outcome he feared. He completed two more works before his death on April 21, 1109. *De processione Spiritus Sancti* (*On the Procession of the Holy Spirit*) is perhaps the most formal of Anselm's works, drawn from his defense of the Latin doctrine of the Spirit's procession from the Father *and* the Son (the "filioque" clause) made against defenders of the Greek position at the council of Bari in 1098. His last work, the *De concordia praescientiae et praedestinationis et gratiae Dei cum libero arbitrio* (*The Concordance of the Foreknowledge, Predestination and Grace of God with Free Will*) returns to themes explored in earlier works, notably the *Monologion*. Anselm left only what have become known as the *Philosophical Fragments* in incomplete form.

Salvation

Salvation is a constant theme in Anselm's writing, the ground and grammar on which his theological and philosophical reflections are founded and the purpose and end of his teaching. Salvation cuts across the genres in which he wrote, from the earliest prayers to his last treatises. At the end of his life, Eadmer records, Anselm was anxious to explore a question about the origin of the human soul, probably concerning traducianism (souls are transmitted through birth) and creationism (all souls are created by God).[7] Anselm's position is not known, but the question is one that relates directly to the post-lapsarian human condition and the broader economy of salvation: what remains after the fall, what is to be saved, and how. Salvation forms part of a nexus of themes essential to the practice and contemplation of the Christian faith which Anselm interlaces and interweaves: sin, justice, truth, freedom, forgiveness.

Scripture

These themes emerge principally from biblical exposition and it is important to emphasize how central and controlling the Bible remained to Anselm's thought. His advocacy of the place and power of human reason in speculative discourse is well-known, forming a consistent part of his intellectual method. Scripture, however, was the fount and source of his questions, and, ultimately, their fulfillment. As he expressed it in the *De concordia*:

> For, indeed, we preach, usefully to our spiritual salvation, nothing that Sacred Scripture, made fruitful by the miracle of the Holy Spirit, has not set forth or does not contain within itself. Now, if on the basis of rational considerations we sometimes make a statement which we cannot clearly exhibit in the words of Scripture, or cannot prove by reference to these words, nonetheless in the following way we know by means of Scripture whether the statement ought to be accepted or rejected. If the statement is arrived at by clear reasoning and if Scripture in no respect contradicts it, then (since even as Scripture opposes no truth, so it favors no falsity) by the very fact that Scripture does not deny that which is affirmed on the basis of rational considerations, this affirmation is supported by the authority of Scripture. But if Scripture unquestionably opposes a view of ours, then even though our reasoning seems to us unassailable, this reasoning should not be believed to be supported by any truth. In this way, then, Sacred Scripture, in that it either clearly affirms them or else does not at all deny them, contains the authority for all rationally derived truths.[8]

Scripture is, therefore, the authoritative measure for human reason. As such, even a treatise such as the *Cur Deus homo*, which advertises the reasoned nature of its exploration of the incarnation, is explored from a biblical basis and within a biblical framework. The purpose of the treatise was, as its author explains, to demonstrate "by rational necessity... that no man can possibly be saved without Him [Christ]" and "with equally clear reasoning and truth" that man, body and soul, were created to enjoy God, and that the possibility of this attaining this end after the fall depends on the Godman.[9] Anselm begins with a reminder that the defense of the faith by reason has biblical, New Testament, force. As stated in 1 Peter 3:15: "But sanctify the Lord Christ in your hearts, being ready always to satisfy every one that asketh you a reason of that hope which is in you" provides the text from which Anselm moves off, and to which he returns. This is reinforced, with caveats, through reference to Wisdom literature, and Ecclesiasticus

3:22 in particular: "Seek not the things that are too high for thee, and search not into things above thy ability: but the things that God hath commanded thee, think on them always, and in many of his works be not curious." Anselm's exploration of the economy of salvation is biblically inspired, infused, and directed toward questions emerging from Scripture.

Sin

Anselm's approach to salvation encompassed a wide range of responses to the implications of sin, original and individual, the hope for redemption through the incarnation of Christ, and the consequences for daily as well as eternal life. His development of a form of prayer and meditation, which placed a keener emphasis on emotional responses to the object or person of devotion, plays a key part in the articulation of the need for, and fear of, salvation.[10] The Anselmian revolution, as it has been termed, was not wholly his invention; there were older contemporaries, such as John of Fécamp (d.1077), who also experimented with forms of expression focusing on the poles of human emotion, especially as evoked in the contemplation of the wretched situation of fallen humanity and what salvation might mean.[11] Joy, sadness, hope, despair, glory, and tragedy became an important part of the way in which the human condition, and its effects on human life, was articulated.

Anselm follows standard patristic and earlier medieval positions: original sin, the disobedience of Eve and then Adam to God's instructions, was responsible for an indelible stain within each human life, an irremovable impediment to the proper role of humanity, to honor and adore the Creator. Humanity was, as a result of Adamic sin, distorted, unable to act as it should, born with both original sin and a propensity to sin, sin strongly, and sin some more. In the words of the *Prayer to St John the Baptist*: "To sin—how evil and bitter that is. Sins—how easy to commit, how hard to give up. Sinners—so misled by sins—are caught by their fetters."[12]

In his *Prayer to Saint Peter*, Anselm asks his addressee to look kindly on his supplication, in passages rich with the imagery of broken humanity, and ends with a surprising reminder of Peter's own weakness in denying Christ when questioned.

> Peter, good shepherd,
> do not be difficult of access;
> do not turn away your merciful eyes.
> Have a care, I pray you,
> lest you throw down the penitent,
> and delay to hear a suppliant.
> Because his [the supplicant's] soul loathes the life-giving pasture,
> he grows weak for lack of strength;
> because he indulges in what is unhealthy,
> he attracts tormenting diseases.
> Full-grown ulcers, open wounds, putrid decay,
> draw him swiftly to death.
> Wolves have tasted his blood and now they lie in ambush,
> Watching, and plotting his overthrow.
> His enemy, "as a roaring lion", goes about seeking him,
> so that he "may devour him".
> Faithful shepherd, look upon him,
> and recognise that he has been committed to you.
> He at have strayed but at least it is not he
> who has denied his Lord and Shepherd.[13]

Anselm's vivid, visceral bodily description of sin, and its consequences, is characteristic of his style and authorial design. The focus and intensity of his language and imagery was of significant influence on subsequent generations, writing in both Latin and vernacular languages.[14]

The majority of the prayers and meditations direct an appeal for advocacy with God to particular Apostles and Saints (John the Baptist, Peter, Paul, twice to John the Evangelist, Stephen, Nicholas, Benedict, Mary Magdalene), thrice to the Virgin Mary and to Christ.[15] In all of them, the drama revolves around Anselm, the appellant, God the Judge, and the Holy intercessor. A character to which Anselm gives no especial place in his meditations on sin is the devil. While not absent (Anselm does for example make use of biblical imagery for temptation and the tempter, such as the "roaring lion" above), the devil is given a limited and circumscribed place in Anselm's writings as a whole.[16] The treatise *De casu diaboli* (*On the Fall of the Devil*) is concerned with questions of liberty, free will, and the understanding of evil as privation and "constitutive of no thing."[17] Evil, Anselm explains, is not something, even though the word is used in ordinary speech in ways that might imply the opposite.[18] A comparison between Eadmer's description of the genesis of the *Proslogion* and Anselm's own is instructive in this regard. Eadmer relates of Anselm's struggle to articulate his argument that he eventually "supposed that this line of thought was a temptation from the devil." Anselm mentions no such thing; the intellectual struggle had exhausted him before finally "what I had despaired of, appeared, in my strife-torn mind in such way that I eagerly embraced the thinking which I, as one who was anxious, had been warding off."[19]

The Devil

The absence, or indeed removal, of the devil from the economy of salvation finds its most detailed articulation in the *Cur Deus homo*. A dominant strand of patristic thought on the alleviation of original sin gave the devil a significant role. Humanity, having sinned, came under the jurisdiction of the devil. By sending Christ to die, who, although he was God, appeared as man, the devil could be trapped into trying to extend his jurisdiction to that over which he had no rights, that is, God. Having wrongfully tried to claim Jesus, as Man, when he was also God, the devil relinquished all rights over humanity; restitution was therefore achieved. Amongst the Greek Fathers, Gregory of Nyssa established the image of the human Christ as the bait of a divine hook, an image that was adopted amongst Latin authorities, from whom the early medieval west drew inspiration.[20] These included Rufinus of Aquileia, who at the turn of the fourth century offered a straightforward image derived from Gregory of Nyssa:

> So that the divine virtue of the Son of God, like a kind of hook hidden in the form of human flesh . . . could lure the prince of the world to a contest; that the Son of God might offer him his human flesh as bait, and that the hidden divinity might hold him fast with its hook.[21]

The image was adapted also by Augustine in a sermon on the miracle of the loaves and fishes. Moving through a sequence of mysteries connected to Christ, who is, for example, the bread who came down from heaven, Augustine reaches a discussion of Christ as Trader, giving life and resurrection, receiving birth, toil, and death:

> We had stumbled, you see, upon the prince of this world. Who had led Adam astray and enslaved him, and was beginning to possess us as his home-born slaves. But along came the redeemer, and conquered the deceived. And what did our redeemer do to our captor? To pay our price, he set the mousetrap of his cross; as bait he placed there his own blood. While the devil, though, was able to shed that blood, he did not earn the right to drink it. And because he shed the blood of one who was not his debtor, he was ordered to release those who were his debtors; he shed the blood of the innocent one, he was required to withdraw from those who are by no means innocent. The Lord, indeed, shed his own blood precisely for this purpose, to cancel our sins. So the very reason for which the other held us captive was canceled by the blood of the redeemer.[22]

Anselm, by contrast, pivots the economy of salvation not on the role of the devil, but in a transaction between humanity and God. Anselm's closer forebears—in this line of thought—are Irenaeus of Lyon, Athanasius of Alexandria, and Gregory Nazianzen.[23] The latter, in *Oration 45*, the second Easter Oration, a text that had been translated from Greek to Latin in the later fourth century, questions the role of the devil:

> If therefore a ransom is made for no-one except for the detainer, I ask to whom was this paid and for what reason and if any was paid to the evil one damn the injustice—for it was an injustice not to God alone. But the deceiver receives redemption in the form of God himself and an illustrious reward for his tyranny on account of which it had seemed that it was withheld from us.[24]

Anselm takes this position further, removing all mention of the devil. Only man should pay for original sin, but the sin was of such magnitude that only God could; God should not pay for original sin, since he was sinned against, by man the sinner. The solution is a God-man, who encompasses both the need and the capacity to pay the debt of sin.[25]

The economy of salvation as expressed in *Cur Deus homo* draws on a distinctive language of debt and payment, of obligation rendered and of justice enacted.[26] Anselm's vision in this sense was, especially after the Reformation, criticized for a rather legalistic framework in which God demands his due, without much emphasis on the incarnation as an act of love. Anselm sees the justice and the mercy of God as two aspects of the same question, and in the *Meditatio de humana redemptione*, the dynamic of love and the goodness of God are placed more to the fore. Anselm's economy of salvation relies both on honor and satisfaction, and, equally, on hope and love. In all of this, the man-ward nature of the transaction is heavily emphasized. Anselm states that human nature was exalted in the incarnation, rather than the divine nature humbled. The man-ward aspect is underlined by the language of debt and payment, which is the case even in the *Meditatio de humana redemptione*: "He [Christ] had what was above all beings that are other than God, and he took on himself all the debt that sinners ought to pay, and this when he himself owed nothing, so that he could pay the debt for the others who owed it and could not pay."[27]

Christ's atonement for original sin is that which allows for the redemption of creation. In the temporal world, it is baptism that is carried as the mark and mechanism of forgiveness for Adam's sin. In this context Anselm's theology of salvation contains, and operates through, a strongly expressed ecclesiology. In the *Prayer to St John the Baptist*, this is emphasized:

> You, God, take away the sin of the world,
> and you, his friend [John the Baptist], say,
> "Here is he who takes away the sin of the world.
> Behold, before you,
> him who is burdened with the sin of the world".
> You bear the sin—and you proclaim that he bears it.
> Behold me, whose sin you bear as John proclaims.
> Behold, healer, and the healer's witness, here am I—
> behold, the sick servant of the healer and his work
> petitions here the healer and his witness.
> True healer, I pray you heal me;
> true witness, I beg you to pray for me.[28]

Authority

The preface to the *De incarnatione* illustrates the centrality of ecclesiastical authority for Anselm and its theological role. As the preface directed to Pope Urban II (c.1042–1099) explains, Anselm had been moved to write the treatise to defend himself against the implications of remarks made by his younger contemporary Roscelin of Compiègne (c.1050–c.1125). Roscelin, having been accused by others of a tri-theistic position on the Trinity, claimed in his own defense that he had used Anselm's works in coming to his position. Anselm was horrified, and in the preface strongly emphasizes the stability of the faith as the basis on which rational inquiry is possible, and the grounds on which its limitations are set.

> Indeed, no Christian ought to question the truth of what the Catholic Church believes in its heart and confesses with its mouth. Rather, by holding constantly and unhesitatingly to this faith, by loving it and living according to it he ought humbly, and as best he is able, to seek to discover the reason why it is true. If he is able to understand, then let him give thanks to God. But if he cannot understand, let him not toss his horns in strife but let him bow his head in reverence.[29]

Salvation according to Anselm was to be hoped for and prayed for, in the course of baptized Christian life. For Anselm, baptism is an essential qualification: Unbaptized infants, because of the transmission of original sin, are subject to damnation.[30] Once baptized, Christian life is to be lived properly, to the extent possible.

In the definition of a proper Christian life, Anselm's view is influenced strongly by his monastic vocation. A life led properly is a life of obedience to God's will; the discipline of obedience more easily adopted within a monastery. As Anselm reminded a monk of St. Werburgh's, Chester, a dependent priory of Bec, the prayers of one obedient monk were worth more than ten thousand from one who is disobedient.[31] Not that Anselm should be imagined as withdrawn from the world, as Prior and Abbot of an expanding monastic house in Normandy in the period just after the Norman Conquest of England, and then, to a much greater extent, as Archbishop of Canterbury, he was in charge of institutions with a significant worldly as well as spiritual economy.[32] Debt, payment, and the obligations incurred within transactions were part of his daily life, materially as well as spiritually. Indeed, the two are part and parcel of the same economy: for Anselm and his contemporaries, action in the world had eternal consequences for good or ill.

Influence

Anselm's posthumous influence is the subject of ongoing research; the traditional assessment of a rather limited immediate impact on a rather limited number of pupils and followers no longer holds. Collections of his sayings and sermons were made by a number of his closer companions, principally Eadmer and Alexander, another monk of Canterbury, which circulated in various versions throughout the Middle Ages.[33] In the case of the doctrine of the atonement, where difference has often been emphasized between Anselm and Abelard, their positions are far closer than general discussions acknowledge. On questions of redemption and free will Anselm also formed a significant model for Hugh of St. Victor, albeit one that was not unquestioned.[34]

The characteristically Anselmian insistence on the removal of the devil from the economy of salvation was not adopted by Peter Lombard in his *Sentences*. The *Sentences* became ubiquitous within medieval theological training from the second half of the twelfth century until the Reformation. Lombard took a more Augustinian line and insisted on the devil's illegitimate usurpation of his rights over mankind by applying them to Christ. A dominant metaphor for Lombard is litigation; the image of a court of law was used explicitly to explain the relationships between Man, God, and the devil.[35]

During the second half of the twelfth and beginning of the thirteenth century, Anselm's *Cur Deus homo* became a standard reference work for the necessity of the incarnation and the atonement, and was frequently paired in manuscript with John of Damascus's *De Fide Orthodoxa* (*On the Orthodox Faith*).[36] The influence of Anselm's thought was prominent in that of Robert Grosseteste, whose heavily annotated copy of the *Cur Deus homo* survives in the library of St. John's College, Cambridge, Manuscript 17. Grosseteste also disagreed with Anselm over the rights of the devil, including them as a matter of course in discussions of the economy of salvation.[37] Of greater significance though was the transformation of Anselm's theology of redemption into a theology of creation. In the 1230s, Grosseteste developed the Christocentric organization of theology in his *Hexameron*. He turned to the question of the incarnation in his *De cessatione legalium*, in which he argued that Christ would have been incarnate even without Adam's sin, as he who unites Creator and Creation.[38]

In the later Middle Ages, as Chaucer's pilgrims made their way to Canterbury, Anselm is quoted in the *Parson's Tale* as part of a discussion of how contrition should be induced. Fear of hell forms the third cause, and a passage from Anselm's *Meditatio ad conitandum timorem: Terret me vita mea* (*Meditation to Stir Up Fear: My Life Terrifies Me*) forms the vehicle.[39] Anselm's original words come from the final section of the meditation:

> Alas for me, here are sins accusing me—there is the terror of judgment. Below the horrible chaos of hell lies open—above is the wrath of the judge. Inside is the burning of conscience—outside is the burning of the world. Scarcely shall the just be saved,—and thus overtaken, where can a sinner turn?

Impossible to hide, intolerable to view, wanting to hide with nowhere to go, Anselm is left appealing for the Savior.

> But it is he himself, he himself is Jesus. The same is my judge between whose hands I tremble. Take heart, sinner, and do not despair. Hope in him whom you fear, flee to him whom you have fled. . . . For what is Jesus except to say Saviour? So, Jesus, for your own sake, be to me Jesus. You have made me, do not let me perish. You have redeemed me, do not condemn me. You created me by your goodness, do not let me perish by my wickedness . . . Have mercy, Jesus, while the time of mercy lasts, lest in the time of judgment you condemn. For what profit is there for you in my blood, if I go down to eternal corruption? O most desired Jesus, admit me to the number of your elect, so that with them I may enjoy you, with them I may praise you, and glorify you.[40]

Salvation defines Anselm's theological vision, developed over his whole writing career, with consistent stress on a Christocentric position, and a powerful sense of the contradictory consequences of sin which evoke joy and despair, fear and hope, in equal measure. Emphasizing the enormity of sin underlines for Anselm the miraculous nature of Christ's sacrifice and the possibility, for the elect, of salvation.

NOTES

1. The research for this chapter was made possible by the Norwegian Research Council, and was carried out under the aegis of the following research project: Svein H. Gulbekk, professor and project manager, "Religion and Money: Economies of Salvation in the High Middle Ages" (project number 222545, University of Oslo).
2. Eadmer, *Vita Anselmi*, ed. and trans. R. W. Southern (Oxford: Oxford University Press, 1972), ii.15.
3. Eadmer, *Vita Anselmi*; Eadmer, *Historia novorum*, ed. M. Rule, The Rolls Series (London: Longmans, 1884), *History of Recent Events in England*, trans. G. Bosanquet (London: Cresset Press, 1964): this is a translation of books i–iv; v–vi remain untranslated.
4. Anselm, *Cur Deus homo*, Preface. All quotations are taken from *Anselm of Canterbury: Works*, ed. and trans. J. Hopkins and H. Richardson, 4 volumes (Toronto: Mellen Press, 1976), with emendation. The standard critical edition for Anselm's works remains the *Opera omnia S. Anselmi Cantuariensis archiepiscopi*, ed. F. S. Schmitt, 6 vols. [vol. 1 printed at Seckau 1938; vol 2. at Rome 1940, all reset for the Nelson edition] (Edinburgh: Nelson, 1946–1961), reprinted with new editorial material as *S. Anselmi Cantuariensis archiepiscopi opera omnia*, 2 vols (Stuttgart-Bad-Cannstatt: F. Frommann, 1968–1984). The *Library of Latin Texts* through Brepols publishers makes the Schmitt edition available online (with subscription). Dr. Samu Niskanen's forthcoming re-edition and translation of Anselm's letters will supersede the Schmitt edition. Concerning the preliminary discussion for the edition, S. Niskanen, *The Letter Collections of Anselm of Canterbury* (Turnhout: Brepols, 2011).
5. Gilbert Crispin, *Disputatio Iudei et Christiani* in *The Works of Gilbert Crispin Abbot of Westminster*, ed. Anna Sapir Abulafia and G. R. Evans, Auctores Britannici Medii Aevi VIII (Oxford: Oxford University Press), 1–61 (including the Continuation).
6. As for example Peter Abelard's *Dialogus inter Philosophum, Iudaeum, et Christianum* (*Dialogue between the Philosopher, Jew and Christian*), of which the standard critical edition is Peter Abelard, *Collationes*, ed. Giovanni Orlandi and trans. John Marenbon (Oxford: Oxford University Press, 2001). The most comprehensive treatment of Jewish-Christian intellectual relations in the high medieval period is by Anna Sapir Abulafia, *Christians and Jews in the Twelfth-Century Renaissance* (London: Routledge, 1995), *Christians and Jews in Dispute. Disputational Literature and the Rise of Anti-Judaism in the West (c. 1000–1150)* (Aldershot: Ashgate,

1998), and *Christian-Jewish Relations, 1000–1300 Jews in the Service of Medieval Christendom* (London: Longman, 2011).
7. Eadmer, *Vita Anselmi*, Book II.66. The question was explored by Gilbert Crispin, as noted by Southern in the *Vita* p. 142 n.1, where Gilbert supports traducianism, a position that would be firmly rejected in later scholastic writing: Gilbert Crispin, *De anima* in *The Works of Gilbert Crispin*, 156–164.
8. Anselm, *De concordia*, III.6.
9. Anselm, *Cur Deus homo*, Preface.
10. See *The Prayers and Meditations of Saint Anselm of Canterbury*, trans. Benedicta Ward (London: Penguin, 1973) and her "Inward Feeling and Deep Thinking": The *Prayers and Meditations* of St. Anselm Revisited, *Anselm Studies* I (1983), 177–184 (repr. in B. Ward, *Signs and Wonders: Saints, Miracles and Prayer from the 4th Century to the 14th*, Variorum Collected Studies Series (Basingstoke: Ashgate, 1992). R. W. Southern, *Saint Anselm and His Biographer* (Cambridge: Cambridge University Press, 1963), 34–47, and *Saint Anselm A Portrait in a Landscape* (Cambridge: Cambridge University Press, 1990), 91–112.
11. The "Anselmian Revolution" was coined in R. W. Southern, *Saint Anselm and His Biographer*, p. 42. On John of Fécamp, see Jean Leclerq and Jean-Paul Bonnes, *Un maître de la vie spirituelle au xiesiècle: Jean de Fécamp* (Paris: Vrin, 1946). Jean de Fécamp, *La confession théologique*, trans. Philippe de Vial (Paris: Cerf, 1992) makes available a French translation of his *Confessio theologica* which, like Anselm's near-contemporary *Proslogion*, has elements of both prayerful theology and theological prayer. Hugh Feiss, "John of Fécamp's Longing for Heaven" in *Imagining Heaven in the Middle Ages*, ed. Jan Emerdon and Hugh Feiss (New York: Garland, 2000), 65–82, emphasizes the fascination that sin, death, and judgment held for John.
12. Anselm, *Prayer to St John the Baptist*, trans. Ward, *Prayers and Meditations*, 131.
13. Ibid., 137.
14. For the vernacular transmission of Anselmian thought see Margaret Healy-Varley, "Anselm's Afterlife and the Middle English *De custodia*," in *Saint Anselm of Canterbury and His Legacy*, ed. Giles E. M. Gasper and Ian Logan (Toronto: Pontifical Institute of Mediaeval Studies, 2012), 239–257, and Evelien Hauwaerts, "The Middle English Versions of Saint Anselm of Canterbury's *Prayers and Meditations*," in Gasper and Logan, *Anselm and His Legacy*, 258–275.
15. In addition, prayers are addressed to God, to the Holy Cross, to patron saints of churches by a bishop or abbot, on behalf of friends, on behalf of enemies, and before receiving Eucharist.
16. 1 Peter 5.8: "Be sober and watch: because your adversary the devil, as a roaring lion, goeth about seeking whom he may devour."
17. Anselm, *De casu diaboli*, 1.1.
18. Ibid.
19. Eadmer, *Vita Anselmi*, i.XIX; Anselm, *Proslogion*, Preface. For an analysis of the circumstances of the *Proslogion*'s composition see Giles E. M. Gasper, "Envy, Jeal-

ousy, and the Boundaries of Orthodoxy: Anselm of Canterbury and the Genesis of the *Proslogion*," *Viator*, 41 (2010), 45–68.
20. Gregory Nyssen, "*The Great Catechism*," In *Gregory of Nyssa: Dogmatic Treatises*. 2nd Series, Vol. V of Nicene and Post-Nicene Fathers (Edinburgh: T&T Clark, 1892 [repr., Grand Rapids, MI: Eerdmans, 1994]), 24. John of Damascus also used the image in his *Exposition of the Orthodox Faith* which was translated into Latin, although after Anselm's lifetime, Nicene and Post-Nicene Fathers, 2nd Series, Vol. IX (Grand Rapids, MI: Eerdmans, 1989), III.27.
21. Rufinus, *Expositio Symboli*, in *CCSL*, vol. 20, Turnhout, 1961.16.
22. Augustine, *Sermon 130*, *The Works of Saint Augustine*, Part III, *Sermons*, Vol. 4, trans. Edmund Hill, ed. John E. Rotelle (New York: New City Press, 1992), 130.2.
23. See Giles E. M. Gasper, *Anselm of Canterbury and His Theological Inheritance* (Aldershot: Ashgate, 2004), Chapter 5, "The Christological Frame."
24. Gregory Nazianzen, *Or. 45, The Second Oration on Easter, Orations, Sermons, Letters*, Nicene and Post-Nicene Fathers, 2nd Series, Vol. VII (Grand Rapids, MI: Eerdmans, 1989), 22. For details of the Latin translation see B. Gain, *Traductions latines de Pères grecs: La collection du manuscrit "Laurentianus San Marco 584,"* (Berne: Peter Lang, 1994).
25. This is expressed succinctly in Anselm, *Cur Deus homo*, ii.6.
26. John McIntyre demolished the criticism of Anselm's argument as "feudal" in his *St. Anselm and His Critics: A Re-interpretation of the Cur Deus homo* (Edinburgh: Oliver and Boyd, 1954), pp. 202f. The origins of an analogy do not affect the validity of the argument they are marshalled to support. While Anselm's linguistic expression is replete with contemporary terminology, it is also worth stressing the extent to which a great deal of what looks feudal is in fact biblical, from the language of debt and servitude, to formulations for kingship and dominion.
27. Anselm, *Meditatio de humana redemptione, Medietation on Human Redemption*, trans. Ward, *Prayers and Meditations*, 233.
28. Anselm, *Prayer to St. John the Baptist*, trans. Ward, *Prayers and Meditations*, 133.
29. Anselm, *De incarnatione Verbi Dei*, 1.
30. Anselm, *De conceptu virginali*, 28. The position, while not rejected in the later Middle Ages, was softened: Not all are imagined as suffering equally in hell.
31. Anselm, *Letter*, 232.
32. Giles E. M. Gasper and Svein H. Gullbekk, "Money and its Use in the Thought and Experience of Anselm, Archbishop of Canterbury (1093–1109)," *Journal of Medieval History* 38 (2012), 155–182.
33. *Memorials of Saint Anselm*, ed. R. W. Southern and F. S. Schmitt, Auctores Britannici Medii Aeui I (Oxford: Oxford University Press, 1969). A translation of this volume is under preparation by Sister Benedicta Ward SLG. See also G. R. Evans, "*Sententiola ad aedificationem*: The *Dicta* of St Anselm and St Bernard," *Révue Bénédictine* 92 (1982), 159–71.
34. See J. Dunthorne, "Anselm and Hugh of St Victor on Freedom and the Will," in *Saint Anselm of Canterbury and His Legacy*, ed. Giles E. M. Gasper and Ian Logan

(Toronto: Pontifical Institute of Mediaeval Studies, 2012), 114–132. Dunthorne extends this analysis in *Anselm of Canterbury and the Development of Theological Thought c.1070–1141* (unpublished PhD dissertation, Durham University, 2012).

35. Peter Lombard, *The Sentences Book Three On the Incarnation of the Word*, trans. Giulio Silano (Toronto: Pontifical Institute of Mediaeval Studies, 2008). The standard critical edition remains *Sententiae in IV libris distinctae*, 2 vols. I. Brady, ed. (Grottaferrata: Editiones Collegii S. Bonaventurae ad Claras Aquas, 1979–1981). For further discussion of Lombard, see P. W. Rosemann, *Peter Lombard* (Oxford: Oxford University Press, 2004) and *The Story of a Great Medieval Book: Peter Lombard's "Sentences,"* (Toronto: University of Toronto Press, 2007) and Marcia Colish's magisterial *Peter Lombard*, 2 vols. (Brill: Leiden, 1994).
36. Thomas H. Bestul, "The Manuscript Tradition of Anselm's *Cur Deus Homo*," in *Cur Deus Homo: Atti del Congresso Anselmiano Internazionale*, ed. Paul Gilbert, Helmut Kohlenberger, and Edgar Salmann, Studia Anselmiana 128 (Rome: Centro Studi S. Anselmo, 1999), 285–307.
37. Robert Grosseteste, *Dictum 10*, available online on the Electronic Grosseteste website: www.grosseteste.com (accessed August 3, 2015).
38. Robert Grosseteste, *On the Six Days of Creation*, trans. C.F.J. Martin, Auctores Britannici Medii Aevi VI (2) (Oxford: Oxford University Press, 1996), I.1; *On the Cessation of the Laws*, trans. Stephen M. Hillenbrand, The Fathers of the Church Medieval Continuation, 13 (Washington, DC: Catholic University of America Press, 2012), III.1.1–22.
39. Geoffrey Chaucer, *The Parson's Tale*, in *The Riverside Chaucer*, ed. Larry Dean Benson and F. N. Norris (Boston: Houghton Mifflin, 1987), 10 (1) 2: 168–73, at 291. For an illuminating commentary on this meditation, see Burcht Pranger, *The Artificiality of Christianity* (Stanford: Stanford University Press, 2003), 107–135.
40. Anselm, *Meditatio terret me vita mea; Meditation to stir up fear* (trans. Bendicta Ward), 224.

9

Saint Thomas Aquinas

R. JARED STAUDT

Thomas was a Master in Theology (Magister in Sacra Pagina) at the University of Paris, engaged in the tasks of teaching (primarily commenting on Sacred Scripture), leading public disputations, and preaching.

Thomas Aquinas was born circa 1225 in the castle of Roccasecca. His parents were of noble lineage, and were kin to the Emperors Henry VI and Frederick II. As a young boy, he was sent to the care of the monks at the Benedictine monastery at Monte Cassino, where he displayed an unusual precocity in intellectual and spiritual matters, not to mention a mastery of the liberal arts. Around 1236 he began study in the University of Naples, where he became acquainted with the nascent Order of Preachers. Despite the attempts of his aristocratic family (two of his brothers were soldiers of Frederick's army) to dissuade him from a life of voluntary poverty, he joined the Dominican order in the early 1240s. In fact, at his mother's behest, Thomas's brothers kidnapped him and held him under house arrest, even tempting him with, as legend has it, the introduction of prostitutes into his chamber, whom he chased away with a firebrand. Undeterred, Thomas was allowed to return to Naples and pursue the religious life among the friars, with whom he studied the works of Aristotle, recently reintroduced to the Latin west through the work of Arabic commentators and translators, the *Sentences* of Peter Lombard, and the Holy Scriptures.

In the first of several sojourns in Paris, Thomas came under the tutelage of the eminent Dominican thinker Albertus Magnus, with whom he traveled in 1248 to establish a new studium generale in Köln. As was typical at the time, his early academic life was taken up with lecturing on the Lombard's *Sentences*, then the classic textbook of medieval theology, and on the Scriptures. From 1252 until his death in 1274, Thomas produced a range of works extraordinary in both number and ingenuity, which demonstrate a mind of the highest conceivable order, brilliance, and devotion to Christ's church. These include the two great Summae: the *Summa Contra Gentiles*, and his crowning achievement, the *Summa Theologiae*, left unfinished at the time of his death. Among his many other works are commentaries on several Old Testament books, on the Pauline epistles and two gospels, numerous commentaries on works of Aristotle, a commentary on Lombard's *Sentences*, *Quaestiones* on truth, evil, the virtues, and others, the liturgy for the Feast of Corpus Christi, and other works far too numerous to mention.

According to tradition, in December 1273, while en route to the Council of Lyons, called to resolve some theological disputes between the Eastern and Western churches, Thomas experienced a vision of such overwhelming power that he resolved never again to write another word, declaring everything he had written as "so much straw" compared to what he had seen. It was in fact a vision that ultimately cost him his life, for he became increasingly debilitated, and by January 1274 he was no longer able to travel, and died in the Cistercian monastery at Fossanova on the seventh of March. After a series of controversies regarding the interpretation of some of his theses, he was canonized in 1323, and in 1567, Pius V declared Thomas a "doctor of the universal church." His feast is celebrated January 28.

Introduction

Salvation is a central theme in the thought of St. Thomas Aquinas (1225–1274).[1] His approach to salvation can be seen most completely in his masterpiece, the *Summa Theologiae* (*ST*), which will serve as the foundation for approaching his thought in this chapter.[2] The question of salvation is rooted primarily in two places in the *Summa*: first, in Aquinas's presentation of justification within the treatise on grace (*ST* I-II, qq. 109–114) and, second, in his discussion of the effects of Christ's Passion within the treatise on Christ (*ST* III, qq. 1–59). These two topics are central to Aquinas's teaching on salvation, for Aquinas explains that "there is no salvation but to those who are justified," and further that "the death of Christ is . . . the universal cause of human salvation."[3] Salvation, thus, has a twofold aspect: the internal liberation from sin by which the soul is renewed and justified (that is, made just by grace), and the cause of that justification which is participation in the justice of Christ's own soul, effected by his work of salvation.

Justice and Justification

Aquinas treats justification most directly within the question on the effects of grace (*ST* I–II, q. 113).[4] Before examining this question directly, it is necessary to examine how Aquinas understands the nature of justice, because justification literally means "to make just."[5] Aquinas makes the link between justification and justice clear when treating the moral commands or precepts of the Old Law, or covenant. His response to the question of whether the Old Law justifies provides his first explanation of this issue in the *Summa*: "Justification means first and properly the causing of justice."[6] This can happen in two ways, "first, according as man is made just, by becoming possessed of the habit of justice: secondly, according as he does works of justice, so that in this sense justification is nothing else than the execution of justice."[7] The two types of justice described here concern, first, the interior state of the soul and, second, the actions that proceed from that state. In the first sense, insofar as justification makes one "to be just before God," it must flow from an "infused virtue... caused by God Himself through His grace."[8] The moral precepts of the Old Law could not bring about this state, although they did manifest the will of God by commanding just actions, namely "that which is just."[9]

Because the understanding of justification depends so much on the nature of justice, it is important to examine Aquinas's treatment of justice as a virtue (*ST* II–II, q. 58). To begin, Thomas accepts and clarifies the classic definition of justice from Aristotle that it consists in the "habit whereby a man is said to be capable of doing just actions in accordance with his choice."[10] To this Aquinas adds the medieval maxim that justice is "the perpetual and constant will to render to each one his due."[11] As the question on the virtue of justice proceeds, Aquinas shows that justice pertains to the right ordering of the soul within itself and ultimately to the right ordering of the soul to God and to its neighbor.

On the first point—that the just soul is itself well ordered—Aquinas once again turns to Aristotle, this time for his definition of metaphorical justice. This kind of justice refers to the right relation of the parts of the soul to one another. Aquinas describes this as follows:

> In one and the same man we may speak metaphorically of his various principles of action such as the reason, the irascible, and the concupis-

cible, as though they were so many agents: so that metaphorically in one and the same man there is said to be justice in so far as the reason commands the irascible and concupiscible, and these obey reason; and in general in so far as to each part of man is ascribed what is becoming to it.[12]

This kind of interior justice can be described as a right ordering within oneself. What this means first is that the passions are governed by reason, both in their desires for things (the concupiscible) and its confrontation with difficulties (the irascible).[13] Further, metaphorical justice brings peace and right order to the soul generally and between its parts, the lower parts subordinate to the higher. Justice is therefore crucial not only to the life of society, rendering to another what is due or owed, but also to the life of the soul, by bringing about what is right or due within and thus enabling the soul to live as it should.

We begin to see the all-encompassing scope of justice when Aquinas describes it as a general virtue. Justice is not simply giving one particular individual what is due, but more generally it is referring all of one's actions to their right end. In the case of earthly justice, this general end is the common good by which "the good of a part can be directed to the good of the whole."[14] Quoting St. Augustine, Aquinas shows how this earthly justice relates to God and neighbor: "Justice is the love of God and our neighbor which pervades the other virtues, that is to say, is the common principle of the entire order between one man and another."[15] Indeed, the whole understanding of justice laid out so far applies to God more than to any other. Every good thing comes from God and is ordered back toward him in justice. Therefore, Aquinas argues that "religion . . . is the chief part of justice," "whereby man is duly directed to God, Who is the last end of man's will."[16] God is the end toward which all things are directed, and justice demands a right ordering toward him. Within this ordering also comes right relations with neighbors: "Just as love of God includes love of our neighbor, as stated above (II–II, q. 25, a. 1), so too the service of God includes rendering to each one his due."[17] The supernatural order of the soul to God can be understood through the lens of justice, by which the soul is rightly ordered in itself, to God, and to neighbor.

With this background on justice, Aquinas's teaching on justification emerges more clearly.[18] Aquinas applies the nature of justice to the question of sin and grace, seeing justification as a movement of the ungodly from a state of sin to a state of justice.[19] Aquinas again uses the term "metaphorical justice" from Aristotle, but understands the interior ordering of the soul in light of Romans 4:5, where Paul speaks of God justifying the ungodly. The transformation that occurs in the ungodly is real, bringing about "a certain rectitude of order in the interior disposition of a man, in so far as what is highest in man is subject to God, and the inferior powers of the soul are subject to the superior, i.e., to the reason."[20] The process of conversion is called *justification*; it is named for justice rather than for faith or love because it brings about a "general rectitude of order," especially in relation to God.[21] The breaking from sin is understood by Aquinas to be a removal of injustice.[22]

Although he employs the term *justice* for conversion, Aquinas is clear that salvation occurs through grace, not a natural virtue. Aquinas explains that justification occurs only through the free gift of God's love: "Now the effect of the Divine love in us, which is taken away by sin, is grace, whereby a man is made worthy of eternal life, from which sin shuts him out. Hence we could not conceive the remission of guilt, without the infusion of grace."[23] In addition to the gratuitous nature of justification, Aquinas also stresses the role of free will, because justification also occurs "according to the condition of . . . human nature."[24] Rather than seeing grace and free will in competition, Aquinas understands grace to enliven free will and invite its cooperation: "Hence in him who has the use of reason, God's motion to justice does not take place without a movement of the free-will; but He so infuses the gift of justifying grace that at the same time He moves the free-will to accept the gift of grace, in such as are capable of being moved thus."[25] This movement of the free will is propelled by faith and charity, a movement of the soul in both the intellect and will. Of course, even this cooperation itself is the result of grace.[26]

Deification and Merit

Justification, the making just of the soul, culminates in nothing less than the soul's participation in the life of God, a concept known as deification.[27] Toward the end of his treatment of justification, Aquinas makes the qualified claim that the gift of grace to the ungodly is the greatest of all God's works both because of the great distance of the sinner from

God and also because of the greatness of the effect: "The justification of the ungodly ... terminates at the eternal good of a share in the Godhead."[28] In fact, Aquinas believes that justification begins a participation in the divine life even upon earth. The justified soul is infused with all the virtues so that the new life begun in grace can be ordered completely to God. This ordering, though understood as a kind of justice, actually occurs through the virtue of charity, which orders all things not to an earthly common good, but to a heavenly one: "It is charity which directs the acts of all other virtues to the last end, and which, consequently, also gives the form to all other acts of virtue: and it is precisely in this sense that charity is called the form of the virtues."[29]

Charity is one of the theological virtues, along with faith and hope.[30] Aquinas understands virtue as a habitual, good disposition of the soul, which brings happiness. Aquinas recognizes virtues that help us to act well in accord with our nature, and also virtues that are infused to help us act rightly in accord with our supernatural sharing in the life of God. The highest of the infused virtues are the theological, which are central to Aquinas's understanding of deification. In addition to a kind of natural happiness of living well in the world, Aquinas speaks of another "happiness surpassing man's nature, and which man can obtain by the power of God alone, by a kind of participation of the Godhead, about which it is written (2 Peter 1:4) that by Christ we are made 'partakers of the Divine nature.'"[31] Unlike justice, the theological virtues do not simply have God as their end by ordering actions toward him, but actually have God as their object.[32] To have God as their object means that the theological virtues "reach God" and "attain" him in their acts: knowing God, hoping in him, and loving him.[33] In faith, the intellect knows not just about God, but also knows God in a supernatural way to the point that Thomas considers faith to be a participation in God's own knowledge of himself.[34] Aquinas goes so far as to say that the soul becomes conformed to God in a "spiritual union, whereby the will is, so to speak, transformed into that end—and this belongs to charity. For the appetite of a thing is moved and tends toward its connatural end naturally; and this movement is due to a certain conformity of the thing with its end."[35] The theological virtues, especially charity, create this conformity of the soul to God, so that it acts in a manner in accord with the life of God, making the soul divine in its participation in the life of God.

Having looked at the effect of grace in deifying the soul, the proper context has been provided to understand merit.[36] Aquinas's assertion that one merits eternal life as a reward may sound controversial, but he makes it clear that merit must be understood also in terms of deification: "And the worth of the work depends on the dignity of grace, whereby a man, being made a partaker of the Divine Nature, is adopted as a son of God, to whom the inheritance is due by right of adoption, according to Romans 8:17: 'If sons, heirs also.'"[37] Acting in a divine manner on earth merits a further share in the divine life in heaven. The divine life of grace exceeds the natural capacities of human nature, though it also involves cooperation. This cooperation, by which one acts in accord with the gift of charity, forms the basis of merit.[38]

Although Aquinas speaks in terms of justice in relation to merit, this justice itself is a gift: "Hence a man can merit nothing from God except by His gift."[39] The justice of merit is not one of strict equality, which justice normally seeks when it renders what is due, but rather is a justice by which God rewards what he has commanded in the life of grace.

> Now it is clear that between God and man there is the greatest inequality: for they are infinitely apart, and all man's good is from God. Hence there can be no justice of absolute equality between man and God, but only of a certain proportion, inasmuch as both operate after their own manner. Now the manner and measure of human virtue is in man from God. Hence man's merit with God only exists on the presupposition of the Divine ordination, so that man obtains from God, as a reward of his operation, what God gave him the power of operation for, even as natural things by their proper movements and operations obtain that to which they were ordained by God.[40]

Thus, Aquinas can claim that eternal life is merited in justice without jeopardizing the dependence of the soul upon God in grace for salvation. In what seems like a side question in relation to merit, Aquinas asks if human persons can merit for one another. Although the answer is generally "no," there is one crucial exception to that rule, which actually reveals the foundation for all merit: "But Christ's soul is moved by God through grace, not only so as to reach the glory of life everlasting, but so as to lead others to it, inasmuch as He is the Head of the Church, and the

Author of human salvation."[41] Ultimately the graced actions of the soul have to be seen as a participation in the actions of Christ.

The Source of Salvation in Christ

We have looked at justification and how it culminates in deification. We now must turn to the source of salvation from which these realities spring. Ultimately, Aquinas says that God alone is the cause of grace, because "it is as necessary that God alone should deify, bestowing a partaking of the Divine Nature by a participated likeness, as it is impossible that anything save fire should enkindle."[42] God as the source of salvation, however, is complemented by the central importance of mediation in Aquinas's understanding of salvation. In fact, it is not an exaggeration to say that justification and deification come to the soul precisely through the mediation of Christ by the soul's sharing in the grace and merit that Christ possessed: "Now the interior influx of grace is from no one save Christ, Whose manhood, through its union with the Godhead, has the power of justifying."[43] This mediation continues as Christ bestows his grace and merits through the Church and its sacraments:

> As in the person of Christ the humanity causes our salvation by grace, the Divine power being the principal agent, so likewise in the sacraments of the New Law, which are derived from Christ, grace is instrumentally caused by the sacraments, and principally by the power of the Holy Ghost working in the sacraments, according to John 3:5: "Unless a man be born again of water and the Holy Ghost he cannot enter into the kingdom of God."[44]

It is in the third part of the *Summa* that Aquinas unfolds the meaning of Christ's mediation, uniting God and humanity, by discussing the nature and consequences of the Incarnation, Christ's life, and the sacraments.[45] Although it will not be possible to do justice to such a large amount of material, a few central aspects of Christ's mediation of grace will be presented, especially concerning the salvific nature of the Incarnation and Christ's work of salvation in his death and resurrection.

In presenting the fundamentals of the Incarnation, Thomas makes it clear that Christ became incarnate precisely to save humanity. Although he shows caution in assigning absolute necessity to the Incarnation (God in his omnipotence could act otherwise), nonetheless, Aquinas asserts, "the work of Incarnation was ordained by God as a remedy for sin."[46] Thus, there is a necessary link between the Incarnation and salvation. In particular, Aquinas sees the humanity of Christ as a conjoined instrument of the Second Person of the Trinity, the Son of God. The use of the term *instrument* does not demean the Incarnation, but precisely shows its significance: "The Divine Nature makes use of the operation of the human nature, as of the operation of its instrument; and in the same way the human nature shares in the operation of the Divine Nature, as an instrument shares in the operation of the principal agent."[47] The humanity of Christ is thus given its ability to save by sharing in the operation of God as its instrument. One can say that Christ's entire incarnate life has salvific value; this is why Aquinas walks through all the major events of Christ's life.[48] Nevertheless, the Paschal Mystery of Christ's death and resurrection stand out as the primary events of salvation.

The united operation of the divine and the human natures in the incarnate Christ points directly to the way in which Christ acts as savior. Aquinas describes the humanity of Christ as the point of mediation between God and man.

> Properly speaking, the office of a mediator is to join together and unite those between whom he mediates: for extremes are united in the mean [*medio*]. Now to unite men to God perfectively belongs to Christ, through Whom men are reconciled to God. . . . And, consequently, Christ alone is the perfect Mediator of God and men, inasmuch as, by His death, He reconciled the human race to God.[49]

In this work of mediation, God and humanity are brought together in Christ. Christ's very existence as the God-man is a bringing together and joining of what was held apart by sin. Although Christ has solidarity with all of humanity in the Incarnation, the work of mediation is appropriated by those who are joined to Christ as members of his Body, the Church. In this way the grace of Christ is said to "overflow into His members" and furthermore that "Christ's works are referred to Himself and to His members."[50] Following Paul, Aquinas notes that Christ is a new Adam who acts as the "head of all men in regard to grace."[51]

In order to explore this theory further, it is helpful to define the ways in which Aquinas describes that this mediation occurs: satisfaction, merit, atonement, sacrifice, and redemption:

Satisfaction

"Being adequate to make good the fault committed."[52]

Merit

"Whosoever suffers for justice's sake, provided that he be in a state of grace, merits his salvation thereby, according to Matthew 5:10: 'Blessed are they that suffer persecution for justice's sake.'"[53]

Atonement

"He properly atones for an offense who offers something which the offended one loves equally, or even more than he detested the offense."[54]

Sacrifice

"Something done for that honor which is properly due to God, in order to appease Him."[55]

Redemption

"The price, by which [one] ransoms himself or someone else from sin and its penalty."[56]

There are two key elements that explain how Christ mediates for humanity based on the preceding points. First, humanity is in bondage to sin and cannot on its own resolve this dilemma: "Man was held captive on account of sin in two ways: first of all, by the bondage of sin. . . . Secondly, as to the debt of punishment, to the payment of which man was held fast by God's justice."[57] Second, Christ, on behalf of humanity, compensates for sin and all its associated debts in a superabundant way. Aquinas notes that Christ offers "what was of greatest price—Himself—

for us" in sacrifice as both priest and victim.[58] Even the sacrifice of his body appeases the Father "as it was God's flesh, the result of which was that it was of infinite worth."[59] But much more than his flesh, the highest worth of the sacrifice is found in the interior disposition of the priest: "But by suffering out of love and obedience, Christ gave more to God than was required to compensate for the offense of the whole human race."[60] The overarching emphasis of how Christ achieves salvation is that his love both for the Father and for humanity draws them together through his mediation on the Cross.

Aquinas links the discussion of Christ's work of redemption to the question on justification, not only through the focus on the remission of sin, but also on the justice that belongs particularly to Christ and which he bestows upon those who believe in him: "Man was set free by Christ's justice."[61] His obedience and love achieve perfect justice because they rightly render to God what is owed by humanity for salvation. The overall effect of the work of Christ's redemption is the blotting out of sin, the bestowal of saving grace, and the perfection of glory.[62] The first two points have already been addressed, but the final point is reserved for Christ's resurrection. The resurrection "complete[s] the work of our salvation," or justification, by serving as "the cause of newness of life, which comes through grace or justice."[63] Christ's resurrection also completes the work of salvation by causing the resurrection and glorification of the body, the final step in the restoration and perfection of humanity.

As was evident in Aquinas's teaching on grace, the work of salvation is not accomplished without human cooperation. It is necessary to be drawn into Christ's saving actions, which Thomas thinks need "to be applied to each individual."[64] Often he speaks especially of obedience and love as examples; these examples are not just for edification, but are meant to be participated in because Christ is "the model for our justification."[65] Aquinas insists on this so strongly that he says: "In order to secure the effects of Christ's Passion, we must be likened unto Him."[66] This likening happens when one is joined to Christ as part of his Body: "Christ's satisfaction works its effect in us inasmuch as we are incorporated with Him, as the members with their head."[67] Aquinas specifies even further how this occurs: "Christ's Passion works its effect in them to whom it is applied, through faith and charity and the sacraments of faith."[68] In this way, the soul does not just receive the benefits of Christ's saving action, but is incorporated into Christ so that these actions can belong to the soul through its union with Christ.

Conclusion

Conformity to Christ shapes Thomas Aquinas's theology of salvation. The soul is justified by being made just interiorly, acting in accord with that justice in meritorious action, which essentially flows to the soul from the saving action of Christ. The humanity of Christ mediates this saving grace to the soul from God, so that the soul may consequently share in the very life of God through deification. Aquinas's teaching may be summarized by saying that the soul is saved or justified by participation in the life and justice of the Incarnate Word, Jesus Christ.

NOTES

1. For two more comprehensive works on the topic of salvation in Aquinas, see Romanus Cessario, O. P., *The Godly Image: Christ and Salvation in Catholic Thought from Anselm to Aquinas* (Petersham, MA: St. Bede's Publications, 1990); Matthew Levering, *Christ's Fulfillment of Torah and Temple: Salvation according to Thomas Aquinas* (Notre Dame, IN: University of Notre Dame Press, 2002). For a general introduction to Aquinas, see Jean-Pierre Torrell, *St. Thomas Aquinas*, vol. 1, *The Person and His Work*, trans. Robert Royal (Washington, DC: Catholic University of America Press, 1996).
2. For a brief overview of the structure and content of the *Summa*, see J. P. Torrell, O. P., *Aquinas's Summa: Background, Structure, and Reception*, trans. Benedict M. Guevin (Washington, DC: Catholic University of America Press, 2005). The *Summa Theologiae* is divided into three parts, but the second part is divided into a further two parts (I–II and II–II). Each part is divided into a series of questions, which in turn is divided into articles. The structure of the article generally consists of posing a question, listing objections that answer the question in a way contrary to the later solution, a *sed contra* ("on the contrary"), which provides a short, authoritative rebuttal of the objections, Aquinas's own response or solution to the question (corpus), and then finally a response to the objections (referenced as *ad* with a number corresponding to the prior objection). A normal citation of the *Summa* would be listed as follows, and will hereafter be cited as such: an abbreviation of the title, the part, the question, the article, and section of the article: *ST* I, q. 1, a. 1, corpus. The translation used in this chapter is that of the Fathers of the English Dominican Province (New York: Benziger, 1947).
3. *ST* I-II, q. 106, a. 2, *sed contra*; St. Thomas Aquinas, *Summa Contra Gentiles*, book 4, ch. 56, no. 1, trans. Charles J. O'Neil (New York: Hanover House, 1957). Aquinas generally uses the word *salutem* for salvation, which can have the connotation of

wellness, not simply deliverance from sin. He uses *salutem* 1,740 times throughout his corpus, but the word *salvatio* only 10 times.

4. It is important to note that Aquinas's position on justification exerted wide influence in the Catholic response to the Reformation, as seen in the Council of Trent's "Decree on Justification." For one comparative study, see Stephen Pfurtner, O. P., *Luther and Aquinas on Salvation*, trans. Edward Quinn (New York: Sheed and Ward, 1964).

5. For an overview of the virtue of justice in the *Summa*, see Jean Porter, "The Virtue of Justice (IIa IIae, qq. 58–122)," in *The Ethics of Aquinas*, ed. Stephen J. Pope (Washington, DC: Georgetown University Press, 2002), 272–86.

6. *ST* I–II, q. 100, a. 12, corpus.

7. Ibid.

8. Ibid. Aquinas references Romans 4:2, which uses Abraham as an example of justice as an infused virtue. The full answer about the law and justification only comes when Aquinas discusses the New Law in question 106. In article 2, he asks whether the New Law justifies and states: "There is the chief element, viz. the grace of the Holy Ghost bestowed inwardly. And as to this, the New Law justifies." For more on the way that Christ fulfills the precepts of the old law for Aquinas, see Levering, *Christ's Fulfillment of Torah and Temple*, 51–79.

9. Ibid.

10. *ST* II–II, q. 58, a. 1, corpus, quoting Aristotle's *Nicomachean Ethics* 5.5.

11. *ST* II–II, q. 58, a. 1. Translation slightly altered. This definition comes from Justinian's legal code, the *Digest* (D1.1; De Just. et Jure 10), and is transmitted to Western theology by Isidore of Seville's encyclopedia, *Etymologiae*.

12. *ST* II–II, q. 58, a. 2, corpus.

13. In the next article, Aquinas explains this subordination to reason in more detail: "For a man's act is made good through attaining the rule of reason, which is the rule whereby human acts are regulated" (*ST* II–II, q. 58, a. 3, corpus).

14. *ST* II–II, q. 58, a. 5, corpus. In article 6, Aquinas says that justice even "directs the acts of the other virtues to its own end, and this is to move all the other virtues by its command." This reveals the way that charity acts like justice, insofar as it directs all things not to an earthly common good, but to the divine good: "Charity may be called a general virtue in so far as it directs the acts of all the virtues to the Divine good" (ibid.).

15. *ST* II–II, q. 58, a. 8, ad 2, quoting Augustine, *Eighty-Three Questions*, q. 61.

16. *ST* II–II, q. 122, a. 1; a. 2.

17. *ST* II–II, q. 58, a. 1, ad 6.

18. For a treatment of justification in Aquinas that places his thought within the theological framework of the Middle Ages, see Alister E. McGrath, *Iustia Dei: A History of the Christian Doctrine of Justification*, second edition (New York: Cambridge University Press, 1998). McGrath notes that Aquinas continues "Augustine's understanding of *iustitia*," which "embraces practically the entire ordering of the universe, so that justification can be understood as the restoration of man to his

correct place in the hierarchy of being, including the establishing of the correct relationship between the various existential strata within man" (46).
19. The movement from sin to justice can be understood as a process (*processus iustificationis*) with four major components: "There are four things which are accounted to be necessary for the justification of the ungodly, viz. the infusion of grace, the movement of the free-will towards God by faith, the movement of the free-will towards sin, and the remission of sins" (*ST* I–II, q. 113, a. 6, corpus).
20. *ST* I–II, q. 113, a. 1, corpus.
21. *ST* I–II, q. 113, a. 1, ad 2.
22. *ST* I–II, q. 113, a. 1, ad 1. Aquinas devotes a whole article in this question to the simultaneous turning to God and turning away from sin: see a. 5.
23. *ST* I–II, q. 113, a. 2, corpus. In the response to the second objection of this article, Aquinas makes clear that grace is not simply an act of the will, but an effect within the soul: "God's love consists not merely in the act of the Divine will but also implies a certain effect of grace" (ibid., ad 2). For a fuller treatment of the nature of grace, as both a motion of God and an abiding quality within the soul, see *ST* I–II, q. 110. For an overview of the topic of grace from a Thomistic perspective, see Charles Journet, *The Meaning of Grace* (New York: Scepter Publishers, 1997).
24. *ST* I–II, q. 113, a. 3, corpus.
25. Ibid.
26. *ST* I–II, q. 113, a. 4, corpus. Aquinas specifies that faith and charity are infused by God at the moment of justification: "The movement of faith is not perfect unless it is quickened by charity; hence in the justification of the ungodly, a movement of charity is infused together with the movement of faith" (ibid., ad 1). Aquinas's teaching on predestination follows a similar pattern. Although predestination is considered to be a necessary, certain, and infallible movement of the divine will, it occurs in such a way that "free-will is not destroyed" (*ST* I, q. 23, a. 6, corpus).
27. For a general overview of the theology of deification, see Daniel K. Keating, *Deification and Grace* (Ave Maria, FL: Sapientia Press, 2007). For a more specific treatment of Aquinas on this topic, see A. N. Williams, *The Ground of Union: Deification in Aquinas and Palamas* (New York: Oxford University Press, 1999).
28. *ST* I–II, q. 113, a. 9, corpus.
29. *ST* II–II, q. 23, a. 8, corpus.
30. The scriptural locus for these virtues can be found in 1 Corinthians 13:13.
31. *ST* I–II, q. 62, a. 1, corpus.
32. *ST* I–II, q. 62, a. 2, corpus.
33. *ST* II–II, q. 81, a. 5, corpus.
34. In the first question of the *Summa*, Aquinas describes the way in which sacred doctrine is a wisdom received in faith from God himself: "But sacred doctrine essentially treats of God viewed as the highest cause, not only so far as He can be known through creatures just as philosophers knew Him . . . but also as far as He is known to Himself alone and revealed to others" (*ST* I, q. 1, a. 6, corpus). Although this deifying union with God through knowledge begins through faith, it

increases further in what Aquinas calls the light of glory: "By this light the blessed are made 'deiform'—i.e. like to God, according to the saying: 'When He shall appear we shall be like to Him, because we shall see Him as He is' (1 John 2:2)" (*ST* I, q. 12, a. 5, corpus).
35. *ST* I–II, q. 62, a. 3, corpus.
36. For more on merit in Aquinas, see Joseph P. Wawrykow, *God's Grace and Human Action: 'Merit' in the Theology of Thomas Aquinas* (Notre Dame, IN: University of Notre Dame Press, 1995).
37. *ST* I–II, q. 114, a. 3, corpus.
38. See *ST* I–II, q. 114, a. 5. There Aquinas states: "Hence the merit of eternal life rests chiefly with charity" (*sed contra*).
39. *ST* I–II, q. 114, a. 2, ad 2. Likewise, Aquinas states: "And hence it is that no created nature is a sufficient principle of an act meritorious of eternal life, unless there is added a supernatural gift, which we call grace" (ibid., corpus).
40. *ST* I–II, q. 114, a. 1, corpus.
41. *ST* I–II, q. 114, a. 6, corpus.
42. *ST* I–II, q. 112, a. 1, corpus.
43. *ST* III, q. 8, a. 6, corpus. In fact, deification itself is a participation in the deification of Christ's human nature: "Christ is the true God in Divine Person and Nature. Yet because together with unity of person there remains distinction of natures, as stated above, the soul of Christ is not essentially Divine. Hence it behooves it to be Divine by participation, which is by grace" (*ST* III, q. 7, a. 1, ad 1). For more on the inner life of Christ and its importance for Aquinas, see Elders, Leo Elders, S.V.D., "The Inner Life of Jesus in the Theology and Devotion of Saint Thomas Aquinas," in *Faith in Christ and the Worship of Christ: New Approaches to Devotion to Christ*, ed. Leo Scheffczyk, trans. Graham Harrison (San Francisco: Ignatius Press, 1982), 65–79.
44. *ST* I–II, q. 112, a. 1, ad 2. For more on Christ's mediation through the Church, see Lawrence J. Welch, *The Presence of Christ in the Church* (Naples, FL: Sapientia Press, 2007).
45. Aquinas never completed the third part of the *Summa*. The text breaks off during the discussion of the Sacrament of Penance (Confession).
46. *ST* III, q. 1, a. 3, corpus. See the prior article of this question for Aquinas's argument that the Incarnation, although not absolutely necessary, was most fitting for salvation. This is one modification in Aquinas's appropriation of St. Anselm's famous theory of satisfaction outlined in Anselm's *Cur Deus Homo* (*Why God Became Man*). Aquinas offers a brief summary of satisfaction that largely follows Anselm in ST III, q. 1, a. 2, ad 2. For a more in-depth analysis of Aquinas's relation to Anselm and of how the theories of both theologians differ from Protestant understandings, see Rik van Nieuwenhove, "St. Anselm and St. Thomas Aquinas on 'Satisfaction': or How Catholic and Protestant Understandings of the Cross Differ," *Angelicum* 80 (2003): 159–76.
47. *ST* III, q. 19, a. 1, corpus. In the response to the first objection, Aquinas uses Pseudo-Dionysius to explain this further: "Dionysius places in Christ a thean-

dric, i.e. a God-manlike or Divino-human, operation not by any confusion of the operations or powers of both natures, but inasmuch as His Divine operation employs the human, and His human operation shares in the power of the Divine." In relation to salvation particularly, Aquinas states that "all Christ's actions and sufferings operate instrumentally in virtue of His Godhead for the salvation of men" (*ST* III, q. 48, a. 6, corpus).

48. Torrell makes clear that "Thomas thinks that nothing is without meaning for salvation which the Incarnate Word lived" (*St. Thomas Aquinas*, vol. 2, *Spiritual Master*, trans. Robert Royal [Washington, DC: Catholic University of America Press, 2003], 131). See *ST* III, q. 48, a. 6.
49. *ST* III, q. 26, a. 1, corpus. Aquinas quotes Paul twice in this corpus: "According to 2 Corinthians 5:19: 'God was in Christ reconciling the world to Himself'"; "Hence the Apostle, after saying, 'Mediator of God and man, the man Christ Jesus,' added: 'Who gave Himself a redemption for all (1 Tim 2: 5).'"
50. *ST* III, q. 48, a. 1, corpus.
51. *ST* III, q. 19, a. 4, ad 1. The entire response reads: "The sin of an individual harms himself alone; but the sin of Adam, who was appointed by God to be the principle of the whole nature, is transmitted to others by carnal propagation. So, too, the merit of Christ, Who has been appointed by God to be the head of all men in regard to grace, extends to all His members."
52. *ST* III, q. 1, a. 2, ad 2.
53. *ST* III, q. 48, a. 1, corpus.
54. *ST* III, q. 48, a. 2, corpus.
55. *ST* III, q. 48, a. 3, corpus. Aquinas also links the word *reconciliation* to sacrifice, noting that humanity is reconciled to the Father through the appeasement of Christ's sacrifice on the Cross (*ST* III, q. 49, a. 4).
56. *ST* III, q. 48, a. 4, corpus.
57. Ibid.
58. Ibid. Aquinas devotes an entire question to the priesthood of Christ: *ST* III, q. 22.
59. *ST* III, q. 48, a. 2, ad 3.
60. *ST* III, q. 48, a. 2, corpus. The importance of obedience for justification is expounded upon further: "It was befitting that Christ should suffer out of obedience. First of all, because it was in keeping with human justification, that 'as by the disobedience of one man, many were made sinners: so also by the obedience of one, many shall be made just,' as is written Romans 5:19" (ST III, q. 47, a. 2, corpus).
61. *ST* III, q. 46, a. 1, ad 3. Romanus Cessario notes that in Aquinas's first major work, his *Commentary on the Sentences* of Peter Lombard, he links satisfaction to the virtue of justice: "When applied to satisfaction, this proportioned equality establishes in the one performing the satisfactory deed a kind of balance or equilibrium in relationships with others. Thus, Thomas includes satisfaction as part of that justice which exists between one individual and another" (*The Godly Image*, 54). See also Cessario's discussion of satisfaction as the "key-notion" of Christ's redemption, 149–66.

62. *ST* III, q. 22, a. 2, corpus.
63. *ST* III, q. 51, a. 1, corpus; q. 56, a. 2, ad 4. Romans 4:25 is quoted by Aquinas to prove that the resurrection does indeed contribute to justification.
64. *ST* III, q. 49, a. 1, ad 4. Rik van Niewnhove emphasizes this point in his overview of Aquinas's soteriology, as evidenced by his title, "'Bearing the Marks of Christ's Passion': Aquinas's Soteriology," in *The Theology of Thomas Aquinas*, 277–302. He remarks, for instance: "Although salvation is from God alone, through Christ's satisfaction we begin to participate in God's redeeming work: satisfaction is an inchoative participation in our abiding with God" (ibid., 291).
65. St. Thomas Aquinas, *Commentary on the Gospel of St. John*, vol. 2, trans. Fabian R. Larcher, O.P. (Albany, NY: Magi Books, 1998), ch. 13, lec. 3, no. 1781.
66. *ST* III, q. 49, a. 3, ad 2.
67. *ST* III, q. 49, a. 3, ad 3.
68. *ST* III, q. 49, a. 3, ad 1.

10

Julian of Norwich

KERRIE HIDE

Julian of Norwich is one of the English mystics, who was born in 1346 and died around 1420. She lived in England at the eve of the Reformation, through a time of enormous suffering, poverty, plague, war, and Church schism. Little is known about Julian's background, although she is thought to have been a Benedictine nun, or a titled Lady who married and had children. At some stage in her life she became an anchoress, a recluse attached to the Church of St. Julian, in Norwich. We do not know her name, but only her title given to her as an anchoress. As an anchoress she prayed the liturgy of the hours and lived a life of silence and prayer. She also counseled people who sought her wisdom through her window that opened onto the outside world.

At age thirty-and-a-half, Julian suffered an illness so severe she believed she was going to die. In that experience, she received a series of sixteen showings or visions that she later recorded. The earliest, more succinct short text has a strong, immediate, visionary nature, while the later, long text, *A Revelation of Love*, is a deeply theological exploration of the nature and meaning of salvation. The original texts were lost, but later copies of both texts, along with various compilations, were preserved. There are two main variations of the long text: *Sloane 1*, kept in England; and the Paris manuscript, preserved in Paris.

The past fifty years has seen a revived interest in the creativity of Julian's theology for informing systematic theology, placing her *Revelations* among the great soteriologies of Christian theology.

Introduction

"Here I saw a great oneing between Christ and us."[1]
Julian of Norwich

At the beginning of her *Showings*, Julian of Norwich leads her reader to ponder the mystery of love and suffering by entering into a shadowy room. Julian describes herself as languorous, suspended in time between life and death, for three days and three nights.[2] Evoking the atmosphere of the *tridiuum* of Christ's dying and rising, Julian invites anyone who desires to be Christ's lover to be stirred and comforted by this vision of salvation.[3] It is an intimately personal experience[4] and at the same time theologically profound and universal. A climax is reached at the *poynte* of Julian's dying (ii: 42). Physically she is fading, her body feels numb, and she is leaning propped on pillows so her heart may feel open. Emotionally, she surrenders into Love as all she longs for is to "assent fully with all the will of her heart to be at one with God's will" (ii: 16–17). A parson comes to anoint her, holds a sculptured image of Christ on the cross before her face, and says: "Daughter I have brought the image of your saviour; Look upon and reverence the image of your saviour who died for you and for me" (ii: 25–28). As Julian sets her eyes on the face crowned with thorns, light shimmers through the shadows. The compassionate moment of suffering with the crucified Christ becomes a liminal space, a point in between, where suspended between life and death, she beholds and enters into an expansive new way of seeing salvation. Julian realizes that "all my pain was taken away from me, and I was all whole, in every part of my body as I was before. I marvelled at this change, for I knew it was the inner (privy), working of God" (ii: 42–45). As Julian contemplates the meaning of this experience of becoming whole and well "for twenty years or more" (14.51.86), she explores the meaning of salvation and develops a contemplative soteriology of *oneing*. Christ advises Julian to "take the meaning, be comforted by it and trust it" (16.70.26–7).

A Soteriology of Oneing

This chapter will examine Julian's interpretation of salvation as oneing. Her personal experience of suffering informed and shaped her understanding of the salvific role of Christ. The cross is the centering principle that initiates and expands her understanding of salvation. Through the three *beholdings* of the cross as suffering, love, and joy, Julian came to envisage salvation as the oneing of love that is integral to the loving of the Trinity. For Julian, salvation is a great oneing with which human beings cooperate through contemplative prayer. Salvation is not an afterthought to the divine plan initiated because we went astray. Salvation is integral in the journey of *exidus reditus*, oneing from God the One, to God, in who all is One.[5] Salvation is endless, personally transformational, cosmic, and evolutionary.

Julian has a unique contribution to make to the soteriologies that have been presented so far, because her theology of redemption emerges directly from her experience of suffering and contemplative visionary experience of Christ. She gives a classic example of how to discern the salvific movement of the Spirit in personal experience. Fortunately, during the twentieth century and into the twenty-first there has been careful scholarship into the genre of mystical literature[6] and the nature and role of woman's visionary experience as discourse for theology.[7] So, within the context that human beings can and do experience the presence of God and are shaped and formed by the experience, it is important to focus directly on the soteriology that emerges from Julian's text. What is crucial, though, in order to interpret Julian, is to explore what Julian says about how she "*beholds* and sees," in order to illuminate her understanding of salvation.

Beholding and Seeing

Julian's *showings* are visual and expressive, with an unusual emphasis on "bodily sight." In her text, sensual bodily wisdom initiates spiritual and theological insights that are intrinsically complex, "elusive and allusive."[8] They are paradoxical and can only be interpreted through beholding in harmony with the way Julian beholds in the showings. In general usage, *beholding* is looking, gazing, seeing a visual appearance, applying the mind in thought, meditation, and contemplation.[9] In Julian's hands beholding becomes profoundly contemplative. In her introduction Julian affirms the crucial nature of "*beholding* and *seeing*." She explains, "he means: *behold* and *see*, for by the same power, wisdom and goodness that I have done all this, by the same might, wisdom and goodness I shall make well all that is not well, and you shall *see* it."[10] Emphatically, Julian asserts that it is the desire of Christ that human beings behold, and see with the knowing of the heart, how the crucified Christ makes all things well.

Julian clarifies the threefold nature of her beholding: "All this was shown in three parts, by bodily sight, and by words formed in my understanding, and by spiritual sight. For the spiritual sight I cannot nor may show as truly as I can" (16.73.2–5; 9.29–32; vii: 1–5).[11] Beholding is not simply observing the physical crucified body of Christ, but participating in "the body of Christ," in the Pauline sense, of Christ as the center who holds all things together (Col 1:17). For Julian, *beholding* involves gazing at the crucified body, compassionately entering into the physical and emotional experience of Christ, surrendering beyond conscious control deeper into Christ, abiding, until the effects of simply being in Christ flow into conscious beholding and understanding emerges from the spiritual depths of her loving. Through beholding, Julian gains deep participatory knowledge of how one, human beings are "in" Christ. She presents a Christophany[12] that identifies Christ as the mid-person who is the ground of human nature (14.53.32),[13] the point where we are *knit* and *oned* in the dynamic ground of the oneing of the Trinity. In a wonderful interplay of bodily and spiritual infusion, beholding with Julian awakens a limitless interior space where the consciousness of oneing arises, which the reader knows in the deep ground of his or her heart. Beholding awakens awareness of oneing.

Oneing

Oneing is a dynamic Middle English term that has returned to contemporary theological discourse.[14] In common usage it means to be one, united, joined, blended, or fused,[15] but these terms do not encapsulate the dynamic interpenetration of the divine and human that preserves unique identity. Oneing is "ordained beyond the beginning."[16] It is expressed ontologically in the oneing of the Trinity and in the life of our soul when humanity was "preciously knit to God in the making, with a knot so subtle and so mighty that it is *oned* into God. In this *oneing* it is made endlessly holy."[17] This knitting and oneing continues now, as the Trinity desires that "all the souls that shall be saved in heaven without end be *knit* in this *knot* and *oned* in this *oneing* and made holy in this holiness" (14.53.59–64). Human beings are eternally knotted and oned in God. Living in this knitting and oneing is natural. It belongs to our essence as human beings. Like the oneing between Christ's humanity and his divinity (see 8.20.2–3), Christ knits and ones our substance (the essence of who we are in God) and sensuality (the responses of our sensual earthy nature) and makes us whole. We experience this oneing now, existentially, as we participate in Christ who is the ground of our nature. In the deepest sense of who we are, we are already one, and at the same time we are being drawn into an endless oneing. As Brant Pelphrey points out, oneing is the forerunner of the word "atonement," literally suggesting *at-one-ment* with God.[18] Oneing is salvific. Oneing creates at-one-ment.

As Julian recovers from her illness and surrenders into her encounter with Christ day by day, she is continually drawn back to the cross. In her three beholdings of the cross, Julian sees suffering, love, and joy. The cross becomes the centering ground that expands her understanding of salvation.

Oneing through the Crucified Christ

Julian distinguishes three interrelated revelations of the crucified Christ, as a beholding of suffering, a beholding of love, and a beholding of joy. These three beholdings interrelate and become one kenosis of desire. They reveal how we become one with Christ through the pouring out of love on the cross. They also disclose how creation and creatures participate in the oneing love in the body of the crucified Christ in the Trinity "for where Jesus appears the blessed Trinity is understood" (1.4.15).

Oneing through Suffering

The first beholding Julian presents of "the hard pain that he suffered with contrition and compassion" (8.20.34–35) holds all the revelations that follow. Christ is like the suffering servant of Isaiah (Is 42–53), disfigured and dying, as he pours himself out in love. At first it appears that Christ is a distant, sacrificial victim who resolutely carries the sin of the world. Increasingly, as the colorful images glow like medieval illuminations, Christ becomes surprisingly intimate and homely, evoking the wounds Julian prayed for herself, of contrition, compassion, and longing for God (See 1:2.6–7). Initially, Julian describes in vivid detail "red blood running down from under his garland, hot and freshly, plenteously and lively" (1.4.3–4), "in the painful changing of his deep dying" (1.8.9–10) until "the pain dried up all the lively spirit in Christ's flesh" (1.8.21–22). This powerful portrayal of the physical suffering and the continual drying of the spirit in Christ's flesh draws Julian to hear Christ's words: "I thirst" (8.17.2–4). This drying of the spirit in the body of Christ that leaves his body "like a cloth blowing in the wind" (1.8:40) expresses the bodily and spiritual thirst of Christ for human beings. Resonating with the great Philippian hymn of kenosis (Phil 2:7),[19] this compassionate desiring of Christ loving human beings expressed in his bodily and spiritual thirst becomes a great kenosis of desire. Christ as lover empties himself and draws Julian and all creation into the one outpouring of love.

As the showing continues, Julian's appreciation of the meaning of Christ's thirst expands:

> Here I saw a great *oneing* between Christ and us . . . for when he was in pain we were in pain, and all creatures that might suffer pain suffered with him, that is to say all creatures that God has made for our service the firmament and the earth failed in sorrow in their nature at the time of Christ's dying. (9.18.14–18)

Strikingly, Julian does not see Christ as separate from human beings; rather, she perceives "a great *oneing*." All, human beings, creatures, and all creation feel sorrow and are one with Christ in suffering. This oneing is "great" because the identification of Christ with creation is so profound that there is only one suffering. It is impossible for anything to happen to the body of Christ in isolation from creation, because creation is already one in the one body of Christ. An understanding emerges that "we are now in our Lord's meaning in his cross with him in our pain and in our passion dying" (9.21.11–21). Creation is never isolated from Christ in suffering. We can choose to desire oneing with Christ in suffering and consciously continue in the oneing of the cross.

Julian also sees Christ immersed in contrition. In Middle English, contrition describes being bruised with heartfelt sorrow for the condition of sin.[20] Julian is haunted by the question of sin, wondering why sin was not prevented. She pursues her uncertainties. Christ's response is extraordinary, as he does not mention human sinfulness, and he dismisses Julian's struggle with his confronting words: "Sin is behouley (necessary) but all shall be well, and all shall be well and all manner of things shall be well" (13.27.13–14). Julian then perceives how sin is "all that is not good" (13.27.15–16). She continues: "But I did not see sin, for I believe it has no manner of substance, no part in being, nor may it be known but by the pain that it causes" (13.27.26–28). Because God does not create sin, it has no substance, no being. Sin is an illusion.[21] In contrast to *beholding* the crucified body of Christ, sin cannot be beheld because it has no essence. It is "*nothing*" (xxiii: 26). It is "*naked*" (13.27.14) and "*unnatural (unkind)*" (14.63.16). Contrary to our natural oneing, sin distorts desire, disturbs the harmony between substance and sensuality, and blinds us to our substantial oneness in God. Sin annihilates and can only be seen by the pain it causes.

In the example shown in the fourteenth revelation, "The Parable of Lord and the Servant" (14.51.1–331), this sense of non-being becomes clearer. In this retelling of the myth of the fall, the servant, who is Adam and humanity, does not willfully separate himself from the Lord. He accidently falls into the dell when he seeks to do the will of the Lord. He "runs in great haste for love to do his lord's will. And accidently he falls in a slade into great sorrow and groans and moans and wallows" (14.51.15–16). Caught in an illusion of separation from the Lord, the servant suffers in isolation. He loses his vision of love. Yet, the servant is never left alone, because Julian realizes that the servant is also Christ. When the servant fell in the dell, Christ also fell into the ground of the womb of the maiden. As servant, Christ works ceaselessly on the earth to restore contemplative vision. The parable reveals to Julian how the fall is the great accident: a collapse into a confusing pit of meaninglessness, which causes the servant as human beings to be unable to see reality and to turn and face the love of the Lord. The heartfelt desire of the Lord is that the servant as humanity may see the fullness of his identity as servant and enjoy the love in his midst.

Julian's exploration of sin is distinctive because instead of focusing on human guilt, Christ rejects the popular images of Julian's day that stressed human willfulness as well as developed extensive lists and categories of sin. Christ simply says, "sin is behouley," often translated to mean that sin is necessary,[22] in the sense that sin is inescapable with respect to the circumstances of destiny. All sin takes place within the context of the centering love of the cross, which has the power to place love where there is non-being and to make all things well. The accident of the fall occurred, but we are always kept safe (13.37.10), one in Christ, so "all shall be well." There is no sense here of Christ focusing on sin or blaming or condemning human beings. Christ sees the nothingness of sin, lovingly enters into the pain that it causes, and makes all things well. Human nature does not need to focus on sin, but on the desire of Christ who is love. Salvation is about loving.

In beholding suffering, Julian experiences the kenosis of the desire of Christ thirsting for human beings. She sees how in his outpouring of love all creation suffers in the one suffering. Creation is never left alone in suffering. Humanity, creatures, and all creation are one in this wonderful expression of love.

Oneing through Love

The intensity of Christ's suffering and the extravagance of his thirst and compassion continue to captivate Julian, until a climax occurs that transforms her understanding of the nature and work of salvation. Julian sees in "the second beholding in his blessed passion, the love that made him suffer . . . this love was without beginning and without end" (9.22.45–49). This showing of the heart of Christ, in the tenth revelation, has a centrifugal force that expands into a dynamic "Christogenesis"[23] of all things coming together in Christ. There is a profound self-emptying in Julian as she follows divine desire into Christ's side, which she later identifies as "beholding in his blessed side enjoying" (14.60.43–44). Beholding takes Julian deeply into Christ:

> With good cheer our Lord looked into his side and beheld with joy, and with his sweet looking led the understanding of his creature forth through the same wound, within, into his side. And there he showed a fair and delectable place large enough for all humankind who shall be saved to rest in peace and love. (10.24.3–7)

In contrast to the very active beholding of suffering, this showing begins in silence, with each movement revealing a transformation in Julian as her understanding is drawn into the wound.[24] Note how the "sweet looking" of Christ catches Julian's gaze and leads her through the "same" wound into his side. The "same" wound suggests that Christ and Julian, all humanity, and all creation share the one wound of love.[25] The wound becomes an enclosure, the ground of prayer that awakens Julian to participatory knowledge that tastes of the divine essence. The wound opens into Christ's heart, revealing boundless oneness, where all rest in peace and love. Julian's personal experience infuses into universal experience, as she sees that the heart of Christ is not a home for a select few, it is large enough for all to rest in peace and love. A melody of love then rings out from the silence, as Christ says "Lo, how I love you" (10.24.15–16). This love, Julian explains, is the kind and gracious loving of Christ, the deep wisdom of the Trinity our mother, who "bares us into joy and endless life" (14.60.19–20). Later in the showings, Julian describes the wound "as a sweet opening which shows us in part the godhead and the joys of heaven with the spiritual sureness of endless bliss" (14.60.39–41). Christ's open wound inspires trust as it immerses Julian in joy and offers a taste of heaven.

The wound leading into the heart-womb of Christ expands on Julian's portrayal in the first revelation of human beings enfolded and enclosed in Christ, who "for love wraps around us and winds about us, holds us and encloses us in tender love, so he may never leave us" (1.5.4–6). This same sense of enclosure occurs in the fourteenth revelation where she sees how, "by the endless intent and assent of the Trinity, the mid person would be the ground and head of this fair kind out of whom we all come, in whom we are all enclosed, into whom we shall all go" (14.53.30–34). In the final revelation, Christ is then enclosed in us, as he sits in our soul in the midst of our heart "evenly in rest and peace" (16.68.9). "The place that Jesus takes in our soul he will never remove without end because it is his homeliest home and his endless dwelling" (16.68.15–16). Christ is the home of humankind and humankind is the home of Christ. The heart of Christ is the ground of oneness from where we all come and where we will all go. This beholding of entering into the heart of Christ further awakens a Trinitarian consciousness of how ". . . we are *closed* in the Father and we are *closed* in the Son, and we are *closed* in the Holy

Spirit. And the Father is *be-closed* in us, the Son is *be-closed* in us and the Holy Spirit is *be-closed* in us " (14.54.23–26). "Closed" stresses permanence, showing how human nature is substantially hidden within the Father, Son, and Holy Spirit in eternity, while "be-closed" emphasizes the active enfolding and sharing of love that creates mutual indwelling.[26] This beholding of love imparts joy.

Beholding love takes Julian into Christ. It awakens her to Christ's desire to draw all to rest in peace and love, in the ground of his heart. It returns her to her natural home. Her vision of salvation becomes joyful because of the reciprocal indwelling between Christ and human beings in this great kenosis of loving. The revelation offers hope for a life where through, with, and in Christ, all may live in the joy of life, closed and be-closed in the Trinity.

Oneing through Joy

The third beholding of the joy of crucified love, recorded in revelation nine, further infuses Julian's understanding in "the joy and bliss that makes him like it" (9.23.7–8). She understands how joy arises from the depths of suffering because its source is the endless, boundless, oneness of love. "*Bliss*" reinforces the enstatic and ecstatic, expansive and enlightening quality of joy, highlighting the blessing, pleasure, and wellbeing.[27] In a remarkable dialogue with the risen Christ, Julian appreciates how the cross becomes a *glorious asseth*, or glorious satisfaction. The beholding occurs in a lively vocal exchange. Christ asks:

> Are you well apayed that I suffered for you? I said yes Good Lord have mercy. Yes Good Lord blessed may you be. Then Jesus our Good Lord said: If you are apayed I am apayed. It is a joy, a bliss, an endless liking to me that ever I suffered the passion for you; and if I might suffer more, I would suffer more. (9.22.2–7)

In the popular theology of her day the interpretation of redemption as a commercial exchange,[28] that evolved from a version of Anselm of Canterbury's (1033–1109) *Cur Deus Homo?*,[29] emphasized the need for Christ to become human to suffer and die as reparation to restore God's honor. As in a monetary exchange, Christ buys back, or pays retribution to

God the Father.³⁰ Here, Julian adopts this language of "buying" humanity. However, as she struggles to understand the reason for Christ's suffering, she does not interpret Christ's suffering as payment to the Father. Nor does she stress the need for Christ to suffer and buy back sinful human beings. Rather, Christ asks Julian, not the Father, is she *"apayed."* Furthermore, there is no sense of Christ paying Julian in an economic exchange. All Christ desires is to please, delight, and satisfy her heart. So Christ's question becomes, are you at peace now?³¹ Can you rest in my heart in peace and love? Being apayed is being given the gift of peace.

Later, Julian tells us that apayed resonates with Christ's words, "if I could suffer more I would suffer more." They are spoken as a loving mother baring humanity "into joy and endless life" (14.60.19–20), into the fullness of life in the Trinity. Mirroring Julian's initial experience, the cross becomes the liminal space of "again *making*" (2.10.55–6) or "again *buying*" (14.42.35). It becomes the point in time where Christ, as deep wisdom and mother, recreates and gives birth to all creation into joy, bliss, and endless life. As deep wisdom, Christ is the expression of the eternal wisdom of the Trinity. As mother, he is constantly giving birth to humanity into the fullness of oneing love. And so the three beholdings of the passion expand into three beholdings of Christ, who is mother of kind in being the ground of our nature in our first making, mother of mercy and grace recreating us in our *again making*, and mother of working in spreading grace to *"the length and breadth, height and depth without end for love"* (14.59.47–48). Through the cross, Christ, deep wisdom and mother, births us into the fullness of oneing love.

The joy of divine presence magnifies in revelation eleven, when Julian encounters a spiritual sight of a serene and imageless presence of Christ. Christ speaks in words full of light:

> It is I. It is I (*I it am*). I am the one who is highest. I am the one you love, I am the one you like. I am the one you serve. I am the one you long for. I am the one you desire. I am the one who is your meaning. I am the one who is all. I am the one holy church preaches and teaches. I am the one who showed myself to you before. (12.26.7–11)

In this encounter with the luminous, creative, risen presence, like the risen Christ in the gospels, Christ identifies himself intimately and tenderly: "It is I," or literally "I it am." This alludes to God's words to Moses at the burning bush (Ex 3:14). Additionally, it alludes to the "I am" passages in John where Christ distinguishes himself as I, the subject of all that is. He is the one who holds all meaning, the one who is all. Later in the revelation, the litany of "It is I" continues to reinforce how "as truly God is our Father, as truly God is our mother" (14.59.12). Christ continues: "It is I the might and goodness of fatherhood, it is I the wisdom and kindness of motherhood, it is I the light and grace that is blessed love. It is I the Trinity; it is I the unity" (14.59.13–16). In the risen Christ the qualities of father and mother unite beyond gender into a Trinitarian unity, in Christ the one who is all.

Christ reassures Julian of the sureness of his salvific presence, stressing the mutual indwelling of each person of the Trinity. He continues: "I may make all things well, and I can make all things well, and I shall make all things well, and I will make all things well, and you shall see yourself that all manner of things shall be well" (13.31.3–6). The repetition of "*well*" creates a mantra that rings from the essence of joy. In common usage, to be well is to live in good health.[32] In the context of the cross, to be well is a dynamic synthesis of all the qualities that enhance and give life.[33] To be well is to live in Christ, in suffering in love becoming joy, in the oneing love of the Trinity. In this wellness, we are undisturbed by the illusive non-being of sin, because we know our substantial and sensual souls are always being oned in Christ, who is our "I," the ground of our being.

Julian then sees how the risen Christ, as our "I," places us in the reciprocal indwelling of the Trinity. Together, the whole Trinity work in an evolutionary sense to make all things well.

> Where he says I may, I understand the Father, where he says I can, I understand the Son, where he says I will, I understand the Holy Spirit; and where he says I shall, I understand all the blessed Trinity, three persons and one truth. And where he says you shall see yourself, I understand the *oneing* of all human kind who shall be saved into the blessed Trinity. (13.31.11–12)

The strength of the power and sureness of the Trinity making all things well conveyed in the verbs may, can, will, and shall is lost in contemporary English.[34] But Julian is assured that just as the Trinity created all things from nothing, so the Trinity is faithful to its promise and will make well all that is not well, and we shall see it. The ongoing creative desire of the Trinity has the power in fulfilling its universal salvific will,[35] that all may come to rest in peace and love in the heart of Christ, in the Trinity.

The beholding of joy reaffirms for Julian that the suffering in love of the crucified Christ is not a juridical response to the accident of the fall, but rather a joy for Christ. The passion is an expression of joy because Christ, deep wisdom and mother, recreates and showers us in grace. It is a joy because Christ's loving empowers the *great oneing*. This salvific work continues now as the risen Christ, indwelling all that is as our all, is making all things well.

Living the Great Oneing

Though Julian's revelations begin with suffering and immerse the reader in the suffering of Christ, this is not a strange preoccupation with suffering. It is a model of redemption that takes the ambiguity of life seriously and shows how, through Christ entering into the wound of human suffering, humanity is drawn more fully into the oneing of the mutual indwelling of the divine in the human. Julian engages with the language of the tradition, and at the same time, trusting her own prayerful experience, draws together creative, expansive insights into the nature of divine love and the desire of the Trinity to make all things well. Julian envisages Christ's suffering as a great oneing, a kenosis of desire in which all creation participates, so intensely that there is only one suffering. In loving and thirsting for humanity, Christ does not focus on the non-being of sin, but on the presence of love drawing all into a great oneing.

As the beholding of suffering fades into the central luminous beholding of love, Julian is drawn into the intimacy of oneing in Christ's heart, where she sees room for all to rest in peace and love. This intimate enclosure infuses an awareness that Christ is also enclosed in her heart, which opens into the reciprocal closing and be-closing in the Trinity. In the final beholding of joy, all the colors of the light of the cross unite, as Julian comes to understand how the risen Christ is Christ, deep wisdom of the Trinity and our mother, who through the cross, births us into joy, bliss, and endless life. Now, crucified and risen, Christ is intimately present as I, the ground and subject of all being, who draws all into himself, and as our all, makes all things well. It is crucial for Julian that her readers, her "*even Christians*" (vi: 1–2), know this oneing. So, a study of Julian's soteriology would be incomplete without also exploring how human beings, one in creation, now participate in and live in the wellness of this great oneing through prayer.

Julian's understanding that *all shall be well* is not simply a future reality, but the great oneing that continues now in all our living. Human beings learn to see again, and become aware of our innate oneness and wellness through contemplative prayer. Although "all our living is prayer" (14.41.47), Julian says clearly: "prayer ones the soul to God" (14.43.2). She encourages us, "though you feel nothing, see nothing, and think you will not" (41:44–45), to respond to Christ's desire that we pray. She presents a way of prayer that enables all our living to be prayer because we live oned to Christ. Julian specifically identifies the prayer of *beseeking*[36] as "the gracious lasting will of the soul, *oned* and fastened into the will of our Lord by the sweet inner working of the Holy Spirit" (14.41.30–32). More passive than seeking, "beseeking" is a gentle yet responsive movement into our soul in the midst of our heart,[37] where in silence and stillness, we seek Christ our center. In beseeking we activate our *godly will* (13.37.15–17), our responsive loving that is already one with the will of Christ. Our godly will naturally responds to the pouring out of love we see on the cross.

When Julian presents her teaching on prayer at the beginning of revelation fourteen, she places all prayer in Christ, who as the subject of all that is, says: "I am the ground of your *beseeking*" (14.41.11.26; 14.42.5).[38] As the ground of our being, the ground of all suffering love and joy, and the ground of all prayer, Christ desires that we take "our place and our dwelling" (14.42.31–32) in his ground. Julian then illuminates a threefold movement of beholding that is essentially a reflection of Christ pouring out himself in love. First, Christ says, "*It is my will*" (14.42.6). This will of Christ is his loving. It is eternal and powerful. Our role in prayer is to consciously respond through "turning our will into the will of our Lord, enjoying" (14.42.7–9). Notice how this movement of turning into Christ is an act of loving that mirrors Julian's experience of turning into the wound of Christ. As we turn within, in stillness and silence, into the indwelling of Christ, we are infused in joy. "Enjoying" emphasizes the endlessness of enjoying oneness in returning to the ground of our original oneing. "The fruit and end of our prayer is to be one and like Christ in all things" (14.42.11–12). Julian's way of prayer enables us to be one, Christ-like, and to continually live in the fullness of joy in the great oneing.

Conclusion

The salvific nature of Julian's earliest and most love showing of a little thing, like a hazelnut lying in the palm of her hand (1.5.9–33), becomes clear. Although it looks like it will fall into nothing, she realizes, "what did I *behold*, truly the maker the keeper and the lover" (1.5.19). This is the salvific work of oneing, making, loving, and keeping. We are made, knit and, oned in the Trinity, loved in the creative outpouring of desire in the passion, and kept in reciprocal indwelling, evolving into the one love of the Trinity. In prayer we come to behold the reality. All is well.

NOTES

1. Edmund College O.S.A. and James Walsh S. J., *A Book of Showings to the Anchoress Julian of Norwich*. Part Two (Toronto: Pontifical Institute of Medieval Studies, 1978), *9.18.14*. Translations are my own. I have translated Julian's Middle English quite literally in order to draw out the rich theological implications that are often lost in translation. Hereafter cited by revelation, chapter and line number. The short text has the chapter in Roman numerals.
2. ii: 4–5.
3. i: 1–5. I have chosen to consistently use the Christological term Christ because Julian's crucified Lord is always Christ, crucified and risen, not Jesus of Nazareth.
4. "Experience," as I use the term in keeping with O'Collins as an aspect of immediacy; it implies direct contact and must be entered into and lived. Experience and reflection on the experience, though distinct, are not separate. See Gerard O'Collins, *Fundamental Theology* (London: Darton and Todd, 1981), 33–6. I appreciate, however, that any language that describes an experience is already in some sense an interpretation.
5. *Exidus reditus* is a Plotinian principle widely adapted into Christian theology that stresses how creation is in a circular movement from God, the One to God. Everything derives from the One and everything returns to the one. See Andrew Louth, *The Origins of the Christian Mystical Tradition* (Oxford: Clarendon Press, 1981), 38.
6. Christian Mystical literature assumes a belief that it is possible to experience a sense of presence or union with God in this life. See Bernard McGinn, *The*

Presence of God: The History of Christian Mysticism. Vol. 1 *The Foundations of Mysticism* (New York: Crossroad, 1991), xvii. Although Kevin Magill and Denys Turner do not want to keep the term mystic, see Denys Turner, *Julian of Norwich, Theologian* (New Haven: Yale University Press, 2011), 28. I use it in the sense that all human beings are mystics because, as we will see, *oneing* is essential to human nature.

7. See Elizabeth Petroff, *Medieval Women's Visionary Literature* (Oxford: Oxford University Press), 1986.
8. Nicholas Watson and Jacqueline Jenkins, eds., *The Writings of Julian of Norwich: A Vision Showed to a Devout Woman and A Revelation of Love* (University Park: Pennsylvania State University Press, 2006), ix.
9. Kerrie Hide, *Gifted Origins to Graced Fulfilment: The Soteriology of Julian of Norwich* (Collegeville, MN: Liturgical Press, 2001), 23–26. Maggie Ross, *Writing the Icon of the Heart: In Silence Beholding* (Abingdon: Bible Reading Fellowship, 2011, p. 1), affirms this way of interpretation when she says that we need to recover the lost word "behold" and restore it to its central place in Judeo-Christian textual tradition.
10. Citations from the Long Text include revelation number, chapter and line numbers. This citation (1.37–40) is in the introduction, before the revelations begin. The Short Text is in the traditional lower case, e.g. (ii: 25–28).
11. This is not a progression from imaginative to contemplative prayer. For Julian the "bodily sight of Christ is always important." See Julia A. Lamm, "Revelation as Exposure in Julian of Norwich's *Showings*" *Spiritus A Journal of Christian Spirituality*, Vol. 5 (2005), 56–57.
12. I use this term in the manner of Raimon Pannikar, *Christophany The Fullness of Man* (Maryknoll, NY: Orbis Books, 2010), 27–35, who stresses how "Christophany" holds the dynamism of seeking Christ in ourself by emptying ourself of our self, going out of ourself to enter into Christ, discovering the Christ as thou, to seeking Christ in ourself as our deepest thou, to discovering Christ in ourself as I.
13. Julian uses the word "ground" repeatedly, e.g.: Christ is the ground of all our whole life in love (39.44), our steadfast ground (14.49.54), the ground in whom our soul stands (14.56.12). Christ wants our understanding to be grounded in him (14.42.30). This sense of Christ as the ground of human nature is crucial for Julian's soteriology.
14. When I first explored a soteriology of oneing in the 1990s, as far as I knew, oneing was not part of spiritual vocabulary. It was always translated as union, so I needed to argue a case for adopting the term. Now, thanks to the journal of Richard Rohr called *Oneing*, the term has become part of contemporary spiritual vocabulary. See Hide, *Gifted Origins*, 52–54.
15. *The New Shorter Oxford English Dictionary on Historical Principles*, ed. Lesley Brown, Vols. 1 and 2 (Oxford: Clarendon Press, 1993), 1998. (Hereafter cited as NSOED.)
16. 14.55.26–27.

17. 14.53.59–64.
18. Brant Pelphrey, *Love Was His Meaning: The Theology and Mysticism of Julian of Norwich* (Salzburg: Institut fur Anglistik und Amerikaristik), 132–134. Pelphrey points out that the atonement has connotations of separation, subsequent reconciliation, and the mending of division which Julian does not develop.
19. This self-emptying we will see is not a diminishment of Christ but a *oneing*. See Turner, *Julian of Norwich, Theologian*, 252n10, who stresses how in classical Christologies in the medieval period self-emptying does not imply a diminishment in Christ or humanity. In the Philippians hymn the divine in the human is no less than is the divine in the Trinitarian source of *kenosis*.
20. NSOED, 499.
21. This sense of the being of God as distinguished from the non-being of sin occurs in Augustine. *The Confessions of St. Augustine*, translated by F. J. Sheed (London: Sheed and Ward, 1949), 3.7.12; 7.12.18.
22. Hans Kurath, Sherman Kuhn, and Robert Lewis, eds., *Middle English Dictionary* (Ann Arbor: University of Michigan Press, 1954–), 844.
23. I use this term in the sense of the ongoing creation of life in Christ.
24. Julian describes here the grace of becoming single focused in beholding. Though she does not give details, there is a sense of turning into Christ as she advises in prayer. Her conscious mind becomes still so that the deep understanding of the knowing of her soul in the midst of her heart awakens beyond conscious control. Her beholding is informed by the oneness she experiences with Christ.
25. This beholding that draws Julian into the heart of Christ resonates with the earlier iconography of the sacred heart familiar in mystical literature, such as Gertrude of Helfta (1256–1302), and expressed in the more contemporary theology of Teilhard de Chardin (1881–1955).
26. Traditionally "*beclose*" is to close, to shut what is open, enclose, confine, enwrap. n.m.wiktionary.org.
27. *Middle English Dictionary* online, quod.lib.umich.edu. "*Bliss*" includes a happy condition of existence, well-being, prosperity, good fortune, as well as the splendor and majesty of God and the beatitude of the blessing of heaven.
28. See for example *The Letters of Clare of Assisi* (1194–12–53), where Clare adopts the language of an economic exchange and envisages Christ's suffering as the great exchange of love.
29. See chapter 8 of this book.
30. It is not clear whether Julian knew of Anselm's writings, but this terminology was naturally in the language of Julian's day. See Joan Nuth, "Two Medieval Soteriologies: Anselm of Canterbury and Julian of Norwich," *Theological Studies* 53 (1992), 611–45.
31. See my discussion of this in *Gifted Origins*, 111–12, that explores why peace is a more accurate translation than satisfied because it has connotations of Anselm's theology of redemption.
32. NSOED, 3654.

33. Hide, *Gifted Origins*, 184.
34. NSOED, 325, 1721, 2808, 3686.
35. There are hints of *apokatasis* or universal salvation in Julian, but she also wants to align herself with Holy Church so she never discounts the possibility of damnation for sinners and she considers the fiend to be eternally damned. See Hide, *Gifted Origins*, n.8, 185.
36. Julian's way of "beseeking" is not petitionary prayer. See Patricia Clinkskel Wait, *Meeting God: An Interpretation of 'Wound' In the Mystical Writings of Julian of Norwich and John of the Cross* (PhD dissertation, Melbourne College of Divinity, 2013), 117–20. "*Beseeking*" is a deep contemplative *kenosis* of seeking oneness with the desire of Christ, the ground of all prayer.
37. This is how Julian describes her inner life in God, as we saw in the indwelling of Christ (16.6815–16).
38. Though it is unclear whether Julian knew of Eckhart's *grunt*, however, her use of "ground" resonates with Eckhart in *Die Deutchen Werke* 90; 113–114. "In the inner most intellect God's ground is my ground and my ground is God's ground. After all the knower and the known are one in knowledge." See Kelly, *Meister Eckhart on Divine Knowledge* (Berkeley: North Atlantic Books, 2009), 26.

PART III

Reformation and Catholic Counter-Reformation

11

Theologies of Salvation in the Reformation and Counter-Reformation

An Introduction

FRANK A. JAMES III

The Context of Salvation

Theology can be a dangerous occupation. Theological discussions are all too often enveloped in an ambiance of debate and contention. What might begin as friendly dialogue can quickly degenerate into sordid name-calling, as in the case of the medieval Thomist who buttressed his theological arguments by adding that his opponent was a "boorish dog, an infernal worm, a delirious wasp and a dung-eating pig."[1] In extreme circumstances, soteriological differences can result in persecution or even death. Among the theological loci, soteriology (the study of salvation) is among the most dangerous of all. To take a stance on the meaning of salvation is especially serious business because it touches the most vital religious nerve—where one spends eternity. To err on this topic may very well entail condemnation to eternal hellfire and damnation.

Salvation and Other Biblical Metaphors

Salvation is not merely a theological construct, but is indeed a biblical term. From an Old Testament perspective, it most often has the connotation of rescue from adverse circumstances such as oppression, destruction, or captivity. Drawing on this OT theme, New Testament writers extend the notion of salvation beyond its historical referent, by granting it substantive theological significance. The Synoptic gospels represent the ministry of Jesus in salvific terms: "The Son of Man came to seek and to save the lost."[2] The idea of salvation is specifically bound up with Jesus and the "forgiveness of sins."[3]

The salvific mission of Jesus is manifested through a variety of New Testament metaphors—justification, reconciliation, regeneration, and redemption. Each of these NT metaphors focuses more narrowly on some aspect of the broader concept of salvation.[4] But in the sixteenth-century reformation, the metaphor of justification became the primary expression of salvation.

Late Medieval Soteriologies

The language of salvation belonged to the vocabulary of the early church fathers (they less frequently refer to justification), but it was not until Augustine's conflict with Pelagius that soteriology received focused attention. Over time, the medieval church specifically linked salvation with the sacraments. Baptism was the first plank of salvation, which removed the guilt (*culpa*) of original sin but not sinful proclivities. Sins committed after baptism placed the individual in jeopardy of eternal punishment. But there is a second plank of salvation, the sacrament of penance. The sinner must be contrite, confess to a priest, and perform satisfactory acts of penance commensurate with the gravity of the sin in order to receive absolution. This two-plank salvation scheme means that salvation is both an event and a constant process that is only as effective as one's last penance. Should the sinner die without completing the full satisfactory penance for all sins, there remains the punishment of a fiery purgatory which endures for as long as it takes to complete the penance due for sins.[5] In this understanding, salvation was intimately tied to a highly developed ecclesiology. Consequently, it became the practical dogma that there was no salvation outside the institutional church (*extra ecclesiam nulla salus*).

Protestantism: Salvation from Anfectungen

There is little doubt that Luther's conception of salvation emerged from his own battles with *Anfectungen*—the relentless search for forgiveness and peace with God. At the heart of his inner turmoil was the terror that God was going to judge and condemn him. Luther describes this intense spiritual struggle with God, which the monks called "the bath of Satan."

Though I lived as a monk without reproach, I felt like I was a sinner before God with an extremely disturbed conscience . . . I did not love, yes, I hated the righteous God who punishes sinners, and secretly, if not blasphemously, certainly murmuring greatly, I was angry with God. I said to myself: "it is not enough that miserable sinners, eternally lost through original sin, are crushed . . . by the law of the decalogue, without having God add pain to pain . . . by the gospel threatening us with his righteousness and wrath!" Thus I raged with a fierce and troubled conscience.[6]

It is one of the intriguing twists of history that these spiritual travails of an obscure university professor morphed into an ecclesiastical fissure that changed the course of Western civilization. Luther's spiritual desperation was so crippling that he could find no respite apart from a new understanding of salvation. He acknowledged: "I did not learn my theology all at once, but I had to search deeper for it, where my *Anfectungen* took me . . . [It is] not understanding, reading or speculation, but . . . dying and being damned [that] make a theologian."[7]

Luther found salvation in his doctrine of justification which in turn became the centerpiece of his Protestant movement. For him, this discovery represented a fundamental recovery of the true meaning of the Christian gospel. Justification was, as Luther famously stated, the article by which the church stands or falls (*articulus stantis et candentis ecclesiae*). This doctrine became the soteriological fulcrum to which every other teaching was subservient. He once said that he would kiss the feet of the Pope, if only the Holy Father would embrace justification by faith alone.[8]

Luther's doctrine of justification cannot be fully grasped until one understands something of the medieval soteriology that gave rise to his *Anfectungen*. It is important to note that a moderate Augustinianism had been the prevailing soteriological inclination in the medieval church at least since the Second Council of Orange in AD 529. The Augustinian legacy continued in the following centuries through such Augustinian stalwarts as Gottschalk of Orbais, Thomas Bradwardine, and Gregory of Rimini. The later writings of Aquinas also must be included in this Augustinian stream.[9]

Luther, however, was trained in the nominalist school of thought, which was quite far removed from the Augustinian soteriological stream. Indeed, nominalism inclined toward a Pelagian soteriology. As the young Luther was taught, the sinner must take the initial step toward God no matter how paltry the effort (*facere quod in se est*). In response, God would bestow justifying grace, thus enabling the performance of meritorious works by which the sinner is justified. It was this first trifling step in the nominalist process of justification that prompted Luther's *Anfectungen*. He could not conceive how a sinful human could take that first step without God's grace.

As he was grappling with *Anfectungen*, Luther discovered in Augustine a new soteriological vision of divine grace. Fortified with a renewed Augustinianism, he turned to an intensive study of the Apostle Paul, which led to his own distinctive doctrine of justification, unprecedented in the history of the Christian church. By 1519, he came to understand that the righteousness of God (*iustitia Dei*) does not refer to divine judgment but to a divine act of grace toward the hapless sinner. As he developed his understanding, distinctive features emerged. Perhaps his most distinctive idea was the concept of *iustitia Christi aliena* (the alien righteousness of Christ). Luther argued that justification is not based on one's own righteousness but upon a righteousness that is alien or extrinsic to the sinner. He insisted that, because of the fall, individuals have no righteousness in themselves and therefore, if one is to be justified, it must be based entirely on an external righteousness, by which he meant the perfect righteousness of Christ. This perfect righteousness of Christ belongs to the Christian (in an external not internal sense) because of his/her union with Christ. There is for Luther a "wonderful exchange" that takes place in this union between the Christian and Christ: Individual sins are exchanged for the righteousness of Christ.

This wonderful exchange takes place by faith. This faith is not viewed as a human work and as such cannot be considered as the cause of justification; rather, faith is understood as the instrument by which one is justified. Above all, Luther's assertion that justification is by faith *alone* (*sola fide*) and the notion of the alien righteousness of Christ underscore that justification has everything to do with God's grace and nothing to do with human merit.

Many fail to appreciate that Luther envisioned justification as both an event and a process. What later Protestants were inclined to separate, Luther kept together, at least initially. He was quite clear that there is a moment when the sinner is actually justified by faith, that is, when the alien righteousness of Christ has been transferred to the sinner. But this is only the beginning of a process in which the Christian makes moral progress until the final resurrection when he will possess a perfect righteousness created in him by the Holy Spirit. Especially in his early writings, justification is often conceived as a healing process in which God regards the sinner as totally righteous in anticipation of the perfect righteousness to come at the final consummation. At points, the relationship between justification and sanctification is so closely drawn that Luther does not hesitate to use the rubric of justification to include the process of sanctification as well as the event of justification.[10]

One of the important historiographical insights garnered from an historical analysis is the fact that the Protestant doctrine of justification was not static, but went through a process of theological development. To be sure, Luther set the course that others would follow, but a proper understanding of this period must recognize that Luther's initial insights provoked decades of Protestant refinement from both Lutheran and Reformed theologians.

In the 1530s, Luther's close friend and colleague at the University of Wittenberg, Philip Melanchthon, made a fundamental refinement to Luther's doctrine (initially in his *Apology*, 1530) which then became normative for both Lutheran and Reformed branches of Protestantism. Instead of viewing justification as a process of "healing" as Luther earlier had maintained, Melanchthon recast justification in a forensic framework. Whereas Augustine and the medieval church taught that the sinner is *made* righteous in justification, Melanchthon taught that he is *declared* or *pronounced* righteous on the basis of the imputed righteousness of Christ. Melanchthon drew a sharp distinction between justification (the event of being declared righteous) and sanctification (the process of being made righteous). This refinement of Luther's doctrine represents a further break from the teaching of the church up to this point. This forensic conception of justification was taken up by virtually all subsequent Protestant reformers and came to represent a standard difference between Catholics and Protestants.

Luther did not inaugurate a single reformation; he actually prompted a number of interrelated but distinctive reformations throughout Europe. Despite theological variations, historians have typically identified two branches of Protestantism: Lutheran and Reformed. The reformation movement that looked to Luther naturally took his name and most of his ideas. The Reformed branch, however, did not look to a single leader, but rather to a coterie of theologians whose theological perspectives had a general coherence. The initial impetus for this branch came from the Zurich pastor, Ulrich Zwingli, but the definitive expression of the Reformed branch centered on the collaboration of Martin Bucer, Heinrich Bullinger, John Calvin, and Peter Martyr Vermigli. Richard Muller designates them as the "codifiers" of Reformed theology.[11]

These Reformed "codifiers" were largely second generation Protestants. They hailed Luther as a modern-day Apostle and yet they could not fully embrace his soteriology. These second-generation reformers had the opportunity to process Luther's doctrine of justification and in doing so they realized they had to make refinements before they could make it their own. Both the Catholics and the Anabaptists had raised the specter of antinomianism—that a forensic doctrine of justification minimized the role of good works. At times Luther's rhetoric supplied ample ammunition, but a careful reading demonstrates that he fully affirms good works, not as the cause of justification but as the natural consequence.

Although the Reformed theologians were in basic agreement with Lutherans on the matter of justification, they did not give it the same prominence in their soteriology. Moreover, Reformed thinkers tended to configure the doctrine in substantially different ways. The later Luther and confessional Lutheranism tended to stress the distinction between justification and sanctification, while Reformed tended to stress the positive connection between the justified and a moral life.[12] Zwingli, Calvin, Bucer, Bullinger, and Vermigli all envisaged a close relationship between sanctification and justification.[13]

Vermigli's three-tiered conception is one of the more intriguing Reformed articulations of justification.[14] He clearly affirms a forensic justification, but also includes internal moral renewal (regeneration) and good deeds (sanctification), all under the general rubric of justification.[15] What is clear is that Vermigli does indeed include a transformational element in his understanding of justification. For him, the proper understanding of justification is one that includes both the act and its consequences. Vermigli's soteriology was very much shaped by his Augustinian understanding of original sin. Because sin was not only a legal violation but a moral infraction as well, he invests justification with the comprehensiveness equal to the magnitude of original sin.

The version of justification that eventually gained ascendancy in the Reformed branch was that of Calvin. He revived Luther's emphasis on the believer's union with Christ (*insitio in Christum*) through faith as the means by which that union is achieved. This union has a twofold effect, which Calvin called "double grace." The first effect of the believer's union with Christ leads directly to forensic justification. Through the imputed righteousness of Christ, the believer is declared to be righteous in the sight of God. But there is a second simultaneous effect of this union, namely, that because of the union with Christ—and not because of his justification—the believer begins the process of being made like Christ through sanctification (or, as he sometimes calls it, regeneration). Instead of giving priority to either sanctification or justification, Calvin turned his attention to their common source, union with Christ, which granted them equal standing, distinct, but not separate. For Calvin, where there is justification there also will be sanctification.

In light of these various Protestant configurations of justification, one would be hard pressed to conclude that there was a single uniform Protestant doctrine of justification.[16] Add to this the variety of soteriological perspectives among Anabaptists and the doctrinal diversity is even more pronounced.

Catholic Counter-Reformation: Salvation as Sacramental Process

If Protestants could not come to a consensus on justification, there was little prospect that Catholics would. The Council of Trent was summoned in 1545 in order to formulate a comprehensive response to Luther, especially his doctrine of justification. The sixth session of Trent reached its definitive conclusions regarding justification on January 13, 1547. Against Luther, Trent strongly defended the traditional view that justification is the process of renewal that brings about a change in both the outer status and the inner nature of the sinner. For the theologians at Trent, justification was not only "forgiveness of sins" but also "regeneration and sanctification" through the voluntary reception of grace. They strenuously argued that sinners were justified on the basis of an internal righteousness graciously infused or imparted to the sinner by God.

There was one remarkable effort at Trent for a more moderate stance. The Vicar-General of the Augustinian Hermits, Girolamo Seripando, put forward a doctrine of "double justification" for consideration. Such an idea was first proposed at the Colloquy of Regensburg in 1541, where Catholic theologians led by Cardinal Contarini met with Protestants led by Melanchthon and supported by Martin Bucer and John Calvin. The doctrine of double justification asserted that there were two causes of justification: the external righteousness of Christ (the Protestant view) and an internal righteousness of the sanctified believer (the Catholic view). Remarkably, Protestants and Catholics reached agreement.[17] However, neither the Pope nor Luther accepted this configuration of the doctrine and when it was revived at Trent, the same response was given.

Perhaps the key to understanding the reaction of Trent is their fear that Luther's view of justification would lead inevitably to antinomianism. Justification by faith alone inevitably conjured up the prospect that one could be justified without any need for obedience, good works, or spiritual renewal. To these theologians, Luther's concept of justification undermined all morality. For Trent, Luther's view on justification was so vile that it incurred a curse: "If anyone says that the sinner is justified by faith alone . . . let him be anathema."[18] By the final session at Trent, the doctrinal battle lines had been drawn.

Concluding Thoughts on Sixteenth-Century Theologies of Salvation

It will not be possible to properly understand the development of the Reformation doctrine of justification without recognizing that it was articulated in a period of intensive theological transition. Sixteenth-century Protestant theologians were pioneers who were in the process of casting off traditional medieval theological notions and braving the new world of Protestant theological exegesis. In the midst of this dynamic intellectual ferment, the Protestant doctrine of justification remained unusually dynamic. To be sure, Luther set the course that others would follow, but a proper understanding of this period must recognize that Luther's initial insights provoked opposition from Catholics and decades of Protestant refinement from both Lutheran and Reformed theologians.

Despite the soteriological diversity among Protestants, they shared the unifying conviction that salvation was by grace, not works. They were united in their belief that the ground of justification rested exclusively on the righteousness of Christ. That was non-negotiable. Protestants also shared a fundamental theological presupposition, namely, an intensive Augustinian anthropology. As far as Protestants were concerned, one of the basic errors of Roman Catholic conceptions of justification was the failure to view original sin with the seriousness it deserved. In the final analysis, Protestants believed the only way to avoid *Anfectungen* was to embrace justification by faith alone.

NOTES

1. Denis Janz, "Late Medieval Theology" in *The Cambridge Companion to Reformation Theology*, edited by David Bagchi and David C. Steinmetz (Cambridge, UK: Cambridge University Press, 2004), 5–6.
2. Luke 19:10.
3. Luke 7:48.
4. There is also an eschatological dimension to the NT conception of salvation in which a tension exists between the already completed deliverance through faith in Christ in the present, but which has not yet been fully implemented and will not be fully implemented until Christ returns.
5. Hans J. Hillerbrand, ed., *Oxford Encyclopedia of the Reformation*, (Oxford: Oxford University Press, 1996), III: 242.
6. *Luther's Works* (St. Louis: Concordia, 1955–), vol. 34, 336–337 (hereafter cited as *LW*). *Weimarer Ausgabe* (Weimar: H. Böhlhaus Nachfolger, 1883–), 54, 185 (hereafter cited as *WA* followed by volume and page). Cf. Bernhard Lohse, *Luther's Theology: Its Historical and Systematic Development* (Minneapolis: Fortress Press, 1999), 90–91.
7. WA *Tischreden* (= TR), I: 146; WA 5, 163. Cf. Timothy George, *Theology of the Reformers* (Nashville: Broadman and Holman, 1988), 60–61.
8. Alister E. McGrath, *Iustitia Dei: A History of the Christian Doctrine of Justification* (Cambridge: Cambridge University Press, 2005), 2: 10. The key text is *WA*, 56: 502–503.
9. See *Aquinas the Augustinian*, ed. Michael Dauphinais, Barry David, and Matthew Levering (Washington, DC: Catholic University Press, 2007).
10. G. W. Bromiley, "The Doctrine of Justification in Luther," *Evangelical Quarterly* 24 (1952), 95, writes:

    As he [Luther] saw it, the divine gift of righteousness is at one and the same time both justification and regeneration, and the one term justification may quite well be used to cover what are essentially two aspects of the one thing.... Righteousness is imputed when the sinner believes. But also when the sinner believes the righteousness of Christ is inwardly received in regen-

eration, initiating and indeed involving the development of holiness which is the very essence of the Christian life.
11. Richard Muller, *Post-Reformation Reformed Dogmatics*, vol. 1, *Prolegomena to Theology* (Grand Rapids: Baker Book House, 1987), I. 28–40.
12. McGrath, *Iustitia Dei*, 2: 32–39, characterizes early Reformed views as "moralistic."
13. Alister E. McGrath, "Justification," in *Oxford Encyclopedia of the Reformation*, ed. Hans Hillerbrand (Oxford: Oxford University Press, 1996), 2: 365. See also W. P. Stephens, *The Holy Spirit in the Theology of Martin Bucer* (Cambridge: Cambridge University Press, 1970), 52–53, and W. P. Stephens, *The Theology of Huldrych Zwingli* (Oxford: Oxford University Press, 1988), 159–163.
14. Peter Martyr Vermigli, *In Epistolam S. Pauli ad Romanos commentarii doctissimi* . . . (Basel: P. Perna, 1558), 86–87. Vermigli's own distinctive juxtaposition of justification, regeneration, and sanctification especially resonates with Martin Bucer, with whom Vermigli spent his first five years as a Protestant.
15. Vermigli, *Romanos*, 539.
16. Muller, *Post-Reformation Reformed Dogmatics*, vol. 1, 28, states that the early period of Reformed theology (1523–1563) "defies harmonization of its various theologies into a single analysis of doctrine." Cf. McGrath, *Iustitia Dei*, 2: 32–39.
17. A. N. S. Lane, *Justification by Faith in Catholic-Protestant Dialogue: An Evangelical Assessment* (Edinburgh: T. & T. Clark, 2002). Cf. Bruce L. McCormack, ed., *Justification in Perspective: Historical Developments and Contemporary Challenges* (Grand Rapids, MI: Baker, 2006).
18. H. J. Schroeder, O. P., ed., *The Canons and Decrees of the Council of Trent* (Rockford, IL: Tan Books, 1978), 43.

12

Martin Luther

CARL R. TRUEMAN

Born in Eisleben, Germany, Martin Luther (1483–1546) was baptized on the feast day of St. Martin of Tours, for whom he was named. From 1501 to 1505, Luther attended the University of Erfurt, where he earned Bachelor and Master of Arts degrees. At his father's urging, he embarked on the study of law, but soon left and joined the mendicant order of Augustinian Hermits. He took final vows shortly afterward, and in 1507 was ordained a priest. Luther was intellectually gifted, but a keen awareness of his own sinfulness left him frequently melancholy and fearful of God's wrath. His superior, Johannes von Staupitz, a significant theologian in his own right, ordered Luther to undertake advanced study in theology, in part to take his mind off his spiritual struggles. In 1512, Luther received a doctorate in theology and assumed the chair in Bible at the University of Wittenberg. Lecturing intensively on Scripture, he soon developed a deeply Augustinian but in some ways radically new understanding of sin, grace, and faith. In 1517, he protested the plenary indulgence that was being proffered for the building of a new St. Peter's basilica in Rome. The ensuing controversy—the so-called Luther affair—soon embroiled much of Christendom in heated dispute. Luther was brought before the Diet of Worms (an Imperial Congress under the leadership of the new Holy Roman Emperor, Charles V) and condemned in 1521. Afterward, however, the princes of Electoral Saxony protected him from extradition, and Luther lived out his life preaching and teaching in Wittenberg, even serving as dean of the faculty there. In 1525, he married Katharina von Bora, and their happy home, into which six children were born, instantly epitomized the emerging Protestant parsonage. Luther personally taught much of the first generation of Lutheran ministers, shaping their outlook decisively on such matters as biblical authority, the right of clerical marriage, the real presence of Christ in the sacrament of Holy

Communion, and much more. His Smaller and Larger catechisms have been used to teach the Christian faith among Lutherans down to the present. In 1534, the "Luther Bible" brought the Scriptures into middle-high German; it remains a classic. Luther also commented or preached on most of the Bible. The still incomplete critical edition of his works comprises well over 100 massive volumes, including letters and "table talks," and it continues to fuel the endeavors of a small army of scholars.

Introduction

Martin Luther is the single most important figure for Protestant theologies of salvation. Although not all Protestants are Lutherans, his understanding of justification by grace through faith and its implications was foundational for how later Protestants of all confessional varieties understood such matters as sacraments and church authority. Whether such agreed with Luther or not, all defined themselves to a significant degree in relation to him. His understanding of justification, of the Word, and of the sacraments basically established the framework for later discussions of these matters, both Lutheran and Reformed; and the broad contours of his soteriology still define the nature of the most basic differences between Roman Catholics and Protestants.[1]

Because Luther was an occasional theologian who addressed issues as he had to confront them in his roles as professor, pastor, and church statesman, and because he had a long and dramatic career, it is not an easy task to reconstruct his understanding of salvation. The student of Luther is always faced with the twin problems of over-systematizing his thought in a way that fails to do justice to development over time or of failing to give due weight to areas of consistency within his writings. Therefore, a sketch of the most significant points in Luther's thought will be illuminating, while leaving room for further study.[2]

Medieval Background

Much of the most fruitful scholarly work on Luther since the 1950s has addressed his relationship to the medieval background. Central to this is the role of nominalism and the *via moderna* (modern way), the intellectual traditions within which the young Luther himself studied. While these terms cover intellectual movements that embraced a variety of perspectives, the crucial point for understanding Luther is the way in which they weakened the overall sacramental and substantial emphases in medieval theology. Put simply, the kind of theology articulated by Thomas Aquinas placed great emphasis upon the vital necessity of the sacraments, especially the Mass, in effecting a gracious transformation of the recipient into someone who was in a state of grace. From the late thirteenth century onward, however, an emphasis upon the will of God among certain thinkers weakened confidence in human reason and, as a collateral result, weakened the need for the sacraments. Luther, who was deeply rooted in this late medieval voluntarism and profoundly influenced by the writing of Gabriel Biel (ca. 1420–95), came increasingly to accent the divine will as determinative of reality. This was an epistemological point: What it did was to make God's actions unpredictable from a human perspective (he *could* do anything he wished) and thus focused attention on what he had chosen to do (as made manifest in his revelation).[3]

The most significant aspect of this for understanding Luther is the development of the *pactum* idea. One of the perennial problems of theology is how the finite can be connected to the infinite. In the realm of salvation, the question is acute: How can finite human beings merit eternal life or even God's good pleasure here on earth, given the finite and indeed sinful nature of their works? Biel's solution was to argue that for the individual Christian to achieve an initial state of grace whereby the sacraments could be taken with benefit, God has established a pactum between himself and human beings whereby God would not deny grace to the one who "did what was in him," i.e., did his best.[4] This had a twofold impact. First, it dramatically attenuated the necessary link between the sacraments and coming to be in a state of grace. One could attain the state of grace, one could do what was in one, without the use of the sacraments. Second, it rooted being in a state of grace not in anything intrinsic in the individual Christian but in the extrinsic determination of God himself. This latter point clearly provides the conceptual foundation for Luther's later understanding of justification by grace through faith. Spiritual realities are determined by what God decides that they are, not so much by what they intrinsically are. This is critical because it opens the way for understanding justification to depend upon extrinsic declaration by God.

The Crucial Period of 1514–1520

While scholars debate what Luther's "Reformation breakthrough" was, when it occurred, and even whether it occurred at all, it is clear that the years 1514–1520 are critical in the development of what would be his mature theology of salvation. During this period, Luther struggled with the deeply personal and existential question of how he, a sinner, could stand before a righteous God. The agonies of this struggle, known by the German term *Anfechtungen*, would torment him for his entire life, though they found resolution in his transformed understanding of the gospel and the Christian life. During this crucial period, a number of themes emerge in his writings.

Baptism

First, his understanding of baptism undergoes a significant shift, indicating a profound change in his understanding of the problem faced by fallen human beings. Luther had been taught by his medieval masters that indwelling sin was a *fomes*, a piece of tinder, which was extinguished by baptism. Lecturing on Paul, as his career as a university professor required him to do, led him to change his opinion on this. He came to see sin as involving the status of death and thus baptism as not being a washing or dampening process but rather as involving death and resurrection. The dead person does not need to be washed but to be resurrected. Thus, the signification of baptism is that of dying and rising: "The significance of baptism is a blessed dying unto sin and a resurrection in the grace of God, so that the old man, conceived and born in sin, is there drowned, and a new man, born in grace, comes forth and rises."[5]

It is worth noting that this shift was not simply an intensification of the idea that Luther had been taught but was fundamentally discontinuous with it. Weakness is an attribute of something else, a corruption of substance. Death is a status. One can be a little bit weak, or slightly injured. One is either dead or alive. This comports with the linguistic philosophy Luther inherited from Biel, which deals with reality in terms of extrinsic declaration (status) rather than intrinsic quality (substance). Yet, even as it was consistent with Biel it raised the stakes considerably because it had obvious implications for the moral ability of human beings. Human beings could only operate within the extrinsic status that they possessed.

Humility

This led to the second important development. Flowing from his conviction that human beings were *dead* in trespasses and sins, Luther came to identify the "doing what is in him" of the pactum with the individual's total despair of being able to do anything to merit salvation. In other words, the condition of the pactum is humility, the acknowledgment that grace and salvation must come from outside, from God. Only as the individual casts himself upon God's mercy are the conditions of the pactum met, and the positive aspects of salvation must therefore be fulfilled by a declaration of God. This is clear from the Heidelberg Disputation of April 1518. Theses 16 to 18 make essentially this point:

16. The person who believes that he can obtain grace by doing what is in him adds sin to sin so that he becomes doubly guilty.
17. Nor does speaking in this manner give cause for despair, but for arousing the desire to humble oneself and seek the grace of Christ.
18. It is certain that man must utterly despair of his own ability before he is prepared to receive the grace of Christ.[6]

Thus, humility—despair of one's own righteousness—is the precondition to receiving grace. This is not quite justification by faith but represents a decisive break with the anthropology (and thus soteriology) of the late medieval school of Biel.

Scholars debate at which point humility morphs into faith in Luther's thinking. It is probably some time between the Romans lectures of 1515–1516 and the *Freedom of the Christian Man* of 1520. This is one of the reasons why seeking the breakthrough moment in his thought is so problematic. Luther's Reformation theology is the result of a complex of related theological shifts, all of which are necessary for the later mature doctrine of justification. The famous "Autobiographical Fragment" of 1545 purports to recount events circa 1519 where Luther makes this transformative discovery about the exegesis of Romans 1:17, but, strange as it may sound, it is clear to scholars of Luther that it did not really happen that way. The chronology of the passage is confused and, even if Luther did have a deep existential experience with regard to his reading of Romans 1:17, that "breakthrough" was only one part of the larger network of theological shifts and revisions that took place as part of his Reformation discovery.

In fact, Luther's later understanding of faith perhaps subsumes and expands the earlier notion of humility: Faith involves both abandonment of any pretentions to meriting God's favor and the embrace of God's word of salvation in Christ. It is arguable that Luther's ongoing development underlies his famous protest of October 31, 1517, against the sale of indulgences, with its emphasis on repentance as something that embraces the whole of the Christian life. Nevertheless, the *Ninety Five Theses Against Indulgences* is not a particularly Protestant tract by the standards of even 1520. It is rather the work of a mind undergoing rapid theological transformation.[7]

A better candidate for the moment at which we see the public emergence of the foundations of his later theology is the disputation at Heidelberg in April 1518. Here, at a regular chapter meeting of the Augustinian Order, Luther prepared a series of theses for debate on theological and philosophical topics. The emerging contrast in Luther's thinking between the Law (commands) and the Gospel (promises) is evident; free will (meaning humanity's unaided ability to perform works of merit before God) is denied. This is clearly continuous with what will be Luther's mature Reformation theology. The Law commands and is set forth both to reveal God's holiness and to reveal the moral impotence and indeed depravity of fallen human beings. Once broken by the Law, the Gospel brings the promise of Christ. All that is needed is belief in that promise to receive salvation.[8]

Toward the end of the Heidelberg Disputation, and immediately after the radical revision of the pactum theology noted above, Luther draws a famous contrast between theologians of glory and theologians of the cross:

19. That person does not deserve to be called a theologian who looks upon the invisible things of God as though they were clearly perceptible in those things which have actually happened [Rom. 1:20].

20. He deserves to be called a theologian, however, who comprehends the visible and manifest things of God seen through suffering and the cross.
21. A theologian of glory calls evil good and good evil. A theologian of the cross calls the thing what it actually is.
22. That wisdom which sees the invisible things of God in works as perceived by man is completely puffed up, blinded, and hardened.[9]

What Luther is articulating here is building upon the theology of the cross articulated by Paul in 1 Corinthians. There are two basic ways of understanding the cross: through the lens of human reason, or through the lens of divine revelation. As with his background in the *via moderna*, Luther places a high premium on God's revelation of how he acts as opposed to human speculation as to how he might act. The distinction between the two kinds of theologian rests in large part upon the linguistic approach Luther learned from Biel. Reality is what God declares it to be, not what it intrinsically is or empirically appears to be. God's revelation is the key to knowing reality, not human reason.[10]

At Heidelberg, however, he combines this revelational emphasis with his renewed Augustinian understanding of sin. The nature of human knowledge and the power of human sin come together. The epistemologies of glory and of the cross are not simply matters of incorrect and correct analysis; they reflect fundamentally opposed moral standpoints. Theologians of glory think in a particular way in order to make themselves the measure of God. Theologians of the cross despair of their own ability to know God on the basis of their own autonomous reason and look rather to where and how he has revealed himself: in the incarnate Christ, broken and hanging on the cross at Calvary. It is only in that weak, broken flesh that Luther believed one could find a God who was truly gracious and merciful. Outside of that God was the hidden God of wrath and righteousness.[11]

This moral and epistemological revolution turns theological vocabulary on its head. The theologian of glory thinks of God's power as analogous to the power of the world: raw, coercive, irresistible. That is the result of his basic theological assumption: God is made in man's image and can thus be understood in terms of the natural order of things. But the theologian of the cross understands God in terms of how God has revealed himself to be. On the cross, God reveals that his power is of a different order: revealed in weakness, hidden to the eyes of all but those of faith. Luther has taken the late medieval epistemological insight into the priority of revelation and made it also a moral issue. True knowledge of God is only available to the eyes of faith.

This revolution in theological vocabulary is epitomized in the final theological article of the *Heidelberg Disputation*: "The love of God does not find but creates that which is pleasing to it. The love of man comes into being through that which is pleasing to it."[12] There is a sense in which this single statement contains the fundamental principles of Luther's theology in miniature. Here the inversions of the cross come to the fore. Human love is reactive: I see an attractive object and I am thus drawn to love it. We might perhaps say that human love is thus empirical: It is motivated by intrinsic qualities, real or imagined, which it perceives to exist in another. Divine love, however, is creative: God does not see something attractive and then love it; he loves something in itself unattractive and thus makes it lovely. This captures the essence both of electing love and of justification by grace through faith. Both root divine action in divine sovereignty and priority, undergirded by Luther's powerful sense of human beings as dead, and thus spiritually unresponsive and unattractive.[13]

At the same time as Luther was elaborating the theology of the *Heidelberg Disputation*, he was also teasing out its broader implications for the Christian life. Bringing the anti-sacramental tendencies of Biel and company to their logical conclusion, Luther rooted justification in despairing of self and placing trust in Christ. This oriented the church away from the primacy of the sacraments to the primacy of the Word read and preached. It was in the speech of God, in his verbal declarations, that one found reality. God's work was a creative power, constitutive of what was actual and real.

Now, even as a Reformer, Luther retained a high view of the sacraments. On baptism he considered the Roman error to be that of trivialization: Rome relegated baptism to the chronological start of the Christian life and, when its salutary effects wear off, the believer needs to move on to the other sacraments.[14] Luther was certainly highly sacramental in many ways, and considered his baptism to be the moment he became a Christian. Later in life, when tempted by the devil, he used his baptism as proof that he belonged to God.[15] Yet, for Luther, while baptism happened only once with water, it encapsulated the whole of the Christian life. Every moment of the life of the Christian was to be one of baptism: dying to sin and self, rising to Christ. And the efficacy of baptism lay in grasping the promise attached to baptism by faith.[16]

As to the Mass, the problem with medieval theology was that it understood Mass to be a sacrifice, not a promise. The priest offered the crucified Christ to God in a recapitulation, or reapplication, of the sacrifice of Christ. This made what should be gospel (a promise we believe, based on what God has done and will do) into law (something we do to please God).[17] Transubstantiation, while an error, was problematic because it denied the presence of bread and wine, not because it asserted the presence of the whole Christ.[18] Luther needed the whole Christ in the elements because only in the flesh of Jesus was God revealed as gracious to his people. The whole Christ had to be present and there had to be a clear promise attached to that presence for the Mass to be effective to salvation.[19]

Yet, his sacramentalism was still subordinated to the word, theologically and liturgically. As noted, the efficacy of the sacraments lay in the fact that they held forth the promise of Christ. Thus, it was the declaration of the word in the reading and the preaching of the Bible that was the central practical element in salvation. This meant that liturgies should be set in the vernacular and that preaching should hold pride of place in public worship. Indeed, for Luther it was grasping Christ by the promise of his word, which places the person in a state of justification. In a powerful passage in *The Freedom of the Christian Man* (1520), Luther expresses this idea as follows:

> Christ is full of grace, life, and salvation. The soul is full of sins, death, and damnation. Now let faith come between them and sins, death, and damnation will be Christ's, while grace, life, and salvation will be the soul's; for if Christ is a bridegroom, he must take upon himself the things which are his bride's and bestow upon her the things that are his. If he gives her his body and very self, how shall he not give her all that is his? And if he takes the body of the bride, how shall he not take all that is hers?[20]

As the individual grasped the word of God by faith, Luther believed that a joyful exchange took place, whereby the believer's sins were taken by Christ and Christ's righteousness was taken by the believer. This was an act of imputation: The believer was not intrinsically righteous as Christ was, any more than Christ was intrinsically sinful as the individual was. While later Protestant theology under the influence of, among others, Luther's younger colleague, Philip Melanchthon, tended to favor understanding this in terms of a law court (thus the idea of forensic justification), Luther sets justification within the context of the Pauline analogy between Christ and the church and the union of a husband and wife.[21]

This justification by faith in the word also led to a fundamental revision of the ethical imperatives of the Christian life. Whereas older patterns of justifications had been predicated on the notion that one is righteous by doing righteous things, Luther turned that approach on its head. For him, the one declared to be righteous subsequently did righteous things. He argued this in brief compass in his *Sermon on Two Kinds of Righteousness* in 1519 and at much greater length in the treatise of 1520, *The Freedom of the Christian*. In this work, he argued that works were to be done in response to God's prior justification of the individual and not as a constitutive part of that justification. As a good tree bears good fruit, so the justified person does good works. The motive is simple gratitude and love to God, with Adam before the fall being the best analogy that Luther could find.[22]

Yet for Luther the justified person is always simultaneously a sinner and a righteous man. Indeed, every human being, justified and unjustified, is such. The unjustified man is confident in his own ability to stand righteous before God. He is outwardly respectable, at least in his own eyes and probably in the eyes of society. Yet inwardly he is a sinner, filthy and incapable of coming before a righteous God. One might say that he is justified before the world and damned before God. The believer, however, understands the depth of his own filth and depravity and knows that he is unworthy to stand before God. Outwardly, he is despicable; inwardly he is righteous by faith, clothed with Christ. Damned in the eyes of the world, justified before God.

The theology of human impotence and divine agency that is expressed throughout the *Heidelberg Disputation* reaches its most elaborate expression in Luther's major treatise of 1525, *On the Bondage of the Will*.[23] This work was a response to the 1524 treatise of Erasmus of 1524, *Diatribe on Free Will*. Luther's treatise is perhaps the most complex of all his writings and certainly one of only a handful of his compositions (along with his two catechisms) that he felt would be worthy of preservation after his death.

While the work contains a large number of interrelated themes, the two central elements are the fact that the human will is subordinate to the will of God, such that God is the one who raises up to heaven or casts down to hell; and that Scripture is perspicuous in its teaching of the basic and necessary elements of the gospel. This latter point is crucial. At a debate at the University of Leipzig in 1518, Luther's opponent, John Eck, had successfully pressed him on the issue of authority, such that Luther not only rejected papal authority but also conceded the fallibility of church councils. In effect, this left Scripture alone as the authority for the church's proclamation. That in itself required a further doctrinal refinement if it was to be coherent, and that refinement was scriptural perspicuity.

In the *Bondage of the Will*, Luther makes a twofold distinction with regard to perspicuity. There is external perspicuity, which refers to what we might call the public aspects of interpretation: vocabulary, grammar, syntax, genre, context, etc. This is open to all, regardless of their spiritual state, who have the relevant technical competencies. Internal perspicuity refers to the faith relation. This is an act of the Holy Spirit and is available only to believers. The relationship and the difference between the two is that of believing that Christ rose from the dead and believing that Christ rose from the dead *for me*.[24]

As to the former point, the impotency of the human will to take any initiative in moving toward God was crucial to the maintenance of Luther's Law-Gospel distinction upon which his understanding of justification and, indeed, the Christian life depends. To allow that the human will could respond positively to the Law at any level would be to enervate the dialectic and blur the Law with the Gospel—something that Luther saw as Erasmus's most basic and fundamental error.[25]

Luther certainly articulates a position that is most consistent with a double predestinarian view of salvation. The basic logical structure of his argument is this: Everything God foreknows, he must first will;

God foreknows everything; therefore he must first will everything. It is "fundamentally necessary and salutary for a Christian, to know that God foreknows nothing contingently, but that he foresees and purposes and does all things by his immutable, eternal, and infallible will."[26] That would seem to demand a determinist and thus by implication a double predestinarian approach to salvation. Yet it must also be noted that double predestination plays little or no role elsewhere in Luther's writings. It is the Law-Gospel dialectic, and the need to maintain that absolute distinction, that is central to his theology.

Given Luther's careful and clear division of Law and Gospel, and his early emphasis upon works as the grateful and free response of human beings, shaped by love to God and to neighbor, to their prior justification, the question of the continuing role of the Law in the Christian life is a somewhat complicated one. Several points need to be taken into account.

First, because human beings are always both sinners and righteous, the Law retains its importance as a means of exposing sin and tearing down any attempt at self-justification. Luther is no advocate of a conversionist or victorious life form of Christianity. Thus, the preacher needs to proclaim both Law and Gospel every time he or she mounts the pulpit.

Second, Luther's own theology was a work in progress. So radical were the pastoral implications of his insights into salvation that we need to understand that his Reformation thought raised questions that he then needed to work out over some time. On the issue of good works and the role of the Law, the key developments took place in the late 1520s, when a visitation of the Lutheran parishes in Electoral Saxony was authorized by the Elector. This revealed the worrying fact that the preaching of justification by faith was not leading to any significant moral reformation of the people.[27]

As a result of the visitation, Luther produced his two catechisms. The *Small Catechism* was a very basic introduction to the faith, built around the standard catechetical elements of the Decalogue, the Apostles' Creed, and the Lord's Prayer (in that order, thus respecting the Lutheran priority of Law over Gospel). The *Large Catechism* was far more elaborate, more akin to a set of thematically arranged homilies and clearly designed to help ignorant and unlearned pastors have something to say to their flocks.

What is interesting about these two works is that they were specifically produced in a context in which Luther was very disillusioned with the immorality that was rife in the parishes and that seemed to look to Lutheran preaching as a specious justification. Thus, both catechisms contain not simply a clear statement of the Law but also specific applications of the Law to various callings and situations that would be familiar to the congregation. While Luther does not go as far as to formalize this as the so-called third use of the Law, it is clear that he expects his preachers to give clear guidance on what works of love look like. And they look rather like works shaped by the Decalogue. This is hardly surprising, for love as a virtue requires content.

The situation was exacerbated in the 1530s, in the so-called Antinomian Controversy. The details need not detain us here, but suffice it to say that the problem was that Johannes Agricola of Eisleben was preaching Gospel without Law.[28] As Luther made clear, this leads purely to presumption. There is a place for moral imperatives in the Christian life and Luther did not want his theology of justification to eliminate any need for growth in outward righteousness. In a passage of powerful rhetoric, he declares his verdict on grace only preaching:

> For they, having rejected and being unable to understand the Ten Commandments, preach much about the grace of Christ, yet they strengthen and comfort only those who remain in their sins, telling them not to fear and be terrified by sins, since they are all removed by Christ. They see and yet they let the people go on in their public sins, without any renewal or reformation of their lives. Thus it becomes quite evident that they truly fail to understand the faith and Christ, and thereby abrogate both when they preach about it. How can he speak lightly about the works of the Holy Spirit in the first table—about comfort, grace, forgiveness of sins—who does not heed or practice the works of the Holy Spirit in the second table, which he can understand and experience, while he has never attempted or experienced those of the first table? Therefore it is certain that they neither have nor understand Christ or the Holy Spirit, and their talk is nothing but froth on the tongue, and they are as already said, true Nestoriuses and Eutycheses, who confess or teach Christ in the premise, in the substance, and yet deny him in the conclusion or *idiomata*; that is, they teach Christ and yet destroy him through their teaching.[29]

The question of good works in Luther is complicated and likely to remain a source of debate.[30] Certainly, from his earliest Reformation writings he was aware of the antinomian danger and so was careful to emphasize the importance of good works and the renovative work of grace in the life of the believer.[31] Yet it is clear that by the late 1520s, Luther is dissatisfied with the renovative impact of Lutheran preaching and sees fundamental imbalances emerging among the preachers who take their cue from his work. This is a timely reminder that Luther's own theology and practice were works in progress and themselves subject to constant, probing reformation.

Conclusion

Like Augustine, Luther's writings, occasional as they are, exerted a decisive influence on later theology. Indeed, when it comes to discussions of salvation, if Augustine provides the basic parameters for debating grace, then Luther does the same for justification. Yet even a brief survey such as this shows that Luther's understanding of justification and salvation demands much more than a simple reorientation of part of the medieval church's theology. In fact, as it had its roots in shifts in his understanding of sin and baptism, so it ultimately demanded a wholesale revision of sacraments, liturgy, ethics, and indeed expectations of the Christian life.

NOTES

1. On Luther's life, see Martin Brecht, *Martin Luther*, trans. James L. Schaaf (Minneapolis: Fortress, 1985–93); also Heiko A. Oberman, *Luther: Man Between God and Devil*, trans. Eileen Walliser-Schwarzbart (New Haven: Yale University Press, 2006). The standard edition of Luther's writings is the *Weimarer Ausgabe* (Weimar: H. Böhlhaus Nachfolger, 1883–). Given the introductory nature of this chapter, I will cite from the standard English edition, *Luther's Works* (St. Louis: Concordia, 1955–), hereafter cited as *LW* followed by volume and page numbers.
2. There are numerous excellent studies of Luther's theology. Gordon Rupp, *The Righteousness of God: Luther Studies* (London: Hodder and Stoughton) is still worth consulting, as is Paul Althaus, *The Theology of Martin Luther*, trans. Robert C. Schultz (Minneapolis: Fortress, 1966). More recent studies include Bernhard Lohse, *Martin Luther's Theology: Its Historical and Systematic Development*, trans. Roy A. Harrisville (Minneapolis: Fortress, 2006) and Oswald Bayer, *Martin Luther's Theology: A Contemporary Interpretation*, trans. Thomas H. Trapp (Grand Rapids, MI: Eerdmans, 2008).

3. The best study of Biel's theology as providing the context for Luther is still that of Heiko A. Oberman, first published in the 1960s: *The Harvest of Medieval Theology: Gabriel Biel and Late Medieval Nominalism* (Grand Rapids, MI: Baker Academic, 2001).
4. The Latin phrase was "Facienti quod in se est, Deus gratiam non denegat."
5. *LW* 35, 30.
6. *LW* 31, 40.
7. Thesis 1 reads: "1. When our Lord and Master Jesus Christ said, 'Repent' [Matt. 4:17], he willed the entire life of believers to be one of repentance." *LW* 31, 25. Yet the disputation as a whole clearly rests upon many conventional medieval positions, such as the authority of the Papacy and the reality of purgatory.
8. He is not righteous who does much, but he who, without work, believes much in Christ. The law says, "do this," and it is never done. Grace says, "believe in this," and everything is already done.' *LW* 31, 41.
9. *LW* 31, 40–41.
10. Luther's commitment to reality as the construct of divine speech is clear in his *Lectures on Genesis*, where he uses the idea of the divine rule of language as that which determines reality. E.g., his comment on the creation of birds in his *Lectures on Genesis*: "Who could conceive of the possibility of bringing forth from the water a being which clearly could not continue to exist in water? But God speaks a mere Word, and immediately the birds are brought forth from the water. If the Word is spoken, all things are possible, so that out of the water are made either fish or birds. Therefore any bird whatever and any fish whatever are nothing but nouns in the divine rule of language; through this rule of language those things that are impossible become very easy, while those that are clearly opposite become very much alike, and vice versa." *LW* 1, 49.
11. The classic treatment of Luther on this point is that by Walther von Loewenich, *Luther's Theology of the Cross*, trans. Herbert J. A. Bouman (Minneapolis: Augsburg Publishing House, 1976). A more recent treatment which has proved highly influential in the church at large is Gerhard O. Forde, *On Being a Theologian of the Cross: Reflections on Luther's Heidelberg Disputation* (Grand Rapids, MI: Eerdmans, 1997).
12. *LW* 31:41.
13. This is also part of Luther's understanding of divine speech as creative, in contrast to that of human beings. Also see his comments on the first day of creation in his *Lectures on Genesis*: "We, too, speak, but only according to the rules of language; that is, we assign names to objects which have already been created. But the divine rule of language is different, namely: when He says: 'Sun, shine,' the sun is there at once and shines. Thus the words of God are realities, not bare words." *LW* 1, 22.
14. *LW* 36, 57–58.
15. E.g., "[The devil says,] 'Behold, you are weak. How do you know, therefore, that God is gracious to you?' Then the Christian must come and say, 'I have been

baptized, and by the sacrament I have been incorporated [in Christ]; moreover, I have the Word," *LW* 54, 86.
16. *LW* 36, 58–59.
17. *LW* 36, 35.
18. *LW* 36, 34–35.
19. This is why the symbolic view of the Lord's Supper advocated by Zwingli was so egregious to Luther. Zwingli's denial of the objective presence of the humanity of Christ in the elements essentially turned the sacrament into something human beings do—an act of remembrance—rather than something God does—offer his incarnate Son to us in accordance with his promise.
20. *LW* 31, 351.
21. On the relationship between Luther and Melanchthon on the issue of justification, see Timothy J. Wengert, "Melanchthon and Luther / Luther and Melanchthon," *Lutherjahrbuch* 66 (1999), 55–88; Bengt Hägglund, "Melanchthon versus Luther: The Contemporary Struggle," *Concordia Theological Quarterly* 44 (1980), 123–33; Carl R. Trueman, "*Simul peccator et Justus*: Martin Luther and Justification," in Bruce L. McCormack (ed.), *Justification in Perspective: Historical Developments and Contemporary Challenges* (Grand Rapids, MI: Baker, 2006), 73–97.
22. 'We should think of the works of a Christian who is justified and saved by faith because of the pure and free mercy of God, just as we would think of the works which Adam and Eve did in Paradise, and all their children would have done if they had not sinned . . . . the freest of works, done only to please God and not to obtain righteousness, which Adam already had in full measure and which would have been the birthright of us all' *LW* 31, 360.
23. The Latin title, *De Servo Arbitrio*, is typically translated *On the Bondage of the Will*, but the Latin term *arbitrium* is not a precise equivalent of the English term *will*. It has connotations of *judgment* that the latter lacks. Thus, a better translation is *On the Bondage of Judgment*.
24. *LW* 33, 28. The rhetoric of Scripture's clarity pervades the opening sections of Luther's work. He sees it as the foundational difference between himself and Erasmus.
25. E.g., *LW* 33, 106–07.
26. *LW* 33, 37.
27. On the Visitation, see Carl R. Trueman, *Luther on the Christian Life: Cross and Freedom* (Wheaton, IL: Crossway, 2015), 164–66.
28. On the Antinomian Controversy, see Timothy J. Wengert, *Law and Gospel: Philip Melanchthon's Debate with John Agricola of Eisleben over Poenitentia* (Grand Rapids, MI: Baker, 1997).
29. *LW* 41, 147.
30. The most recent scholarly engagement on this point is associated with the Finnish School of Luther interpretation, which has been promoted in the English-speaking world by Robert W. Jenson. In summary, this approach argues for a close analogy between Luther's understanding of justifying righteousness and

Eastern Orthodox notions of theosis. It relies heavily upon early, pre-1518 Luther texts and also posits a radical discontinuity between the thought of Luther and Melanchthon. See Tuomo Mannermaa, *Christ Present in Faith: Luther's View of Justification*, ed. Kirsi Stjerna (Minneapolis: Fortress, 2005). This was originally published in Finnish in 1989. Also Carl E. Braaten and Robert W. Jenson (eds.), *Union with Christ: The New Finnish Interpretation of Luther* (Grand Rapids, MI: Eerdmans, 1998). For a critical response, see Carl R. Trueman, "Is the Finnish Line a New Beginning? A Critical Assessment of the Reading of Luther Offered by the Helsinki Circle," *Westminster Theological Journal* 65 (2003), 231–44.

31. E.g., the argument concerning the twofold aspect of Christ, grace and "the gift," one that forgives, the other that heals, in his work *Against Latomus* (1520).

13

John Calvin

J. TODD BILLINGS

John Calvin (1509–1564) was born in Noyon, France, and was trained in the study of law at Orleans and Bourges. During his legal studies, Calvin also developed a love of Latin and Greek classical literature. After his sudden conversion to the evangelical movement started by Martin Luther, Calvin used his skill in languages to teach doctrine and interpret Scripture for the evangelicals in France. Calvin was called to be a reader of Scripture and a pastor in Geneva in 1536. He and his colleague Guillaume Farel were expelled from Geneva in 1538, and Calvin spent the next three years in Strasbourg, where he taught in the new Academy and was the pastor of the French congregation in that city. Calvin was called back to Geneva in 1541, and spent the rest of his life in that city as its head pastor and teacher. Calvin produced many editions of his primary teaching manual, the *Institutes of the Christian Religion*, culminating in the final edition of 1559. He also published commentaries on the whole of the New Testament (except 2 and 3 John and Revelation) and lectures and commentaries on the books of Moses, the Psalms, and the Prophets. Calvin preached hundreds of sermons on many of the books of the Old and New Testaments, including Genesis, Deuteronomy, Job, and Galatians. He was one of the major teachers of evangelical theology of his time, and has exercised a profound influence on the subsequent Western Christian tradition, especially in the English-speaking world.

Introduction

What is "salvation" in the thought of John Calvin? There is a wide-ranging answer to that question; Calvin's theology of salvation intersects with many doctrinal loci—including the Trinity, creation, election, covenant, the law, and the Christian life. But there is also a shorter answer to that question, as Calvin himself describes the "sum of the gospel" as the "newness of life" and "free reconciliation," which "are conferred on us by Christ, and both are attained by us through faith."[1] To draw from elsewhere in his writing to expand this summary, the gospel is the double grace of justification and sanctification accessed through union with Christ by the Spirit, received through the instrument of faith.

On the one hand, this "sum" of the gospel points to a thread that runs through much of Calvin's doctrinal work: The double grace of union with Christ is a simple yet expansive description of salvation, for it combines forensic and transformational images of salvation, without absorbing one category into the other. Calvin claims that there is no temporal gap between the gifts of justification and sanctification—they are inseparable, yet distinguishable. Moreover, the context for this formulation is both Trinitarian and Christocentric. One of Calvin's favorite images for salvation, adoption, displays its Trinitarian character, for, in salvation one receives both the legal declaration of becoming a child of the Father (as one united to Christ) and the inheritance of adopted children by receiving the Spirit who conforms believers ever more into the image of Christ. Yet, it is unmistakably Christocentric: All of this takes place in the context of union with Christ, through participation in Christ by the Spirit.

On the other hand, Calvin was not a "systematic theologian" in the sense of placing one article of doctrine at the center and deducing the rest from this point of doctrine. Calvin wrote as an exegetical theologian, organizing his teaching into a series of topical common places (loci communes) in the *Institutes* but deriving his teaching from exegetical expositions of Scripture through his commentaries. As such, Calvin's account of salvation develops a very wide range of biblical descriptions and analogies. Calvin derives his theology through the exegesis of Scripture in dialogue with the earlier exegetical and doctrinal traditions, in light of the pastoral and polemical challenges of his day. This chapter will focus upon Calvin's "sum of the gospel" of the double grace of union with Christ by the Spirit. Even this "sum" is far-reaching and expansive.

Scope of the Language of "Union with Christ"

First, the nature and scope of the topic need to be sharpened so as to avoid the projections of modern categories onto Calvin's thought. There is a sense in which Calvin did not have a sharply defined "theology" of "union with Christ" as a distinct doctrinal locus, in the same way that he has a theology of baptism, or even a theology of justification by faith. The phrase "union with Christ" is best seen as shorthand for a broad range of themes and images that occur repeatedly through a wide range of doctrinal loci. These images are often clustered together—like participation in Christ, ingrafting in Christ, union with Christ, adoption, and participation in God. Yet, the images function differently in different doctrinal and, at times, polemical contexts. Moreover, this pattern of images does not present a Christ-and-the-individual mysticism. Instead, Calvin gave a distinctly communal accent to these images for salvation (incorporated into Christ means being incorporated into Christ's communal body, the church), functional within a Trinitarian framework with a strong emphasis upon the Spirit's role in uniting believers to Christ. Calvin used these images in relation to a very wide range of doctrinal loci.

Union with Christ in Calvin's Early Work

In Calvin's early writing, he made significant use of union with Christ imagery in his account of justification. Calvin spoke of believers being adopted as children of the Father, engrafted into Christ, and experiencing such "participation in him [Christ] that, although we are still foolish in ourselves, he is our wisdom before God; while we are sinners, he is our righteousness; while we are unclean, he is our purity."[2] Adoption, engrafting, and participation in Christ are all images used in expositing justification, and the way in which believers are declared righteous before God is based upon the righteousness of Jesus Christ.

To set the proper context for understanding Calvin's doctrine of justification, it is important to examine the doctrine that Calvin inherits as a second-generation member of the evangelical movement. Justification by grace through faith alone was a key exegetical and doctrinal insight of Martin Luther, developed by Philipp Melanchthon, and incorporated into the Reformed tradition by Calvin, Vermigli, Bucer, and others. Although the Reformation was in many ways a revival of Augustinianism, on the point of justification, Scripture was seen as providing a corrective to Augustine and a later Augustinian tradition of Scriptural interpretation.

Reformers such as Luther shared with Augustine a strong theology of sin and grace—that the will was in bondage to sin apart from the effectual, regenerating work of the Spirit. But Luther departed from the received interpretation of Augustine on the significance of the biblical term "justification." According to these interpretations of Augustine, justification refers to the process of internal renewal by the Spirit in the believer.[3] In contrast to this, Luther made two moves. Both are apparent by 1520 in his work *The Freedom of the Christian*.[4] First, Luther argued that the righteousness that justifies believers is alien and external—contained in Jesus Christ himself—and thus received by faith as a fully sufficient gift. Second, for Luther the process of growth and renewal in Christ became notionally distinct from that of "justification." In this view, justification is not an internal transformation of the believer but a change in status before God because of the alien righteousness of Christ, so that believers are at once holy "saints" and still "sinners" in need of redemption. Luther's doctrine of justification by faith operated within a theology of union with Christ. But frequently, justification itself became the focus since the Augustinian approaches that Luther opposed also worked within a theology of union with Christ, but with a different theology of justification.

Melanchthon had significant continuity with Luther on justification.[5] But he also developed the theme by emphasizing the forensic (legal) character of justification and clarifying the notional distinction between justification (as a legal "declaration of righteousness," as in a courtroom), and sanctification or regeneration (the internal work of the Spirit in believers). For Melanchthon, the distinction between these two is crucial. For if our own works (sanctification) become even a small part of the basis of justification, then Luther's central insight, that our justifying righteousness is contained in Jesus Christ alone and not in ourselves, is lost. Thus, we are justified by grace, which faith alone is sufficient to access. Justification, as the forgiveness of sins through the imputation of Christ's righteousness, must be kept distinct from good works performed by the Spirit. Yet, Melanchthon also sought to clarify the common misunderstanding that justification by faith alone means that justification is not accompanied by good works. Justification by faith necessarily leads to good works.[6] But the good works come as part of the Spirit's gradual healing and redeeming work, not as the ground for God's judgment of believers as righteous in God's sight.

As a second-generation reformer, Calvin shares a great deal with Luther, Melanchthon, and early Lutheranism on the doctrine of justification, over and against Rome. Calvin argues that justification does not refer to the Spirit's gradual healing of the sinner, and it is not based on the good works of the Christian. Instead, "we explain justification simply as the acceptance with which God receives us into his favor as righteous men. And we say that it consists in the remission of sins and the imputation of Christ's righteousness."[7] This 1543 definition would be prohibited by the Council of Trent in 1547, and yet Calvin retained it through the final edition of the *Institutes*.[8] While in Calvin's *Antidote to Trent* he insisted that justification is inseparable from sanctification,[9] he continued to insist upon describing justification as "the gratuitous acceptance of God" grounded wholly in the imputation of Christ's righteousness.[10] In terms of the doctrine of justification, it is clear that Calvin sought to be "orthodox" by an early Reformational (Lutheran and Reformed) standard, affirming that justification involves God's free pardon of sin because of the external righteousness of Jesus Christ imputed onto believers.

This conviction about justification is sustained throughout the course of Calvin's work.[11] As he entered into his program of writing commentaries and revising the *Institutes*—along with various doctrinal disputes—this doctrine of justification became increasingly incorporated into a larger theological fabric in which the cluster of images related to union with Christ is key.

Expansion of Theme through Calvin's Program of Biblical Exegesis

Calvin's exegesis of the book of Romans was crucial for the expansion and development of his theology of union with Christ and the double grace. Calvin was working on his *Romans* commentary at the same time as his 1539 *Institutes*, the edition of the *Institutes* that moves it from a catechism to an ordered set of theological loci. In the prefaces to these two works, he outlines his "program," which he would follow for the next two decades. The commentaries would strive for "lucid brevity" in unfolding "the mind of the writer" in Scripture.[12] The *Institutes* include a "sum of religion" to prepare readers to profit from Scripture, organized into a series of exegetically derived "common places," or loci communes. The ordering of the loci in the *Institutes* appears to emerge largely from Calvin's reading of the book of Romans.[13] Indeed, Calvin is open about the exegetical centrality of Romans for his program: "If we have gained a true understanding of this Epistle, we have an open door to all the most profound treasures of scripture."[14]

Thus, it is not surprising that in the 1539 and 1543 *Institutes* the cluster of images related to union with Christ expanded greatly—not only in his section on justification, but in sections on the sacraments, the imago dei, the Trinity, Christ, and the Spirit as well. Because of the centrality of Romans, the images of union, participation, and ingrafting are spread throughout the *Institutes*. Moreover, as Calvin continued writing biblical commentaries in the 1540s and the 1550s, these images form a cluster that appears in numerous commentaries as complementary images, even where there is no warrant from the immediate biblical context for this clustering.[15] The book of Romans was used by Calvin as an exegetical key to the rest of Scripture, as well as a doctrinal key for the *Institutes*.

In light of this, it is worth examining how, exactly, Calvin expounded justification, sanctification, and union with Christ in his commentary on Romans. According to Calvin's analysis, the first five chapters of Romans focus upon "the main subject of the whole Epistle," namely, "that we are justified by faith."[16] In Calvin's exposition of these chapters, there is particular emphasis upon the inadequacy of human works to make us righteous before God—we are in need of "the righteousness of faith" which is, in fact, "the righteousness of Christ."[17] Yet, faith is not a work meriting God's pardon, but the instrument for receiving God's mercy offered to sinners in Jesus Christ.

> When, therefore, we are justified, the efficient cause is the mercy of God, Christ is the substance (materia) of our justification, and the Word, with faith, the instrument. Faith is therefore said to justify, because it is the instrument by which we receive Christ, in whom righteousness is communicated to us.[18]

Thus, faith is the mode to apprehend Christ, who alone possesses the righteousness by which sinners are justified. In these chapters, Calvin argues that it is imperative to understand that justification takes place by grace through faith, because "men's consciences will never be at peace until they rest on the mercy of God alone."[19]

It is in the exposition of Romans chapters six and eight that sanctification and the double grace enter prominently into Calvin's commentary. In Calvin's reading of Romans, the earlier chapters on justification provide the indispensable context for these chapters.

With the image of being united with Christ in chapter 6 (glossed by Calvin as an "ingrafting" into Christ),[20] we see how "no one can put on the righteousness of Christ" in justification "without regeneration. Paul uses this as the basis of exhortation to purity and holiness of life."[21] Thus, although believers are not declared righteous on the basis of their good works, the Spiritual renewal and works of regeneration always accompany God's free pardon in justification. "The truth is that believers are never reconciled to God without the gift of regeneration. Indeed, we are justified for this very purpose, that we may afterwards worship God in purity of life."[22] In the *Institutes*, passages from Romans 6 are later incorporated into a section that explains how the doctrine of justification does not dampen zeal for good works, but frees persons to actually serve God with their works rather than performing works as acts of merit.[23] This fits into Calvin's view of Christian obedience in which the conscience is allowed to rest from the "perpetual dread" of fulfilling God's law (because of justification), empowered by the Spirit to obey God "cheerfully and in great eagerness," performing good works in gratitude, not because it is required for justification.[24] While Calvin emphasized that justification and sanctification are inseparable in his reflections on Romans 6, he also suggested an order (which is not temporal) of being "justified" for the purpose that "afterwards" the life of holiness lived would not be focused on acquiring righteousness before God but on serving God in eager gratitude.[25]

In Romans 8, many of the earlier themes related to justification and sanctification continue, but several key features are added which characterize Calvin's theology of union with Christ. First, the Spirit is portrayed as the agent of union with Christ; apart from the Spirit's work in believers, Christ is like a "dead image or a corpse."[26] The Spirit dwells in believers, and mediates Christ to believers. Second, union with Christ is set in the Trinitarian context of adoption. Calvin stresses the Trinitarian dimensions of the Spirit, enabling believers to call out to God as

"Abba, Father" as adopted children of God (who are one with Christ). Third, this section includes emphatic statements about the inseparability of justification and sanctification. "We must always bear in mind the counsel of the apostle, that free remission of sins cannot be separated from the Spirit of regeneration. This would be, as it were, to rend Christ asunder."[27] "Let believers, therefore, learn to embrace Him [Christ], not only for justification, but also for sanctification, as He has been given to us for both of these purposes, that they may not rend Him asunder by their own mutilated faith."[28]

Thus, not unlike the two natures of Christ defined by Chalcedon as "without confusion" or mixture, and yet "without division" and "without separation," Calvin argued for the inseparability (yet distinction) of the double grace based upon the oneness of Jesus Christ himself. Thus, also in 1539, Calvin wrote: "By partaking of him [Christ], we principally receive a double grace: namely, that being reconciled to God through Christ's blamelessness, we may have in heaven instead of a Judge a gracious Father; and secondly, that sanctified by Christ's spirit we may cultivate blamelessness and purity of life."[29] In this short passage, it is clear that the inseparability of justification and sanctification is found in the person of Christ. By participation in Christ through faith, believers enter into a Trinitarian drama of encountering a gracious Father who pardons our sin because of Christ's blamelessness (justification) and a powerful Spirit who sanctifies believers for new life (sanctification). Both of these aspects are accessed through participation in Christ, but both aspects would be dramatically altered if the two sides of the double grace were combined or collapsed into one another.

Many of the continued extensions and expansions of this theme of union with Christ continue along the lines presented above, particularly following the themes from the book of Romans. For example, as Calvin continued his exegesis of Romans, he gave a broadly Augustinian account of adoption and election in commenting on Romans 8:29 through Romans 11. One should not "foolishly" assert "that God has elected none but those whom he foresaw would be worthy of his grace."[30] Christians are not elect out of "worthiness" that they have in themselves; instead, God's election freely flows from "God's good pleasure."[31] In this way, salvation "depends on the free adoption of God as the first cause."[32] As Calvin's exegetical work developed and controversies with theologians such as Jerome Bolsec emerged, he continued to expand his defense and exposition of election as an aspect of his theology of salvation in Christ. Moreover, other aspects of union with Christ came to be developed in occasional works, such as his works on the Lord's Supper, in relation to both Gnesio-Lutherans and Zwinglians. In all of this, the cluster of images and themes related to union with Christ are extended and expanded in later editions of the *Institutes*, including his discussions of the Incarnation, the atonement, and the resurrection, along with the earlier topics of justification, baptism, the Lord's Supper, the imago dei, predestination, and the Christian life.[33]

For the purposes of our focus on the double grace in union with Christ, there are three developments that are particularly significant: Calvin's use of the church fathers on union with Christ, the double grace in writings on the Christian life, and Calvin's polemic against Osiander in the 1559 *Institutes*.

Calvin's Use of the Church Fathers on Union with Christ

The topic of Calvin's use of the church fathers is a broad and complex one, and space does not allow a complete overview of Calvin's use of the patristic writings. Yet, it is worth noting that Calvin did make use of patristic material on the theme of union with Christ and the double grace, incorporating patristic language (and at times patristic distinctions) into his account.

Like other sixteenth-century interpreters of the church fathers, Calvin did not approach them in a "disinterested" way. He was interested in finding commonality between his own theology and patristic writings as much as possible—thus vindicating his claim (contra Rome) that the Reformation is not a "new" movement, of "recent birth."[34] Yet, Calvin sought to be clear about Scripture as the final authority, so he was quite willing to point out "errors" in the patristic writings when he judges them as inconsistent with Scripture.

On the topic of union with Christ, Calvin engaged patristic authors such as Augustine, Cyril of Alexandria, and (although in the medieval period, functioning in a similar way) Bernard of Clairvaux. Augustine, in particular, was a major figure of engagement for Calvin. Calvin, like Luther, is deeply indebted to Augustine's overall theology of sin and grace. In addition, on the double grace, Calvin draws upon particular passages about faith and Jesus Christ as the righteousness of believers.[35] Yet, Calvin openly parted from Augustine on the issue of justification (in a similar way to Luther, above).[36] With Cyril of Alexandria's writings, Calvin made selective use of his union with Christ theme on the Lord's Supper, repeatedly drawing upon Cyril's image of the body and blood of Christ as life-giving for the receiver.[37] Finally, Bernard's work was a resource for Calvin as he exposited a theology of union with Christ, criticized a Roman Catholic theology of merit, and exposited the justifying qualities of faith.[38] In all of these cases, Calvin drew upon patristic writings with the learned sensitivity of a humanist scholar, but also for the doctrinal and polemical purposes that suited his needs. Yet, the fact that Calvin incorporated their language into his positive position, and drew additional distinctions for his position while engaging their thought, indicates that his interaction with patristic writings did influence his thought.[39]

The Double Grace and the Christian Life

Through the development of Calvin's program, the soteriological movement within the double grace appears increasingly in Calvin's writings on the Christian life. For the most part, he did not seek to give precise doctrinal schemas in these sections as much as pastoral instruction. Nevertheless, it is important to see how Calvin was arguing for a consistent piety in these different areas, grounded in the double grace and accessed through union with Christ by the Spirit.

For example, Calvin's chapter on prayer in the *Institutes* was expanded significantly in the course of his theological program. With reference to Romans 8, Calvin writes in the 1559 edition "to pray rightly is a rare gift"—properly done in and through the power of the Spirit, for "our natural powers would scarcely suffice." Yet, believers must also be watchful in prayer—expending great effort—for saying that the Spirit empowers prayer should not lead us to "vegetate in that carelessness to which we are all too prone."[40] Stated differently, prayer is a Spirit-enabled human activity, one in which the Spirit activates human beings to pray to God as Father by the Spirit's power. But the indispensable context for this action is that our confidence to approach God in prayer is provided by justification. While Calvin admonished his readers to include a confession of sin in prayer, it must be done in the confidence that characterizes prayer overall, confidence derived "solely from God's mercy."[41] "For if anyone should question his own conscience, he would be so far from daring intimately to lay aside his cares before God that, unless he relied upon mercy and pardon, he would tremble at every approach."[42] Why should we have this confidence? Because we pray as those who belong to the Mediator, Jesus Christ, who offered a sufficient blood sacrifice on our behalf. For God was "appeased by Christ's intercession, so that he received the petitions of the godly."[43] In light of this, Calvin frequently warns against the sin of ingratitude in prayer,[44] and readers are admonished to offer prayers as a "sacrifice of praise and thanksgiving."[45] Prayer is an act of Spirit-empowered gratitude, an act in which the conscience is calmed, because prayer is an act aware of the fully sufficient Priestly sacrifice and intersession of Jesus Christ, a sacrifice for forgiveness received in justification.

A very similar logic is followed in Calvin's polemic against the Mass in *Institutes* 4:18, when he sharply distinguished between the once for all sacrifice of the cross, to "wash sins and cleanse them that the sinner ... may return into favor with God," and the "sacrifice of praise" performed in grateful thanksgiving to God.[46] The sacrifice of praise, which includes the whole life of sanctification and "all the duties of love," has "nothing to do with appeasing God's wrath, with obtaining forgiveness of sins, or with meriting righteousness."[47] For Calvin, the Mass reprehensibly confused the two forms of sacrifice, offering the Mass as a sacrifice acquiring merit. In doing so, the Mass mixed the two sides of the double grace—failing to see that our righteousness before God is found in Jesus Christ alone and his once for all sacrificial work, and that the Christian life as a "sacrifice of praise" is a life of gratitude in response to Christ's sacrifice. These reflections flesh out the pastoral implications of the double grace for the Lord's Supper.

While many other texts could be cited reflecting the influence of the double grace of union with Christ upon Calvin's view of the Christian life, it is worth noting that the method of presentation in these sections reflects a greater emphasis upon pastoral instruction than systematic, doctrinal exposition. In the section on prayer above, Calvin did not begin with a precise statement of the double grace, but he interwove these themes amidst giving practical "rules for prayer" and an exposition of the Lord's Prayer. In a similar way, when Calvin included material about the mortification and vivification of the believer in the final edition of the *Institutes* (as part of regeneration, 3:3–10), he included it before his discreet chapter on justification. This ordering has puzzled some commentators, since as can be seen from the material surveyed above, the grace of regeneration takes on its character as Spirit-empowered gratitude in light of justification. Yet there are pedagogical reasons for exploring regeneration first, such as countering the practical objection that justification by faith alone leads to laxity rather than good works.[48]

Nevertheless, in this section, Calvin still defines justification very clearly as the "free imputation of righteousness" in contrast to regeneration.[49] Calvin provides sufficient clarity in these sections to counter a view of the Christian life based on the calculus of works-righteousness, but in this context he does not broach the more technical disputes about the nature of justification and sanctification. His focus was to give pastoral instruction about the Christian life, being clear that while faith alone justifies, faith necessarily leads to an active life of pursuing holiness by the Spirit's power. The logic of this pastoral instruction fits with what he states in his chapter on justification: that sanctification is the "second of these gifts" of the double grace, for until one understands "the nature of his [God's] judgment concerning you, you have neither a foundation on which to establish your salvation nor one on which to build piety toward God."[50]

Osiander Controversy

Calvin expanded and developed his theology of the double grace as part of a polemic against Andreas Osiander in the 1559 edition of the *Institutes*. Osiander himself died in 1552, thus the timing may appear strange for a heated dispute. The reason is that during the 1550s, Calvin was accused by his Lutheran opponents of being Osiandrian in theology.[51] Osiander was a Catholic priest who had converted to Lutheranism, and then was disowned by his fellow Lutherans for denying a forensic doctrine of justification by faith. Osiander argued that the righteousness of Jesus Christ is infused to believers by faith such that they "participate in the divine nature" (2 Pet. 1:4) through union with Christ. As such,

Jesus Christ is the righteousness of salvation, but his righteousness is infused into believers, not forensically imputed. With the loss of forensic imputation, a key Reformational feature of the doctrine of justification by faith was lost, and there was no longer ground to clearly distinguish between justification and sanctification. According to Osiander, they were both part of a process of the infusion of Christ's righteousness, received in union with Christ.

Calvin was determined to prove the "Osiandrian" accusation false and reaffirm his Reformational orthodoxy on the issue of justification by faith alone. Yet, there is no doubt that he had some commonalities with Osiander. With Osiander, Calvin used emphatic language about the oneness of believers with Christ and the indwelling of Christ by the Spirit. Indeed, for Calvin, the double grace is not a set of abstract benefits acquired in themselves. This double grace is acquired as part of an intimate union with Christ. "He [Osiander] says that we are one with Christ. We agree."[52] In fact, in his 1559 polemic against Osiander, Calvin goes on to write one of his most emphatic statements about affirming the reality of this union with Christ:

> Therefore, that joining together of Head and members, that indwelling of Christ in our hearts—in short, that mystical union—are accorded by us the highest degree of importance, so that Christ, having been made ours, makes us sharers with him in the gifts with which he has been endowed.[53]

Thus, Calvin affirms a "mystical union" of intimacy with the believer, of Christ dwelling within the believer. In this union with Christ, the gifts of justification and sanctification are received by believers.

But for Calvin, an intimate union with Christ should not lead one to downplay the forensic character of justification as the imputation of Christ's righteousness. Indeed, Calvin claims that Osiander makes serious exegetical and doctrinal errors by rejecting the forensic character of justification. First, in Osiander's conception of union by the infusion of Christ's divine nature, "he [Osiander] does not observe the bond of this unity," namely, "to be united with Christ by the secret power of his Spirit."[54] For Calvin, union with Christ is always by the work of the Holy Spirit. Second, Osiander's infusion of Christ's nature approach results in a "confusion of the two kinds of grace" in union with Christ, namely, justification and sanctification[55]—a distinction Calvin goes on to defend against Osiander on Scriptural grounds.[56]

Third, and perhaps most decisively, Calvin complained that Osiander grounds the justifying work in Christ's divine nature, to the exclusion of his human nature. This moves deeply against the logic of Jesus Christ as the Mediator in his divine-human state.[57] But even more significant for Calvin is that this diminishes a crucial Scriptural and doctrinal connection: the cross of Christ and the forgiveness of sins. Here, Calvin argues "we are justified in Christ, in so far as he was made an atoning sacrifice for us."[58] Yet, this act of atonement is not performed simply in the divine nature. "For even though Christ if he had not been true God could not cleanse our souls by his blood, nor appease his Father by his sacrifice, nor absolve us from guilt . . . yet it is certain that he carried out all these acts according to the human nature."[59] This final point is significant for Calvin because it shows that he maintained a strong link between the cross of Christ and justification. By the instrument of faith, believers are justified in union with Christ. But they are not simply united to a "divine nature" that is righteous because it is divine, or even a second Adam who lived a righteous life and hypothetically could have died a natural death. Rather, the righteousness of Jesus Christ is the righteousness of the cross—the mystery of the cross connected to the "wondrous exchange" language that is so closely related to imputation—in which the sin of sinners is imputed upon Christ and the righteousness of Christ is imputed to sinners. As Calvin writes elsewhere, "that, receiving our poverty unto himself, he [Christ] has transferred his wealth to us; that, taking the weight of our iniquity upon himself (which oppressed us), he has clothed us with his righteousness."[60]

Conclusion

John Calvin has a complex and multifaceted theology of salvation. It does not emerge from one central dogma (such as election, or even union with Christ) and then extend into deductive inferences from that dogma. Rather, it is expansive because of the way it fits into his program of coordinated biblical commentary and theological exposition of Christian loci in the various editions of the *Institutes*. In the midst of this, his engagement with the church fathers and in controversies with theologians such as Osiander added to the clarity and precision of his developments.

In his exegetically derived account, the book of Romans played an especially central role. Particularly key in his exegesis of Romans was the theology of justification, adoption, sanctification, and election—all held together with his theology of union with Christ. Through the development of this theology over the course of his career, Calvin expounded upon both his Reformational orthodoxy and his broad catholicity: With Lutheran and Reformed reformers, he insisted upon a forensic account of justification by faith, in which God's declaration of righteousness is based upon the righteousness of Jesus Christ. With earlier Catholic theologians, he championed the Spirit's work in indwelling, transforming, and glorifying human beings in Christ. He framed this as a second gift of the double grace of union with Christ. This approach enabled Calvin to embrace both forensic and transformative images for salvation in Scripture and the earlier tradition, insisting that justification and sanctification are distinct yet inseparable. For Calvin this theology of union with Christ had a far-reaching influence upon a wide range of doctrinal loci, and it had profound significance for his approach to the Christian life of prayer, love, and gratitude. Thus, amidst all of the complexity of Calvin's biblical, theological, and pastoral writings, Calvin's "sum of the gospel" of justification and sanctification in union with Christ does illuminate key aspects of his account of salvation.

NOTES

1. John Calvin, *Institutes of the Christian Religion*, 1559, ed. J. T. McNeill and F. L. Battles (Louisville, KY: Westminster John Knox, 1960), 3:3:1. Unless otherwise noted, English translations of the *Institutes* are from this source (hereafter cited as *Institutes* followed by book, chapter, and section numbers).
2. *Institutes*, 1536 edition, trans. F. L. Battles (Grand Rapids, MI: Eerdmans, 1986), 37.
3. Calvin, for his part, largely conceded that Augustine does not properly distinguish justification from regeneration; see *Institutes* 3:11:15.
4. For an exposition of Luther's doctrine of justification in 1520, its notional distinction from sanctification, see Carl Trueman, "*Simul peccator et justus*: Martin Luther and Justification," in *Justification in Perspective*, ed. Bruce L. McCormack (Grand Rapids, MI: Baker Academic, 2006), 75–92. Luther's notional distinction between justification and sanctification becomes particularly pronounced by the time of his 1535 commentary on Galatians.

5. The degree to which Melanchthon has continuity with Luther on justification is a point of dispute. For a brief statement of the case for strong continuity, see Trueman, "Martin Luther and Justification," 88–92.
6. While Luther makes this point as well, it becomes emphatic in Melanchthon. See McGrath, *Iustitia Dei*, 2nd ed. (Cambridge: Cambridge University Press, 1998), 214.
7. *Institutes* 3:11:2.
8. Trent condemns those for whom justification is "either by the sole imputation of the righteousness of Christ or by the sole remission of sins, to the exclusion of grace and charity ... or that the grace by which we are justified is only the goodwill of God." Translation from Alister McGrath, *Historical Theology* (Blackwell: 1998), 192.
9. "It is not to be denied, however, that the two things, Justification and Sanctification, are constantly conjoined and cohere; but from this it is erroneously inferred that they are one and the same." "Antidote to Trent" (sixth session), trans. Henry Beveridge (Edinburgh: Calvin Translation Society, 1851), quoted from *Tracts and Treatises in Defense of the Reformed Faith* (Grand Rapids, MI: Eerdmans reprint, 1958), vol. 3, 115–116.
10. *Tracts and Treatises*, vol. 3, 116.
11. *Institutes* 3:11.1.
12. *Calvin's New Testament Commentaries: Romans and Thessalonians*, trans. Ross MacKenzie (Grand Rapids, MI: Eerdmans), 1 (hereafter cited as CNTC: Romans).
13. See Richard Muller, *The Unaccommodated Calvin* (Oxford: Oxford University Press, 2000), 119–130.
14. CNTC: Romans, 5.
15. See J. Todd Billings, *Calvin, Participation, and the Gift: The Activity of Believers in Union with Christ* (Oxford: Oxford University Press, 2007), 93–94.
16. CNTC: Romans, 5.
17. Ibid., 73.
18. Ibid.
19. Ibid., 71.
20. Ibid., 124.
21. Ibid., 8.
22. Ibid., 122.
23. *Institutes* 3:16:2.
24. *Institutes* 3:19:4–5.
25. CNTC: Romans, 122. For an exposition of this ordering of justification and sanctification, see Richard A. Muller, *Calvin and the Reformed Tradition: On the Work of Christ and the Order of Salvation* (Grand Rapids, MI: Baker Academic, 2012) 209–12, 239.
26. CNTC: Romans, 164.
27. Ibid.

28. Ibid., 167. The image of rending Christ is also used in Calvin's commentary on Romans 6:1.
29. *Institutes* 3:11:1, 1559 edition. Note the way in which sanctification is received "secondly."
30. CNTC: Romans, 180.
31. Ibid., 181.
32. Ibid., 180.
33. See *Calvin, Participation, and the Gift*, 101, and 108–116 on prayer and the Christian life. On predestination, see *Institutes* 3:24:1, 4.
34. See Calvin, *Institutes*, 1536 edition, 5–6.
35. For example, see *Institutes* 3:12:3, 3:12:8, 3:14:4.
36. *Institutes* 3:11:15.
37. For an account of this, see Billings, *Calvin, Participation, and the Gift*, 49–50.
38. For example, see *Institutes* 3:12:3, 3:12:8, 3:13:4, 3:15:2. See Dennis E. Tamburello, *Union with Christ: John Calvin and the Mysticism of St. Bernard* (Louisville, KY: Westminster John Knox, 1994).
39. For further exploration of this point, see Billings, *Calvin, Participation, and the Gift*, 43–53.
40. *Institutes* 3:20:5.
41. *Institutes* 3:20:9.
42. Ibid.
43. *Institutes* 3:20:18.
44. *Institutes* 3:20:14, 19, 28, 41.
45. *Institutes* 3:20:28.
46. *Institutes* 4:18:13.
47. *Institutes* 4:18:16.
48. For a judicious treatment of this issue, arguing that Calvin displays a "pedagogical purpose" in his ordering of his topics on the *Institutes* related to union with Christ, see Muller, *Calvin and the Reformed Tradition*, 211–12.
49. *Institutes* 3:3:1.
50. *Institutes* 3:11:1.
51. See David Steinmetz, *Reformers in the Wings* (Philadelphia: Fortress Press, 1971), 91.
52. *Institutes* 3:11:5.
53. *Institutes* 3:11:10.
54. *Institutes* 3:11:5.
55. *Institutes* 3:11:6. In this section, Calvin gives a response to Osiander's reading of Romans 4:4–5 and 8:33 in support of his interpretation.
56. *Institutes* 3:11:12.
57. *Institutes* 3:11:8.
58. *Institutes* 3:11:9.
59. Ibid.
60. *Institutes* 4:17:2.

14

The Catholic Reform

DONALD S. PRUDLO

The Catholic Reformation is a period in the history of the Roman Catholic Church that dealt with issues stemming from the rise of Protestantism. Though Catholic reform predated the coming of Luther, nonetheless the challenge of the reformers led the Church to make serious and sustained changes. The focus of the Catholic Reformation—also known as the Counter-Reformation—was the Council of Trent (1545–1563). This Council left few areas of Catholic life untouched. It issued far-reaching dogmatic decrees on the sacraments, the scriptures, justification, and church government, in addition to passing numerous ordinances on internal church reform. So thoroughly did Trent do its work that the loss of Catholics in Europe was largely stanched, catechesis and priestly formation became more systematic, and doctrine was well clarified in opposition to Protestant ideas. Indeed, the whole period from Trent until at least the nineteenth century can really be called the Counter-Reformation in the Catholic Church.

Various occurrences were associated with the Catholic Counter-Reformation. The first was the foundation of the Jesuit order, an elite group of intellectual priests that grew quickly and became commonplace both in the highest echelons of European society and on the front line of missionary territories. There was an explosion of Catholic education with the foundation of seminaries and schools. The vulgate Latin edition of the scriptures was updated to agree more fully with ancient texts, and the Catholic liturgy was simplified and systematized throughout the Catholic world. A proliferation of missionary efforts in Africa, Asia, Latin America, and Canada more than made up for numerical losses sustained in northern Europe, and made Roman Catholicism a worldwide religion. The Church also continued its patronage of the arts, especially in relation to the Baroque style and to polyphonic music. While portrayed by many as a reactionary period in the Church's history, it was at the same time a healthy and innovative age for Roman Catholicism.

Introduction

"As God knows, we seek nothing else, we propose nothing else in celebrating this Council, except the honor of God, the recovery and the salvation of the sheep that are scattered, and the perpetual tranquility and repose of the Christian commonwealth."[1] Such were the words of Pope Pius IV (r. 1559–1565) in his Bull convoking the last sessions of the Council of Trent (1545–1563). In the final analysis, the end of all Christian movements in the century of the Reformations—no matter what confession—was salvation. Though variously conceived and vigorously contested, salvation was the underlying conception that rooted all the theological and historical actions undertaken during this very Christian, yet very divisive, century. All of the diverse and contested points that so animated the age—justification, the sacraments, mediation, scripture, hierarchy, and even saints and sainthood—ultimately can be reduced to the question "What must I do to inherit eternal life?" (Matt. 19:16). The question of the rich young man echoed down the centuries, reverberating with particular force in the 1500s. The chief controversy of the age was how one should understand salvation. The Catholic Church—operating in the context of immemorial tradition—had ideas about salvation that ran very deep when it came to concepts about the ecclesial community and intrinsic sanctification, yet at the same time it was utterly unprepared for the challenge of Protestant arguments about individual and extrinsic salvation. The Catholic Church would have to come to terms with such ideas in order to more fully understand its own long-held doctrines.

Long before the Council of Trent—or even the Reformation itself—Roman Catholics had deeply rooted and well-considered beliefs about the nature of human salvation. Their answers were grounded in the conception of individuals rooted in an ecclesial community, under the invisible headship of Christ and visible headship of the hierarchy, working out their salvation "in fear and trembling" (Phil. 2:12). The earthly community of the Church mediated this salvation, through the ministry of the priesthood, and in contact with the material world. Catholics had a rich sense of both the vertical (divine) and horizontal (ecclesial) components of the reality of salvation and possessed the common premodern conception of religion as a communitarian undertaking.[2] The Church as a whole was marching toward salvation, on an earthly pilgrimage, led by the priests and bishops—considered to be the successors of the Apostles. If a premodern Catholic was confronted by a modern Evangelical and asked the question "are you saved?" they would be puzzled, and could conceivably even answer in the negative. This very disjunction lays bare the necessity for proper definitions of the terms of the debate.

A sophisticated premodern Catholic would answer in the way that the Council of Trent would later speak about human salvation: that it was both an event and a process. In the first place salvation had already occurred. Christ's incarnation and Paschal mystery had redeemed human nature, and he had paid the penalty due for human sins, opening the gates of heaven by being the "firstborn on the dead" (Col. 1:18). In that sense, salvation was a reality that had transpired in the past; the redemption of human nature has been accomplished by the blood of Christ. Yet that very redemption—along with its merits—had to be applied concretely to individual human persons. As men and women began to enter into the Paschal mystery themselves through baptism and the celebration of the sacraments, salvation became a present and progressive reality. Salvation was something that was happening now. It is important to stress that the event of "First Justification," usually connected to the celebration of baptism, was merely a beginning. The new Christian then had to cooperate freely with the graces sent by God and begin to perform good works in charity. They had to frequent the sacraments—which were the ordinary channels of grace—and they had to increase in holiness, in order to conform themselves to the exemplar. In this sense, salvation was an ongoing reality in the life of the Christian, usually going by the name "sanctification." There was still a third sense of the word salvation used in the pre-Reformation Church, one that was the most commonly accepted understanding of the term. Salvation in this sense referred to the completion of a Christian's earthly life in a state of habitual grace. Purified of sin and its effects, a personal judgment by Christ Himself at the moment of death permitted the justified and sanctified person admittance into the heavenly kingdom of God. This is the denotation that most premodern Catholics had when they considered the word "salvation." In this sense, salvation was yet to be accomplished; it was rather the object of one's efforts, prayers, and the subject of one's Christian hope. So, for the Catholic Church of the premodern period, salvation had already happened, was happening now, and was also yet to come.

Developing Doctrine

Indeed, for many Catholics, salvation was an issue that had been hashed out in the Patristic period, punctuated by the towering figure of Augustine (354–430).[3] He had battled the Pelagians, who had denied the reality of intrinsic grace and emphasized the role of free will in choosing our own salvation. Augustine also had helped to delineate Catholic teaching on Original Sin and the correlative doctrine of the irreducible necessity of the grace of God for salvation. Because of him, the Western Church was deeply committed to the idea of salvation through the graces that Christ merited on the Cross. At the same time, however, Augustine may have objected to some of the later Protestant views on salvation, such as the complete denial of the reality of human freedom, or of the stern necessity of reprobation before foreseen demerits;[4] nor did he ever see justification as merely an event, but rather as an unfolding process through further sanctification. The Catholic Church was determined to take Augustine's *via media* in describing justification, such as the contention that the justice we receive is "not that by which God himself is just, but that by which he makes us just."[5] Augustine's theology is not one of imputed righteousness. Augustine's emphases remained throughout the next one thousand years, being confirmed and deepened by St. Thomas Aquinas (1225–1274).[6] At the same time, both of the great theologians of the Catholic tradition had stoutly defended the sovereignty of God and the weakness of the human will.[7] However, by the beginning of the 1300s, a new form of philosophy, fed by nominalism and voluntarism, was challenging traditional conceptions of salvation. Called by the name *via moderna*, this movement tended to obscure the traditional Augustinian emphasis on our absolute dependence on grace in favor of stressing the role of human action in the process of salvation.[8] Such meditations led to the famous phrase "Do what is in you, and God will not withhold his grace."[9] By the turn of the sixteenth century, such meditations had begun to smack of outright Pelagianism. In addition, one could point to popular strains of religious behavior that stressed personal performance of meritorious works without a concomitant emphasis on the priority of divine grace, such as those found in the carefully worked-out systems of Thomas and Augustine. Adding fuel to the fire was the position of many otherwise orthodox humanists, and especially Desiderius Erasmus (1466–1536), who concentrated on the ethical development of mankind through the application of free will.[10] The key problem in the late medieval Catholic tradition then was the foregrounding of certain ideas, which came to be overemphasized by some groups, leading to a diminution of reliance on the balanced theologies of Augustine and Thomas. Had such balance been present, the Reformation might have been quite different indeed.[11]

Contesting the Reformation

The confrontation with the thought of the Lutheran and Reformed traditions forced the Catholic Church to take stock not only of its theology, but also of the very meanings of the terms that it used to describe it. During their first confrontations with Luther, Catholic apologists seemed to be talking past him.[12] Luther and his associates were using traditional terms in wholly new and provocative ways. The radically individualist model of salvation in Luther's theology was shocking and wholly divergent from the more communitarian models of the historical Christian experience. Only gradually did the Church move past sloganeering to approach a deeper understanding of the problem posed by the German Augustinian. Ironically, this more profound apprehension came about as a result of the chaotic efforts to assemble an ecumenical council to deal with the question. From the very beginnings of the signs of dissent against the institutional Church, men on both sides of the issue had been clamoring for an ecumenical council to deal with the issues being raised. The papacy, for its part, was terrified of the specter of fifteenth-century conciliarism (a movement seen as subverting papal authority by appeal to a general council). In addition, the Roman bishops were apprehensive about the motives of the various political forces, in particular those of the King of Spain and Holy Roman Emperor, Charles V (1500–1558). While Charles V would later be one of the strongest Catholic opponents of Luther, during the early part of his reign, Rome was suspicious of his intentions and wary of his immense power, chafing at his constant demands for the convocation of a Council.

Leo X (r. 1513–1521) excommunicated Martin Luther in 1520 for a variety of heresies centered on his new conception of soteriology, particularly forensic justification by the imputed alien righteousness of Christ. In the face of that crisis, and in spite of nation after nation falling into the hands of the Protestants, the Church still dithered. One could say the popes, particularly the hapless Clement VII (r. 1523–1534), fiddled while Rome burned. Twenty-five years were to elapse before the Church would convoke an ecumenical council at Trent, a small northern Italian city lying in the alpine passes between Germany and Italy.[13] In spite of the massive damage wrought by the Protestants in the preceding generation, this delay in the convocation of the council allowed Catholics room to breathe. Trent would be no knee-jerk reaction, no simple reactionary riposte to sophisticated and serious Protestant challenges. Instead, it would be a considered, careful, and comprehensive synod, dedicated to making the best defense and explanation of the Catholic faith that it could offer. The delay also permitted a more profound appreciation of the content of Protestant doctrine, and even gave birth to an abortive effort to come to some soteriological consensus.

Even before the coming of Luther, theologians had been debating the exact nature of our justification. They posed the question concerning whether we were made just by the justice of Christ or our own intrinsic justice flowing from our works done in cooperation with grace. Such sentiments produced an ecumenical effort at the Diet of Regensburg in 1541. In an attempt to come to grips with the Lutheran contention of salvation by the imputed justice of Christ with the Catholic demand for genuine, inner regeneration, a group of Catholics and Lutherans articulated a doctrine called "Double Justification." Martin Bucer (1491–1551), a Lutheran theologian, and Cardinal Contarini (1483–1542), an early proponent of Catholic Reform, led the conference. Together they worked out a personal agreement that, although it was to have a short life in both confessions, it nonetheless demonstrated a willingness to understand alternative positions and to work together for unity. Jointly, they developed a theory that included the Catholic conception of the infusion of charity, which heals our will so that we can do good works.

It was not this which, in the end, granted salvation. Instead, there was a second justification by the imputed righteousness of Christ, and only because of this could one be certain of justification. The compromise pleased no one, for it had one foot in both camps: Both Luther and Trent rejected it. Still, it did show that the Catholics were beginning to take Protestant conceptions seriously.[14]

The Tridentine Council

Though the Regensburg accord was a non-starter, Catholics were finally preparing to assemble an ecumenical council. After waiting for 25 years, a small group of papal legates, together with a few dozen bishops, convoked the Ecumenical Council of Trent on December 13, 1545. The long interval between the appearance of Luther and the calling of the Council had brought clarity. The Fathers knew exactly where they had to focus their initial energies. They placed reform decrees, declarations on the sacraments, saints, and indulgences, and various other issues in the background. The initial topics brought up for analysis and discussion surrounded the Catholic belief on the initiation, progress, and confirmation of justification for a Christian; in other words, "how is one saved?"

The first question that the Fathers had to address was that of the subject of salvation: the human person. In order to understand the transition (in theology known as the *ordo iustificationis*) from sinner to saved, the Fathers had to explore the Catholic doctrine of man's original condition. They had to address the natural state of man without grace, and for this reason, they turned to original sin. During the fifth session in 1546, the Council solemnly defined several dogmas on the subject. The first three are interesting in that they confirm the perennial doctrine of the Church, and indeed even Protestants could assent to them: the reality of original sin, the transmission of original sin to all men, and the idea that human nature was changed for the worse by it. One should note that Trent always begins its most important decrees on points of agreement. This was not only intended to reaffirm commonalities with the Protestants, but to situate the synod in the deep tradition of the Christian Church. The fourth canon affirms infant baptism and maintains that it really effects the forgiveness of sins. The Council directed this canon against some Protestant innovators, such as the Anabaptists. The final canon is critical for understanding Tridentine soteriology.[15] Contrary to Lutheran concepts of justification, Trent declared that after receiving the laver of baptism, not only is sin removed, but the baptized have nothing hateful in them, and they are a friend of God, pure and immaculate, and joint heirs with Christ.[16] Trent would have none of Luther's theology of extrinsic imputation, nor of his famous expression "simul iustus et peccator," i.e., "at the same time just and a sinner." The council also differed with Luther on the matter of concupiscence. For the Reformer, the concupiscence that remained after baptism was itself a sin, whereas Trent defined that it is merely an inclination toward sin (or, as St. Thomas called it, the "tinderbox" of sin). Some Council Fathers, including two of the papal legates, attempted to soften the conciliar language on the regeneration of the baptized. They attempted to insist that concupiscence was a grave sickness—even in those justified after baptism—and that it hindered their performance of good works.[17] The Council Fathers rejected these considerations and affirmed "God hates nothing in the reborn."[18] In spite of concupiscence remaining in the soul, the baptized person was sinless and a friend of God, regenerated by the water of the sacrament. In terms of salvation, Trent had reaffirmed Catholic doctrine that the unbaptized person comes into the world deprived of the grace by which one is justified and made a friend of God. The Council reaffirmed the impossibility of salvation in such a condition, and tied salvation to the absolute necessity of baptism. Those stained with original sin are excluded from heaven, making baptism a necessity of means for eternal life with God. The Council would later expand upon its theology of original sin in the decrees on the sacrament of Baptism.

Justification and Catholic Doctrine

With the preparatory material on original sin established, the Fathers quickly advanced to the salient issue of the day—that of justification. The Council gave this matter perhaps the most thorough theological analysis of any of the multitude of topics that arose at Trent. A thorough analysis and definition of the terms in the debate was necessary before serious discussion could begin. Since Luther and his followers had altered the theological denotations of many concepts, it was critical to establish ironclad expositions from the Catholic perspective. While many theological viewpoints from within the tradition were present at the Council, there were some broad, overarching agreements. In the first place, all of the assembled bishops and theologians agreed that in some way justification was intrinsically transformational, in opposition to Lutheran theories of extrinsic imputation. That means that those who are justified *actually* became righteous before God, rather than merely being reputed as just because of the external merits of Christ. They also generally agreed that one cannot be absolutely certain of one's own justification (and hence of one's own salvation). These considerations were intimately related to questions of the communication of grace through the sacraments. Indeed, the interpretive key to the Tridentine doctrine of justification is to read its declarations in tandem with those on the sacramental theology of the Catholic Church. The regeneration attained in the first justification in baptism could be recovered in the sacrament of Confession, and augmented unto holiness and salvation through the celebration of the other sacraments. Yet the articulation of justification had to come first, before the consideration of the ordinary means of sanctification.

For nearly six months the Fathers and theologians assembled at Trent debated the meaning of justification and discussed a suitable response to Protestant ideas. They explored the definitions of key terms in light of the Catholic tradition. For them, the transition from a state of sin and alienation from God had real, internal effects in a person. This was best expressed by the perennial Catholic understanding of the saving effects of God as described by St. Paul in Galatians 5:6, "fides quae per dilectionem operatur," or "faith which works through love." Theologians at Trent repeatedly turned to this passage in order to undermine Protestant conceptions of saving faith as simple trust in divine mercy. Once again, this demonstrates a commitment to salvation and justification as *processes* in the Catholic Church, rather than simple events. The Tridentine Council would be faithful to the Catholic tradition in insisting that justification was a process, that it effected an internal change, and that such salvation could be increased (by cooperation in the performance of good) or even lost (through serious sin). While some of the Fathers attempted to advance the Double Justice doctrine worked out at Regensburg (in particular the Augustinian Cardinal Seripando),[19] the consensus of the Fathers was against it. They saw imputed justice as foreign to tradition and an unwarranted innovation by the Lutherans. Gradually the Double Justice defenders acquiesced and abandoned that ineffective theological compromise.

Closing Ranks

Two fundamental matters remained. In the first place, the Fathers had to negotiate the Protestant contention that Catholic doctrine was Pelagian, with men relying on themselves for their own salvation instead of on Christ. Further, the Council was eager to soften the impact of Luther's individualistic model of salvation and reaffirm the communitarian and ecclesial aspects of the question. Wrangling for months on this difficult topic, the Fathers worked out a masterful synthesis, through particular application of biblical imagery. They asserted that there was only one justice whereby we are justified, eliminating the theological straddling of the Double Justification theory. They followed the Augustinian model that it was not the justice of Christ that was infused into us, but rather that called "inhering justice" (or, by another name, habitual sanctifying grace). This is distinct from the justice of Christ, but critically depends on it as a meritorious cause. We can have no justice if we are not rooted in the justice of Christ. While we ourselves are justified, that justification is nullified if we are not grafted branches onto the "true vine" (John 15:5). We become living members of the mystical body of Christ by being incorporated into his body: the Church (Col. 1:18; Eph. 1:22–23). In this way, the justice by which God makes us just is distinct from His own justice and distinct from Christ's own merited justice. That is to say, it is really our own, but depends for its very existence on the justice merited for us by Christ. Our relationship to Christ is not extrinsic or accidental, but ontological, for we really become adopted sons of God and co-heirs with Christ. In this way, the Council establishes but one formal cause (to use its precise terminology), rather than two.[20] In addition, the Council asserted the irreducible centrality of Christ to our own salvation in order to counter Protestant accusations of Pelagianism, while at the same time using biblical imagery to underscore the communal nature of that salvation by employing the metaphors of the Vine and of the Mystical Body of Christ. The results of the Tridentine dialogue on justification were a significant tour de force and one of the most sophisticated theological achievements of any Ecumenical Council in history.

By the end of 1546, the Fathers were ready to begin to mold the Decree on Justification into its final form. Many months had been spent making thorough inquiries, both to answer Protestant objections and in free debates on the subtleties of the Catholic position. McGrath notes that the final decree, confirmed on January 13, 1547, was a departure in conciliar history, being the first time a list of condemned propositions was accompanied by a thorough theological exposition of Catholic teaching.[21] The document is significant in several other ways. First, it did not create new division where none yet existed, refusing to deepen the already serious split with the Protestants. Second, it did not judge among disputed positions among theological schools within the Church, preferring to allow free debate within the boundaries of Catholic dogma.[22] Finally, the Council attempted to avoid the rarefied language of late medieval scholasticism to avoid antagonizing the dissidents who scorned what they saw as pedantry. In order to do this they adopted broadly biblical and patristic language, lending the declaration ecumenical possibilities for the future, while at the same time rooting the decree in the tradition of the Church. At the same time, it retained the exceptionally helpful apparatus of Aristotelian causality in order to make its decisions particularly plain. Even apart from its content, for all of these reasons, the decree on Justification is one of the signal achievements of the Council of Trent and of the whole of the Catholic Reform.

The introduction of the final decree sees the Council Fathers continuing their considerations from their previous declaration on Original Sin. Once again nodding to the Lutheran claims of late medieval Pelagianism, the decree opens with a declaration of the absolute inability of man to achieve his own salvation: Works without grace are useless unto eternal life. In the first section, Protestant concerns about Catholic doctrine being infected with heresy are met. Any interpretations of the faith must in the future be rigorously purified of any Pelagianism; in this, the Council was certainly looking back upon the inadequate soteriologies of people such as Ockham and Biel, acknowledging that some of the criticisms of the Reformers regarding certain strains of scholasticism had merit. With that said, however, the Council defended the reality of human freedom. While weakened by original sin, it was not destroyed, and in cooperation with grace, can make a real preparation for justification and, after justification, claim a real title to merit, for the Catholic position had always been that grace perfects nature, not destroys it. God, in His providence, had created the world in such a way that, by grace, man's own will would be healed and empowered to make free and meritorious decisions. Such a position could not be further removed from Luther's outright denial of free will, and calling free "in name only."[23]

In their defense of human freedom, the Council Fathers also were responding to inchoate developments in the churches of the Reformation. In the first place, Trent's defense of free will went back to the doctrine of Augustine: that evil is not imputable to God, and that sin entered the world because of the imperfection of human choice. This means that humanity is free to reject the graces that are sent by God for our salvation, denying the incipient Reformed doctrine of the irresistibility of Grace. Having free will—for Trent—means having the ability to resist the grace that God gratuitously bestows upon one for salvation.[24] This doctrine is a corollary of the universality of the salvific will of God (1 Tim. 2:4). In response to theories of limited atonement, the Council maintained that Christ died for all, and offers salvation to all, and because of free will some are able to turn down this invitation.[25] Indeed, some who become justified can later lose that justification through serious sin. This fall, though, is a result of their own doing, and therefore there is no "predestination to evil." Predestination is indeed a Roman Catholic doctrine, but reprobation before consideration of demerits is a heresy in the Catholic tradition.[26] The topic of the manner of Predestination would be one of the fundamental issues in the post–Tridentine Church. At Trent, the Church had worked out a substantive refutation of the Reformed doctrine of salvation, long before its classical formulation at the Synod of Dordt.[27] Trent here made a fine distinction in terms of our salvation. Without the gratuitous and unmeritable grace of justification, it is impossible to be saved, but one is able to be damned by one's own free refusal to accept that gift.

The Nature and Content of Justification

Having explored the reception of the gift of justification, however, the Council proceeded to a thorough examination of the nature and content of that gift. This is the crucial seventh chapter of the Decree on Justification, and there one can find the heart of the Council's doctrine. There the Fathers address both the Lutheran forensic imputation theory and the Double Justification model proposed by the colloquy at Regensburg. They reject both and declare that the sole and only formal cause of justification is not the justice of Christ, nor that justice whereby God himself is just, but rather that justice by which he makes us just.[28] With this, the Double Justification model becomes defined as heresy. Yet this has deeper ramifications for the manner of our justification. First, justification is not merely a non-imputation of sins, and is certainly not merely external and forensic. Indeed, for Trent, justification was twofold, involving first a real and genuine purification of our sins. Not merely covered over by the external righteousness of Christ, one's sins were wholly purged and one was washed utterly clean of them. But justification did not simply end with this purification, for it went hand-in-hand with an infused sanctification and renovation, so that the justified person was in a real way a "New Man." As Trent succinctly states, when this happens "we are not only reputed, but are truly called, and indeed *are* just."[29]

From this flows the concept that justification can increase or, through sin, be lost. Justification then is both event and process for Trent, which is why Catholics have tended to call an increase in justification by the term "sanctification," even though for Trent, both of those words are essentially convertible (indeed, for our purposes, one can add a third, "salvation"). Put another way, our personal salvation begins at baptism with the infusion of sanctifying grace, we intensify our salvation by cooperation with the continuing free gifts of grace from God, we lose our salvation by serious sin (and can have it restored by the sacraments), and have our salvation consummated in the particular and general judgments of Christ. The Council clearly agrees with the Lutheran contention that the beginning of justification is faith, without which such a transition would be impossible. Yet after the first justification, the faithful cooperate with the grace of Christ in the mortification of the flesh, the pursuit of virtue, and the performance of good works. By these works, the Council declares that the faithful increase in justice (read also "holiness" and "salvation") and that the person becomes further justified.[30]

Trent also asserts that one can never be certain of one's own justified condition (read as a condemnation of the assertion "I am saved" understood in a final and unalterable sense). For individuals have to continue to work out their own salvation, and Trent repeats the Catholic doctrine that the final perseverance of the justified is itself a gift and grace from God. Further, when tied to the doctrines of human free will defined above, several necessary correlatives arise. In the first place, man is always free to reject the grace of God, even after first justification. By the movements of God's grace, continually offered to sinners, a person can turn from their sin and, through sacramental absolution (or—*in extremis*—simply the desire for it), one can be justified anew. Also, apart from the loss of grace inherent in serious sin, Trent affirms that faith remains, even in the sinner. Yet at the very end of the extraordinary explanatory chapters, Trent ends with the fruits of justification. By using one's free will, elevated, purified, and directed by grace (which perfects nature, not destroys it), one grows in holiness by the performance of good works. Trent states that man genuinely acquires a title of merit to those good works that he performs in a state of grace, and always preceded by grace. Still, those merits all depend on the free grace of God. In a real sense, one's genuine merit, and one's ability to become holier and "more saved," is itself a gift of God. Here Trent lays out the Johannine image of Christ as the vine and the justified believers as the branches. All life flows from Christ to us, his grace "precedes and accompanies, and follows" all of our works and, because of that, those works of ours become meritorious. Though we gain real merit, and perform genuine good deeds freely, all of that utterly depends on the grace of God. Indeed, the sixteenth and last chapter of the Decree is a masterpiece, framing in biblical language the Catholic doctrine, and answering Protestant objections about a lack of Christocentricity in its teachings.

Justification and the Sacraments

The Decree on Justification was in a certain sense a gateway for the consideration of the sacraments of the Catholic Church, for all of them were intimately involved in the transition from "enemy to friend" of God.[31] The sacraments were the ordinary manner in which this passage was accomplished. "First Justification" was intimately associated with the sacrament of baptism, and the council emphasized the material and communitarian aspects of the ritual, along with its internal sanctifying effect against extrinsic models used by the Protestants, and against any spiritualizing tendencies. Yet at the same time, the Council, in accord with Catholic tradition reaching back to the fathers, affirmed the validity of baptisms performed by heretics, so long as the proper matter and form were used. The salvation of the human race was too irreducibly critical to adopt a Donatist or puritanical attitude to the sacrament that was the gateway to heaven itself. So insistent was the Council on the universal availability of baptism, it even determined that the sacrament could be received not only by water, but also by a simple desire for the sacrament. This would lead to fruitful post-conciliar theological development about salvation by implicit desire even outside the bounds of the visible Church community. It also evinces the sincere desire for the Council Fathers not to restrict access to salvation in any way, for God had died for all men, and made provision for sufficient grace for every human being.

In light of the Catholic doctrines on human nature, freedom, and the possible loss of justification, the sacrament of Confession attracted the particular attention of the Fathers.[32] Protestants had attacked confession from a variety of angles, including priestly ministration, indulgences, and allegations of works-righteousness. In the Catholic context, penance and confession were absolutely critical for salvation. For when one lost the grace of justification, and no longer possessed sanctifying grace, there had to be a "second plank," as Tertullian had called it, for those who made "shipwreck of their faith." Sacerdotal confession of all mortal sins restored the sinner to sanctifying grace or, to put it another way, justified them anew and made them subjects of salvation. Just as in the decree on baptism, the Council Fathers made a point to emphasize, against Protestant claims to the contrary, that the spirit of penance, the desire for the sacrament, and the ability to reform were all movements of God's grace. This grace always preceded, accompanied, and purified the human will in order to reach its final end in the Triune God.

All of the remaining sacraments, called by Catholics "sacraments of the living," were there in order to accompany the journey of the believer in deepening the grace of initial justification. Christ had given marriage, orders, extreme unction, confirmation, and most particularly the Holy Eucharist so that a person could become more holy—always through the cooperation of God's grace. In a real sense then, by cooperating with grace and through participation in the sacraments, one became sanctified or "more and more saved." These moments of salvation found their epicenter in the Mass, which was for Roman Catholics the meeting of heaven and earth: the unbloody re-presentation of the one sacrifice of Christ on Calvary across time and space. Through the Holy Sacrifice of the Mass, the faithful on earth received a "foretaste of heaven," certainly through participation in the offering of the Mass with the priest, but most intimately and uniquely when they partook of the Eucharistic banquet by eating the flesh of Christ. Taking Christ's commands in John 6 literally, the historical Churches of the Christian tradition had adopted the doctrine of the real presence. To participate in receiving the Eucharist was to be sanctified by Holiness itself. It was a privileged moment in the ongoing sanctification of the Christian, for in that sacred exchange, the Catholic received the one whose very name means "salvation."

In the end, for the Council the consummation of the Christian life was eternal happiness with God in heaven, accomplished through the transition from enmity to friendship realized in baptism, and augmented through participation in the means of grace established by Christ himself. By not interposing obstacles to the operation of grace, and by employing one's elevated and purified free will, one acquired real merit before God, all the while referring all the glory back to God and his free gift. This done, one would die in a state of grace, purified from the temporal effects of sin, and able to have a claim on the reality of eternal life. In this then Trent laid out the road map, through first and second justification, subsequent sanctification, unto heaven itself. Trent had reaffirmed the complexity of the Catholic understanding of salvation: first, already accomplished through the purification and elevation of human nature through the Incarnation and Paschal mystery ("*we have been saved*"); second, beginning with justification and unfolding as a lifelong process ("I am being saved"); and the final consummation after the particular and final judgments when one can say definitively "I am saved." Trent is careful to explain that all of these types of salvation are undertaken in and through a community. Human nature was redeemed as a whole; we are saved in and through the Church, in contact with other humans, our neighbors and fellow-travelers. We become holy by pursuing virtue lived out in communities, and we will become part of the "heavenly Jerusalem" (Rev. 21:20), the whole mystical body of the Church, all together making up the "spotless bride of Christ" (Eph. 5:27). It was not that the doctrines of salvation by grace alone, or salvation by faith, or even the individual standing before the all-holy God, were not true. In one way or another, Trent reaffirmed them all. The problem was that those accounts were incomplete, and Trent supplied the concomitant realities of the cooperation of human free will *under the influence* of grace. This meant salvation by charity working through faith manifested in good works and participation of the sacraments, and salvation within the context of the dense vertical and horizontal community of relations that we experience as human beings. Members of the mystical body, and branches engrafted into Christ—these were the biblical visions of the Christian life offered by the Fathers at Trent.

As a result Trent achieved a number of things. In the first place, it was a wholesale reaffirmation of lived Christianity in all its manifestations: hierarchical, liturgical, traditional, and mystical. It was a solid and robust defense of the Catholic faith against Protestantism but, at the same time, it was not needlessly divisive. It was not reactionary or rigid, nor were its decisions merely a string of unanalyzed *anathemata*. Rather, the Council spent months on each issue, carefully considering all sides and crafting responses that were theological masterpieces. Where the Protestants had a point, their positions were affirmed—such as in the repeated and solemn condemnations of Pelagianism. Where there was difference, Trent provided explanation of and support for the Catholic position. Trent also successfully avoided the technical terminology of late scholasticism and provided a basis for dialogue by rooting its teachings on salvation in biblical and patristic imagery. Further, the Fathers of Trent did not close off intellectual debate by siding with one particular theological school over another. Where there was genuine disagreement within the Catholic tradition, Trent refused to rule, choosing rather to allow doctrine to continue to develop in the context of the continuing history of the Church, something that can be clearly seen in the post-Tridentine developments about soteriology.

The Tridentine Age

The Church, purified by Trent, was then equipped for a major internal reform. Seminaries were created, liturgical books were normalized, and new forms of piety were encouraged. The Tridentine Church had indeed been shorn of much of northern Europe, but it made astonishing gains elsewhere around the globe—in Africa, in Asia, and particularly in the Americas. Upon its closing in 1563, Trent had considerable room left for interpretation. Questions about merit, preparation for justification, and predestination all came up over the next century. The decrees of the Council had set the boundaries for discussion; it would be up to the theologians of the Church, particularly in their response to dissidents, who would help to refine the Council's bold view of Christian salvation.

The Council held to the Christian imperative of retaining seemingly paradoxical doctrines. Christ was God *and* man, God was One *and* Three, Grace *and* nature must both be maintained. Trent accepted this normative tension in Christian theology. Most particularly, it insisted that grace *and* free will are both dogmatic realities, that human freedom *and* infallible divine predestination must be accepted. Trent's genius lay in refusing prematurely to come to an understanding of how those realities operated in the human drama of salvation. There were still many controversies to assess: the condition of man in his prelapsarian nature, the precise manner of preparation for justification, and the manner in which grace operated upon the human will.

One of the most famous post-Tridentine controversies was over the Catholic dogma of predestination.[33] A major dispute arose between the Thomist theologians of the Friars Preachers and those of the young Jesuit order.[34] The Thomists, following Augustine, taught predestination *ante praevisa merita*, that is, God predestines us to heaven before our foreseen merits. In this way, the Thomists preserved the sovereignty of God and the primacy of grace. The Jesuits, led by Luis de Molina (1535–1600), proposed predestination *post praevisa merita*, which means that God predestines us to heaven only after consideration of our merits. In this way, Molinism preserves human freedom. Both sides adhered to constant Catholic teaching that reprobation to hell only occurred after consideration of a person's demerits (God does not send us to hell, we send ourselves). The arguments got relatively heated, with the Molinists accusing the Thomists of crypto-Calvinism, and the Thomists coining the term *semipelagian* to use against the Jesuits. The arguments became so tense that the papacy intervened in 1607 to silence both sides, preventing them from condemning the positions of the other. Any system could be called Catholic if it preserved the sovereignty of God, the primacy of grace, and the reality of human freedom. It has proven to be one of the most intractable of theological issues, but the institutional Church, as it has done numerous times throughout Church history, has insisted that both grace and free will be retained as the basis for any answer to the question of salvation.

Jansenism

One further post-Tridentine movement deserves mention, and that is the phenomenon of Jansenism. In the 1600s, Augustine's ideas were in the air, for both Protestants and Catholics claimed him as representing their position. A Dutch bishop named Cornelius Jansen (1585–1638) was thoroughly familiar with Calvinist thought, and concluded that Saint Augustine was entirely in favor of a type of limited atonement and irresistible grace. By the 1630s, he had written a massive work called *Augustinus* to present his theses.[35] It was not published until after his death, but proved to be the founding theological document of a movement known as Jansenism.[36] Jansen and his followers, using a literalist reading of Augustine's very late anti-Pelagian treatises, saw human nature as radically vitiated by the fall of Adam. They saw it as nonsense to talk about inefficacious grace for, in their opinion, that would rob it of its very name. This led them down a path to Calvinism, particularly in their conclusion that because of these things, Christ only died for the elect. This position drove the papacy to act, and in a series of documents, it further refined Catholic doctrine. In 1653, Pope Innocent X formally condemned the doctrines of limited atonement and irresistible grace, refining and explaining what had lain in seed in the Tridentine declarations. Also condemned was the idea that human nature was so shattered that free will could not merit anything, even when accompanied by grace. The Church reacted strongly against this rigoristic soteriology, which seemed very much like Catholic Calvinism.

Conclusion

Trent remains one of the fundamentally defining moments in the history of the Roman Catholic communion. While there are still debates about whether or not Trent introduced a comprehensive Catholic doctrine of justification, it is clear that the Council offered a coherent account of salvation from the Catholic perspective, rooted in biblical and patristic tradition. After having to refine its positions against Protestant contentions, Trent had made plain many assumptions that had been dormant in the medieval Church. The Council corrected the course of the Church away from any influence of late scholastic Pelagianism, purified the ecclesiastical institution, and solidified the doctrine that missionaries would carry to the four corners of the earth. Worldwide Catholicism was—by definition—Tridentine Catholicism, purified, elevated, and clear in its beliefs. The salvation that was offered by the Catholic Church of the early modern period was cleansed of late medieval dross, while at the same time it retained the liturgical and mystical tradition that had characterized it from the beginning. To be saved was to be a member of a pilgrim community, worshipping as embodied persons, reveling in the goodness of a world created by God and sanctified in the Incarnation, and directed toward God as the final end of all humanity.

NOTES

1. "Nihil, ut Deus scit, quaerentes aliud, nihil propositum habentes in hoc concilio celebrando, nisi honorem ipsius Dei, dispersarum ovium reductionem ac salutem, et perpetuam Christianae reipublicae tranquillitatem ac quietam." Pius IV, *Ad ecclesiae regimen*, 30 November 1560, in *Canons and Decrees of the Council of Trent*, ed. H. J. Schroeder, O.P. (St. Louis: Herder, 1941), 397. The corpus of work done at and around the Council is edited in *Concilium Tridentinum actorum*, ed. Sebastien Merkle et al. 13 vols. (Fribourg: Herder, 1901–1967).
2. For robust explorations of the communitarian and ritual implications of Roman Catholic soteriology, see Augustine Thompson, O.P., *Cities of God: The Religion of the Italian Communes 1125–1325* (University Park: Pennsylvania State University Press, 2005); and Eamon Duffy, *The Stripping of the Altars: Traditional Religion in England c. 1400–c. 1580* (New Haven: Yale University Press, 1992).
3. By far the most complete account of the development of the soteriological doctrines of Christianity can be found in Alister E. McGrath, *Iustitia Dei: A History of the Christian Doctrine of Justification*, 2 vols. (Cambridge: Cambridge University Press, 1986) (hereafter cited as McGrath, *Iustitia Dei*). For Augustine, see vol. 1, 17–36, esp. 27–31 for doctrines materially related to the sixteenth-century controversies.
4. The Reformers and Catholic apologists heavily contested the meanings of Augustine's theology, and indeed he is difficult to pin down, not being a systematic theologian. One can see definite emphases during his life, including an optimism about human nature during his early debates with the Manichees, and a decided pessimism as the debate with the Pelagians dragged on, particularly in the writings of his last three years AD 427–430.

5. Augustine, *De Spiritu et Littera*, 18–19, in Patrologia Latina 44, 220. For this phrase in Augustine's thought, see Christopher Malloy, *Engrafted into Christ* (New York: Peter Lang, 2005), 25, fn. 15. See also McGrath, *Iustitia Dei*, vol. 1, 30–32.
6. For St. Thomas, see Rik Van Nieuwenhove, "'Bearing the Marks of Christ's Passion': Aquinas' Soteriology," in *The Theology of Thomas Aquinas*, ed. Rik Van Neiuwenhove and Joseph Wawrykow (Notre Dame, IN: University of Notre Dame Press, 2005), 277–302.
7. Ibid., 44–48.
8. Ibid., 65–89.
9. For late medieval theology, see Heiko Oberman, *The Harvest of Medieval Theology: Gabriel Biel and Late Medieval Nominalism* (Durham, NC: Labyrinth, 1983; 1963); and David Steinmetz, *Luther and Staupitz: An Essay in the Intellectual Origins of the Protestant Reformation* (Durham, NC: Duke University Press, 1980).
10. For the great schism between Luther and the humanists on the topic, see *Luther and Erasmus: Free Will and Salvation*, ed. E. Gordon Rupp et al. (Philadelphia: Westminster Press, 1969).
11. I am particularly thinking of the provocative positions of Otto Pesch that had Luther known Thomistic theology more comprehensively, rather than being educated in the *via moderna*, his soteriology may have worked itself out according to more traditional models. See Pesch, *Theologie der Rechtfertigung bei Martin Luther und Thomas von Aquin* (Mainz: Matthias-Grünewald, 1967); Pesch, *The God Question in Thomas Aquinas and Martin Luther* (Philadelphia: Fortress, 1972); and most particularly, Pesch, *Martin Luther, Thomas von Aquin und die reformatorische Kritik an der Scholastik: zur Geschichte und Wirkungsgeschichte eines Missverständnisses mit weltgeschichtlichen Folgen* (Hamburg: Vandenhoeck & Ruprecht, 1994). Luther's grasp of Thomas is explored in Denis R. Janz, *Luther on Thomas Aquinas: The Angelic Doctor in the Thought of the Reformer* (Stuttgart: Steiner, 1989).
12. McGrath, *Iustitia Dei*, vol. 2, 54–55. The pre-Tridentine Catholic response is examined in detail in Vinzenz Pfnür, *Einig in der Rechtfertigungslehre?: die Rechtfertigungslehre der Confessio Augustana (1530) und die Stellungnahme der Katholischen Kontroverstheologie zwischen 1530 und 1535* (Wiesbaden: Franz Steiner, 1970), 273–368. In particular Leo X's 1520 Bull of Excommunication "Exsurge Domine" seems to be very scattershot and unfocused.
13. The standard history of the Council of Trent is Hubert Jedin, *Geschichte des Konzils von Trient*, 4 vols. (Freiburg: Herder, 1951–1975), first two volumes are translated in Hubert Jedin, *A History of the Council of Trent*, trans. Dom Ernest Graf O.S.B., 2 vols. (St. Louis: Herder, 1957–1961). The tortured history of its convocation can be found in id., vol. 1, 166–544. A new history of the Council is John O'Malley, S.J., *Trent: What Happened at the Council* (Cambridge, MA: Harvard University Press, 2013). This volume is highly readable and handy, but derives significantly from Jedin, while at the same time offering insights into the role of the Jesuits at the Council, and current debates over the historiography of the period.

14. For the doctrine of Double Justification see McGrath, Vol. 2, 56–63; also Walther von Loewenich, *Duplex Iustitia: Luthers Stellung zu einer Unionsformel des 16. Jahrhunderts* (Wiesbaden: F. Steiner, 1972); and Anthony Lane, "Twofold Righteousness: A Key to the Doctrine of Justification?," in *Justification: What's at Stake in the Current Debates*, ed. Mark Husbands and Daniel Trier (Downers Grove, IL: InterVarsity Press, 2004). For an excellent Catholic perspective on the Double Justification dispute, see Malloy, *Engrafted into Christ*, chapter 2, passim.
15. "Tridentine" is a common adjective for the Council and indeed the whole postconciliar period. It comes from the Latin name for Trent, "Tridentinum," and the Council, "Concilium Tridentinum." For this theological move, see Jared Wicks, S.J., "Dogma and Theology" in *Catholicism in Early Modern History*, ed. John. O'Malley, S.J. (St. Louis: Center for Reformation Research, 1988), 229.
16. "Si quis per Iesu christi domini nostri gratiam quae in baptismate confertur reatum originalis peccati remitti negat aut etiam asserit non tolli totum id quod veram et propriam peccati rationem habet sed illud dicit tantum radi aut non imputari: anathema sit. In renatis enim nihil odit deus quia nihil est damnationis iis qui vere consepulti sunt cum christo per baptisma in mortem qui non secundum carnem ambulant sed veterem hominem exuentes et novum qui secundum deum creatus est induentes innocentes immaculati puri innoxii ac deo dilecti filii effecti sunt heredes quidem dei coheredes autem christi ita ut nihil prorsus eos ab ingressu coeli remoretur." Canon 5, Session 5, "Decree on Original Sin."
17. Jedin, *A History of the Council of Trent*, Vol. 2, 146–162; Malloy, *Engrafted into Christ*, 63–64.
18. "In renatis enim nihil odit deus," Canon 5, Session 5, "Decree on Original Sin."
19. For the attempt to assert the doctrine at Trent, see Hubert Jedin, *Papal Legate at the Council of Trent: Cardinal Seripando*, trans. Frederick C. Eckhoff (St. Louis: Herder, 1947) 326–392.
20. Malloy notes that the rejection of Double Justification was an ecumenical service of the Council for it, like Luther, had seen the inadequacy of a position that attempted to please all sides, and ended up minimizing the genuine positions of each. Now both Protestant and Catholic positions on these critical issues would be clear and accessible: Malloy, *Engrafted into Christ*, 73–74.
21. McGrath, *Iustitia Dei*, Vol. 2, 80–81.
22. I am personally of the opinion that a large portion of the *via moderna* directly traceable to Ockham, through Gabriel Biel, falls under the condemnation of the Decree, but there is a large plurality of opinions on this matter.
23. McGrath, *Iustitia Dei*, Vol. 2, 81. See the canon: "Si quis liberum hominis arbitrium post Adae peccatum amissum et extinctum esse dixerit aut rem esse de solo titulo immo titulum sine re figmentum denique a satana invectum in ecclesiam, anathema sit." Trent, Session 6, canon 5.
24. "neque posse dissentire, si velit." Ibid.
25. In this the Council followed the teaching of Augustine against the Pelagians, "God is good, God is just. He can save a person without good works, because he

is good; but he cannot condemn anyone without evil works, because he is just." St. Augustine, *Contra Julianum*, 3, 18, 35. Patrologia Latina, 44, 721.

26. "Si quis dixit quod iustificationis gratiam non nisi praedestinatis ad vitam, contingere dixerit reliquos vero omnes qui vocantur, vocari quidem, sed gratiam non accipere utpote divina potestate praedestinatos ad malum." Trent, Session 6, Canon 17. This declaration paralleled that of the Council of Orange, 1,000 years before, in AD 529, "We not only do not believe that any are foreordained to evil by the power of God, but even state with utter abhorrence that if there are those who want to believe so evil a thing, they are anathema."

27. For a recent scholarly survey of the Synod of Dordt, see *Revisiting the Synod of Dordt (1618–1619)*, ed. Aza Goudriaan and F. A. van Lieburg (Leiden: Brill, 2011).

28. The Council sidestepped the debate between Scotists and Thomists about whether justification was the establishment of a created habit or divine acceptation. Once again Trent wanted no division where there already was none, nor was it simply to settle disputes between theological schools. McGrath, *Iustitia Dei*, vol. 2, 83.

29. "non modo reputamur sed vere iusti nominamur et sumus iustitiam." Trent, Session 6, chapter 7. Italics my own.

30. Ibid., chapter 10.

31. For an analysis of Trent on the sacraments, see my chapter "The Sacramental Theology of the Catholic Reform," in *Christian Theologies of the Sacraments*, ed. Justin S. Holcomb (New York: New York University Press, 2015).

32. See *Decree on the Most Holy Sacraments of Penance and Extreme Unction*, Council of Trent, Session 14 (1551).

33. For an excellent introduction to the Catholic position, see Matthew Levering, *Predestination: Biblical and Theological Paths* (Oxford: Oxford University Press, 2009); for this debate in particular see 98–134.

34. For an introduction to this debate, see McGrath, *Iustitia Dei*, vol. 2, 92–96.

35. For Jansen, see Jean Orcibal, *Jansénius d'Ypres (1585–1638)* (Paris: Études augustiniennes, 1989). The *Augustinus* was reprinted by Minerva Verlag in 1964.

36. For a good overview see William Doyle, *Jansenism: Catholic Resistance to Authority from the Reformation to the French Revolution* (Basingstoke: Macmillan, 2000).

PART IV

Eighteenth to Twenty-First Centuries

15

Theologies of Salvation from the Eighteenth to Twenty-First Centuries

An Introduction

RYAN M. REEVES

Few theological debates are as crucial as those that center on salvation. The salvation wrought through Christ on the cross is so central to the Christian story that it would be impossible to envision any Christian theology that does not, in some way, address the subject of salvation. Christian theology is *salvation theology*. The issue, of course, is how we conceive of salvation. Over the centuries, the church has weathered severe storms related to these topics—especially in the Pelagian controversy (fifth century) and the Lutheran Reformation (sixteenth century). Each of these debates centered on the issue of faith and works, yet if we pull the lens back further and consider the issues of Christology, creation, and eschatology—to name only three—we see how a number of threads come together to comprise a deeper context of salvation in Christian theology. The period covered in this introduction—the eighteenth to twenty-first centuries—is not unique in the extent to which theologians struggled with the theology of salvation. These centuries are unique, however, in several of the strategies employed by theologians to express the central conviction of salvation in the Christian witness.

Context: The Eighteenth Century and the Rise of Evangelicalism

The eighteenth century provides the context of issues that will be raised in theology in subsequent centuries. In particular, this backdrop included a new emphasis on holiness and a reorientation of theology away from several key tenants of early Reformation theology—represented especially in the figure of John Wesley (1703–1791).[1] By 1700 the split between Catholic and Protestant theologies appeared irrevocable, as the hope of ecumenical dialogue had ceased by the end of the sixteenth century.[2] Catholic theology had galvanized its essential teachings in the Council of Trent (1545–1563), but within Protestantism there was no single authoritative voice. As time wore on, the rise of new theological traditions was always a possibility, and the rise of the Wesleyan movement became the most influential example of a new Protestant voice. The eighteenth century also saw the flourishing of Enlightenment theories of rational discourse and a trend toward marginalizing religious influence in philosophical thinking. Much of the war between "faith and science" would not be manifested until after the Darwinian revolution in the late 1800s, but there are already rumblings about the limits of reason and the perils of rationalism by the end of the 1700s. The progress in technology—especially in machinery and the creation of a new global economy—led to the subjugation of foreign nations in the Far East and in Latin America, as well as the steady rise in the African slave trade to the New World. This colonial impulse would eventually subside, though the residual issues of oppression and liberation would carry on until today.

Each of these factors reveals the length and depth of the issues in the modern world. They also reveal the need for theologians to probe how the Gospel addresses these fundamental issues, first in the nature of salvation itself and then in the effects of salvation on the liberation of both individuals and people groups. There exists, too, the question of the appropriate method for theological reflection in the light of modern concerns for rational, empirical thinking.

We begin with the teachings of Wesley, one of the most influential theological voices in the entirety of the eighteenth century.[3] Wesley frequently focused his teaching on the reorientation of Christian living around the concept of holiness. Wesley's theology began with many of the same traditional Protestant categories: the overwhelming weight of sin, the inability of humanity to save itself, and the need for faith in Christ's atoning work.[4] Wesley, though, was the inheritor of the Arminian rejection of Calvinistic teachings, which centered on the Dutch church schism and the Synod of Dordt (1618–1619). Several of the same criticisms of Reformed teachings had been present in England since at least the reign of Charles I (r. 1625–1649), who struggled to check the influence of English Puritanism. Wesley received many of these critiques and wove them into his own Arminian theological outlook.

What is perhaps the most unique feature of Wesley's theology, though, is his optimism about the sanctification of the Holy Spirit, or the holiness of life that comes as God works in us after justifying us in Christ. Wesley's teachings were not entirely unique—Protestants had always affirmed the renovation of the heart during the Christian life. Wesley, though, rejects the allergy of early Protestantism (especially Luther) in discussing holy living in an optimistic tone. After his conversion at Aldersgate in London in 1738, Wesley came temporarily under the influence of Moravian and Pietist practices found in German Lutheran areas. Pietism had arisen out of the context of confessional Lutheranism and had resisted the dogmatism of the church and its emphasis on Law and Gospel. Pietism was the mother of the later Moravian movement, but both stressed the need for a renovation of the emotional life (i.e., piety) and the need for an immediate experience of Christ. Though he ultimately rejected Moravian theology, Wesley too became a promoter of immediate, emotional engagement with Christ. Wesley's theology was thus marked by a Protestant vision that placed an accent on the necessity of an increasingly holy life for the Christian—to the point that he would speak of a certain "Christian perfection."[5]

Driven by his theological vision, Wesley also signaled later Christian engagement with the application of the Gospel to social ills, especially the plight of subjugated peoples. Wesley was a staunch opponent of the American slave trade—even trading letters with William Wilberforce about the appalling practice he witnessed in the Colonies. Wesleyan pastors such as Francis Asbury became defenders of abolition, and the holiness traditions that were spawned by Methodist circuit riders helped lead the way, in time, for advocating women's suffrage, improvement in labor conditions, education and literacy, temperance, and a number of issues related to social justice.

An appropriate contrast to Wesley is the teaching of Friedrich Schleiermacher (1768–1834).[6] Schleiermacher is the most influential example of a theologian who felt the acute pressure of the political, social, and theological upheavals of the Enlightenment era. As a result, he strove to place Christian theology on a new footing—one he felt would prepare it to confront the modern world. Schleiermacher's approach to Christian theology, and the views he put forward, created some of the most influential (and controversial) teachings of the eighteenth century.

Schleiermacher descended from a lineage of Reformed pastors and, like Wesley, came under the influence of the Moravian movement and Pietism in his early education. Also formative for Schleiermacher was the rising tide of Enlightenment thinking. The works of Immanuel Kant (1724–1804) were published in his lifetime, and Schleiermacher made concerted efforts to read these and other philosophical texts. The context of this theological formation—of emotional Pietism and Enlightenment rationalism—forms the context of Schleiermacher's transformation of Christian theology.

Schleiermacher's most notable work was *The Christian Faith* (1830–1831),[7] which he wrote while serving as professor of theology at the University of Halle. In this work, the influence of Pietism on the one hand, and of the demands of the Enlightenment on the other, form a unique fusion of dogmatic inquiry. From the start Schleiermacher grounds Christian theology in the affections or emotions. Theology itself is no longer the grammar of the faith, revealed through scripture, and embodied in the life of the church and in concrete confessions, but rather "the account of religious affections set forth in human speech."[8] From this foundation, the focus throughout the entire book is the experience of individual Christians in community. The role of experience in Christian theology, then, becomes the foundation of all subsequent theological discourse, including salvation. Schleiermacher also was concerned to place Christian theology within a more limited framework to the other disciplines of academic inquiry, especially philosophy. His intentions for grounding salvation and theology in the emotions were therefore also an attempt to limit the claims of Christianity over against the Enlightenment. By his efforts, Schleiermacher hoped to place Christian theology at once on a more intellectually credible foundation and on a more emotionally vital experience.

Tensions: The Nineteenth Century

For the development of modern theology, the nineteenth century is too often overlooked as the intellectual bridge between the concerns of the eighteenth and twentieth centuries. In particular, the intellectual and political crises of the twentieth century were coming into existence in the 1800s. The rapid advances in the scientific revolution began to raise concerns about the subjugation of people for manual labor and, by the end of the 1800s, with the increased territorialism of various nations that would lead to the World Wars.

The developments within the worlds of science and technology continued to drive a wedge between traditional claims about Christianity and established science. It was the nineteenth century, for example, that witnessed the maturation of the studies of archaeology and geology, which not only discovered the first fossilized records of primordial humans, but also discovered the first evidence of dinosaurs. Charles Lyell (1797–1875) categorized geological eras such as the Paleozoic period and was one of the first to date Earth as older than 300 million years old. Lyell's close friend Charles Darwin (1809–1882) followed similar evidences to determine his theory of the evolution of the species—which has ever since been synonymous with his name.[9] As a result, several of the bedrock assumptions about the Bible and its history came under scrutiny to the point of jeopardizing trust in the scriptures themselves. It was in the late 1800s, then, that a deep rift between "science and religion" began to materialize in both Protestant and Catholic circles. Tensions and fights had been part of the history of the church since the 1500s, but it was in the 1800s that these tensions became, for some, a campaign of total war.

In actuality, the kaleidoscope of different Christian opinions about modern science and philosophy are not easy to categorize. There were a significant range of options beyond merely rejecting science (fundamentalism) and embracing all the claims of Enlightenment rationalism (progressivism). In Protestant and Catholic circles there arose a number of strategies of accommodation to modern science—for example in the relationship of faith to modern psychoanalysis—that was neither hostile nor fully accepting of every claim. The vast majority of later Christian theology will not often be pitched between either extreme, but will often look for a dialectical relationship between modern thinking and Christian faith.

The nineteenth century also gave rise to the context for later aggressive forms of political supremacy, fueled by the technological advances of devastating, mechanized warfare. By the end of the 1800s various nations in Europe began an arms race to offset one another, and a new hagiography of nationalism began to emerge in the majority of the developed world. In the early 1900s this gave rise to World War I, which introduced mustard gas and other biological strategies on the battlefield. But the wars that ravaged the twentieth century were not born in a vacuum and often came as a result of the intellectual and political revolutions of the 1800s.

Contemporary Theology: The Twentieth Century

One of the most important theologians of the twentieth century was Karl Barth (1886–1968). Barth's theology in many ways embodies the tensions that Europe and America inherited from the nineteenth century.[10] It would be wrong to suggest that Barth is merely a "reactionary"—as if his theology were merely the overthrowing of the corrosive elements of modern Liberalism and the rediscovery of Orthodoxy. Barth did reject certain elements of progressive theology, but his criticisms of Liberalism were based on more than hostility to their conclusions. Moreover, in terms of Christian theology, Barth was as concerned with the tensions in Protestant theology inherited from the Reformation as he was with finding new paths of exploration from within this heritage. The influence of Barth's theological project might be said to rest on his unique theological vision, which exposed flaws in a number of different modern theological trajectories, both in Liberalism and fundamentalism.

Barth's approach to salvation is both nuanced and complex. Modern interpreters can find his approach initially frustrating because he, at times, refuses to abide by the traditional separation of categories found in earlier Protestant theologies. The method undergirding Barth's categories—and at times the question of which categories are most important—are the main features in scholarly debate on Barth. Central to Barth's theology of salvation, though, is the concept of the revelation of God in the Word, which is wrapped up in the coming of God himself as the Word in the humanity of Christ. In this important move Barth unites the theological categories of creation and redemption into a theology of salvation that is not concerned only with legal guilt and God's election of sinners. Barth therefore can speak of salvation history as beginning with creation itself.[11] God is always turning graciously toward humanity, and so creation and eschatology are not separate theological issues but centerpieces of a fully biblical account of salvation.

Similar instincts (but divergent answers) can be found in early-twentieth-century Roman Catholic theology. Two of the most influential Catholic theologians during this century are Karl Rahner and Hans Urs von Balthasar.[12] Both were trained as Jesuits and were steeped in the more traditional methods of "neo-scholasticism"—an amorphous Catholic movement from the 1800s that strove to revive the heritage of the medieval scholastic synthesis of Bonaventure, Scotus, and Aquinas. The general approach of neo-scholasticism was to stress the heritage of the medieval witness and, especially, to stress the view that Catholic doctrine does not change over time. This perspective was ratified in Pope Leo XIII's *Aeterni patris* (1879): Catholic doctrine was already established; what was missing is the proper imitation of these sources in modern theological studies. At its most excessive, neo-scholastic theology served as a mere reaction to the fears of modernism. The answers given to the modern world, then, were almost entirely negative—as in the "Anti-Modernism Oath" promulgated in 1910 by Pope Pius X.

Rahner and Balthasar each react against this neo-scholastic training, not because they felt Catholic theology needed fundamental change, but because they felt Catholic articulation of the faith was not enshrined in the medieval world. Rahner and Balthasar therefore are two of the best representatives of a new path for Catholic theology in the modern world—a movement often known as *Nouvelle Théologie*. Rahner was equally a critic of neo-scholasticism and a theologian more interested in finding an accommodating stance toward modern philosophy. Balthasar by contrast was less interested in critique and more interested in describing a new synthesis of Christian theology focused on the revelation in Christ and its parallels in the true, the good, and the beautiful. Both shaped new paths for Catholic theology in the twentieth century that were embodied in Vatican II.

A New Focus: Liberation and Salvation

Of all the issues addressed in the early twentieth century, one of the most underdeveloped was the role of salvation in the freedom of oppressed peoples. To be clear, Protestants and Catholics both engaged in social justice at various stages in their history since the 1500s, but what was lacking was a robust articulation of how these practices unite with the work of Christ in salvation. Also lacking were voices from within the context of oppression that could raise awareness to dominant cultures about the sufferings of others.

Within the American world the central concern was the plight of black Christians in the aftermath of the Civil War. The various Jim Crow laws throughout the South, and the decision in favor of "separate but equal" in *Plessy v. Ferguson* (1896), carried on some of the worst practices of oppression even after the end of slavery. Racism was present throughout every region of America, but the South was marked by a violent streak of racial hostility, and there was often fierce opposition to black denominations in these areas. As a result, the dominant voices in the subsequent Civil Rights movement were those of black pastors and theologians who advocated for the liberation of blacks in society through a meditation on the theology of salvation. Martin Luther King, Jr. was the central pastoral voice during the Civil Rights era, but from the context of academic theology it is James Cone (b. 1938) who became a crucial voice in advocating Black Liberation. The variety of opinions of African American theologians was always complex, and the development of new perspectives continues until today.

There are parallel movements for liberation and change both in the West and around the globe. One of the most important voices for what would become known generally as Liberation Theology,[13] though, is Gustavo Gutiérrez (b. 1928). Gutiérrez focused attention in salvation on the restoration of broken community, first between humanity and God and then between people groups. Salvation is not only the focus on the freedom of individuals from legal guilt but also the eradication of practices and contexts that dehumanize people groups. Gutiérrez follows similar threads to Rahner and Balthasar, which viewed the Thomistic separation of "nature" and "supernatural" as creating a false dichotomy by denigrating the natural order of creation as being little more than the touchstone of salvation. Instead, Gutiérrez argues, salvation should be seen as integral to this world and therefore capable of creating radical change in sociopolitical oppression.

Conclusion

The role of salvation in modern theology is as significant as any other single issue. The vital issues that arise through the context of the modern world, though, gave rise to a number of salient features within modern Christian theology that reshape the conversation in new directions. Often the complexity of interpreting modern theologies of salvation turn on the question, not only of the evolution of Protestant and Catholic views, but also with the relative influence of modern social, political, and philosophical ideas on individual theologians. Therefore, while modern theologies of salvation are not entirely unique, they nevertheless are at times concerned with issues not seen before in Christian history.

NOTES

1. Cf. Mark Noll, *The Rise of Evangelicalism* (Downers Grove, IL: InterVarsity Press, 2010).
2. The ecumenism of the twentieth century is quite unique in the history of post-Reformation theology, driven both by the changes brought about by Vatican II and an increased willingness of multiple Protestant branches to engage in ecumenical dialogue.
3. This is not to deny the importance or influence of figures such as George Whitefield or Jonathan Edwards, both of whom had enormous impact in the 1700s. Still, Wesleyan churches and subsequent holiness movements dominated the new American nation. On Wesley, see Stephen Tomkins, *John Wesley: A Biography* (Grand Rapids, MI: Eerdmans, 2003).
4. The Protestant qualities of his teachings on salvation are dealt with in this book in chapter 16.
5. 'Christian perfection' is a wildly misunderstood teaching of Wesley and is often mischaracterized as if Wesley believed in pure perfection. The nuances of this phrase are discussed in chapter 16.
6. For an introduction to Schleiermacher, see Jacqueline Mariña (ed.), *Cambridge Companion to Schleiermacher* (Cambridge: Cambridge University Press, 2005).
7. The first (and much shorter) edition appeared in 1820–1821, though it has never appeared in English. It is the expanded version of 1830–1831 that became the definitive edition.
8. Friedrich Schleiermacher, *The Christian Faith*, ed. H. R. Mackintosh and J. S. Stewart (London and New York: T & T Clark, 1999), 1.4.
9. On this background, see Jonathan Hodge and Gregory Radick (eds.), *Cambridge Companion to Darwin* (Cambridge: Cambridge University Press, 2009).

10. Two influential perspectives on Barth's theology can be found in George Hunsinger, *How to Read Karl Barth* (Oxford: Oxford University Press, 1993), and Bruce McCormack, *Karl Barth's Critically Realistic Dialectical Theology* (Oxford: Clarendon Press, 1997).
11. On Barth, creation, and salvation, see chapter 18 in this volume.
12. On the scholarly backdrop of their theology, see chapter 19 in this volume.
13. There is no singular Liberation Theology, properly speaking, but rather a variety of perspectives about liberation from the context of theology. On this, see chapter 20 in this volume.

16

John Wesley

THOMAS H. MCCALL

John Wesley (1703–1791) and Charles Wesley (1707–1788) were co-founders of the Methodist movement, the former a noted preacher and the latter a hymn-writer poet. Sons of the Anglican clergyman, Samuel Wesley, and the incomparable Susanna, both were educated at Christ Church, Oxford, and ordained to the priesthood of the Church of England. They spearheaded a movement of renewal in the life of the eighteenth-century church combining a warm-hearted evangelical piety and a dynamic Eucharistic fervor. Charles founded the so-called Holy Club while a student at Oxford, the leadership of which was taken over by John.

John traveled more than 250,000 miles on horseback during his lifetime, preaching a message of faith working by love across the British Isles. In 1745, John and Charles jointly published *Hymns on the Lord's Supper*, a collection of 166 hymns that expound their Eucharistic theology. The spirituality of both brothers revolved around the concept of perfect love, or Christian perfection. John Wesley's *A Plain Account of Christian Perfection*, often considered his *magnum opus*, summarizes his teaching on the subject. His *Journal*, letters, sermons, and treatises are available in many editions.

Introduction

John Wesley's doctrine of salvation is not utterly unique in the history of Christian thought (recognizing this, he regarded it as a good thing). Nor is it a carbon copy of some earlier view. Instead, it is eclectic; it is unmistakably Protestant in some very important ways (perhaps most notably with respect to the doctrine of justification), but it is also grounded in the theology of the early church while incorporating important themes from Roman Catholic and Orthodox theology (particularly with respect to the doctrine of sanctification).[1] His soteriology does, however, have several powerful emphases that make it distinctive.

The Theological Framework of Wesley's Soteriology

Wesley is utterly convinced that humans are created in the image of the Triune God—and he is just as confident that the purpose for that creation is nothing less than communion with the God who is Father, Son, and Holy Spirit. As Wesley says, "God is love: accordingly man at his creation was full of love . . . God is full of justice, mercy, and truth; so was man when he came from the hands of his Creator." Humanity was made for fellowship and communion with the Triune God whose essence is holy love; they were created full of "righteousness and true holiness."[2] He is also certain that humans have turned away from their Creator in rebellion and thus have "fallen," that they are desperate and helpless sinners, and that they cannot save or redeem themselves. Indeed, he says that his own doctrine of sin is not even a "hairs-breadth" different from John Calvin's doctrine,[3] and he says that humanity is "filled with all manner of evil," "wholly fallen," and "totally corrupted."[4] Thus, we cannot save ourselves; if we are to have any hope of salvation, it is by divine action. And the good news—the gospel, for Wesley—is precisely this: God indeed has taken decisive and drastic action for us. The Triune God, whose essence is holy love, has poured out his grace upon us. This grace first prepares the way,[5] and it then convicts of sin, justifies, sanctifies, and glorifies. We are saved *for nothing* less than communion with the Triune God, and thus we are saved *from* the sin that would separate us from God's holy love.

Predestination and Election

Wesley's soteriology is marked by pointed differences between the common "Reformed" (or "Calvinist") views of predestination and his own understanding of the doctrines of election and predestination. Specifically, he disagrees with the doctrines of unconditional election, limited atonement, and irresistible grace as these are expressed in such confessional statements as the Canons of Dordt and the Westminster

Confession of Faith (as well, of course, as prominent theologians such as Calvin, Piscatorius, Twisse, Vermigli, Zanchi, and Zwingli).[6] He understands the appeal of the standard Reformed accounts. After all, many Christians seem to experience something like "irresistible grace" in their own conversions and should desire that God take all the credit in salvation. And, of course, there are various biblical texts that may be interpreted in ways that support the Reformed doctrines.[7] He insists upon the importance of the "catholic spirit" in these discussions. Clearly he recognizes that "Calvinists" are members of the same family or body and are deserving of deep respect and even affection. Indeed, Wesley affirms that "many Calvinists are pious, learned, and sensible men," and he exclaimed that it is both "sin and folly" to use the term "Calvinist" as a "term of reproach."[8]

Notwithstanding his appreciation of Reformed theology, however, Wesley strongly and famously disagrees with their doctrines of predestination. He argues against the Reformed account on several grounds. He appeals directly to Scripture; he lays out page after page of biblical text that he takes to directly challenge, undercut, or contradict Calvinism. Here he argues from the biblical witness to the will of God that all be saved (e.g., Job 36:5; Ps. 145:9; Prov. 1:23; Isa. 45:2f; Ezek. 33:20, 23; Matt. 22:9; Mark 16:15; Luke 19:41; John 5:34–40; Acts 17:24; Rom. 5:18; 10:12; 1 Tim. 2:3–4; 4:10; 2 Pet. 3:9), from what seem to be clear affirmations that Christ died for all humanity (e.g., John 1:29; 3:17; 12:47; Rom. 14:15; 1 Cor. 8:11; 2 Cor. 5:14; 1 Tim. 2:6; Heb. 2:9; 2 Pet. 2:1; 1 John 2:1–2; 4:14), and from numerous passages that make no sense apart from conditionality (e.g., Gen. 3:17; 4:7; Deut. 7:9, 12; 11:26–28; 30:15f; 2 Chron. 15:1–2; Ezra 9:13–14; Ezek. 33:11).[9] In addition to what he takes to be straightforward and quite obvious biblical evidence against Calvinist soteriology, he also raises distinctly *theological* arguments against it. In particular, he finds Reformed soteriology to be opposed to an adequate conception of divine justice (including divine truth and sincerity). For, as he understands the Calvinist position, he thinks that it entails that God makes sin inevitable for people and then holds them responsible for that sin, that God withholds grace from them and then faults them for not accepting it, and that God invites them to repent while not making it truly possible for them to do so. Indeed, he concludes that the "Calvinist" account "flatly contradicts, indeed utterly overthrows, the Scripture account of the justice of God."[10] Anticipating the response that people are damned for their own rebellious unbelief, he retorts,

> But could they believe? Was not this faith both the gift and the work of God in the soul? And was it not a gift which he had eternally decreed never to give them? Was it not a work which he was of old unchangeably determined never to work in their souls? Shall these men be condemned, because God would not work; because they did not receive what God would not give? Could they "ungrasp the hold of his right hand, or force omnipotence?"[11]

Moreover, if the doctrine of limited (or "definite") atonement is true, then,

> Christ did not die for these men. But if so, there was an impossibility, in the very nature of the thing, that they should ever savingly believe. For what is saving faith, but "a confidence in God through Christ, that loved me, and gave himself for me?" Loved thee, thou reprobate! Gave himself for thee! Away! . . . There never was any object for thy faith; there never was anything for thee to believe. God himself (thus must you speak, to be consistent with yourself), with all his omnipotence, could not make thee believe Christ atoned for thy sins, unless he had made thee believe a lie.[12]

Divine justice cannot, for Wesley, be marginalized or compromised by appeal to other divine attributes (e.g., divine sovereignty), for the divine attributes are "inseparably joined."[13] And, as he sees the matter, the standard Reformed account is simply inconsistent with the justice of God.

> How could they even thus have escaped from sin? Not without that grace which you suppose God had absolutely determined never to give them. And yet you suppose him to be sending them into eternal fire, for not escaping from sin! That is, in plain terms, for not having that grace which God had decreed they should never have! O strange justice! What a picture you draw of the Judge of all the earth![14]

Wesley rejects the Reformed account on biblical and theological grounds, and he is convinced that he is not alone. For, while "Augustine sometimes speaks for it, and sometimes against it," nonetheless "all antiquity for the first four centuries" is opposed to it, "as is the whole Eastern Church to this day." Moreover, he takes the Church of England to be officially opposed to the determinism that he sees in Calvinism; he interprets not only such Anglican stalwarts as Hooker and Latimer but also the "Catechism, Articles, and Homilies" to be inconsistent with it.[15]

When considering purported biblical evidence for the Reformed doctrine, Wesley works to interpret Scripture with Scripture and according to the rule of faith. Doing so, he finds such texts to be either inconclusive or supportive of his own view. Wrestling with Romans 9 (and 9–11), he makes a case for a corporate reading. He observes that Paul's quotation "the elder shall serve the younger" (9:12) works only with a corporate reading: "it is undeniably plain, that both these Scriptures relate, not to the persons of Jacob and Esau, but to their descendants . . . In this sense only did 'the elder' (Esau) 'serve the younger'; not in his person, (for Esau never served Jacob,) but in his posterity. The posterity of the elder brother served the posterity of the younger."[16] For, while the historical individual "Esau" did not (so far as we know from Scripture) ever serve Jacob, Esau's descendants in fact did serve Jacob's progeny. Accordingly, Wesley concludes, Romans 9 is referring to corporate entities rather than the individuals. Wesley finds that this interpretation coheres well indeed with his own doctrine of election. In addition to a broadly corporate understanding (whereby a people are chosen for a specific and appointed purpose), he sees two senses of election in Scripture. The first is the "divine appointment of some particular men, to do some particular work in the world." This election, Wesley maintains, "is not only personal, but absolute and unconditional."[17] The second sense, he explains, is of "a divine appointment of some men to eternal happiness." This sense, he insists, is conditional rather than unconditional.[18] Wesley is confident that such a doctrinal formulation is consistent with straightforward biblical teaching as well as a proper understanding of the nature and character of God.

So Wesley is opposed to the common Reformed doctrines of election and predestination, and he is sure that he rejects these doctrines on solid biblical, historical, and theological grounds. In its place, he proposes a broadly corporate and conditional doctrine. But as he does so, he insists that Methodists "come to the very edge of Calvinism" in these ways: "in ascribing all good to the free grace of God," in "denying all natural free will, and all power antecedent to grace," and "in excluding merit from [humans]."[19] He also continues to insist on the importance of the "catholic spirit":

> As far as is possible, let us join in destroying the works of the devil, and in setting up the kingdom of God upon earth, in promoting righteousness, peace, and joy in the Holy Ghost . . . let us unite in destroying the works of the devil, in bringing all we can from the power of darkness into the kingdom of God's dear Son. And let us assist each other to value more and more the glorious grace whereby we stand, and daily to grow in that grace and in the knowledge of our Lord Jesus Christ.[20]

Justification

Nowhere is Wesley more obviously and decidedly *Protestant* than in his doctrine of justification.[21] In sharp contrast to his disagreements about predestination, he holds that his own view is in full agreement with Reformed (and Lutheran) accounts. As he puts it: "I think on Justification . . . just as Mr. Calvin does. In this respect I do not differ from him a hair's breadth."[22] Wesley understands human sinners to be legally condemned before God, and unable to do anything of themselves to avoid this condemnation or escape this punishment. But, while we are unable to do anything to help ourselves, God acts for us. In justification, God declares that we can stand righteous and without condemnation before him. Because of Christ's work, our guilt can be removed and our condemnation itself condemned. Wesley understands the biblical language of justification in a heavily legal sense, and he takes it to be a vitally important element of the doctrine of salvation.

More specifically, Wesley makes a case for federal headship; all humans share a legal relation with Adam due to original sin, and all humans potentially share a legal relationship with Christ by virtue of God's gracious provision of justification. He argues for the "ground" of the doctrine in an affirmation of (penal) substitutionary atonement.[23] For Wesley, justification is to be distinguished clearly from sanctification. While both are essential elements of the doctrine of salvation, they are distinct in important ways: Justification refers to what God does on our behalf in changing our position or legal status, while sanctification is what God does *in us* by making us truly just or righteous and holy.

Who is justified? For Wesley, there is only one answer to this question: *Sinners*, and *only sinners*, are graciously justified. Just as justification and sanctification are not to be confused for Wesley, neither should we think that sanctification somehow precedes and enables justification. God justifies *sinners*; he graciously justifies those who are not yet actually pure and holy. Justification is "pardon, the forgiveness of sins. It is that act of God the Father, whereby, for the sake of the propitiation made by the blood of his Son, he 'showeth forth his righteousness (or mercy) by the remission of sins.'"[24] Our sins are imputed to Christ, and Christ's righteousness (both active and passive) is imputed to us.[25] The righteousness of the incarnate Son is given or accredited to us as

> The bestowing (as it were) [of] the righteousness of Christ, including his obedience, as well passive as active . . . in the privileges, blessings, and benefits, purchased by it; so a believer may be said to be justified, by the righteousness of Christ imputed. The meaning is, God justifies the believer, for the sake of Christ's righteousness, and not for any righteousness of his own.[26]

And *how* are sinners justified? Wesley is clear and emphatic: Sinners are justified *by grace alone*, and this gift is received by *faith alone*. "Faith," he insists, "is the *necessary* condition of justification. Yea, and the *only necessary* condition of justification."[27] On this point, Wesley is unwavering: "I believe justification by faith alone, as much as I believe that there is a God."[28] Accordingly, Wesley's "Methodist Articles of Religion" leave Article 11 of the Anglican Thirty-Nine Articles unchanged: "We are accounted righteous before God, only for the merit of our Lord and Savior Jesus Christ by faith, and not for our own works. Therefore, that we are justified by faith is a most wholesome doctrine and very full of comfort."[29]

For Wesley and early Methodist theology and piety, truly this doctrine of justification was "very full of comfort." Indeed, it shone with a luminous beauty, and this is reflected in the hymnody. As Charles Wesley's famous hymn "And Can It Be?" puts it,

> No condemnation now I dread,
> Jesus and all in him is mine;
> Alive in him my living head,
> And clothed with righteousness divine;
> Bold I approach the eternal throne,
> and claim, through him, the crown my own.

So Wesley offers resounding affirmation of a broadly Protestant account of justification, and he is convinced that there is no genuine gospel without it. But, he also denies that salvation can be reduced to justification. It is not the mere removal of any accusation. And he stoutly denies that it is legal fiction. Wesley argues that while justification is distinct from sanctification, it never occurs apart from genuine regeneration and progressive sanctification.

Regeneration and Sanctification

Wesley is convinced that justification changes our legal status before God. While this divine act is distinct from sanctification and must not be confused with it, neither can it be separated from God's work in regeneration and sanctification. The doctrines of justification and regeneration are, for Wesley, of such importance that "if any doctrines within the whole compass of Christianity may be properly termed fundamental, they are doubtless these two."[30] Justification refers to what God does *for* us, "in forgiving our sins," while regeneration refers to "the great work which God does *in us*, in renewing our fallen nature" and working *real* change within us.[31]

How is regeneration related to justification? For Wesley, justification *logically* precedes the new birth, but they share a temporal beginning.[32] Sanctification begins at the "same time that we are justified."[33] For "in that instant we are born again, born from above, born of the Spirit: there is a *real* as well as a *relative* change."[34]

The new birth is what makes someone a genuine Christian rather than an "almost Christian." Genuine Christianity is not, for Wesley, merely a matter of having good manners or commendable ethics. It is not—and cannot be confused with—honesty, justice, and care for others. As wonderful as such characteristics are, they are not a substitute for regeneration. Nor is it what Wesley calls the "form of godliness"; for the person who abstains from profane and evil language, avoids sexual sins, resists temptations to substance abuse and gluttony while also attending Christian worship may yet be an "almost Christian" rather than a genuine child of God.[35]

To the contrary, the truly regenerate person—the "altogether Christian"—is the one who is filled with the love of God and the love of neighbor. The genuine Christian loves the Lord with all their "heart, mind, soul, and strength."[36] Indeed, "such love of God is this, as engrosses the whole heart, as takes up all the affections, as fills the entire capacity of the soul, and employs the utmost extent of all its faculties."[37] Particularly important here is Wesley's focus on the affections; he is convinced that genuine regeneration involves a reorientation of our affections. This love for God cannot, for Wesley, ever be separated from a love for neighbor that is both genuine and genuinely new. Wesley is persuaded that Jesus will not allow us to separate the love of God from love of neighbor (even though they are distinct), and he is insistent upon the centrality of love of neighbor. Who is our neighbor? According to Wesley, the scope of our obligation to hospitality extends to all—even to the enemies of Christianity.[38]

Why must we be born again? For Wesley, the "foundation of this doctrine" is "as deep as the creation of the world."[39] We were made in God's image; as God is "love, accordingly man at his creation was full of love," as God is "full of justice, mercy, and truth, so was man when he came from the hands of his Creator." God is spotless in purity and holiness, "and so man was in the beginning pure from every sinful blot."[40] But while good, humanity was not *necessarily* good and thus was able to be tempted and to fall. When by "willful act of disobedience" the original human parents sinned against God, they "died to God, the most dreadful of all deaths." For here Adam "lost the life of God: he was separated from him, in union with whom his spiritual life consisted."[41] This fall into sin has impacted all of Adam's progeny, and now all are "dead in trespasses and sins." Thus "we must be born again."[42]

How may we be born again? Just what is this strange-sounding new birth? Wesley strives hard to give what he calls a "plain scriptural account" of the nature of regeneration. In reference to the question of Nicodemus (John 3:9), Wesley emphasizes the spiritual and supernatural nature of the new birth. To be "born from above, born of God, born of the Spirit" is analogous to natural birth.[43] Spiritual regeneration is a "quickening" by the Holy Spirit that enlivens the sinner to a genuinely new life and future. The picture Wesley draws echoes the creation account. It is a picture of resuscitation, for "God is continually breathing, as it were, upon the soul; and his soul is breathing unto God."[44] In summary, regeneration is "that great change which God works in the soul, when he brings it into life; when he raises it from the death of sin to the life of righteousness. It is the change wrought in the whole soul by the almighty Spirit of God, when it is 'created anew in Christ Jesus,' when it is 'renewed after the image of God, in righteousness and true holiness.'"[45] It is a supernatural act, a gracious work of the Triune God to rescue and renew what sin has enslaved and ruined. And it changes everything.

The new birth is not necessarily to be equated with baptism, nor does it always and automatically accompany baptism. Moreover, it is possible to deny our baptism.[46] Nor yet can good works take the place of the new birth. Thus all sinners—no matter how self-righteous or industrious for good deeds they might be—must be born again. Wesley concludes his sermon "The New Birth" with this characteristic exhortation: "Without this, nothing will do any good to your poor, sinful, polluted soul."[47] To the person who appeals to his own observance of the sacraments and alms-giving, Wesley replies: "It is well you do: but all this will not keep you from hell, except you be born again. Go to church twice a day; go to the Lord's table every week; say ever so many prayers in private; hear ever so many good sermons; read ever so many good books; still, you must be born again."[48]

Wesley is absolutely convinced of both the reality and the power of the new birth, but he is also frank about the fact that sin remains in genuine believers. Recognizing that the doctrine of original sin is taught in Scripture and affirmed in the theology of the early church as well as the Articles of his own Church of England, he disagrees explicitly with Count Zinzendorf in his insistence that the justified and regenerate are not immediately delivered from all sin.[49] He rejects Zinzendorf's account of instantaneous perfection on three grounds: first, it is "contrary to the whole tenor of Scripture," second, it conflicts with the most obvious deliverances of Christian experience, and third, because it produces the kind of laxity in the Christian life that results in "the most fatal consequences."[50] The regenerate have hearts that are *truly* but not yet *entirely* renewed.[51] As Wesley puts it, "Although we are renewed, cleansed, purified, sanctified, the moment we truly believe in Christ, yet we are not then renewed, cleansed, purified altogether; but the flesh, the evil nature, still *remains* (though subdued) and wars against the Spirit."[52]

Such recognition of sin in believers means that the Christian life is a life of repentance and faith. Just as they are the "gate of religion," so also are repentance and faith "as necessary, in order for our *continuance* and *growth* in grace."[53] This recognition entails the admission that those who have been born again nonetheless have no standing before God apart from the work of Christ. Additionally, it implies a complete reliance upon the work of the Holy Spirit. Indeed, Wesley will go so far as to say that regenerate believers "are no more able now *of themselves* to think one good thought, to form one good desire, to speak one good word, or do one good work, than before they were justified," and "they have still no kind or degree of strength *of their own*; no power either to do good or resist evil."[54] Genuine Christians thus live always and only by the power of justifying, regenerating, and sanctifying grace.

Wesley exhibits a serious optimism about what grace can do in the life of a genuine Christian. Christians are to avail themselves of the "means of grace" which are used by God "to be the ordinary channels" whereby God expresses prevenient, justifying, and sanctifying grace.[55] Such sacraments are "outward sign[s] of inward grace, and a means whereby we receive the same."[56] The "chief of these means" are prayer, study of Scripture, and the reception of the Eucharist.[57] The Christian life, as a life of repentance and faith that utilizes the God-ordained means of grace, is one of genuine growth in godliness.

Just as justification is by grace alone through faith alone, so also is sanctification by grace through faith. We are not justified by our works, and neither are we sanctified by our good works. Wesley is clear about the symmetry between justification by faith and sanctification by faith: "Faith is the condition, and the only condition of sanctification"; faith and faith alone is "sufficient for sanctification."[58] This does not, of course, mean that what we *do* is irrelevant to sanctification; rather, Wesley means to insist that we do not sanctify ourselves by our works. Those good works are indeed necessary, but they are necessary as a consequence.[59] They may be categorized as "works of piety" and "works of mercy." The former include such activities as public worship and prayer, family and private prayer, study and mediation on Scripture, fasting, and reception of the Eucharist. The latter include "feeding the hungry, clothing the naked, entertaining the stranger, visiting those that are in prison, or sick, or variously afflicted" as well as teaching and comforting.[60]

As Christians avail themselves of the means of grace and respond to this grace in faithful obedience, they grow in holiness and righteousness. This is a process that is linear and teleological in nature, and it is one that will be marked by important moments. Regeneration happens at a definite point in time; much like our physical birth precedes and enables our bodily growth, so also does the new birth precede, begin, and enable our sanctification. Thus, regeneration is the "gate" or "entrance" into the process of sanctification.[61] Wesley makes much of this "exact analogy": "A child is born of a woman in a moment, or at least in a very short time: afterwards he gradually and slowly grows." Similarly, "a child of God is born of God in a short time, if not in a moment. But it is by slow degrees that he afterwards grows up to the measure of the full stature of Christ. The same relation, therefore, which there is between our natural birth and our growth, there is also between our new birth and our sanctification."[62]

Thus, sanctification is the work of the Holy Spirit that truly changes sinners into holy people, and it happens as a "gradual work."[63] God has promised full and complete deliverance from sin in Scripture, for God has promised nothing less than the "circumcision of the heart."[64] Christians should have every confidence that God is *able* to do what he has promised; so while it is indeed senseless to think that sinners might purify themselves, nonetheless "with God all things are possible."[65] Moreover, there is available to Christians "a divine evidence and conviction that he is able and willing" to completely sanctify believers. Indeed, we should believe God when he says that he actually does this, for truly "if we walk in the light as he is in the light, we have fellowship one with another, and the blood of Jesus Christ his Son cleanseth us from all sin."[66] God may do it either gradually or instantaneously—and we dare not circumscribe God's ability to cleanse and purify. Wesley concedes that the completion of sanctification most often happens near the point of death, but he insists as well that there is no reason why it cannot happen earlier.[67] Thus, Christians should earnestly seek, and receive gratefully, all that God has provided for their salvation.

Whenever and however exactly it comes from the Lord, Wesley is utterly convinced of the reality of sanctification. Indeed, he refers to full or "entire" sanctification as "Christian perfection." He does so knowing that this terminology will ignite all sorts of misunderstandings and indeed will fuel all manner of accusations, but he is persuaded that fidelity to the biblical portrayal of salvation demands it. For even though "whosoever preaches perfection, i.e., asserts that it is attainable in this life, runs great hazard of being accounted by them worse than a heathen man or a publican," nonetheless the language itself is found in the "oracles of God" and cannot be rejected out of hand.[68] So Wesley insists upon retaining the language, but he is also exercised to avoid misunderstanding. He points out that the biblical sense of perfection does not include freedom from mistakes, ignorance, or infirmities, for even the most sanctified are none the less finite creatures.[69] Nor does Christian perfection imply freedom from temptation.[70] Nor yet should we think that it ever entails a completion so that there is no room for growth in grace.[71]

So what *does* it mean to affirm Christian perfection? Does the concept not die the death of a thousand qualifications? Wesley summarizes his positive account of Christian perfection as perfection in love.[72] The one who is perfect in this sense is "one in whom is 'the mind which was in Christ,' and who so 'walketh as Christ also walked'; a man 'that hath clean hands and a pure heart.'"[73] More precisely, this is the person who "walketh in the light as he is in the light, in whom there is no darkness at all; the blood of Jesus Christ his Son having cleansed him from all sin."[74] So exactly what does it mean to affirm Christian perfection? For Wesley, it is nothing more and nothing less than this: Christian perfection is "loving God with all our heart, and mind, and soul (Deut. 6:5)."[75] Wesley is utterly convinced that God's sanctifying work penetrates to the darkest reaches of human existence, and he insists that God is both able and willing to sanctify his people.

Perseverance and Assurance in the Christian Life

As a pastoral theologian, Wesley is keenly aware of critical issues related to the continued growth in grace and Christian assurance of salvation.

Some Christians are so confident of their salvation that their lives show signs of moral laxity, while other sincere and earnest Christians seem unable to gain any confidence of their salvation. He offers some "serious thoughts" on the doctrine of the "perseverance of the saints," and here he is "sensible [that] either side of this question is attended with great difficulties."[76] Nonetheless, he follows what he takes to be the difficult teaching of Scripture on this issue. Arguing from the "warning passages" of Scripture as well as the apparent examples of people who indeed have made "shipwreck" of their faith, Wesley concludes that it is possible for genuine believers—those who are "holy or righteous in the sight of God himself" as well as "endued with the faith that purifies the heart" and "grafted into" Christ to "so fall away from God as to perish everlastingly."[77]

Does this possibility not remove all assurance from Christian experience? Does not the possibility of apostasy remove all genuine faith and hope? Wesley is alert to such worries, and he is exercised to insist that it is important to understand that God's grace offers genuine and comforting assurance.[78] In fact, the doctrine of assurance became something of a hallmark of Wesleyan theology; Thomas C. Oden even says, "The doctrine of the assuring witness of the Spirit is a quintessentially Wesleyan doctrine."[79] Subsequent Methodist theologians, according to Oden, have found it "exceedingly important" to insist that "God not only gives us this merciful gift of justifying grace through the Son on the cross [but also] works through the Spirit to attest the meaning of the Son's mission and to bring it to full actualization in us."[80]

Wesley is concerned here to avoid dangers from very different directions. On one hand, he sees the skepticism that comes from some quarters (both from rationalistic skeptics and from some theologians who denied that assurance was either possible or healthy). On the other hand, he is very worried about the dangers of fanaticism and "enthusiasm." Resisting both extremes, he proclaims that genuine Christian assurance is both possible and glorious. Wesley is confident that it is God's gracious gift to the children of God who walk in fellowship with God. And it comes in two ways: through the "indirect witness" and through the "direct witness." The "indirect witness" is grounded in Scripture, for there we find that "everyone who has the fruit of the Spirit is a child of God."[81] So if we know that everyone who exhibits the fruit of the Spirit belongs to God, and if we can see that we exhibit the fruit of the Spirit, then we can have confidence that we belong to God. The "direct witness" is also grounded in Scripture, for there we read that "the Spirit itself bears witness with our spirit, that we are the children of God"—and this witness is nothing less than the direct testimony of the Holy Spirit to us that we belong to God.[82] This assurance is not the possession of a few elite saints or mystics; to the contrary, Wesley is convinced that this is the birthright of every child of God.

"Nothing To Do But Save Souls": The Implications of the Gospel and the Hope of Glory

Wesley is deeply convinced that the mission of God included all of creation; therefore, he is passionate about mission and evangelism as well as matters of "social justice" and mercy. His view of the breadth and depth of the holy love of the Triune God compels him to see *every person* as loved by God, and this love impels us to extend God's mercy to both "body" and "soul." In other words, Wesley's theology leads him to be passionate about both evangelism and works of mercy and justice—particularly as these works are expressed to the most vulnerable. Thus he can tell his preachers that they have "nothing to do but to save souls"—while also working tirelessly for the abolition of slavery, fighting poverty, providing medical care for the underprivileged, promoting education, and resisting child labor (among other activities).[83] For all of this is closely related to the gospel: for "Christianity is essentially a social religion; and to turn it into a solitary one is to destroy it."[84] Thus Wesley insists that we are "expressly commanded to feed the hungry and clothe the naked,"[85] and he warns that when we live extravagantly while ignoring the poor and oppressed, we are like those who are "keeping money from the poor, to buy poison for ourselves."[86] The strength of Wesley's conviction on this point is evident in the force of his thunderous statements on the subject. For instance, he says that those who live only for themselves are

> Not only robbing God, continually embezzling and wasting their Lord's goods, and by that very means, corrupting their own souls, but also robbing the poor, the hungry, the naked; wronging the widow and the fatherless; and making themselves accountable for all the want, affliction, and

distress, which they may, but do not remove. Yea, doth not the blood of all those who perish for want of what they lay up, or lay out needlessly, cry against them from the earth?[87]

The breadth of Wesley's vision of God's infinite holy love is vivid in his eschatology. He is well acquainted with the vicissitudes of life; he knows that this planet is inhospitable in many ways and that life upon it is always short and often brutish. But, he is resolute: God is "making all things new"—and we have a glorious future in Christ. God is not rescuing a few people (the "elect") away from creation; instead, God is renewing and restoring creation as a place of *shalom*. Here, once again, Wesley's Trinitarian understanding of reality gives shape and substance to his doctrine of salvation. His vision of the scope and depth of salvation is obvious in his gospel-centered eschatology:

> But the most glorious of all will be the change which then will take place on the poor, sinful, miserable children of men. These had fallen in many respects, as from a greater height, so into a lower depth than any other part of creation. But they shall "hear a great voice out of heaven, saying, Behold, the tabernacle of God is with men, and he will dwell with them, and they shall be his people, and God himself shall be their God." Hence will arise an unmixed state of holiness and happiness far superior to that which Adam enjoyed in paradise. In how beautiful and affecting a manner is this described by the Apostle! "God shall wipe away all tears from their eyes; and there shall be no more death, neither sorrow nor crying, neither shall there by any more pain: for the former things are done away" (Rev. 21:3–4). As there will be no more death, and no more pain or sickness preparatory thereto; as there will be no more grieving for or parting with friends; so there will be no more sorrow or crying. Nay, but there will be a greater deliverance than all this; for there will be no more sin. And to crown all, there will be a deep, an intimate, an uninterrupted union with God; a constant communion with the Father and his Son Jesus Christ, through the Spirit; a continual enjoyment of the Three-One God, and of all creatures in him![88]

Truly, for Wesley, salvation flows from the generous purposes of the Triune God. It is intended for all—the Triune God wants to save and restore all those creatures made in his image (and indeed all creation). Thus we are saved *from* sin, and thus we are saved *for* communion with our Creator. This is Wesley's vision of salvation.

NOTES

1. See Randy L. Maddox, *Responsible Grace: John Wesley's Practical Theology* (Nashville: Abingdon Press, 1994).
2. John Wesley, "The New Birth," in *Wesley's 52 Standard Sermons* (Salem, OH: Schmul Publishing, 1988), 460. The quotations retain Wesley's gender-specific terminology.
3. See the discussion in Barry E. Bryant, "Original Sin," in *The Oxford Handbook of Methodist Studies*, ed. William J. Abraham and James Kirby (Oxford: Oxford University Press, 2009), 534, and more broadly, Thomas H. McCall, "'But a Heathen Still': The Doctrine of Original Sin in Wesleyan Theology," in *Adam, the Fall, and Original Sin: Theological, Biblical, and Scientific Perspectives*, ed. Hans Madueme and Michael Reeves (Grand Rapids, MI: Baker Academic, 2014), 147–166.
4. John Wesley, "Original Sin," in *Wesley's 52 Standard Sermons*, 456.
5. Wesley clearly accepts and extends (and, arguably, adapts in some respects) the Augustinian doctrine of prevenient grace.
6. John Wesley, "Dialogue Between a Predestinarian and His Friend," in *The Works of John Wesley*, Vol. X (Grand Rapids, MI: Zondervan, n.d.), 260–265. Whether or not these are the best (not to mention preferred) doctrinal labels, they are Wesley's currency, e.g., John Wesley, "The Question, 'What Is An Arminian?' Answered. By a Lover of Free Grace," in *The Works of John Wesley*, Vol. X, 358–361.
7. John Wesley, "Predestination Calmly Considered," in *The Works of John Wesley*, Vol. X, 204–205.
8. John Wesley, "What Is An Arminian?," 360–361.
9. Wesley, "Predestination Calmly Considered," 211–216, 224–227.
10. Ibid., 221.
11. Ibid., 223.
12. Ibid.
13. Ibid., 217. Here Wesley comes close to an outright affirmation of the doctrine of divine simplicity (and he does so within a pastoral context).
14. Ibid., 221.
15. Wesley, "A Dialogue Between a Predestinarian and His Friend," 265.
16. Wesley, "Predestination Calmly Considered," 237.
17. Ibid., 210.
18. Ibid.
19. Thomas C. Oden, *John Wesley's Scriptural Christianity: A Plain Exposition of His Teaching on Christian Doctrine* (Grand Rapids, MI: Zondervan, 1994), 253.
20. Wesley, "Predestination Calmly Considered," 259.

21. This section draws upon my summary of Wesley's doctrine in my *Forsaken: The Trinity and the Cross, and Why It Matters* (Downers Grove, IL: InterVarsity Press, 2012), 126–128.
22. Wesley, Letters 4:298 . . . For lucid discussion see Kenneth Collins, *The Scripture Way of Salvation: The Heart of John Wesley's Theology* (Nashville: Abingdon Press, 1997), 86–100.
23. John Wesley, "Justification by Faith," *52 Standard Sermons*, 44.
24. Ibid., 45.
25. For helpful discussion of the controversies surrounding Wesley on the issue of "imputed righteousness," see Collins, *The Scripture Way of Salvation*, 92–100; Allan Coppedge, *Shaping the Wesleyan Message: John Wesley in Theological Debate* (Nappannee, IN: Francis Asbury Press of Evangel Publishing House, 2003), 119–127; and especially Fred Sanders, *Wesley on the Christian Life: The Heart Renewed in Love* (Wheaton, IL: Crossway, 2013), 131–149.
26. John Wesley, "The Lord Our Righteousness," in *52 Standard Sermons*, 196.
27. Wesley, "Justification by Faith," 49.
28. See Collins, *The Scripture Way of Salvation*, 95.
29. See Thomas C. Oden, *John Wesley's Teachings, Volume 2: Christ and Salvation* (Grand Rapids, MI: Zondervan, 2012), 104.
30. John Wesley, "The New Birth," in *52 Standard Sermons*, 459.
31. Ibid.
32. Ibid.
33. Wesley, "The Scripture Way of Salvation," in *52 Standard Sermons*, 441.
34. Ibid.
35. Wesley, "The Almost Christian," in *52 Standard Sermons*, 12–13.
36. Ibid., 15.
37. Ibid.
38. Ibid.
39. Wesley, "The New Birth," 460.
40. Ibid.
41. Ibid.
42. Ibid., 461.
43. Ibid., 462.
44. Ibid., 463.
45. Ibid.
46. Ibid., 464–465.
47. Ibid., 467.
48. Ibid.
49. Wesley, "Sin in Believers," in *52 Standard Sermons*, 118–119.
50. Ibid., 122.
51. Ibid.
52. Ibid., 126.
53. Ibid., 128.

54. Ibid., 133.
55. Wesley, "Means of Grace," 152.
56. Ibid.
57. Ibid.
58. Wesley, "The Scripture Way of Salvation," 444.
59. Ibid., 445.
60. Ibid.
61. Wesley, "The New Birth," 466.
62. Ibid.
63. Ibid., 442.
64. Wesley, "The Scripture Way of Salvation," 446; cf. Wesley, "The Circumcision of the Heart," in *52 Standard Sermons*, 163–171.
65. Wesley, "The Scripture Way of Salvation," 446.
66. Ibid., 447.
67. Wesley, "The Scripture Way of Salvation," 447; cf. Wesley, *Plain Account*, 41.
68. Wesley, "Christian Perfection," in *52 Standard Sermons*, 405.
69. Ibid., 406–407.
70. Ibid., 408.
71. Ibid.
72. Wesley, "Scripture Way of Salvation," 442.
73. Wesley, *Plain Account*, 34.
74. Ibid., 35.
75. Ibid., 40.
76. Wesley, "Serious Thoughts Upon the Perseverance of the Saints," in *The Works of John Wesley*, Vol. X, 285.
77. Ibid., 298.
78. Such worries trouble various theological traditions (not least the Reformed tradition), of course, and they animate theological discussion and controversy. On Jacob Arminius's handling of these issues, see Keith D. Stanglin, *Arminius on the Assurance of Salvation: The Context, Roots, and Shape of the Leiden Debate, 1603-1609*. Brill's Series in Church History, vol. 27 (Leiden: Brill, 2007), and Keith D. Stanglin and Thomas H. McCall, *Jacob Arminius: Theologian of Grace* (New York: Oxford University Press, 2012), 176–188.
79. Oden, *Christ and Salvation*, 128.
80. Ibid.
81. John Wesley, "The Witness of the Spirit, II," in *The Sermons of John Wesley: A Collection for the Christian Journey*, ed. Kenneth J. Collins and Jason E. Vickers (Nashville: Abingdon, 2013), 207.
82. The relation of Wesley's views to "Reformed Epistemology" remains underexplored (although not entirely unrecognized). See, e.g., Alvin Plantinga, *Warranted Christian Belief* (Oxford: Oxford University Press, 2000), 288, 292 n5. See also William J. Abraham, *Aldersgate and Athens: John Wesley and the Foundations of Christian Belief* (Waco: Baylor University Press, 2010).

83. See Robert Coleman, *Nothing To Do But To Save Souls* (Nappannee, IN: Evangel Press, 1990).
84. John Wesley, "Upon Our Lord's Sermon on the Mount, Discourse IV," in *52 Standard Sermons*, 241.
85. Ibid., 249.
86. John Wesley, "Upon Our Lord's Sermon on the Mount, Discourse VIII," in *52 Standard Sermons*, 296.
87. Ibid., 297.
88. Wesley, "The New Creation," 654.

17

Friedrich Schleiermacher's Theology of Salvation

JAMES R. GORDON

Friedrich Schleiermacher (1768–1834) was born in Breslau in Silesia (now Wrocław in Poland). His father was a Reformed pastor with a strong connection to the Moravian community, thus the young Schleiermacher was educated at Pietist institutions in Niesky and Barby (both now in eastern Germany). However, Schleiermacher became increasingly dissatisfied with the restricted Moravian curriculum, and desired to continue his education at a more progressive institution. He enrolled in 1787 at the University of Halle, a stronghold of Enlightenment thinking, where he studied Plato, Aristotle, and Kant. He spent some years thereafter in a combination of personal study, ordination training, and private tutoring, before taking his first pastoral charge in 1796 as the Reformed preacher at the Charité hospital in Berlin. Schleiermacher flourished in the vibrant Prussian capital, finding friends within its cultured salon society and its creative, Romantic circles. In 1799, he published his famous apologetic work *Speeches on Religion to the Cultured among its Despisers*. After a brief period in a further pastoral charge in Stolp in Pomerania (now Słupsk in Poland), he was appointed Extraordinary Professor and University Preacher at the University of Halle in 1804, but the university was closed in 1806 following the city's occupation by Napoleon. Returning to Berlin, where he spent the remainder of his days, Schleiermacher was active in three principal domains. First, from 1809 he was a minister at the Dreifaltigkeitskirche (Trinity Church). He preached weekly, and was heavily involved in the conversation and controversy surrounding the union of Lutheran and Reformed churches in Prussia, a union he advocated and defended. Second, in 1810 he became a founding professor of the University of Berlin. Within the faculty of Theology, he lectured on dogmatics, ethics, exegesis, hermeneutics, church history, and practical theology, and served as dean of the faculty and as rector of the university. In this connection, he produced two editions of his landmark dogmatic work, *Christian Faith*. Third, he was actively interested in political matters, particularly in the areas of education policy and constitutional matters. At times the Prussian state sought to capitalize upon this interest, but at other times viewed it with suspicion. In 1834, while still deeply active on all fronts, Schleiermacher died of pneumonia, five years after the death of his only son. Thousands attended his funeral procession.

Introduction

Friedrich Daniel Ernst Schleiermacher (1768–1834), a Prussian theologian in the Protestant tradition, offers a unique account of salvation in Christ that faces the challenges of Modernity head-on and attempts to mine the rich resources of the Christian tradition to make sense of the way in which believers experience the benefits of Christ the Redeemer. Before proceeding to an exposition of Schleiermacher's understanding of sin and salvation in Christ as outlined in his *magnum opus, The Christian Faith*, we must first make several prefatory comments.

First and foremost, one must understand Schleiermacher within his context. Born to a chaplain and educated in a Moravian school in the conservative pietist tradition, he was raised in a tradition that valued devotion to Christ and expressed a cautionary attitude toward the secular knowledge of the day. As Schleiermacher grew in his education during his time first at Niesky (1783) and later at seminary at Barby (1785), he encountered curricula immersed in the liberal Enlightenment tradition that challenged the faith of his youth and made him question some of the tenants of his conservative education. Yet, despite his humanist education, Schleiermacher did not leave the Christian faith but instead sought to engage the modern academy in order to see how the faith of his youth could be expressed in modern forms of thought; he described himself in a letter to George Reimer in 1802 in the following way: "I have become a Herrnhuter [a Moravian] again, only of a higher order."[1]

What this means is that while Schleiermacher wanted to maintain the best part of his early religious education, he wanted to do so not at the expense of the appropriation of the available forms of knowledge of the day. As a "mediating" theologian, then, Schleiermacher is often considered to be the "Father of Modern Liberal Theology" in that he did not want to bracket off theological knowledge as unsusceptible to the scientific and historic criticisms of the day but instead to state the content of the Christian faith precisely in those thought forms.[2] This gives Schleiermacher the freedom to innovate, revise, and otherwise modify (and, in some cases, reject) the traditional doctrines of the church. More will be said below on how this specifically affects Schleiermacher's approach to sin and salvation in Christ.

However, in maintaining his Moravian pietist heritage, Schleiermacher focuses on the Christian's own religious consciousness in his presentation of redemption (i.e., the believer's own experience of sin and salvation). Since "Christian doctrines are accounts of the Christian religious affections set forth in speech,"[3] and since "Dogmatic Theology is the science which systematizes the doctrine prevalent in a Christian Church at a given time" (§19 proposition), Schleiermacher chooses to focus on religious self-consciousness as the primary way in which doctrine is to be elaborated.

Second, in 1809 Schleiermacher became the pastor of Trinity Church in Berlin, where he would serve for twenty-five years. The church had its origins as a "dual-faith" congregation, with both Reformed and Lutheran pastors and congregants. During Schleiermacher's tenure, the church was united by the king into one Prussian church, and it was his task to facilitate the unification process of a previously divided congregation.[4] This context undoubtedly shaped the way in which Schleiermacher attempted to engage both the Lutheran and Reformed traditions before him and yet to propose a Catholic-Protestant account of the Christian faith that would not divide the church. Since he did not complete the second edition of *The Christian Faith* until 1830, the pastoral context that shaped his work cannot be overlooked.

Sin and Salvation: A Mystical View

Schleiermacher refers to his own view of Christian salvation as a "mystical" view, which lies between the "magical" view on the one hand and the "empirical" view on the other (§100.3). It is important to grasp what Schleiermacher means by the so-called mystical view, since it is quite different than what the term connotes, and it shapes the material content of his entire presentation.

To understand the magical view, it might help to refer to the allegory of John Bunyan's *Pilgrim's Progress*. In the allegory, Christian walks along his journey from the City of Destruction to the Celestial City with a literal burden on his back—allegorically representing sin. Along the way, Christian encounters various figures who instruct him in the best way to remove his burden—such as Mr. Worldly Wiseman, who instructs Christian in moral living as a means of release and freedom from his burden. The burden is not removed, however, until Christian reaches the place of deliverance (representing the cross of Christ).

In a way, Schleiermacher worries that much of the Christian tradition has done something akin to taking Pilgrim's allegorical burden quite literally with regard to sin and salvation: Adam's sin creates an actual backpack filled with the "stuff" of sin that all humans receive insofar as they are participants in the seed of Adam. Over the course of life humans accumulate more sin "coins" in their accounts, and God, as the perfect judge, will condemn anyone whose backpack contains a positive number of sin coins. It is only by Christ's assumption of human nature and his living a life free from the accumulation of sin that he is able to serve as the infinitely valuable redeeming sacrifice. Christ, as the perfect offering, literally takes human sin upon himself, removing the burdens from their backs and imputing his sinless righteousness to them. Schleiermacher refers to this sort of view as a magical view of sin and salvation.

Put differently and somewhat more technically, Schleiermacher wants to avoid the notion that sin and redemption are actual metaphysical entities that can be magically moved around from person to person as if they existed in abstraction from their actual forms in a lived life. However, the opposite error, which he calls the "empirical" view, wants to maintain that nothing *really* happens in redemption; this view seems to follow from a rejection of the magical view. If Christ does not *really* bear the stuff of human sin and does not *really* transfer his righteousness to those he redeems, then perhaps it is the case that Christ only provides some kind of moral improvement for humankind that might rightly be referred to as "redemption." But Schleiermacher is not content with this merely empirical account and so attempts to walk the fine line between the magical and empirical by insisting that the supernatural becomes natural in the person of Christ the Redeemer (cf. §100.3). This means that humans *really* experience redemption and reconciliation in Christ, but they do not do so in any other way than in the natural world processes and the social forms that mediate those processes; Schleiermacher insists that the supernatural becomes natural in the person of Christ such that nothing additional needs to be superimposed on the natural causal structures of the world because God in Christ has determined from all eternity that those structures are an appropriate means for redemption. This will become clearer below, but for now it is vitally important to realize that just because Schleiermacher rejects the traditional metaphysical apparatus by which sin is said to be transmitted and healed *does not mean that he must insist that redemption does not do anything real.*

Sin in Light of Redemption

Finally, before we move to the content of Schleiermacher's understanding of salvation, one additional word needs to be said about the shape of his presentation. While it is the case that Schleiermacher's treatment of human sin comes before his treatment of the redemption and reconciliation offered in Jesus Christ and the way in which believers become conscious of this redemption, the content of his doctrine of sin is already and beforehand shaped and determined by that which redemption accomplishes. In other words, Schleiermacher is a radically Christocentric theologian in that he works backwards, so to speak, from the work of Christ to his account of human sin; his thought process might be summarized in the following way: If redemption consists in x, y, and z, then what must be the case about human sin if redemption is said to repair that which is broken? This order of operation is important for Schleiermacher's account of redemption, but it can be lost if one does not keep the entire structure of *The Christian Faith* constantly in mind. With these prefatory comments behind us, we may now proceed to the content of Schleiermacher's doctrine of salvation.

Sin

For Schleiermacher, any discussion of sin cannot be abstracted from one's personal self-consciousness of it. Sin, accordingly, is anything "that has arrested the free development of the God-consciousness" (§66.1). The continual struggle exists between allowing each moment of finite existence to be determined by the God-consciousness and allowing the consciousness of sin to suppress the God-consciousness. Schleiermacher sees this, simply, as a statement of the struggle between flesh and spirit described by the Apostle Paul in Galatians 5 and Romans 7. A specifically Christian account of sin, and one that is completely in step with that of Schleiermacher, must say "sin consists in our desiring what Christ contemns [sic.] and *vice versa*" (§66.2).

SIN AND THE GOD-CONSCIOUSNESS

In human persons the state of sin exists prior to both the development of the God-consciousness and, therefore, the consciousness of sin. As the God-consciousness develops in a human person, one can reflect on times at which one was completely receptive (and not resistant) to the flesh. Only as the God-consciousness develops does one become aware of those times; that is to say, "we become conscious also of sin as the God-consciousness awakes within us" (§67.2). The spiritual life begins in a conscious decision of the will—a "taking command of one's self"—and acts that do not correspond with such a decision make persons more aware of the "domination of the flesh" (§67.2).

Schleiermacher is clear that his own view is not incompatible with the original perfection of human persons. Rather, since "sin in general exists only in so far as there is a consciousness of it," one must infer that such a consciousness was always and everywhere already determined by a preceding good (§68.2). The notion of the "bad" within persons only exists because of an awareness of that which is better. However, lest one be tempted to claim that the consciousness of sin is merely having insufficiently developed a consciousness of good that comes by particular acts and inner states, Schleiermacher sees such a view as nullifying the reality of sin and, more significantly, "the need of redemption"; such a view "can scarcely be regarded as a Christian view at all" because it "leaves so little room anywhere for the peculiar work of a Redeemer" (§68.3).

Sin, as a derangement of human nature, does not abrogate the possibility of "human perfection evolved without sin," for it is "*he* alone to whom we do not ascribe that common consciousness of sin . . . [who] can exercise redeeming activity" (§68.3). In this way, Schleiermacher's account of sin as derangement is *already constrained by what must be said about the Redeemer*, namely that "the God-consciousness could have developed progressively from the first man to the purity and holiness which it manifests in the Redeemer" (§68.3).

ORIGINAL AND ACTUAL SIN

Finally, the source of sin is both within oneself and outside of oneself. On the one hand, later generations of human persons are dependent upon earlier generations for their own particular dispositions and proclivities, which suggests "the sin of the individual has its source in something beyond and prior to his own existence" (§69.1). On the other hand, Schleiermacher reasons that sin must also have its origins in the individual because it is "the swift movement of a sensuous excitation towards its object without ranging itself with the higher self-consciousness" (§69.1) and because all such occurrences are voluntary actions (§69.2). This twofold relation of sin as originating within oneself and outside of oneself corresponds, according to Schleiermacher, to the church's doctrines of "original" and "actual" sin (*peccatum originis* and *peccatum actuale*) (§69 postscript).

However, Schleiermacher does not think the traditional terminology is helpful, for it suggests that "actual" sin is more "real" than original sin. He certainly wants to posit the "realness" of original sin, but he also wants to make sure his reader understands that "original sin indicates that inherent quality of the acting subject which is a part condition [*sic*] of all his actual sins and is anterior to all action on his part" (§69 postscript). Schleiermacher suggests it might be best to get rid of the unhelpful terminology associated with the two doctrines, but he is also realistic that any such revision must be accomplished gradually and with care.

Schleiermacher claims that original sin is "the sinfulness that is present in an individual prior to any action of his own, and has its ground outside his own being" (§70 proposition). While Schleiermacher maintains that there is no moment in the life of a human person during which the consciousness of sin does not form a "present and operative" part of one's own self-consciousness (§70.1), he is still quick to qualify such original sin with a view toward redemption: "redemption must be regarded as the only thing that can remove the incapacity referred to" (§70.1). To over-emphasize original sin, Schleiermacher thinks, would compromise the true human nature within one and subsequently diminish one's capacity for redemption (§70.2). As such, persons have "the capacity to appropriate the grace offered to us," and the incapacity resulting from original sin refers only to "personal activity . . . and not to our receptivity" (§70.2) (thus avoiding Pelagianism).

But more than merely something inherited from outside of oneself, original sin is also "the personal guilt of every individual who shares in it that is best represented as the corporate act and the corporate guilt of the human race" (§71 proposition). This qualification of sharing in the corporate act and guilt of the human race is important for Schleiermacher, for he worries that many traditional accounts of original sin refer to *individual* guilt that renders one susceptible to eternal punishment. He worries that traditional accounts make it seem as if the guilt inherited in original sin is of such an infinite variety that no amount of actual, accumulated sin in one's life "could add nothing to the penal desert which attaches to everyone on account of this so-called disease" (§71.1).

Original sin is common to all persons—"in each the work of all, and in all the work of each" (§71.2). As such, a doctrine of original sin must not look to individual consciousnesses, for such are the focus of doctrines of *actual* sin; instead, original sin ought to focus on the corporate consciousness (§71.2). Schleiermacher suggests that when one downplays the corporate nature of original sin, "a lower estimate of the redemption wrought by Christ" typically follows (§71.3).

THE FALL

From here, Schleiermacher attempts to give an account of the actual origin of the first sin (the Fall), since his formulation thus far could not apply to the first human pair, as they would not be immersed in a chain of preceding corporate consciousness of sin. After examining some of the traditional accounts of the Fall—such that Satan seduced Adam and Eve or that they misused their free will—Schleiermacher insists that no change in human nature took place at the Fall. When one accepts this, "then the universal sinfulness that precedes every actual sin in the offspring is to be regarded not so much as derived from the first sin of our parents, but rather as identical with what in them likewise preceded the first sin, so that in committing their first sin they were simply the firstborn of sinfulness" (§72.4).

Such an account of original sin allows Schleiermacher to "readily dispense with all those artificial theories which for the most part tend only to lay stress upon the divine justice in imputing Adam's sin to, and exacting its penalty from, his posterity" (§72.4). Instead, he insists that the incapacity for good was something innate to the first human pair even prior to sin, but this in no way violates the original perfection of humans laid out in §60 and §61. Even while the sin of the first human pair did not cause any sort of essential change to human nature, Schleiermacher does allow for the first sin to be a cause for the growth and increase of sin in the human race, which directly relates to his account of redemption, in that "without the entrance into all mankind of an element free from that sinfulness," human nature would be continually dominated by the flesh (§72.5). The Fall, then, as recorded in the Genesis narrative, is a description of the universal narrative of all persons.

Original sin serves as the ground for actual sin, which is manifest in every person in the human race. Even Christ, the Redeemer, is "at no moment free from sin," since he is a constituent member of the human race (§73.1). With regard to the varieties of actual sin, Schleiermacher boils them down into two distinct groups: those that are expressions of particular appetites and those that are obscurations of the God-consciousness (§74.2).

Redemption

In regard to his account of redemption, Schleiermacher notices, first, that all religions prescribe some "device" for getting rid of sin and its effects. There is, in these actions, the idea that the admission of sin requires some accompanying act to rid one of the misery of sin. Such acts, however, only create further misery as one tries to atone for one's own sins, and these futile exercises, Schleiermacher thinks, reveal a longing that is fulfilled in Christianity's conception of the Redeemer (§86.1).

CHRIST'S AND THE CORPORATE LIFE OF BLESSEDNESS
The solution to the misery of sin is found in the state of blessedness in the Christian life: "Every approximation to the state of blessedness essentially includes a relation to Christ" (§87.1), and one's blessedness is "grounded in a new divinely-effected corporate life" (§87 proposition). Christian blessedness is grounded, further, in the twofold reality of the complete removal of the misery of sin and the incorporation into the corporate life of blessedness.

For Schleiermacher, "In this corporate life which goes back to the influence of Jesus, redemption is effected by Him through the communication of His sinless perfection" (§88 proposition). It follows, then, that if the original believers had redemption communicated to them by Christ because of their recognition of his sinless perfection, and if the faith of the church today depends on believers having the same sorts of experiences of the original believers, then "the recognition of the sinless perfection in Jesus Christ . . . must in the same way be still His work" (§88.2). In other words, Schleiermacher needs some mechanism to bridge the gap between the early church, who had experienced Christ's sinless perfection through his immediate personal influence, and the church today, which no longer has Christ with it in the flesh. The faith-producing influence must, in short, be "none other than the influence of the personal perfection of Jesus Himself" (§88.2).

As Schleiermacher has already maintained, sin is transmitted within the community by wholly natural processes as it precludes the development of the God-consciousness. The only way, therefore, for Christ to communicate his perfectly potent God-consciousness to his followers is this: "we must believe that this God-consciousness had a supernatural origin, though only in the sense which has been postulated above" (§88.4).

Crucially, then, analogous to the transmission of sin in the corporate life, "So, too, in relation to the Redeemer Himself, the new corporate life is no miracle, but simply the supernatural becoming natural, since every exceptional force attracts mass to itself and holds it fast" (§88.4). The Redeemer though, insofar as he brings about a renewal in the corporate life of sinfulness, must have come about supernaturally (§88.4). In Christ, there is at the same time "an initial divine activity which is supernatural" and a "vital human receptivity in virtue of which alone that supernatural can become a natural fact of history" (§88.4).

CREATION AND SIN FOR REDEMPTION

But since Christ is the one divine act of God, and since Christ brings about a removal of the misery that accompanies the consciousness of sin, it seems to follow that God, therefore, ordained the consciousness of sin—and, apparently, sin itself—in humanity. God is not the creator of sin, though sin results from the one divine decree whose effect was redemption. In this way, Christ is the Second Adam, "the beginner and originator of this more perfect human life" (§89.1)—a life that never would have arisen on its own out of the natural order of things. Creation, in other words, is creation *for* redemption. The only difference between the Second Adam and the first is that "from the outset He has an absolutely potent God-consciousness" (§89.2).

Schleiermacher turns his attention to "the state of the Christian as conscious of the divine grace." As he has previously elaborated, redemption consists always and only in the corporate life inaugurated in Christ. Schleiermacher foreshadows the two headings under which he will treat redemption in the following sections: Christ and the Christian. Christ's blessedness and sinless perfection "represent a free spontaneous activity, while the recipient's need of redemption represents a free assimilative receptivity" (§91 proposition). God-consciousness unrelated to Christ is not considered Christian God-consciousness. To be related to Christ, then, requires both the cognitive relation of one's God-consciousness to Christ and the incorporate of Christ's saving influence into one's own free activity. But, in order for grace to be grace, the consciousness and activity of the believer cannot originate in that believer, for then they both would fail to be the gracious activity of the Redeemer; as such, Schleiermacher needs a mechanism by which to claim that the free activity of the believer really is the activity of Christ. In short, "all real vital fellowship with Christ, in which He is in any sense taken as Redeemer, depends on the fact that living receptivity for His influence is *already* present, and *continues* to be present" (§91.1).

CHRIST'S PERSON AND WORK

Schleiermacher outlines the way in which a Christian understanding of Christ must proceed, namely, by treating Christ's person and work. If, as Schleiermacher has claimed, the blessedness of the new corporate life founded by Christ proceeds *only* from Christ, then his life must not be divided into isolated moments but considered as whole (§93.1). Further, all of the states of God-consciousness that exist in the corporate life must be present in Christ himself if they are not to be taken as "newly added power[s]" applied later in the community's life (§93.2). Schleiermacher is primarily concerned with these states of God-consciousness existing in Christ in his treatment of Christ's person.

These states, which involve his historical person entering the sinfulness of humanity, are the result of a "miraculous fact" rather than the natural development of the human environment in which he was located. This in no way precludes the natural development of Christ, since the implantation of his God-consciousness is that which cannot be explained naturally. To say that Christ carried a perfectly developed God-consciousness from his first moment of existence is the error of Docetism, which denies Christ a true human life. At the same time, Christ must have always possessed the God-consciousness within him, since if it had been given at a later stage, he would be both the Redeemer *and* the redeemed, which is problematic (§93.3). Furthermore, whereas in human persons the possibility of sinless development is mere counterfactual possibility, in Christ "must have become actual in the person of the Redeemer" (§93.4). Indeed, Christ's sinless development must be the case if the redeeming influence he brought about is equally applicable to all persons (§93.5).

Christ, then, "is like all men in virtue of the identity of human nature, but distinguished from them by all the constant potency of His God-consciousness, which was a veritable existence of God in him" (§94 proposition). If Christ is to be the Redeemer of humanity, then he must share in all that it is to be fully human. Christ came into the corporate life of the world "when it had already advanced far in deterioration," and so his sinlessness could not be attributed to mere positive surrounding influences (§94.1). In order to take away the sinful corporate life, Christ's sinlessness must be essential to himself rather than external to him.

Schleiermacher is careful, however, to maintain that "so far as sin is concerned, Christ differs no less from the first man than from all others" in no way reduces his activity to the same as that of all other humans (§94.1). The reason for this is that "to ascribe to Christ an absolutely powerful God-consciousness, and to attribute to Him an existence of God in Him, are exactly the same thing" (§94.2). The God-consciousness that humanity has within itself is unlike the God-consciousness of Christ in that it is purely passive (i.e., not fully active); therefore, it cannot count as an existence of God. Christ "is the only 'other' in which there is an existence of God in the proper sense" (§94.2). Just as Adam's appearance gave birth to the physical life of humanity, "the appearance of the Second Adam constituted for this nature a new spiritual life" (§94.3).[5]

From this point, Schleiermacher spends a great deal of time handling and critiquing the ecclesiastical formulae of Christ as posited by the church. While much could be—and has been—said about the particular nuances of Schleiermacher's Christology in relation to the classical Chalcedonian formula, for our purposes, it is necessary only to note several important features of that Christology that properly relate to Christ's work of redemption.

First, Schleiermacher revises the traditional talk of natures and persons, which he takes to be less clear than many have taken it to be, to accommodate the particular account of redemption he wishes to give. In particular, he wants to maintain that Christ is in fact an incarnation of God without in any way compromising his true humanity; that is to say, Schleiermacher ensures that Christ is both fully human and fully divine:

> For if the distinction between the Redeemer and us others is established in such a way that, instead of being obscured and powerless as in us, the God-consciousness in Him was absolutely clear and determined each moment, to the exclusion of all else, so that it must be regarded as a continual living presence, and withal a real existence of God in Him, then, in virtue of this difference, there is in Him everything that we need, and, in virtue of His likeness to us, limited only by His utter sinlessness, this is all in Him in such a way that we can lay hold of it. ($96.3)

This, for Schleiermacher, is equivalent to the Pauline claim that "God was in Christ" and the Johannine claim "the Word became flesh" even while it differs from the traditional scholastic formulations of Christology—though, like those Christologies, it avoids both Docetism on the one hand and Ebionitism on the other.

Second, Schleiermacher's account of Christ's person interacts heavily with the notion of Christ's sinless perfection—not because such sinlessness preserves Christ as the sinless offering of the atonement sacrifice, but because such a life of sinless perfection in a fully active God-consciousness *just is* the redemption that Christ brings to humankind. So, because of the way in which Schleiermacher has outlined human original sin (described above), he needs a way to account for Christ's sinlessness. He does this first by suggesting that one need not believe in Christ's "supernatural conception" in order to maintain that he is in fact the Redeemer (§97.2). Since sin does not have some corrupting influence of all human nature after Adam (as in the traditional Augustinian view of original sin), Schleiermacher does not think that Christ needs to be free from any paternal contribution to his life, for such would not exclude Christ from the corporate life of sinfulness (§97.2). Further, the idea that the Virgin Mary was immaculately conceived, thus freeing her nature from the corruption of original sin, has no explanatory power either for Schleiermacher, since "there is no doctrine or tradition of a continuous series of mothers who were conceived, and who remained, without sin" (§97.2). This is not to say, however, that the conception of Christ was just one conception among many other natural conceptions; on the contrary, Christ's conception was a result of "a creative divine activity" that "could alter both the paternal and the maternal influence in such a way that all ground for sinfulness was removed" (§97.2). This means, therefore, that "The general idea of a supernatural conception remains . . . essential and necessary, if the specific pre-eminence of the Redeemer is to remain undiminished" (§97.2).

Every moment of Christ's life was lived as proceeding directly from the being of God in Christ, and "the human nature is only taken up into association with it" (§97.3). And "this 'divine' is the divine love in Christ which, once and for all or in every moment—whichever expression be chosen—gave direction to His feelings for the spiritual conditions of men" (§97.3). All of the active states of Christ proceed directly from the activity of God, and all of those passive states that develop into Christ's activity, too, proceed from this same divine activity.

As a life lived every moment in active God-consciousness, "Christ was distinguished from all other men by His essential sinlessness and His absolute perfection" (§98 proposition). Schleiermacher has maintained that human beings, under the right set of externally conditioned circumstances, can prevent possible sin from becoming active; yet, in such cases, "this happens in such a way that therein we not only remain conscious of ourselves as sinful men, but are even confirmed in this consciousness through this very perception, for it implies a recognition that in our case the *inner* ground for the prevention of sin is lacking" (§98.1). This he describes as *accidental* rather than essential sinlessness. In describing the way in which Christ remains sinless, "Everything," Schleiermacher claims, "depends on determining the point where sin begins" (§98.1). Pleasure and pain, which typically give rise to the internal struggle that is sin, were still part and parcel of Christ's experiences, but they were determined "in the manner appropriate to him," that is, as moments enacted by the divine love within him (§98.1); this is what it means for Christ to be essentially sinless.[6] Christ's work, as the essentially sinless Redeemer, consists in assuming believers "into the power of His God-consciousness" (§100 proposition). And further, the challenge of Christian piety is allowing Christ's acts to become one's own acts (§100.1). Schleiermacher will examine the Christian's experience of being incorporated in the blessedness of the new corporate life in Christ after he examines the way in which Christ accomplishes his work of Redemption.

Schleiermacher views every act of Christ "as a continuation of that person-forming divine influence upon human nature" (§100.2). His view of redemption and the way in which the activity of Christ forms human persons is the mystical view, which is the mean between the magical view on the one hand and the empirical view on the other (§100.3). The magical view isolates redemption from the natural sphere altogether, while the empirical view speaks only to the improvement of humankind by attentiveness to Christ's example (§100.3).

When believers are assumed into the corporate life of blessedness in the God-consciousness of Christ in redemption, they are reconciled in that they receive Christ's "unclouded blessedness" (§101 proposition). This is to say that if redemption establishes a corporate life, reconciliation is "person-forming," in that it establishes in each individual a sense of that corporate life "in that an old man is put off and a new man is put on" (§101.2). Schleiermacher believes that any view of Christ's reconciling activity that says blessedness and forgiveness "are not mediated through vital fellowship with Christ" will inevitably fall into magic (§101.3). Since blessedness cannot originate from within oneself, it follows that if it is not communicated in fellowship with Christ, it must come to one from some other external source; Schleiermacher views this as magical and arbitrary. It is not that Christ's sufferings somehow magically atone for the sins of those who believe, according to Schleiermacher. Instead, there is no redeeming or reconciling activity in any way detached from the directly communicated redemption and reconciliation in the person of Christ experienced in the believing community.

THE INDIVIDUAL'S EXPERIENCE OF CHRIST'S REDEMPTION

Schleiermacher turns his attention away from the person and work of Christ and to the way in which the individual experiences that redeeming and reconciling activity of the Redeemer. His explication of this section is divided into two doctrines, each of which is composed of two theorems. First, the doctrine of regeneration contains the headings of conversion and justification. And second, the doctrine of sanctification contains headings on both the sins and good works of the regenerate person. If the concept of regeneration attempts to describe the process of one's becoming a new creature in Christ, then sanctification speaks to the mitigation of the old life present within one (§106.1).

In one's assumption into living fellowship with Christ (regeneration), change takes place both in one's relation to God (justification) and in one's form of life (conversion) (§107 proposition). The two, while distinct, must be held together as simultaneous occurrences in order to make sense of one's experience of Christ's blessedness (§107.1).

"Conversion," according to Schleiermacher, is "the beginning of the new life in fellowship with Christ" and "makes itself known in each individual by Repentance, which consists in the combination of regret and change of heart; and by Faith, which consists in the appropriation of the perfection of the blessedness of Christ" (§108 proposition). Repentance and faith go together in one's self-experience in a "twofold activity" (§108.1); they represent the ceasing of one's state of being in one's sphere and beginning of existence in another sphere. In repentance one is conscious of one's past and experiences conversion insofar as one experiences Christ's redeeming activity arising out of a vision of his perfection. "Christ awakens a wholly perfect regret just in so far as His self-imparting perfection meets us in all its truth, which is what happens at the dawn of faith" (§108.2). One's change of heart from the fellowship of the life of sin and being brought into the corporate life of blessedness is effected by Christ's receptive activity, since the impulses turning one from regret to faith are in fact the very impulses of Christ (§108.2). Conversion, therefore, can take place over a long period of time, and one need not identify a "moment" of conversion (§108.3). Everything related to conversion, then, depends wholly and entirely on—and indeed *is*—the work of Christ. Conversion can only be communicated by Christ because it is that which originally began in his own life (§108.6). Schleiermacher steadfastly maintains that the human work in conversion is not a co-operative one in the sense that humans contribute anything to that work; rather, grace proceeds and conditions any human act of faith, and "Even the consent accompanying the reception of the Divine Word . . . can be ascribed only to the antecedent work of grace" (§108.6). He does want to insist that a human person is not a "lifeless object" in conversion, so he avoids speaking of it as purely passive. One's God-consciousness is "heightened" by conversion through the impartation of Christ's God-consciousness (i.e., union with Christ) and it eventually becomes one's own spontaneous activity (§108.6).

Schleiermacher wishes to use the language of justification to describe not merely one event in which one is declared righteous before God, but as the whole event in which one receives forgiveness of sins and a positive relation to God on the grounds of one's faith in Christ (§109.1). Justification is "dependent on the whole activity of Christ" and it gives rise to a new consciousness in a believer with regard to sin, namely, forgiveness (§109.2). Specifically, "The new man thus no longer takes sin to be his own"; one's disposition in receiving a new relation to Christ entails that one now identifies the consciousness of Christ as one's new outlook on one's sin (§109.2). While there is no particular change in God with reference to justification, since "God is gracious to the human race in His Son" (§109.3), justification does include a change of the consciousness of the individual's relation to God, which occurs through the means of conversion that Schleiermacher has already specified. In this way, it *just is* faith that saves for Schleiermacher, and this allows him to maintain the Reformation maxim *sola fide*. One's faith is indeed the means by which one is saved, but the faith one exercises is in fact the very faith of Christ the Redeemer.

Sanctification, for Schleiermacher, "is a striving for holiness" rather than a state of being holy (§110.1). While it is true that no new sins develop during the state of one's sanctification, all existing sins are not immediately wiped out from one's life (§110.2). As such, he has to account for both the sins of the regenerate person and the good works of the regenerate person—from whence do they arise, and how can they be explained?

First, with regard to the sins of the regenerate person, Schleiermacher insists "in the state of sanctification there can be no sin which could make regeneration nugatory" (§111.1). The new humanity active in one will always resist, at least in some measure, the sins exercised in the state of sanctification. There is no sense in which one can lose the state of regeneration, even while one may continue to succumb to temptation and sin; all the while one is still an adopted child of God and "conditioned by the liveliness and activity of faith" (§111.4).

Second, with regard to the good works of the regenerate, Schleiermacher maintains that good works are the "natural effect of faith" (§112.1). "To be continuously and receptively open to the influence of Christ, and continuously active in will for His Kingdom, is the life-process of the new man" (§112.1). One additional question arises, however: Since the regeneration one experiences is in fact the faith of Christ made active in her, how can the good works of the regenerate one rightly be attributed to her? Schleiermacher claims "it is self-evident that in virtue of the living fellowship existing between them, what belongs to Christ in a good work cannot be separated from what belongs to the individual; for this would be to dissolve the fellowship" (§112.2). While some might appeal to a use of the Mosaic Law for the Christian in facilitating good works, Schleiermacher suggests that the law can only deal with external actions while love deals with one's inner dispositions. As such, "one may justly say that in the Christian Church it is neither necessary nor advisable to begin instruction about sin, and still less about sanctification, with the Decalogue" (§112.5).

From this point Schleiermacher continues his treatment of the consciousness of grace with reference to "The Constitution of the World in Relation to Redemption," which includes his discussion of the election, the communication of the Holy Spirit, Scripture, proclamation, the sacraments, the relationship between the church and the world, and the last things—all of this before bringing *The Christian Faith* to a close in a discussion of "The Divine Attributes which relate to Redemption" (viz., divine love and wisdom) and, ultimately, the doctrine of the Trinity as the conclusion of a properly Christian dogmatics.[7] So, in one sense, to restrict Schleiermacher's doctrine of salvation to that which takes place in the individual truncates the significance he attributes to Christ's saving work of redemption and reconciliation. Yet, what we have said in the foregoing about Christ's God-consciousness being the means by which salvation is enacted contains the seeds for all that will follow in the remainder of *The Christian Faith*.

Conclusion

Schleiermacher's account of human sin and salvation in Christ, while novel and revisionist, contains many echoes and glimpses of accounts of redemption that preceded him in the Christian tradition. Walter E. Wyman, Jr. is correct in his assertion that "Sin and redemption constitute the heart of Schleiermacher's understanding of Christianity."[8] And, this claim can be taken one step further by noting that, for Schleiermacher, Christ the Redeemer constitutes the undoing of sin and the effecting of redemption. An account of human sin must not be constructed independently of the person and work of the Redeemer, and such a commitment shapes the entirety of what Schleiermacher says on the matter.

NOTES

1. B. A. Gerrish, *A Prince of the Church: Schleiermacher and the Beginnings of Modern Theology* (Eugene, OR: Wipe & Stock, 2001), 26–27.
2. On which, see Bruce L. McCormack, "Introduction: On 'Modernity' as a Theological Concept," in *Mapping Modern Theology: A Thematic and Historical Introduction*, ed. Kelly M. Kapic and Bruce L. McCormack (Grand Rapids, MI: Baker Academic, 2012), 1–20.
3. Friedrich Schleiermacher, The Christian Faith, ed. H. R. Mackintosh and J. S. Stewart (Edinburgh: T&T Clark, 1989), §15 proposition. Citations of *The Christian Faith* hereafter will be noted parenthetically in the text by section.
4. Cf. Catherine L. Kelsey, *Thinking About Christ with Schleiermacher* (Louisville, KY: Westminster John Knox, 2003), 27.
5. For a response to the claim that Schleiermacher has a "low" Christology, see Kevin W. Hector, "Actualism and Incarnation: The High Christology of Friedrich Schleiermacher," *International Journal of Systematic Theology* 8 (2006): 307–322.
6. It is worth mentioning that while traditional Christologies take Christ's resurrection, ascension, and return to be essential to his person (and also, subsequently, to his work), Schleiermacher does not think that such events belong properly to the doctrine of scripture rather than to Christology as such (§99).
7. For a more thorough treatment of the structure of Schleiermacher's *The Christian Faith*, with particular reference to the relationship between his Christology and treatment of the divine attributes, see my "A 'Glaring Misunderstanding'? Schleiermacher, Barth, and the Nature of Speculative Theology," *International Journal of Systematic Theology* 16 (2014): 313–30.
8. Walter E. Wyman, Jr., "Sin and Redemption," in *The Cambridge Companion to Friedrich Schleiermacher*, ed. Jacqueline Mariña, Cambridge Companions to Religion (Cambridge: Cambridge University Press, 2005), 129.

18

Karl Barth

TOM GREGGS

Karl Barth (1886–1968) is considered to be one of the greatest Protestant theologians of the twentieth century. Born in Basel, Switzerland, he began his theological studies at Berne and then continued his education under the direction of many of the prominent liberal theologians of the period, including Adolf von Harnack and Wilhelm Herrmann, at universities in Berlin, Tübingen, and Marburg. In the years before and during World War I, Barth held several Swiss pastorates. While serving as a pastor in the industrial town of Safenwil, he composed his *Römerbrief*, a commentary on Romans, in which he challenged the liberal theology of his earlier training by calling for a radically transcendent view of God. The publication of this work, the first edition in 1919 and the more influential second edition in 1921, has been seen as a turning point in the history of modern theology. In 1921 Barth became a professor in Göttingen, moving to the University of Munster in 1925 and to Bonn in 1930. When Hitler came to power, Barth became one of the founders of the Confessing Church, which resisted the capitulation of the "German Christians" to Nazi propaganda, and he helped to draft the Barmen Declaration of 1934, which affirmed the sovereignty of the Word of God in Christ over against all political ideologies. In 1935, having refused to take a loyalty oath to Nazism, Barth was dismissed from his university chair and forced to flee from Germany. He returned to Basel, where he lived and taught until his retirement in 1962. Barth's massive *Church Dogmatics*, the first volume of which appeared in 1932, is regarded as one of the masterpieces of twentieth-century theology. Other well-known works include *Anselm: Fides Quaerens Intellectum*, *The Word of God and the Word of Man*, and *The Humanity of God*.

Introduction

Although Karl Barth is often caricatured as a theologian who was concerned singularly with the otherness of God and with the doctrine of revelation (someone preoccupied with saying Nein!), it is probably truer to say that Barth is above all else a theologian of the God of salvation. For Barth, theological abstraction consists of any point that is made separate to Jesus Christ—not to Christology, or to conceptions of Jesus Christ, but to the God-man Himself in His life, death, and resurrection. In one sense, it is only out of his prioritization of the reality that there is no god to be known except the God who is the God of our salvation that Barth's concern for revelation exists. For Barth, there is no distant God hidden behind God's economy, no God behind God as He is in His revelation to us in Jesus Christ: God is as God is in His act of revelation. In one sense, therefore, Barth's understanding of salvation is both foundational to and the purpose of his famous concern that theology be orientated only on the revelation of the Word of God. For Barth, the Word of God is the Word of the Creator directed to us, which has become necessary and remains so for the renewal of the original relation between God and humanity. Revelation's purpose, therefore, is that it makes known to us the Word of Reconciliation, the Word of the Reconciler. In this event of revealing Himself to humanity, God promises Himself as the content of our future.[1] Revelation is reconciliation, therefore, in certain ways for Barth.[2] As Barth summarizes in the thesis statement of §15 of *Church Dogmatics* (I/2) on "The Mystery of Revelation": "The mystery of the revelation of God in Jesus Christ consists in the fact that the eternal Word of God chose, sanctified and assumed human nature and existence into oneness with Himself, in order thus, as very God and very man, to become the Word of reconciliation spoken by God to man." Barth is a theologian of salvation in a way comparable to Athanasius and Anselm. His concern is that there is no other God than the God who reveals Himself as for humanity.

Barth's radical maneuver of placing the doctrine of election within the doctrine of God demonstrates precisely this point. We can no longer think of God's act of election as being simply something that God does or wills. Instead, for Barth, election is the decision in which God wills to be and actually is God.³ God is, therefore, gracious in His own self-determination because in this self-determination, God wills to be God solely in Jesus Christ:⁴ "For this self-determination is identical with the decree of His movement towards man."⁵ God is, for Barth, the God of salvation, the God who determines Himself in Jesus Christ.

Even Barth's four-part volume account of creation is premised on salvation. For him, creation and redemption are two points of one ellipse, they are conjoined as part of God's act of grace. Reconciliation and redemption are pre-supposed in creation.⁶ "It would be truer to say that creation follows the covenant of grace since it is its indispensable basis and presupposition."⁷ Creation tells humanity that the creature is predestined to participate in history whose ground and direction is in the will of God.⁸ For Barth, creation is the beginning of the *Heilsgeschichte*, which culminates in Jesus Christ.⁹ Creation should not make us think of salvation as an afterthought, or a second plan after the failure of the principal plan of creation.¹⁰ Quite the opposite: "If by the Son or the Word of God we understand concretely Jesus, the Christ, and therefore very God and very man, as He existed in the counsel of God from all eternity and before creation, we can see how far it was not only appropriate and worthy but necessary that God should be the Creator." Creation is an act of God that is preceded in the divine decrees by God's act of self-determination in His election to be Jesus Christ. Creation follows from God being the God for us, from the actuality that God is the God of salvation.

For Barth, the economy of God is the centerpiece of his thought. There is nothing in theology that cannot and should not be thought of in relation to gracious turning of God in humanity in Jesus Christ. Where Barth differs on this front in his Kantian propensities from his predecessors in the nineteenth century is that he not only speaks of functional Christology, but also sees this as grounded in ontological Christology as well as in the doctrine of God proper. For Barth, it is not simply the case that we can only speak of God as He is for us, but it is also the case that God is God as He is for us. In this chapter, this theme will be explored in relation to Barth's account of the objectivity of salvation in the self-election of Jesus Christ. Following this, Barth's specific account of the doctrine of reconciliation, based on the munus triplex, will be outlined in the second major section of this chapter. A final section of the chapter will provide some comment on the human response to salvation and the extent of salvation in Barth's account.

Election and the God of Salvation: In Christ

George Hunsinger has argued compellingly that to understand salvation for Barth it is necessary to note the centrality of the term "in Christ" to his soteriology. Hunsinger writes:

> Perhaps no single observation can be of more assistance to the careful reader of the Church Dogmatics than to note that Barth always uses the ubiquitous but inconspicuous term "in Christ" (and its cognates) in what is virtually a technical sense. Phrases, sentences, paragraphs, sometimes even entire sections . . . cannot fully be understood, unless it is seen that the argument turns on the objectivist soteriology conveyed by this little phrase.[11]

By soteriological objectivism, Hunsinger means that the life, death, and resurrection of Jesus form the governing way in which salvation is to be understood: Whatever humans do or whatever they experience in relation to salvation (what Hunsinger describes as "soteriological existentialism") can only be understood as being radically subordinated to the person and work of Christ.[12] Salvation should be understood as "entirely constituted, complete, and effective apart from and prior to any reception of it that may or may not occur here and now in our existence."[13] Every account of salvation for Barth is an account of the life of Jesus Christ. This is, in some senses, a classical Reformed way of approaching soteriology: for example, Book II of Calvin's Institutes precedes Book III—the description of the person and the narrative of the life of Christ comes before the explanation of its benefits to humanity. All that soteriology should do is to indicate the narrative of the life of Christ and offer some reflection on it in relation to humanity: To Jesus Christ belongs salvation, and soteriology's role is to point to Him. As Barth puts it:

> "In Christ" means that in Him we are reconciled to God, in Him we are elect from eternity, in Him we are called, in Him we are justified and

sanctified, in Him our sin is carried to the grave, in His resurrection our death is overcome, with Him our life is hid in God, in Him everything that has to be done for us, to us, and by us, has already been done, has previously been removed and put in its place, in Him we are children in the Father's house, just as He is by nature. All that has to be said about us can be said only by describing and explaining our existence in Him; not by describing and explaining it as an existence which we might have in and for itself.[14]

But, Barth sustains the objectivist account of salvation far beyond the imagination of Calvin.

For Barth, the ground of this objectivist salvation rests in his radical account of God's election. As von Balthasar reminds us, election is "the heart beat of Barth's theology."[15] Indeed, Barth makes it clear that his governing soteriological principle "in Christ" rests on his account of divine election:

> "In Him" does not simply mean with Him, together with Him, in His company. Nor does it mean only through Him, by means of that which He as elected man can be and do for them. "In Him" means in His person, in His will, in His own divine choice, in the basic decision of God which He fulfils over against every man.[16]

The ontological ground for salvation is to be found, therefore, in Barth's account of election.[17] By moving the doctrine of election into the doctrine of God, Barth gives content to his account of the divine life: God is the God of election, the God of salvation. Recognizing that it is not necessarily clear that election should be given the place of precedence that Barth affords it, he asserts that election should be considered within the doctrine of God since in election we find the

> primal and basic decision in which He wills to be and actually is God, in the mystery of what takes place from and to all eternity within Himself, within His triune being, God is none other than the One who in His Son or Word elects Himself, and in and with Himself elects His people. In so far as God not only is love, but loves, in the act of love which determines His whole being God elects.[18]

We see in election that God does not simply enact election (and the salvation that follows from it), but that in Barth's actualistic account, this act is the primal self-determining act of God in which God is who God is. This differentiates the Christian understanding of God from all other false and abstract ideas of God.[19] God is the electing God, and in the primal history of the covenant of God in the union of His Son with Jesus of Nazareth, one sees the gracious relating of God to humanity.[20] The will of God cannot be separated from the love of God:[21] Barth does not want to confront humanity with a God who might as well condemn people as save them, who might not be able to allow His deep Yes to overcome His No to sin. At the same time, the love of God cannot be separated from the will of God: God "loves in freedom."[22] Although election is an eternal decision, Barth wishes God's electing to remain a free decision in order to remain gracious: There must still be personhood and a center of self-consciousness behind that loving in freedom,[23] a point much of neo-Protestantism had failed to realize.[24]

But, what is this election like, and how does it relate to salvation? Barth asserts that the doctrine of election must be understood Christologically. It is Jesus Christ who is the Subject and object of election as electing God (der erwählende Gott) and elected human (der erwählte Mensch). The event of Jesus Christ is the first, truest, and fullest reality of election that there can be. Jesus Christ is God in His movement toward and covenant with humanity.[25] In a radical departure from the tradition, the election of Jesus Christ is not passive and confined to His human nature, for Christ, according to Barth, is simultaneously electing God and elected human:[26] Only in the active and passive election of the Son of God does humanity have the basis for its election.[27] Thus, God's election of all humanity is with and in Christ's own election.[28] Christ is the elected human, "before all created reality, before all being and becoming in time, before time itself, in the pre-temporal eternity of God."[29] There is no room for a prior decision of God to create, or elect and condemn before the decision to elect Jesus Christ (no *decretum absolutum*);[30] instead, Jesus Christ is Himself the ultimate *decretum absolutum*.[31] This indicates a singularly positive turning toward humanity, in that it is eternally in Christ that God makes this movement and determines Himself for this covenant of grace. Indeed, in Barth's actualistic inner logics,[32] it might even be stated that God is this movement and turning toward humanity: His economy and ontology cannot be separated.[33] Thus, for God who is love, election is the act of His love in its most glorious forms of condescension, patience, freedom, overflowing.[34] In self-electing, God brings the other upward to Himself, so that He can never again be without it.[35] Election's nature is, therefore, Gospel.[36] Humanity continues to need to be rescued by God in its rejection of Him, but this is now considered in a wholly Christological way, which brings together the Yes and No of God in the simultaneity of the elected and rejected Christ. It is He who demonstrates salvation as its originator and archetype. It is, therefore, in the humanity of the elected Christ that one needs to consider the destiny of human nature.[37]

Furthermore, in the election of Jesus Christ, God elects for Himself the negative part of predestination—perdition, death, rejection, exclusion, and the No of God.[38] These are the things humanity deserves, and yet God decides in His freedom to suffer them on the cross in His self-election in Jesus Christ. Predestination becomes, therefore, not one modus of salvation but the modus of the divine work of redemption, indeed of all of God's works ad extra.[39] In it, Christ has willed to take to Himself rejection in order that rejection can never again become the portion of humanity: "He is the Rejected, as and because He is the Elect. In view of His election, there is no other rejected but Himself."[40] It is this that makes the election of humanity in Christ so radical. Barth posits the integrity of election and rejection and yet unites these in the person of Jesus Christ in a chiastic move in which the elected of God (Jesus Christ) elects rejection in order that the rejected (sinful humanity) may be elect in His election of rejection: Christ suffers rejection on the cross and elects this in order that humanity may be elect even in its rejection of God.

The effects of this on soteriology cannot be underestimated. The election of the community and individuals occurs only in the prior election of Jesus Christ, and cannot be abstractly separated from this. Included in Christ's election is the election of the other—the many "whom electing God meets on this way."[41] Since Barth's account of what it means to be "in Christ" is objectivist, to be "in Christ" cannot be instrumentalized in relation to the resultant identity of Christ with each member of humanity.[42] As Barth writes about Christ's work of salvation: "He really accomplished both His own and our justification and glorification . . . Death could not hold Him, and therefore it cannot hold us."[43]

The Doctrine of Reconciliation

Barth expounds the outworking of his doctrine of election within volume IV of his *Church Dogmatics: the Doctrine of Reconciliation*. This is a work of four-part volumes and around 3,000 pages. Volumes 1–3 were completed, but volume 4 on the ethical material of the doctrine remained incomplete and further fragments were published posthumously. In his preface to the doctrine, Barth asserts that to fail in his articulation of salvation would be to fail everywhere:[44] The reconciling work of God stands at the center of the church's message with creation and redemption as its circumference but the covenant fulfilled in the atonement at its center.[45] Barth wrote to his son that he awoke from a dream at 2 AM with the structure of his doctrine of reconciliation in place, and found himself scribbling the details down.[46] Certainly the layers, interwoven complexity, and elegance of volume 4 makes it exceptional even within the *Church Dogmatics*.

The structure of the three completed part volumes is formed around the *munus triplex* of Christ as Priest, King, and Prophet, but this is developed in an exciting and innovative way related to the Christological confession of Christ as very God, very human, and ontologically one. Each section is then related to a particular aspect of human sinfulness that humans learn from knowing Christ (pride, sloth, and falsehood). And an aspect of the knowledge of the event reconciliation is explained (justification, sanctification, and calling) and related to the work of the Holy Spirit in the community (gathering, upbuilding, and sending), and the being of the Christian (faith, love, and hope).[47] In discussing this event of reconciliation, what Barth believes one will find is "the temporal happening of atonement, God's eternal covenant with man, His eternal choice of this creature, His eternal faithfulness to Himself and to it."[48] In discovering this reality, we find in God's event of reconciliation:

> That its eternity and inflexibility are those of His free grace, and that the glory which He willed to maintain and defend is that of His mercy—His covenant a covenant of grace and His election an election of grace; so that conversely the atonement made in Jesus Christ will be seen to be wholly an act of the grace of God and therefore an act of sovereignty which can-

not be understood in all its profundity except from the fact that God is this God and a God of this kind.[49]

The complex architectonics, which Barth uses to describe the event of reconciliation, are designed to offer us knowledge of the grace of God in which we come to knowledge of the God of salvation.

Barth's account begins, therefore, with the strictly Christological: The governing narrative is that true God truly became true human in the incarnation. *Church Dogmatics IV/1* is orientated to Christ as truly God and the condescension of the Son of God to humanity. It is through this that we are to understand the priestly act of the Son in His substitutionary bearing of the human rejection of and by God: Jesus becomes the "judge judged in our place."[50] This, according to Barth, is the humiliation of God, and through this humiliation, the sin of human pride is overcome. Pride, for Barth, is "the opposite of what God does for us in Jesus Christ in condescending to us, in humbling Himself, in becoming a servant to take to Himself and away from us our guilt and sickness."[51] In this act of the condescension of the Son of God to death upon even the cross, we are able to understand what it is for God to justify the proud sinner:

> Justification definitely means the sentence executed and revealed in Jesus Christ and His death and resurrection, the No and the Yes with which God vindicates Himself in relation to covenant-breaking man, with which He converts him to Himself and therefore reconciles him with Himself. He does it by the destruction of the old and the creation of a new man.[52]

The objective work of justification finds its subjective terminus in the life of the community and the individual, albeit that Barth believes this rests in a very secondary and subjugated place. He approaches this theme in an ordered way, considering first the community and then the individual: Salvation is the salvation of the individual in the community. This community is the historical community of the church that the Holy Spirit awakens as the power of the Word spoken by the Lord who became servant to judge and justify sinners.[53] Only in light of the community can the individual be considered. In terms of this act of justification of individual sinners, it must be noted that for Barth, justification is not a process in which humans become less sinful and more justified; instead, in justification humans are completely and fully both justified and sinner simultaneously (*simul iustus et peccator*).[54] Nevertheless, for Barth, "the question of the subjective apprehension of atonement by the individual man is absolutely indispensable."[55] Under this, he considers the faith of the individual Christian.

The same basic structure of argument is found in *Church Dogmatics IV/2*. Whereas IV/1 begins from the perspective of the true divinity of Christ, IV/2 begins from the perspective of the true humanity of Christ. Through the humiliation and condescension of God in Christ, humanity is exalted:

> As in Him God became like man, so too in Him man has become like God. As in Him God was bound, so too in Him man is made free. As in Him the Lord became a servant, so too in Him the servant has become a Lord. That is the atonement made in Jesus Christ in its second aspect. In Him humanity is exalted humanity, just as Godhead is humiliated Godhead. And humanity is exalted in Him by the humiliation of Godhead.[56]

For Barth, however, these two aspects of the person and work of Christ cannot be divided into two separate or distinctive moments: They are one work that constitutes His person in its two-fold form.[57] This exaltation is the kingly aspect of Christ by which he brings about the sanctification of humankind through His upward movement of the exaltation of humanity in response to the sin of human sloth. Sanctification cannot be thought of as a second or separated moment of reconciliation brought about by the action of individual believers. Instead, it must be thought of objectively in the first instance in relation to Jesus Christ:

> The sanctification of man which has taken place in this One is their sanctification. But originally and properly it is the sanctification of Him and not of them. Their sanctification is originally and properly His and not theirs. For it was in the existence of this One, in Jesus Christ, that it really came about, and is and will be, that God Himself became man, that the Son of God became also the Son of Man, in order to accomplish in His own person the conversion of man to Himself, his exaltation from the depth of His transgression and consequent misery, his libera-

tion from his unholy being for service in the covenant, and therefore his sanctification.[58]

Sanctification thus comes to all humanity *de iure*. However, it takes place *de facto* in the lives of believers in the community, and by this, the community is built up through the work of the Holy Spirit in order to give a provisional representation of the sanctification of all humanity through the event of the life, death, and resurrection of Jesus Christ. In relation to the individual, this sanctification is considered in relation to Christian love as God raises humans up to correspond to His love.

Barth's most daring (and perhaps original) discussion of reconciliation comes in *Church Dogmatics IV/3* (a volume divided and published in two halves because of its length). Having explored the divinity and humanity of Christ in relation to humiliation and exaltation respectively, Barth engages with what it means to say that Christ is one. This is Barth's exploration of the prophetic office of Christ. While the priestly work of the Son of God involves a movement of God from above to below, and the kingly work of the Son of Man from below to above, the prophetic work involves a movement through time, space, and history. This movement and work responds to the human sin of falsehood. Jesus Christ instead makes Himself the "Guarantor of the reality of that which has been done by Him as servant and Lord in that movement from above downwards and below upwards, of the fact that in Jesus Christ God has made Himself the witness of the truth of the atonement."[59] It is under this office of Christ as Prophet that the sending of the community is considered. Barth writes:

> The Holy Spirit as the Spirit of Jesus Christ is the enlightening power of Him who as very God and very man is the Guarantor of the truth of the atonement made in Him—and therefore the summoning power of the promise given in Him to sinful man. When the promise is heard by men, inwardly and outwardly these men are together ordained to be the community sent out as a witness in the world and to the world. The historical reality and inward upbuilding of this community are not ends in themselves.[60]

This is a witness to the whole world of the objective reality of the work of Christ's atonement. Because of this reality, the work of the Holy Spirit in the believer enables the believer to be one who is enlightened in hope. By this, Barth means that the believer is able to move toward her final destiny with an "immediate hope" in Christ.[61]

These three volumes are supplemented with an incomplete part volume published by Barth (*Church Dogmatics IV/4*) on the ethics of reconciliation. The fragment that was published concerns baptism, and is offered as an account of human faithfulness to God in response to God's constant faithfulness to humanity. Again, priority is given to the objective work of God in baptism by the Spirit before the consideration of the subjective aspect of water baptism. This was to be followed by an account of the Christian life in relation to the Lord's Prayer. Lecture fragments of this aspect of Barth's work were published posthumously as *The Christian Life*. For Barth, ethics can never be pried apart from dogmatics: The account of reconciliation requires an account of human in correspondence to the divine event of salvation.

The Life of Faith and the Scope of Salvation

The issue for Barth of human response to God's work of salvation is one that requires further comment. His unprecedentedly strong account of soteriological objectivism could be understood to remove the significance of any human response or existential soteriology. Certainly, it is correct to say that humanity does not contribute anything to salvation. There is no creaturely cooperation in salvation for Barth, since salvation is singularly an act of the grace of God; human response does not condition God into fulfilling salvation for them. However, this does not mean that the existential aspect of salvation and the response of faith are unimportant for Barth. Yes, he wants to state: "The work of atonement, the conversion of man to God, was done for all. The Word of God is spoken to all. God's verdict and direction and promise have been pronounced over all. To that extent, objectively, all are justified, sanctified and called."[62] The conversion of humanity to God takes place on the cross—in the death and resurrection of Jesus Christ. However, Barth qualifies this immediately by stating:

> But the hand of God has not touched all in such a way that they can see and hear, perceive and accept and receive all that God is for all and there-

fore for them, how therefore they can exist and think and live. To those who have not been touched in this way by the hand of God the axiom that Jesus Christ is the Victor is as such unknown. It is a Christian and not a general axiom; valid generally, but not generally observed and acknowledged. Similarly, they do not know their sin or even what sin is, since it can be known only in the light of that axiom.[63]

Although Barth's account of salvation is orientated strongly toward objective soteriology, there is a place for the life of faith and for Christian particularity.[64] It is a work of God the Holy Spirit to relate this moment of salvation to the life of the community and the believer.

Indeed, the motif of being "in Christ" that is so central to Barth's account of the atonement is helpful here. Certainly, Barth is clear that all of history and creation is enclosed within Christ, but he is also clear that "in Christ" there are different ways of being participants. On the one hand, there is *de iure*, objective or passive participation in Christ; on the other hand, there is *de facto*, subjective or active participation in Christ.[65] The former is the ground of the latter. It is not that Barth believes that faith effects our participation in Christ's work of salvation, or that we are unable to participate without Christ; it is rather that faith allows active participation in a reality in which we are already insiders, regardless of whether we recognize ourselves to be or not.[66] This reality meets us in our present and contingent situation by the work of the Spirit within the community and the individual who is enabled by God to engage actively in the life of faith, love, and hope in Christ. In this form, Christians are provisional representatives for the world of the reality of God's event of salvation. There is a life of obedience and correspondence to Christ's work of salvation. This is the conversion Barth speaks about: not a singular moment of decision, but a life of faith that begins anew each day, as the human being in Christ actively shares in His humanity as that which is orientated upon God and upon other humans.[67] This is why election and reconciliation require consideration of their ethical implications for Barth.

The theme of human response and its particular role within Barth's corpus immediately raises a further question—that of the extent of salvation for Barth. His soteriological objectivism determines that what takes place in Jesus Christ takes place for all. As Hunsinger puts it:

Perhaps no theologian of the church since Athanasius, in whom the same strong association of "in Christ" with "for all" is constantly present . . . has so consistently tried to do direct justice to the universalistic aspects of the New Testament witness to Jesus Christ as has Barth. He simply refuses to qualify this aspect for the sake of a tidier conceptual outcome.[68]

Does this amount to universalism for Barth?[69] Barth's description of active and passive, *de facto* and *de iure*, does not make the question a straightforward one. Perhaps reflective of the New Testament itself with the Pauline emphasis on the universal and the Matthean emphasis on decision and choice, Barth's account of salvation contains both universalist and exclusivist statements. Although the logic of his theology clearly seems to point in a universalist direction,[70] Barth himself at various points in his theology emphatically denied that he was a universalist.[71] Nevertheless, it is difficult to deny that his theology tends very strongly in a universalist direction, and he certainly did not display the anxiety that many other theologians display about the doctrine of universal salvation:

> It would be well not to yield to that panic fright which this word seems to have a way of spreading around it, at least before one has come to an understanding with regard to its possible sense or nonsense. . . . It would be well, in view of the "danger" with which the expression is ever and again seen to be encompassed, to ask for a moment, whether on the whole the "danger" from those theologians who are forever sceptically critical, who are again and again suspiciously questioning, because they are always fundamentally legalistic, and who are therefore in essentials sullen and dismal, is not in the meantime always more threatening amongst us than that of an unsuitably cheerful indifferentism or even antinomianism, to which one could in fact yield oneself on one definite understanding of that conception. One thing is sure, that there is no theological justification for setting any limits on our side to the friendliness of God towards man which appeared in Jesus Christ.[72]

To end where this chapter began, one way to think about this tension is to consider Barth's rejection of the category of "universal salvation" as a rejection of any approach to theology in which a principle (universal salvation) replaces Christ as a person: Barth makes clear that while he cannot affirm universalism as a doctrine, he feels he must affirm that "Jesus is Victor."[73] Barth's rejection of universalism is a rejection of any approach to salvation that does not have at its center the particularity of Jesus Christ—a particularity that cannot be gained from a principle, not even that of grace. Furthermore, this emphasis on the particularity of salvation in Jesus Christ ensures that the sovereignty of God is in no way depreciated by the universal election of all humanity: God is under no obligation to elect, and in Jesus Christ, one is able to see the mysterious sovereign will of God. God is not bound to creation by a principle of universal salvation, but chooses to bind Himself to creation in the particular person of Jesus Christ. That Barth rejects dogmatic universalism on occasion does not mean that he posits a limitation of the friendliness of Jesus Christ. Rather, Barth's rejection of universalism posits a limitation of the problems that can arise from such a universal scope for salvation in relation to the freedom and grace of God and the significance of the life of faith. Salvation, for Barth, is a gift of the God of salvation, the God who eternally self-determines to be God in a particular way, to be God in Jesus Christ; the Christian in faith, love, and hope is a proleptic anticipation in time who witnesses to this eternal reality.

NOTES

1. Karl Barth, *Church Dogmatics* (Edinburgh: T&T Clark, 1936–77), Volume I, Part 1, p. 142 (hereafter *Church Dogmatics* will be identified only by volume, part, and page [e.g. I/2, 12)].
2. Cf. I/1, 409–10.
3. II/2, 76.
4. II/2, 91.
5. II/2, 91f.
6. III/1, 42.
7. III/1, 44.
8. III/1, 46.
9. III/1, viii.
10. III/1, 46.
11. George Hunsinger, *How to Read Karl Barth: The Shape of His Theology* (New York: Oxford University Press, 1991), 114.
12. Ibid., 105.
13. Ibid., 114.
14. I/2, 240.

15. Hans Urs von Balthasar, *The Theology of Karl Barth* (San Francisco: Ignatius Press, 1992), 156. The following section is a summary of a section of a previously published chapter: Tom Greggs, *Barth, Origen, and Universal Salvation: Restoring Particularity* (Oxford: Oxford University Press, 2009). For greater detail of the significance of election to Barth's understanding of salvation, see chapters 2, 4, 5, and 7 of that book.
16. II/2, 116–17.
17. Herbert Hartwell, *The Theology of Karl Barth* (Bungay: Richard Clayton & Co, 1964) is correct in asserting the Trinitarian nature of election, however: election takes place "in obedience to the Word, spoken to Him by His Father within the inner-Trinitarian life of God and accepted by Him as the Son in the mutual love of the Holy Spirit" (109).
18. II/2, 76.
19. II/2, 5–7.
20. II/2, 8f.
21. See Trevor Hart, "Universalism: Two Distinct Types," in Nigel M. de S. Cameron, ed., *Universalism and the Doctrine of Hell: Papers Presented at the Fourth Edinburgh Conference on Christian Dogmatics 1991* (Carlisle: Pater Noster, 1992), 1–34. Hart sees this desire not to separate the love and will of God as the heart of Christian universalism (15–16).
22. II/1, §28, emphasis added.
23. II/1, 285 ff.
24. II/1, 288–97.
25. II/2, 7.
26. Barth asserts that Aquinas overlooks this point (II/2, 107). He also states that he differs not in being Christocentric (which he considers Aquinas and indeed Calvin to be), but in seeing a continuity between the Christological centre and the *telos* of God's temporal works, as distinct from those who did not want to bring together the work of God and the eternal presupposition of that work (II/2, 149).
27. II/2, 104–5.
28. II/2, 105–6. Barth cites Scripture to buttress his beliefs: e.g., in Jn. 13.18 and 15.16 and 19, Jesus points to Himself as the one who elects His disciples.
29. II/2, 94.
30. See II/2, 127–45 in terms of Barth's discussion of supra- and post-lapsarianism. In this, Barth sides with supralapsarianism, but in a critical way which almost indicates that the doctrine itself does not go far enough. He rethinks the matter in terms of his own theme of Jesus as the particular Subject and object of election. The "prior" willing of God is not *homo labilis* for the fall, but humanity's "uplifting and restitution by an act of divine power; the demonstration in time, in the creaturely sphere, of His eternal self-differentiation" (142). Cf. Hartwell, *The Theology of Karl Barth*, 106ff. and 139ff.; J. C. McDowell, *Hope in Barth's Eschatology: Interrogations and Transformations Beyond Tragedy* (Aldershot: Ashgate, 2001),

141; Jeannine Michele Graham, *Representation and Substitution in the Atonement Theologies of Dorothee Sölle, John Macquarrie and Karl Barth* (New York: Peter Lang, 2005), 388.
31. II/2, 100–101. On the *decretum absolutum*, see Colin Gunton, "Karl Barth's Doctrine of Election as Part of His Doctrine of God," *Journal of Theological Studies* 25, no. 2 (1974): 382. On Christ as *decretum concretum*, see G. C. Berkouwer, *Triumph of Grace in the Theology of Karl Barth* (London: Paternoster, 1956), 103.
32. On actualism, see McCormack, "Grace and Being: The Role of God's Gracious Election in Karl Barth's Theological Ontology," in John Webster, ed., *Cambridge Companion to Karl Barth* (Cambridge: Cambridge University Press, 2000), 98ff.; and Paul T. Nimmo, *Being in Action: The Theological Shape of Barth's Ethical Vision* (London: T&T Clark, 2007), esp. 4–12. A different account is given by Hunsinger, *How to Read Karl Barth*, esp. 30ff.
33. This point is, however, protected by Barth's continual and emphatic insistence throughout *CD* on the "mystery" of God. See, for example, I/1, 320–21.
34. II/2, 9–10.
35. II/2, 10.
36. II/2, 13–14.
37. II/2, 118 cf. 13.
38. II/2, 166.
39. II/2, 191.
40. II/2, 353.
41. II/2, 195.
42. III/2, 133.
43. II/2, 558.
44. IV/1, ix.
45. IV/1, 3.
46. Eberhard Busch, *Karl Barth: His Life from Letters and Autobiographical Texts* (London: SCM, 1976), 377.
47. An outline of the structure of volume IV is offered in CD IV/1, § 58.
48. IV/1, 80. For a summary of the individual part volumes of CD, see Daniel W. Hardy, "Karl Barth," in David Ford with Rachel Muers, eds., *The Modern Theologians: An Introduction to Christian Theology since 1918* (Oxford: Blackwell, 2005), 21–42.
49. IV/1, 80.
50. IV/1, § 59.2.
51. IV/1, 142.
52. IV/1, 96.
53. IV/1, 151.
54. On this point, and generally on justification, see Trevor A. Hart, *Regarding Barth: Essays toward a Reading of His Theology* (Carlisle: Paternoster, 1999), chapter 3.
55. IV/1, 150.
56. IV/1, 131.

57. IV/1, 133.
58. IV/2, 514.
59. IV/1, 143.
60. IV/1, 152.
61. IV/3, 902.
62. IV/1, 148.
63. Ibid.
64. I have explored this theme in detail in *Barth, Origen, and Universal Salvation*.
65. See Adam Neder, *Participation in Christ: An Entry into Karl Barth's Church Dogmatics* (Louisville, KY: Westminster John Knox, 2009), esp. chapter 2.
66. See George Hunsinger, "A Tale of Two Simultaneities: Justification and Sanctification in Calvin and Barth," in John C. McDowell and Mike Higton, eds., *Conversing with Barth* (Aldershot: Ashgate, 2004), 77.
67. E.g., IV/2, 560ff.
68. Hunsinger, *How to Read Karl Barth*, 108.
69. Space does not allow for a thorough discussion of Barth as a universalist. This is a question I have tackled in detail elsewhere, and the reader is directed to Greggs, "'Jesus Is Victor': Passing the Impasse of Barth on Universalism," *Scottish Journal of Theology* 60, no. 2 (2007): 196–212; *Barth, Origen and Universal Salvation*; and *Theology against Religion: Constructive Dialogues with Bonhoeffer and Barth* (London: T&T Clark, 2011), chapter 5. For further discussion of this theme, Berkouwer, *Triumph of Grace*; Joseph D. Bettis, "Is Karl Barth a Universalist?" *Scottish Journal of Theology* 20, no. 4 (1967); Oliver Crisp, "On Barth's Denial of Universalism," *Themelios* 29 (2003); J. C. McDowell, "Learning Where to Place One's Hope: The Eschatological Significance of Election in Barth," *Scottish Journal of Theology* 53, no. 3 (2000); Hart, *Regarding Barth*, chapter 6, esp. 137–38; and Hunsinger, *Disruptive Grace*, chapter 10, esp. 242 ff.; John Colwell, "The Contemporaneity of Divine Decision: Reflections on Barth's Denial of Universalism," in de S. Cameron, ed., *Universalism and the Doctrine of Hell*; Paul T. Nimmo, "Election and Evangelical Thinking: Challenging Our Way of Conceiving the Doctrine of God," in Tom Greggs, ed., *New Perspectives for Evangelical Theology: Engaging with God, Scripture and the World* (Abingdon: Routledge, 2010), 34–35; and Oliver Crisp, "I Do Teach It, but I Also Do Not Teach It: The Universalism of Karl Barth (1886–1968)," in Gregory MacDonald, ed., *"All Shall Be Well": Explorations in Universal Salvation and Christian Theology, from Origen to Moltmann* (Eugene, OR: Wipf and Stock, 2010).
70. On the logical outcome of Barth's position, see Berkouwer, *Triumph of Grace*; Crisp, "On Barth's Denial of Universalism" and "I Do Teach It."
71. For example, II/2, 417 and 476–77; and also *CD* IV/3, §70.3 "The Condemnation of Man."
72. Karl Barth, *"Humanity of God"* in Karl Barth, *God, Grace and Gospel*, SJT Occasional Papers 10 (Edinburgh: Oliver & Boyd, 1959), 49–50.
73. See my "Jesus is Victor."

19

Hans Urs von Balthasar and Karl Rahner

W. T. DICKENS

Karl Rahner was born in Freiburg im Breisgau, Germany, in 1904. He joined the Society of Jesus at age eighteen. During the next decade, he studied philosophy, Latin, and theology before being ordained a priest in 1932. His early philosophical training included a thorough study of Immanual Kant and Joseph Maréchal. Rahner's Jesuit superiors subsequently sent him to Frieburg to receive a PhD in philosophy. He participated in Martin Heidegger's seminar while there and wrote a dissertation engaging Heidegger's phenomenology from a Maréchalian perspective. Although rejected by his dissertation advisor, this work was later published as *Spirit in the World*. Rahner eventually completed a doctorate in theology at the University of Innsbruck before joining the theology faculty there. After the Nazis closed the University of Innsbruck, he spent the Second World War working as a pastor and lecturing, first in Vienna, then in Bavaria. He returned to university teaching in 1945, and remained a professor of theology, first at Innsbruch, then at Munich, and finally at Münster, until his retirement in 1971. During the Second Vatican Council (1962–65), he served as the official advisor to Cardinal König of Vienna. This work finally brought to a close the official Vatican suspicion that shadowed him for some fifteen years. He was busy until his death in 1984, continuing to lecture, write, and edit several theological encyclopedias and dictionaries, as well as the journal *Concilium*, which he helped launch. For the two decades immediately following the end of Vatican II, Rahner was widely regarded, especially in North America, as the preeminent Catholic theologian. This period coincides with the translation into English of the works by which Rahner is best known, his twenty-one-volume collection of essays, *Theological Investigations*, and the *Foundations of Christian Faith*.

Hans Urs von Balthasar was born into a trilingual, cosmopolitan family in Lucerne, Switzerland in 1905. Torn between studying music—for which he had a remarkable talent, including perfect pitch and a nearly photographic memory—and literature, he chose the latter, eventually writing a dissertation on eschatology in modern German literature. He joined the Society of Jesus in 1929 and was ordained a priest in 1936. When the Second World War began, he declined an appointment as professor of theology at Rome's Gregorian University, preferring to be a student chaplain in Basel. In response to Hitler's book burnings, Balthasar edited and sometimes translated into German a collection of anthologies of European literature and philosophy that grew to fifty volumes. While in Basel, Balthasar came to know Adrienne von Speyr, a talented physician whose mystical visions decisively shaped his theology. Together they founded the Community of St. John, a secular institute for laywomen and laymen hoping to imitate Christ crucified while working in the world. Balthasar left the Society in 1950 after his superiors refused to underwrite his secular institute. Like Rahner, Balthasar labored for years under official Vatican scrutiny, but since no bishop invited Balthasar to Vatican II, he spent the early 1960s working on the *Theological Aesthetics*. This became the first part of the work for which he is best known: the fifteen-volume theological triptych, which also includes the *Theo-Drama* and the *Theo-Logic*. Balthasar's name was cleared of all suspicion once the Council concluded. After his appointment to the Papal Theological Commission, Balthasar began a forceful, sometimes quite vociferous polemic against Rahner's theology, and founded a rival academic journal, *Communio*. John Paul II tapped him to be a cardinal in 1988, but he died a few days before his elevation.

Introduction

Karl Rahner, SJ and Hans Urs von Balthasar were the most prolific and influential Roman Catholic theologians of the twentieth century.[1] This achievement is all the more impressive because each crafted new modes for explicating the Gospel that replaced the neoscholastic theological method in which they were trained. A revived form of the disputational method characteristic of medieval theological inquiry, neoscholasticism enjoyed official Vatican endorsement during the first half of the twentieth century. As students, both Rahner and Balthasar chafed at neoscholasticism's rigid formalism. They found its carefully prescribed list of acceptable theological topics painfully boring and its supposedly unassailable foundation in the history of dogma and scriptural proof texts unpersuasive. Yet they adopted different strategies to ameliorate its worst effects. Rahner sought to render Christian doctrines intelligible in light of modern philosophy's turn to the subject, relying on—occasionally very heavily, depending on his rhetorical purposes—concepts provided by German idealism and phenomenology. Balthasar attempted to interpret the full round of revelation centered in Jesus Christ by means of analogies drawn between it and the true, the good, and the beautiful. Although Rahner spent more time addressing the shortcomings of neoscholasticism than did Balthasar, the differences between these two strategies will serve as our point of departure. Their strategies assume quite different conceptions of the person, which, in turn, shape their distinctive views of sin, the atonement, the Christian life, and the scope of God's reconciliation.

Karl Rahner

Rahner worried that neoscholasticism had so badly distorted the Gospel that Christianity seemed preposterous to many, especially those familiar with modern philosophy, the social sciences, and evolutionary biology. Owing to modernity's distrust of traditional authorities, neoscholastic theologians' recitations of Christian truth claims sound to the modern ear both mythological and heteronomous. To remedy this, Rahner believed it necessary to establish the "a priori possibility on man's part" of being oriented to God.[2] This did not amount to an attempt to prove that one can know and love God on one's own, apart from God's grace. On the contrary, Rahner began, just as the neoscholastics did, with the Church's traditional belief that God both creates and redeems humans, but unlike them, he proceeded to identify what enables humans to know and love God as creator and redeemer. For only so can the propositions cherished by the neoscholastics be rendered "intelligible and assimilable."[3]

To summarize Rahner's argument briefly: Our capacity to reflect upon ourselves in our totality as comprising a host of constitutive factors that are studied by the empirical sciences distinguishes us from the most clever animals and defines what it means for us to be persons and subjects.[4] We stand behind or above these factors, recognizing their significance while refusing to reduce ourselves to any one or all of them. In exercising this capacity to transcend ourselves, we realize we will never capture in thought the subjectivity we are, not only because our questions about our self are infinitely open-ended, but also because our self eludes objectification.[5] Any conception of it that we might present to ourselves is already thereby different from the self who is doing the conceiving. Thus, in realizing our infinite self-transcendence we experience what Rahner calls a pre-apprehension (Vorgriff) of absolute being. We pre-apprehend it because absolute being is not itself a particular object of knowledge, but is what grounds our capacity to know anything at all. Accordingly, we experience the dynamic questioning we are as at once infinite and yet dependent upon the manifestation of absolute being. Since this self-transcendence is mediated historically, our subjectivity is not a fixed, self-identical essence discovered through introspection. It is utterly unique.[6] Rahner's next step is controversial, for he maintained that ingredient to this historically mediated, transcendental experience of absolute being bestowing itself is a transcendental experience of God as holy mystery, a claim that seems to collapse the traditional distinction between being itself and the creator of such. Still, Rahner's polemical point against neoscholasticism's arid propositionalism is clear: All humans, whether we know it or not, are inherently oriented to God as the infinitely incomprehensible ground of our being. Christianity affirms more than that about God, of course, so Rahner next deduced the conditions for the possibility of humans knowing God as redeemer. He argued that if the scriptural proclamations of God's will to save all souls are true, then all humans must in their self-transcendence have a pre-apprehension of God that enables us to recognize and receive God's justifying and sanctifying grace as a gift. Rahner called this capacity our "supernatural existential" to signal that it is at once a gift from God and a constituent element in each human being, whether one affirms it or not.[7] Regardless of whether we consider our pre-apprehension of God as holy mystery or as intimately present as an offer of yet deeper communion, neither form of divine knowledge is a mere postulate of dogmatic theology imposed on us by ecclesiastical authority. Rahner believed he had shown by means of these transcendental deductions that the Christian claim about God's creative and saving deeds, far from being mythological or heteronomous, is compatible with the very structure of our capacity to know ourselves and our world.

Hans Urs von Balthasar

As we have seen, Balthasar shared Rahner's distaste for the arid propositionalism of neoscholasticism. Two aspects of his analogical theology served as fruitful strategies for challenging it. They also provided Balthasar critical leverage against Rahner's view of persons. First, Balthasar used an analogy between revelation and the beautiful to clarify the inadequacies of two conceptions of God's self-communication. One of these, associated with neoscholasticism, highlighted the cognitive content of revelation's historical forms—such as the Exodus or Crucifixion—and treated them as mere signs specifying the articles of belief that the faithful, aided by grace, must accept. This reduces revelation to divine truth claims that, as Rahner has helped us see, have little apparent connection to the spiritual life of humanity. From Balthasar's perspective, Rahner's solution to this problem was also problematical, since it appears to reduce revelation to what fulfills our graced, self-transcendent dynamism. Revelation illuminates a graced state of affairs (the supernatural existential) that has always already been the case.[8] Balthasar sought to combine the strengths of both conceptions (emphasizing the credibility of revelation's historical forms and its ability to soothe our otherwise restless hearts) by likening our encounter with God's self-revelation to being in the presence of stunning beauty.[9] In order properly to appreciate beauty, we must, Balthasar contended, give ourselves to beauty and allow beauty to give itself to us. This demand from beauty that we let ourselves be enthralled by it, that we let ourselves surrender to its effects without attempting to domesticate or master it, foreshadows "what in the realm of revelation and grace will be the attitude of faith."[10] For Balthasar, neoscholasticism and Rahner's transcendental theology[11] both failed to give due credit to God's capacity to captivate a person, leaving her eager to accept the gift of reconciling love made manifest in Jesus Christ. The analogy between revelation and the beautiful thus emphasized God's movement toward someone and her corresponding self-surrender before God, rather than her discovery through self-reflection of God's ongoing presence.

This same dialogical pattern is evident in Balthasar's definition of persons, in the articulation of which he utilized a second important analogy. Balthasar started, as did Rahner, by acknowledging that our identity cannot be captured by combining all the distinctive features that mark us as individuals. But, unlike Rahner, Balthasar's next step was not to examine our capacity for responsible self-transcendence. He regarded not introspection but intersubjective encounters as the gateway to self-consciousness.[12] "It is clear that a conscious subject can only awaken to himself and his distinct selfhood if he is addressed by one or more others who regard him as value or perhaps as indispensable."[13] This can happen to an infant in the presence of her mother's loving smile, which calls her into being. The infant slowly comes to realize that she is a distinguishable self from the one who beckons her forth. This dawning self-awareness yields a conscious subject, but not, so Balthasar held, a person. Conscious subjects do not know with absolute certainty who they are. It is only when "God addresses a conscious subject, tells him who he is and what he means to the eternal God of truth and shows him the purpose of his existence—that is, imparts a distinctive and divinely authorized mission—that we can say of a conscious subject that he is a 'person.'"[14] Balthasar was here trading on the Greek root of the English word person, namely *prosopon*, which refers to the mask donned by an actor in a drama, and, by extension, to the role he takes on. Naturally, the analogy is not meant to imply anything make-believe about one's mission and identity, but to bring out the freedom an actor possesses to interpret his role within the broad confines established by the director and playwright. Balthasar was also drawing a parallel between a mother's beckoning an infant into self-awareness through her loving smile and God's loving call to each person to do his or her part in the ongoing theodrama involving God and the cosmos. Notice once again that Balthasar has subordinated introspection to interpersonal encounters as the means by which we come fully to realize and enact who we are supposed to be. Paradoxically, this means that what is most personal about us is realized not by our looking inward—though inside us it may surely be—but by our being loved by another.[15]

Sin

Both Rahner and Balthasar rejected as simplistic the common notion of sin as a specific deed that violates a divinely ordained and ecclesiastically enforced code of conduct. Both held that such actions, which they unhesitatingly called sins, flow from a prior rejection of God's gracious offer of forgiveness and loving communion, although they accented different features of this offer and its rejection. Hence, they believed sin is best understood as a self-destructive, ruptured relation with God, not a discreet act or even the sum of all one's acts. They also agreed that most people no longer feel guilty before God. Martin Luther's terrified conscience looking for assurance of divine forgiveness is passé. It has been replaced with a sense of alienation (Rahner) in the face of life's seemingly pointless, painful meandering until death or despair (Balthasar) in the face of a loveless world where each serves only himself or a small circle of family and friends. Both construed Luther's description of the faithful Christian as simultaneously justified and sinful (simul justus et peccator) not as a matter of shifting perspectives, as Luther maintained, but of percentages. We are a mixture of both at once, becoming, we hope, less sinful as time goes on. Having adopted teleological interpretations of the Christian life as progressing toward a blessed end, both men failed to grasp that Luther articulated the simul assuming a legal metaphor in which talk of a person being partly guilty and partly innocent is nonsensical. And, finally, both men believed that Christians come to understand the meaning and magnitude of sin only after they have accepted God's offer of forgiveness. Stepping past these similarities, we come to see significant differences that arise from their distinctive definitions of what it means to be a person.

In keeping with his emphasis on the paramount importance of self-transcendence, Rahner understood sin to be the evasion of this fundamental human act that constitutes us as subjects and persons. To be in sin is to avoid accepting that we are ultimately dependent upon something other than ourselves and to shirk responsibility for ourselves as greater than the sum of our parts. The two—radical dependence and autonomy—are, so Rahner argued, not indirectly, but directly proportionate. The more we realize our dependence on God, the more we are freely able to accept responsibility for ourselves as dependent creatures.

In the state of sin, we resolve this seeming paradox by denying either our dependence on God or our autonomy. The former is a typical target of theologians pained by those utterly consumed with the demands and rewards of this world or by those who intuit that this world is open in the direction of absolute being and a loving God, but decline to reflect on that intuition. Rahner shared such concerns, but he was also critical of his fellow Christians who hand over their lives to God in the freedom-denying hope of becoming a mere instrument through which "divinity acts out its own eternal drama."[16] Rahner noted a self-destructive irony at the heart of denying either our dependence or our autonomy since the denial requires a logically prior, albeit unconscious acceptance of both. In order to say "no" to who we are (that is, both dependent on God and autonomous), we must already have said "yes." We must already have accepted ourselves as totalities who, being genuinely free to say no to ourselves and to God, are not closed in on ourselves but open to the divine ground of our being and freedom.[17] So, from Rahner's point of view, sin's self-destruction entails self-delusion: We refuse to engage in self-transcendence all the while transcending ourselves as we do so.

Balthasar maintained that a sinful existence denies its ultimate dependence on God as the creator and arrogates to itself a false freedom. He labeled this false freedom "autonomy" to indicate the error of assuming we govern ourselves when we are in fact at God's disposal. Notwithstanding this terminological difference with Rahner, Balthasar agreed with him that only those who have acknowledged their ultimate dependence on God are truly free. Balthasar spoke of sinners annexing to themselves private domains in which they would brook no interference; prioritizing their ego's values and the relative, finite goods deemed to further them; and creating a fog of half-truths and excuses to obscure the presence of others and of God. Some remain thus curved in on themselves. Others, frustrated by a fruitless search for love in an apparently pitiless world, step beyond privately imposed boundaries to fashion little communities of shared interests and sympathies. But, these are not, so Balthasar claimed, true communities comprising persons, called into being by God, who respond to a prior divine gift of selfless love by pouring themselves out in love for others and God. Sinners are turning away from true love, which is manifest and offered to them in Jesus Christ. For Balthasar, sin is a denial of our creaturely dependence on God and a refusal of God's proffered gift of forgiveness and the promise of communion with God in Christ. This gift takes a unique form for each human being since each of us has a particular role to play in the ongoing drama between finite and infinite freedom. Sin is the refusal to play our part, declining to fight "shoulder to shoulder with Christ against God's enemies."[18] It is, instead, to act on the world's stage, to dress in its costumes and masks and to play the roles it allots us, deluding ourselves that we are thereby free and in control.

Rahner and Balthasar both believed that humans are incapable of not sinning on their own, apart from divine assistance, although Rahner was somewhat more interested in explaining this incapacity in light of the traditional definition of original sin than was Balthasar. Rahner's claim that our transcendental experiences of ourselves as oriented to absolute being and to God are historically conditioned gives his explication of original sin its distinctive shape. The persons, institutions, natural objects, and cultural artifacts with which we deal every day and that constitute the "material" of our free decisions are determined, in part, by the guilt of other free persons.[19] To use his own illustration of original sin, we cannot purchase a banana without being implicated in the environmental destruction and social injustice that paved its route to our grocer's bin.[20] Naturally, Balthasar accepted the Church's teaching about original sin, but in contrast to Rahner, he worried that talk of collective guilt too often served to shield the sinner from God's word that addresses each one of us as a "Thou"—a word not of condemnation but of invitation to step out of the darkness we create "into the light of love."[21] Balthasar was evidently less concerned by an exaggerated emphasis on personal sanctity, which can also lead to a denial of culpability. If my hands are seemingly clean, then of what must I repent? Despite this difference in emphasis—and ironically in Rahner's case, given his more robust definition of original sin—both can be criticized for a relative inattention to sin's social manifestations. Structural injustices, systemic inequities, centuries-long legacies of oppression—none of this evidently merited, in their judgments, the same sustained attention as did the lone sinner standing before God.

Atonement

Rahner and Balthasar disagreed sharply over how the life, death, and resurrection of Jesus Christ reconciled the cosmos with God. For Rahner, human self-transcendence is the lance point of an evolution through which all matter in its unity with spirit reaches beyond itself to become something new, something "qualitatively higher."[22] Although such self-transcendence is the creature's own, it is grounded in God's perpetual, creative self-communication. Thus, a double movement characterizes the entire 15-billion-year history of the universe: the protracted ascendancy of creation to ever higher forms of being and God's patient, welcoming descent, extending divine life to what is not divine. Jesus's life, death, and resurrection—when considered as a whole—culminate the cosmos's self-transcendence and God's self-bestowing communication to the cosmos. In light of Rahner's emphasis on the cosmos's becoming qualitatively new in humanity and being elevated and enabled thereby to sense its constitutive orientation to God, it is not surprising that the Incarnation of Jesus, as distinct from his death and resurrection, would strike some readers as the keystone of Rahner's theory of the atonement.[23] It is true that Rahner shared an affinity with the classical Eastern Christian formulation of the atonement, which highlighted the reconciling significance of the divine Son's assumption of human nature in the Incarnation.[24] He nevertheless remained critical of its seeming disregard for the concrete details of Jesus's life, including what, on his view, culminated and recapitulated that life, Jesus's death on the Cross. According to Rahner, the Cross is salvific not because, as has been commonly supposed in Western Christianity, including neoscholastic theories of the atonement, the death of the sinless God-man was deemed by God an adequate compensatory good to balance the evil wrought by sin. Such a view remained too formal, too abstract, and too legalistic for Rahner.[25] Nor did he regard the death of Jesus as atoning because it offered God an expiatory sacrifice, despite Rahner having acknowledged that some New Testament Christologies construe the death of Jesus this way. He observed that even if we were to suppose that God made Jesus's free self-sacrifice possible and, regarding it as redemptive, granted humans as a consequence the grace to appropriate salvation, we would be left with the odd picture of God being moved to carry out an expiatory sacrifice from a love for humanity so profligate that the need for such sacrifice is eliminated. A God who "loves the sinner originally and without reason" needs no propitiation to reconcile the sinner.[26] If this is so, then how is the death of Jesus causally connected to the reconciliation of the cosmos to God?

Understanding Rahner's explanation of this connection requires that we see death as he did, namely, as the encapsulation and summing up of a person's life. Our lives, he said, attain their validity "through death, not after it."[27] One is most "obedient" to one's graced orientation to God "by accepting his own existence without reservation, and indeed precisely in those areas where freedom risks something which cannot be calculated and controlled."[28] The obedience to God the Father that the incarnate Son demonstrated throughout his life by loving others without reserve reaches its final and definitive expression in his free, resolute acceptance of death. His life thus perfectly reconciled the tensions discussed above between human autonomy and dependence on God. He realized that he simply had to endure death—with its terrifying finality and its annihilation of all that he had done or valued. "In his death he experiences the ultimate God-forsakenness, and in that very situation yields himself and his fate into the Father's hands."[29] The term "God-forsakenness" may suggest to some readers that Rahner tried to rely covertly on aspects of the theory of vicarious punishment, which holds that the sinless Jesus Christ bore the divinely imposed punishment for the sins of humanity. Quite the contrary. In addition to the obstacles to defining atonement either as satisfaction or as expiatory sacrifice voiced above, Rahner would add two additional ones: It is logically incoherent to overcome the evil of sin by creating the evil of punishment, and vicarious punishment violates God's sovereign immutability by supposing that God's mind or heart is changed by what Jesus underwent on the Cross.[30] At most, Rahner would say that whatever punishment Jesus endured was the result of humans loading on to him the burdens of sin. His suffering was not divinely imposed. So what does God-forsakenness mean? The divine abandonment Jesus experienced is the inevitable consequence of sin. As Jesus became sin for humans, he experienced the estrangement from God that every sinner knows.[31]

Christians, of course, insist that Jesus's story does not end there. As Rahner put it, Jesus died into the Resurrection, which is not the restoration to life, but God's final and definitive validation of who Jesus was and what he did and suffered—and therewith God's validation of the entire history of the cosmos's self-transcendence that Jesus recapitulated and finalized. So, the causal connection between the life, death, and resurrection of Jesus, on the one hand, and the reconciliation of the cosmos to God, on the other, is not extrinsic. It is not as though the event of Jesus brought about the reconciliation. Jesus Christ is this promised reconciliation. If we must speak of causality here, we have to think not of an efficient, but of a final, cause. The resurrected Jesus is the goal toward which the cosmos moves and in which, by grace, the cosmos now stands. "In this causality what is signified, in this case God's salvific will, posits the sign, in this case the death of Jesus along with his resurrection, and in and through the sign it causes what is signified."[32] Accordingly, Rahner described the event of Jesus as bearing a "quasi-sacramental" quality, as being what he called a real-symbol, something that points beyond itself while manifesting that to which it points.[33]

Balthasar's works present a very different view of atonement. Before discussing these differences, four important areas of agreement on this issue between Balthasar and Rahner should be noted. They agreed that the event of Jesus Christ was not determined by God in response to sin; the triune God (note, not just the Father) decided upon this way of fulfilling creation before creating the cosmos. Both theologians agreed that the whole event of Jesus Christ is reconciling, not just one aspect of it, although in typically Western Christian fashion they emphasized the centrality of the Cross in its indissoluble connection to the Incarnation and Resurrection. They agreed that the Cross must not be interpreted as God the Father imposing a punishment upon the undeserving, sinless incarnate Son. Finally, they agreed that the triune God is immutable.

Balthasar voiced deep concerns about Rahner's quasi-sacramental view of the atonement. He based his criticism, in part, on the belief that something clearly happened between Good Friday and Easter Sunday. The event of Jesus Christ, therefore, must not be reduced to a mere "manifestation of God's reconciliation with the world, a reconciliation that is constant, homogeneous and always part of the given."[34] Those who advance such symbolic views of the atonement "falsify and diminish the mission of Jesus."[35] This very serious charge falls wide of the mark, at least in Rahner's case, because Rahner clearly believed that something happened in the event of Jesus Christ. It is more than a mere sign of the triune God's desire to save all souls since it bears within itself the salvation that is effected when Jesus freely accepted being paradoxically dependent and free and accepted the offer of God's self in the supernatural existential. God ratified this unique historical event of Jesus Christ in the Resurrection, thereby making it the definitive and final offer of God to humanity. It is hard to square this with Balthasar's intemperate claim that Rahner falsified and diminished Jesus's mission by believing nothing new happened in the event of Jesus Christ. It would have been more accurate had Balthasar said that he and Rahner disagreed over what had to have happened for the event of Jesus Christ to be atoning.

Balthasar also contended that quasi-sacramental or symbolic views of the atonement, such as Rahner's, were out of step with the "realism" of the New Testament passages proclaiming that Christ bore the sins of humanity and that, therefore, such views were not truly Christological (or theological), but merely anthropological.[36] We have already seen how Rahner understood the New Testament passages that identify Jesus Christ as an expiatory sacrifice. We will discuss below how Balthasar handled these same New Testament passages and offer a Rahnerian response. It is important to underline that, for Rahner, God's mind or heart is not changed by the event of Jesus Christ. God has always loved humanity unconditionally—"without reason," as previously noted—and therefore needs nothing done in order to be mollified. So only in that sense is it justifiable to describe his view of the atonement as anthropological rather than theological. Yet it is not simply anthropological because Rahner affirmed that God's Word incarnate is hypostatically united to a real human being in Jesus Christ.[37] Jesus Christ is the climax of both human self-transcendence and God's self-bestowing communication.

Balthasar's view of the atonement shared the ancient eastern Christian emphasis on the redemptive efficacy of the exchange of human and divine properties in the Incarnation. He also accepted the traditional western Christian understanding of the Cross completing this exchange as the Son changes places with the sinner.[38] Accordingly, the triune God's decision to let the Son become incarnate "for us and our salvation," as the Nicene Creed puts it, means not just "on our behalf," but also, and for Balthasar more importantly, "in our stead."[39] Balthasar maintained that legalistic reservations to the idea of one person suffering for the wrongdoings of another fail to consider the mystical union of Christ with humanity that derives from the Son's role in creation as the one through whom all things were made.[40]

When explaining what it means to say that Jesus changed places with sinful humanity, Balthasar repeatedly affirmed that Christ suffered on the Cross at our hands. "If, once the Incarnation has taken place, we ask who burdens the Son, the 'Lamb of God' . . . with the unimaginable load of all the world's No to divine love, the answer . . . must be: men themselves in their darkness."[41] In graphic terms, Balthasar described guilty humanity crushing Jesus Christ with the "power of hammering sin";[42] how the guiltless one "has been put into prison by the world, condemned, spat upon, beaten, bound in chains, crowned with thorns, crucified and mocked for his impotence and Godforsakeness";[43] and how he freely accepted from us "all the God directed hatred, all the accusations showered upon him with cudgels."[44] Such imagery seems contradicted by equally vivid descriptions of God the Father venting his fury at sin upon Jesus Christ. "Can we seriously say that God unloaded his wrath upon the Man who wrestled with his destiny on the Mount of Olives and was subsequently crucified? Indeed we must."[45] The apparent contradiction is resolved when we realize that, for Balthasar, humanity's God-loathing "no" has two consequences, both of which Jesus Christ endured. It entailed humanity turning its back on God and God angrily turning away from humanity, abandoning us in our sin and to its consequences. We have already examined the consequences of humanity turning from God when discussing sin. As for God's turning away from sinners, Balthasar asserted that while on the Cross and in his subsequent descent into hell, Jesus Christ experienced the God-forsakenness of sin even more deeply than do sinners because he endured it as God.[46] God the Son endured estrangement from God the Father so that there is no experience of divine abandonment that God, too, has not undergone.[47]

In what is his most original contribution to discussions of the atonement, Balthasar maintained that in the depths of hell, face to face with the crucified Jesus Christ, both the Father's wrath at sin and sinful humanity's hatred of God are transfigured. "God's anger at the rejection of divine love encounters a divine love (the Son's) that exposes itself to this anger, disarms it and literally deprives it of its object."[48] And while the most embittered sinner hammers away at God in Christ, he comes to realize that his fury is directed at "the impotent form of the crucified brother [who] has been abandoned by God for [his] sake."[49] The sinner thus realizes that God is his highest good because God loves and values him enough to endure God-forsakenness with him and, indeed, more deeply than he does. On Balthasar's telling, redemption thus has both a human and a divine dimension. For humans, the Son's "omnipotent powerlessness" outlasts sin's hatred and eliminates its source.[50] The triune God allows sin to run its course in the Father and the Son, or more precisely, in their relationship, so that they are nearly torn apart by it. All that holds them together is their love for one another, namely, the Holy Spirit, and the triune God's love for humanity.

To Rahner's ear, Balthasar's claim that the Father's wrath was disarmed as the Father beheld the obedient Son's taking the place of sinners would sound very much like God has had a change of heart. To put it polemically, this smacks of God the Father having been placated by the Son. That would appear to violate the principle of divine immutability that Rahner and Balthasar shared. Although Balthasar was at pains to deny that he conceived of God changing, at least in an "intramundane" way, in several places his phrasing suggests divine mutability.[51] For instance, he said that there is "something in God that can develop into suffering" and that the "Trinity does not hover 'unmoved' above the events of the Cross," but is "thoroughly affected" by them.[52] Certainly, Balthasar did not believe that God changed *in se*, that is, ontologically. Rather, the Father's wrath at sin is transformed in the face of the Son's suffering, which means the Father's abandonment of the sinner to suffer the consequences of sin came to an end during the events of the Cross and descent into hell. It is unlikely that Rahner would have found this response persuasive. Although it preserves divine immutability, it assumes that God needed something to happen on the Cross and the subsequent descent into hell in order to be reconciled with the cosmos. This would contradict Rahner's conviction that God loves humanity unconditionally. It also stands in some tension with Paul's claim in Romans 5 that the death of Jesus Christ reconciles humans with God, not God with humans.

Rahner would point out an additional, pastoral problem with Balthasar's views. Balthasar believed that in Jesus Christ's descent into hell, he suffered divine abandonment in his humanity and in his divinity. Rahner wondered whether it helped those who suffer to know that God has suffered too. Do we prefer to be comforted by the God who cannot suffer and whose life-giving power has vanquished sin? For Rahner, the answer seemed obvious. "It does not help me to escape my mess and mix-up and despair if God is in the same predicament."[53] However heartfelt Rahner's views may be, surely the answer one gives to the question of whether one can find comfort from a God who suffers is deeply personal. It would appear, then, that either view of God could be pastorally effective.

The Christian Life

How did Rahner and Balthasar envision the process by means of which someone can come to accept and act in accordance with the gift of forgiveness and deepening communion with God made available in the life, death, and resurrection of Jesus Christ? In the traditional terminology of the Church—at least since the Reformation—this is to ask about their doctrines of justification and sanctification. Neither theologian used these terms frequently. When they did, they agreed that justification is not a mere declaration by God that the sinner is forgiven. Justifying grace ontologically transforms the sinner. It divinizes humans because the gift of forgiveness is the presence of the gift-giver, namely God.[54] For this reason, the sharp distinction drawn in Protestant circles between justification, understood as forgiveness, and sanctification, understood as deepening communion with God, blurred in the works of Rahner and Balthasar. They also agreed that God's offer of forgiveness in Jesus Christ, the acceptance of this offer, and the response to it throughout one's life are empowered by God's gracious presence. Reconciliation with God is emphatically not a reward; it is an unmerited gift. Finally, they agreed that one could have been forgiven by God, and thus transformed, without one being aware that anything has happened.[55]

Rahner believed that at its "core," the Christian life consisted in "an abiding personal relationship with the God-Man."[56] He described this relationship as a life-long task of accepting without reservation our self and our life, with all its injuries and heartbreaks. Indeed, for Rahner, resolutely facing life's incomprehensibilities—especially death—is "identical" with a person's relationship with the risen Jesus.[57] It is not that one's acceptance of life is the result of loving Jesus; it is how one does so. In more traditional terms, Rahner also said that a personal love for Jesus is the "most real actualization and foundation of the love of neighbor which is our mediation to God."[58] Linking the two modes of expression, for Rahner, every act of true love for one's neighbor, which entails giving oneself to another without regard for personal benefit, always already involves freely accepting one's self and one's life in their radical openness to God. For most humans, this happens more or less unwittingly. For those Christians who have tried to make the faith they received govern their deepest sense of self, it happens primarily in the gathered community of their local church. Nevertheless, according to Rahner, loving our neighbor will always disappoint us, since it only "temporarily removes the separation and the chasm which divides us."[59] So, we seek assurance that there is a love that will prove victorious over the self-deceptions and mistrust of others that dog all our relationships. "[T]his ultimate success is pledged and sacramentally present in the church . . . and especially in the Lord's Supper."[60] Rahner's equation of the love of God to love of neighbor and his controversial insistence that "one can love God whom one does not see only by loving one's visible brother lovingly" does not reflect, as Balthasar feared, Rahner's supposed subordination of Christology to anthropology and devaluing the Church, particularly its liturgies.[61] Rahner believed the Eucharist to be the primary locus and means of enacting a Christian's love of neighbor and of God in the risen Christ. This belief grounds Rahner's view of the proper role played by the Church and its sacraments in the life of Christians. He held that only in the Church ("in the profession of faith of Christians, in the cult of Christians, in the community life of Christians") does the faithfuls' experience of God's self-bestowing presence become their salvation "in full measure."[62] The Church is the basic sacrament inasmuch as it is—to follow Rahner's language quite closely—the fruit of an imperishable salvation, the means by which God has chosen to make God's offer of salvation socially and historically tangible, and the ongoing presence of the risen Jesus Christ. It is an efficacious sign or a real-symbol of salvation insofar as it is through it that God both offers salvation as a question to each human and provides God's own positive answer, manifesting the "victorious success of God's self-communication."[63] Whenever the

Church, as the basic sacrament of God's gift of salvation, involves itself in decisive situations in human life, there we find sacraments in the traditional sense of the term. Notwithstanding such positive remarks about the Church, Rahner affirmed, echoing Vatican II, that "we poor, primitive, cowardly people . . . we ourselves are the church."[64] Balthasar, too, could be critical of his fellow Christians, but he refused to criticize the Church as such. His reasons will become apparent in what follows.

Balthasar agreed with Rahner that at the heart of Christianity lies the faithful's personal relationship with Jesus Christ. But in keeping with Balthasar's emphasis on accepting one's unique, divinely bestowed commission and his reliance on a dramatic analogy for depicting the Christian life, he conceived of this relationship primarily in terms of the Pauline image of the faithful being in Christ (*en Christoi*), which Rahner essentially ignored. The risen Christ's Holy Spirit incorporates the faithful into Christ's mystical body, which becomes an "acting area" within which they are empowered to accept freely their "combat role" in God's ongoing battle to liberate the world.[65] This acceptance constitutes the faithful as persons, those who "in God's sight they always are and always have been."[66] The faithful can obey freely God's call because, by the power of the Spirit, they have been stripped of their egos and its idols, which enables them to let the triune divine life flow through them in the service of others. Acting at once in Christ and with him, the faithful thus become co-redeemers, which, according to Balthasar, can include suffering on behalf of others.[67]

In the Eucharist, the faithful are assimilated to the mind of Christ, namely, his thanksgiving and praise for the Father's role in the triune decision to let the Son endure the Father's wrath at sin.[68] "God's anger strikes [the Son] instead of the countless sinners, shattering him as by lightning and distributing him among them," thus completing the Incarnation and rendering him available Eucharistically to the faithful.[69] The faithful are able to experience what has already happened on the Cross as they let themselves be drawn into the Son's self-offering to the Father and the Son's free obedience to the Father's will. The Eucharist, like every sacrament, potentially "clarifies and deepens the grace of sonship vis-à-vis the Father and stirs up God's Spirit in the believer."[70]

By opening themselves to Christ's death and resurrection in the sacraments, the faithful are "in touch with Mary's archetypal faith."[71] For

Balthasar, when Mary said "yes" to being the bearer of God and to its salvific consequences, she did so "in the name" of all humans, even sinners who reject God.[72] Her faith thus undergirds and sustains all humans, "representing and answering for them" and overcoming and compensating for our deficiencies.[73] The similarity between this understanding of Mary's role and the liturgical prayer that God "Look not on our sins, but on the faith of your Church" is not accidental. Balthasar believed that Mary is the Church. He regularly and without hesitation contended that she was at once Christ's Mother and, appropriating the image for the Church in Ephesians 5, his Spotless Bride.[74] This is why he never criticized the Church as such and refused to speak of the Church as sinful.

In contrast to Rahner, Balthasar sharply distinguished the love of God made manifest in liturgical and personal prayer, on the one hand, from the love of neighbor, on the other. He ranked the former higher than the latter, asserting implausibly that only in prayer is God's absolute love returned without ulterior motive.[75] Tellingly, his treatment of the love of neighbor is hedged with cautionary phrases that conjure a brooding, ill-tempered deity quick to find fault. "The issue here is one of interpretation, of making visible all of the presuppositions or consequences implied in our encounter with our neighbor when illuminated by the fire of judgment."[76] Rahner would not have disagreed about the importance of truly loving God in our neighbor, but he evidently did not feel the need to invoke God's judgment when making that point.

Scope

Both Rahner and Balthasar regarded the human species as the apex of creation. Balthasar put it this way: Humans are "the summit of the whole material and organic creation and its mouthpiece before God."[77] Both theologians explained this, following Thomas Aquinas, by identifying consciousness with being. The cosmos is coming to its own fulfillment in and through the self-consciousness of humans, which has reached its climax in Jesus Christ. This conviction warranted for both theologians a unitive anthropology, namely, one that conceives of humans not as souls temporarily inhabiting bodies, but as corporeal persons or concrete spirits, to use Rahner's terms. This led both to affirm that life after death is not the mere prolongation of time for disembodied souls, but the surpassing fulfillment of the human race and, therewith, of the cosmos.[78] Although this anthropology could have underwritten a robust social ethics—because what happens to bodies (war, disease, impoverishment, malnutrition, racism, etc.) matters—neither theologian developed one. A unitive anthropology also could have warranted advocacy for environmentally sustainable practices, but once again, neither theologian pursued this.

Rahner and Balthasar affirmed that God wants to save every human from sin, yet they account quite differently for how God seeks to achieve this end. For Balthasar, the divine desire to have sinful humanity be reconciled with God involved the Son's solidarity in suffering, even in the depths of hell. There is no place, as it were, that God has not been. Thus, the Spirit of God in Christ is found throughout humanity—both within and outside of the visible boundaries of the Church—but it is not universally present in each of us as an offer, as it was for Rahner. Balthasar doubted the possibility of reconciling Rahner's claim, conveyed in the term "supernatural existential," with what Balthasar took to be self-evident: God's anger at sin is so fierce that God turns God's face away from sinners, withdrawing grace.[79] Rahner's response to this criticism highlights the difference between their doctrines of the atonement. God so loved the world, that God became a person who accepted finitude's graced orientation to its ground and goal and its limitations, including a horribly painful death, thereby making the history of the cosmos's self-transcendence God's own. Although God is surely free to withdraw the offer of forgiveness and final communion thus consummated in the event of Jesus Christ, that event indicates, to Rahner if not to Balthasar, that God has no desire and no plans to do so.

Despite their disagreement over whether God's grace is universally present in all humans, Rahner and Balthasar believed that humans are free to reject God's offer of reconciliation.[80] They agreed, then, that a person's love of God cannot be coerced, but disagreed over how God elicits and enables this love. Rahner's notion of the supernatural existential can be likened to a divinely implanted desire that God alone can satisfy. Balthasar sometimes spoke in terms of such desire, as when construing the phrase "image of God," from Genesis 1, to mean that God imparts a natural longing for what transcends humanity as its source and goal. But, Balthasar more typically dwelled on the salvific effect of

God's glory, namely, God's capacity to enthrall humans, leading us freely to accept God's call to obedient discipleship.

Balthasar's emphasis on God's glory stands in some tension with his conviction, shared with Rahner, that it is possible for one to have received the transformative grace of God's forgiveness without being aware of it. It is difficult to understand how one can be unwittingly enraptured by God's beauty. For his part, Rahner famously coined a phrase for those who love God unawares: anonymous Christians. He believed that persons of good will have intimations of God's antecedent grace, namely, the supernatural existential, when they accept their lives as a venture in freedom by loving their neighbors without regard for personal benefit; accept radical powerlessness, especially as it presents itself in death; and hope that eventually the discord within themselves and between them and others will be eliminated.[81] Balthasar rejected the phrase anonymous Christian, asking tartly: "When everything goes so well with anonymity, it is hard to see why a person should still be a name-bearing Christian."[82] In particular, he worried about the martyrs who died in defense of their faith. If there is no salvific significance between being in the Church and out of it, then did they die for naught? Rahner did not have a convincing answer for this question. Nevertheless, he did not deploy the phrase anonymous Christian with this question in mind, but to answer the equally if not more pressing question about how to reconcile the scriptural claim that God wills the salvation of all souls with the fact that most of humanity has not been, is not now, nor ever will be Christian. Rahner was convinced that part of the supernaturally elevated transcendentality of all humans consists in an anticipation of the absolute savior (that is, Jesus Christ), understood as the definitive and unsurpassable offer and acceptance of salvation.[83] As a person of good will accepts the gift of self-transcendence, she implicitly affirms this anticipation and enacts, again implicitly, what Christians would call faith, hope, and love. This experience nevertheless remains anticipatory. It does not rise to the heights offered in an ecclesial, liturgically enriched Christian life, where one "takes the risk and tries to love Jesus in a really personal way by means of the scriptures and the sacraments and the celebration of his death, and by living in the community of his believers."[84] But, the boundary between the one sort of love and the other is "fluid" because baptized Christians fall under the same obligation to bring to conscious reflection their graced experiences as do anonymous ones.[85] The obligation takes a different form, of course, since for the baptized person it entails rigorously thinking through her faith and acting in conformity with it over her entire life. Nevertheless, all Christians, anonymous or baptized, are Christians "in order to become" Christian. This is because the Christian life is a virtuous cycle of self-discovery that enables deeper self-sacrifice, followed by deeper self-discovery, etc.[86] So, in response to Balthasar's rightly pointing out the importance of being a "name-bearing Christian," Rahner would say that such name-bearing does not mean very much, unless a Christian is committed to the lifelong task of faithful reflection and action that being Christian requires.

Rahner's explanation of anonymous Christianity clarifies why his view of the relation between the Catholic Church and other religious groups is described as inclusive. It seems obvious that baptized Christians whose faith remains personally moribund may learn a great deal from their anonymously Christian brothers and sisters, who can be more deeply in love with Jesus (albeit without realizing it) than they are. Initially, this attitude toward non-Christians seems a welcome alternative to Balthasar's views. According to Balthasar, no non-Christian religion besides Judaism is given a role in the theo-dramatic struggle to defeat God's enemies. And he regarded Judaism, with Karl Barth, as nothing but the divinely beloved sign of judgment.[87] He supposed that God is not at work in the world's other religions, except, perhaps, to reduce them to "the dusts of sects, constantly emerging and dissolving or being hollowed out from within, largely as a result of the inroads of Western and technical civilization—which is itself clearly due to the advent of Christianity."[88] Such disdain suggests that Christianity cannot learn anything from these religions; it can only teach. Yet does not Rahner's theory of anonymous Christianity involve paternalism toward members of the world's other religions? Does it not assume that fully self-conscious Christians know what goes on in the hearts of, say, Hindus, better than do the Hindus themselves? At a minimum, neither theologian's explanation of how God might fulfill God's desire to save all souls cultivates among Christians esteem for the beauty, integrity, and plausibility of other religions on their own terms.

NOTES

1. Their discussions of soteriology, which lies at the very heart of Christian thought and so touches on nearly every other theological topic, are spread across their extensive writings. The more focused of these discussions constitute the primary sources for this chapter.
2. Karl Rahner, "Reflections on Methodology in Theology," article 3, *Theological Investigations*, Vol. 11, trans. David Bourke (New York: Crossroad Publishing, 1982), 100 (hereafter cited as TI 11.3).
3. TI 11.3, 93.
4. Karl Rahner, *Foundations of Christian Faith*, trans. William V. Dych (New York: Crossroad Publishing, 1978), 30 and 48.
5. Karl Rahner, "Guilt—Responsibility—Punishment within the View of Catholic Theology," art. 14, *Theological Investigations*, Vol. 6, trans. Karl-H. and Boniface Kruger (New York: Crossroad Publishing, 1982), 202 (hereafter cited as TI 6.14).
6. Rahner, *Foundations*, 48 and 140.
7. Ibid., 129.
8. Rahner, TI 11.3, 93.
9. See Hans Urs von Balthasar, *The Glory of the Lord*, vol. 1: *Seeing the Form*, trans. Erasmo Leiva-Merikakis, ed. Joseph Fessio S.J. and John Riches (San Francisco: Ignatius Press, 1982), passim. Hereafter cited as *Glory* I followed by page number. See also von Balthasar, "Revelation and the Beautiful" in *The Word Made Flesh: Explorations in Theology* I, trans. A. V. Littledale and Alexander Dru (San Francisco: Ignatius Press, 1989).
10. *Glory* I, 153.
11. It is misleading to describe Rahner as a transcendental theologian if by that we mean he confined himself to this mode of doing theology. Yet the results of his transcendental theology, especially as they are manifest in his theological anthropology, established the conceptual boundaries within which the rest of his theology had to operate.
12. Rahner believed introspection of the sort described above does not actualize our transcendental orientation; it brings it to conscious reflection.
13. Hans Urs von Balthasar, *Theo-Drama: Theological Dramatic Theory*, volume 3: *The Dramatis Personae: Persons in Christ*, trans. Graham Harrison (San Francisco: Ignatius Press, 1992), 205 (hereafter cited as TD 3 followed by page number).
14. TD 3, 207.
15. Balthasar's difference with Rahner on this point is one of emphasis. Although Rahner contended that persons become "unique" in their "abiding and personal relationship with the God-Man" [*Foundations*, 309], neither this notion nor his discussion of accepting one's vocation (see *Foundations*, 310–11) received anything like the attention these ideas received within Balthasar's theological corpus.
16. Rahner, *Foundations*, 80; see also 32–33.
17. Ibid., 98–101.

18. Hans Urs von Balthasar, *Theo-Drama: Theological Dramatic Theory*, volume 2: *The Dramatis Personae: Man in God*, trans. Graham Harrison (San Francisco: Ignatius Press, 1990), 164 (hereafter cited as TD 2).
19. Rahner, *Foundations*, 109.
20. Ibid., 110–11.
21. Hans Urs von Balthasar, "Am I a Sinner?" in *Elucidations*, trans. John Riches (San Francisco: Ignatius, 1975), 240–41.
22. Karl Rahner, "Christology in the Setting of Modern Man's Understanding of Himself and of His World," article 9, *Theological Investigations*, Volume 11, trans. David Bourke (New York: Crossroad Publishing, 1982), 224.
23. See, for instance, Karen Kilby, "Balthasar and Karl Rahner," in *The Cambridge Companion to Hans Urs von Balthasar*, ed. Edward T. Oakes, S.J. and David Moss (Cambridge: Cambridge University Press, 2004), 265.
24. This human nature includes, of course, our bodies through which we manifest sin's egoistic disregard for others. See Karl Rahner, "Current Problems in Christology," *Theological Investigations*, art. 5, Vol. 1, trans. Cornelius Ernst, O.P. (New York: Crossroads Publishing, 1982), 196–97 (hereafter cited as TI 1.5 followed by page number). For Rahner's reservations about classical Eastern Orthodox views of the atonement, see "Christology Today?" article 4, *Theological Investigations*, Vol. 17, trans. Margaret Kohl (New York: Crossroad Publishing Company, 1981), 28–29 (hereafter cited as TI 17.4 followed by page number).
25. TI 1.5, 192. It also ignores scripture, as Rahner noted wryly in TI 17.4, 29.
26. Rahner, *Foundations*, 283–84. Compare the following: "[W]e can and also have to understand God's free salvific will as the a priori cause of the Incarnation and of the cross of Christ, a cause which is not conditional upon anything outside of God." (Rahner, *Foundations*, 317).
27. Rahner, *Foundations*, 437; author's emphasis.
28. Ibid., 306.
29. TI 17.4, 32.
30. Rahner, TI 6.14, 215–16. See also *Foundations*, 316–17.
31. See Rahner, TI 1.5, 192 and TI 6.14, 215.
32. Rahner, *Foundations*, 284.
33. Ibid., 284.
34. Hans Urs von Balthasar, *Theo-Drama: Theological Dramatic Theory*, vol. 4: *The Action*, trans. Graham Harrison (San Francisco: Ignatius Press, 1990), 362 (hereafter cited as TD 4 followed by page number).
35. TD 3, 240.
36. TD 3, 517 and von Balthasar, *Love Alone is Credible*, trans. D. C. Schindler (San Francisco: Ignatius Press, 2004), 100.
37. See Rahner, *Foundations*, 197–203, especially 202–203.
38. TD 3, 237–39.
39. Ibid., 241.
40. Ibid., 245.

41. TD 4, 334.
42. Hans Urs von Balthasar, "Eschatology in Outline," in *Spirit and Institution: Explorations in Theology*, Vol. 4, trans. Edward T. Oakes, SJ (San Francisco: Ignatius Press), 421.
43. Ibid., 448–49.
44. Balthasar, *Love Alone is Credible*, 102.
45. TD 4, 345.
46. Hans Urs von Balthasar, "The Descent into Hell," in *Spirit and Institution: Explorations in Theology*, Vol. 4, trans. Edward T. Oakes, SJ (San Francisco: Ignatius Press), 408–9. See also TD 4, 336.
47. Balthasar, "The Descent into Hell," 408.
48. TD 4, 349–50.
49. Hans Urs von Balthasar, "Eschatology in Outline," 456.
50. TD 4, 335.
51. Ibid., 324.
52. TD 3, 328, 333, and 335.
53. Karl Rahner in *Karl Rahner in Dialogue: Conversations and Interviews, 1965–1982*, trans. Harvey D. Eagan, ed. Paul Imhof and Hubert Biallowons (New York: Crossroad Publishing, 1986), 126.
54. See Rahner, *Foundations*, 120 and 389, and TI 1.5, 197 and Balthasar, *Love Alone is Credible*, 103 and TD 2, 314.
55. See Rahner, *Foundations*, 360 and TD 4, 389.
56. Rahner, *Foundations*, 306 and 309.
57. Ibid., 307.
58. Ibid., 308.
59. Ibid., 399.
60. Ibid.
61. TI 16.6, 247.
62. Rahner, *Foundations*, 389.
63. Ibid., 412.
64. Ibid., 390.
65. TD 3, 52 and 231.
66. TD 3, 270; compare *Love Alone is Credible*, 103.
67. TD 3, 247 and 241–42.
68. TD 4, 400.
69. Ibid., 348, 363.
70. TD 3, 432.
71. TD 4, 403.
72. Ibid., 354.
73. Ibid., 361 and *Love Alone is Credible*, 104.
74. See, for example, Balthasar, TD 3, 293.
75. Balthasar, *Love Alone is Credible*, 109.
76. Ibid., 111.

77. Hans Urs von Balthasar, "God Speaks as Man," in *The Word Made Flesh: Explorations in Theology* I, trans. A. V. Littledale and Alexander Dru (San Francisco: Ignatius Press, 1989), 82. Compare this, from Rahner's *Foundations*, 190: "[T]he process by which the cosmos becomes conscious of itself in man . . . [i]n Christian terminology [is called] man's final and definite state, his salvation."
78. TD 3, 20.
79. TD 2, 314; cf. TD 3, 411.
80. See Balthasar, TD 4, 350 and "Eschatology in Outline," 456; and see Rahner, *Foundations*, 198.
81. Rahner, *Foundations*, 295–98.
82. Hans Urs von Balthasar, *My Work in Retrospect* (San Francisco: Ignatius Press, 1993), 56.
83. Rahner, *Foundations*, 319–21.
84. Ibid., 310.
85. Ibid., 306.
86. Ibid.
87. TD 3, 398–401.
88. TD 3, 420. Balthasar's legendary mastery of his sources did not extend to non-Christian religions. The depth of his misunderstanding of Buddhism and Hinduism, in particular, defies summary in a footnote.

20

Gustavo Gutiérrez

MICHAEL EDWARD LEE

Gustavo Gutiérrez (1928–) was born in Lima, Peru of mestizo heritage—part Hispanic and part indigenous (Quechua). After discerning a vocation to the Roman Catholic priesthood, Gutiérrez completed studies in philosophy and psychology in Louvain, Belgium (1951–55) and theology in Lyons, France (1955–59). These studies put him in contact with the *Nouvelle Théologie*, whose retrieval of biblical and patristic sources influenced the Second Vatican Council. When Gutiérrez returned to Peru, his pastoral tasks in a poor parish of Lima and with Peruvian university students sharpened the questions concerning Latin America's widespread poverty and the proper Christian response. Presentations in Petrópolis, Brazil (1964) and Chimbote, Peru (1968), along with his consultory work for the meeting of the Latin American Bishops Conference (CELAM) in Medellín, Colombia (1968), were all important steps toward the formulation of his landmark work, *A Theology of Liberation* (1971).

The following decades saw Gutiérrez clarify his liberation theology (*The Power of the Poor in History*, 1983; *The Truth Shall Make You Free*, 1986), and deepen it, particularly on the themes of: God and God-language (*On Job*, 1986; *The God of Life*, 1989), spirituality (*We Drink From Our Own Wells*, 1983), and a magisterial study of Bartolomé de Las Casas (*Las Casas*, 1992).

Though his work has been held in suspicion within conservative sectors of the Roman Catholic Church, Gustavo Gutiérrez has never been sanctioned officially for any unorthodox writing. On the contrary, his awards and honorary degrees, too numerous to list, include reception of Spain's Prince of Asturias award and admission to the Peruvian Academy of Language, France's Legion of Honor, the American Academy of Arts and Sciences. After joining the Dominican religious order in

1998, he was later bestowed the title, Order of Preachers' Magister Sacrae Theologiae, a title given to Albert the Great and Thomas Aquinas. In what was seen as a powerfully symbolic event, he wrote two chapters in *Poor for the Poor: The Mission of the Church* (2014), a book by Gerhard Müller, the prefect of the Vatican's Congregation for the Doctrine of the Faith, with a preface by Pope Francis.

Introduction

In the last fifty years, no theological movement has made a greater impact than liberation theology. Inspiring deep devotion and generating heated critique, liberation theology is a global, ecumenical, and interreligious approach to theology that, in its Christian iteration, has sought to understand the human struggle for liberation in relation to the gospel promise of salvation. Though it is more accurate to speak of liberation *theologies* than a singular, monolithic entity, perhaps no more enduring and influential an example exists than the theology of Gustavo Gutiérrez. His seminal text, *A Theology of Liberation*, remains the touchstone of this approach, and its categories and concept-structures still inspire theologies even though they might emerge in quite different contexts than Gutiérrez's Latin America.

In *A Theology of Liberation*, Gustavo Gutiérrez offers a basic definition of salvation: "the communion of human beings with God and among themselves."[1] It is a simple phrase, but, like the doctrine of salvation itself in relation to all of Christian thinking, its simplicity belies the complexity with which it permeates Gutiérrez's overall theological vision. How Gutiérrez explicates the communion of human beings with God and among themselves strikes notes that resonate throughout his theological oeuvre and reveals why liberation theology has had such an enormous impact in the last half century. The communion he elaborates is the gracious bestowal of God, but demands the human practice of love. It is deeply tied to a historical process, but its fulfillment is eschatological. It calls for prophetic denunciation, but it is sustained in utopian hope. It requires commitment and critical analysis, but ultimately rests in the mystery of God. However one assesses the ongoing future of liberation theology, the balance, depth, and prophetic power of Gutiérrez's work have made an unmistakable contribution to the Christian tradition.

Key to Gutiérrez's theology is a method that prioritizes the lived experience of Christians as a principal moment of God's self-revelation. Theology is a "second moment," and should be understood as a "critical reflection on Christian praxis in light of the Word."[2] Therefore, the struggle for liberation from the crushing, dehumanizing conditions of poverty serves as the catalyst for Gutiérrez's revolutionary rethinking of Christian soteriology. It is illuminating to examine this theology to see how the key terms "salvation" and "liberation" are understood in Gutiérrez's work, particularly as part of the reworking of Roman Catholic theology that took place in the twentieth century. These will serve to clarify the role of the church and Jesus Christ in his theology of salvation. Ultimately, all of these ideas coalesce in the notion, and spirituality, of the preferential option for the poor.

Integral Salvation

Receiving seminary training in the 1950s, Gustavo Gutiérrez would normally have been schooled in the deductive method characteristic of the theological manuals dominant since Pope Leo XIII's *Aeterni patris* (1879) established neo-scholastic thought as the preeminent mode of Roman Catholic theology. However, when Gutiérrez was sent to Europe for formation, he studied under figures such as Yves Congar, M. D. Chenu, and Henri de Lubac, and their *ressourcement* theology meant a return to biblical and patristic sources and a more dynamic approach to theology.[3] Out of this training, Gutiérrez forged a theology of salvation seeking to overcome the dualist tendencies in neo-scholastic thought and toward a more integral notion of salvation.

The theological developments concerning nature and grace were particularly important for Gutierrez's theology. Since the Reformation, the Thomistic distinction between the natural and supernatural had become reified such that Catholic thought did not recognize a basic orientation to grace in human beings, but, at best, it allowed for a "nonrepugnance."[4] In contrast, the work of figures such as Henri de Lubac and Karl Rahner came to see creation itself as a graced act, and thus, the notion of "pure nature" a remainder concept.[5] For Gutiérrez, these theological advances meant moving away from speaking about human destiny in the language of a "supernatural end" to one of "integral salvation."

In Gutiérrez's thinking, the shift away from a dualistic notion of salvation represents a double achievement: a move away from a quantitative view of salvation, and acceptance of a qualitative one.[6] By moving away from the quantitative, Gutiérrez indicates the recognition of the universality of God's salvific will for humanity such that the possibility of salvation cannot be exhausted by explicit membership in the church. All human beings are called to salvation, and though many questions remain, such as the role of faith or the status of non-Christian religions, Christian theology can no longer assume an exclusive grasp on the possibility of salvation.

Moving away from the calculus inherent in the quantitative view of salvation, Gutiérrez's theology is emblematic of the shift to a qualitative sense of salvation. The dynamic of salvation involves, not merely a juridical judgment or economic transaction of an aggrieved party, but the relationship forged in response to God's gracious self-offer. Practically, this means that grace is not an object to be gained through meritorious acts, a viewpoint that permeated pre-Conciliar Catholic piety, but it is acceptance of God's self-revelation and participation in the communion that inheres in this divine revelation. Christians are called not to "earn" salvation in acts to allay an offended God, but rather, are called to participate in fostering relationships and conditions under which God's will for human freedom and flourishing takes place ever more fully.

If, for the European theologians of the Council the central problematic of salvation revolved around the role of the non-believer, for Gutiérrez and his Latin American counterparts, it focused on the non-person.[7] This difference in perspective means that Gutiérrez's thought moves from an individualist discourse to one of sociality. Participation in grace never ceases to be a profound personal encounter; however, it also never excludes human social and structural interactions. Salvation involves the communion of human beings with God and among themselves, and these cannot be separated.[8] The contrast with much modern theology is pronounced. For Gutiérrez, the problem is not how the human subject relates to God as infinite horizon. Though he would not deny the important ideas brought out by transcendental reflection, Gutiérrez insists that the problem posed by the reality of Latin America (and indeed, the world today) is how to encounter the mystery of God in the face of widespread injustice and suffering. Christian theology must wrestle with death not just as an individual, existential question, but with early and unjust death as the fate of the majority of the world's population.

The sociality of Gutiérrez's thought implies not merely a need to think in terms of larger human communities, but to reflect on the very unity of history itself.[9] Another dimension of dualist thinking in prior theologies was the distinction and even division between human (profane) history and divine, salvific (sacred) history. Gutiérrez affirms the unity of human history and divine (salvation) history as part of salvation's integral character.[10] The biblical examples of the Exodus, the prophets, and Jesus's preaching of God's reign indicate how human beings participate in a partial historical fulfillment of God's promises, promises that are also oriented to an eschatological end. By affirming the complex unity of history, Gutiérrez performs a twofold task. He validates the importance of acting in history as participating in the reign of God. At the same time, he acknowledges a dimension of salvation beyond immediate historical acts. Gutiérrez thus puts forward a theology of salvation that eschews the extremes of either a spiritualism that empties human agency of any salvific meaning or an immediatist-activism that does not recognize any wider or future dimension of human salvation.[11]

The notion of integral salvation brings together different insights, among them: the universal call of humanity; the unity of history; the efficacy of human action; and the gratuitousness of God's self-revelation. All of these insights cohere in Gutiérrez's theology of salvation. However, they are also interrogated by the recognition of profound human suffering. Gutiérrez, from the perspective of a so-called Christian continent, sees the scandal of widespread poverty and Christian cooperation in the mechanisms of oppression and repression that sustain it, and rightly asks, "What does it mean to say, 'God loves you,' to the poor?"[12] The reality of the poor thus plumbs the depths of Christian soteriology by asking what exactly Christians mean when they speak of salvation. Salvation from what? For what? For Gutiérrez, the most useful language to answer these questions today is the language of liberation.

Liberation From, Liberation For

In its famous opening lines, *Gaudium et spes*, Vatican II's Pastoral Constitution on the Church in the Modern World states, "The joys and the hopes, the griefs and the anxieties of the people of this age, especially those who are poor or in any way afflicted, these too are the joys and hopes, the griefs and anxieties of the followers of Christ."[13] While many commentators have properly understood these lines as a radical shift from a view of the church as separated or above the world, they often fail to note the priority given to the collective experiences of those who are *poor or in any way afflicted*. This failure is important because of the soteriological significance the document places upon these joys, hopes, griefs, and anxieties understood as "signs of the times."[14]

In the twentieth century, no term better represented the expectations and anxieties of Latin America than "liberation." The long history of Iberian colonization, mixed results of revolutions of the previous century, grave inequalities in the industrialization process, unfulfilled promises (and crushing debt) of failed development projects after World War II, and repressive violence of Cold War national security states were all part of a complex set of factors that made liberation a powerful concept in Gutiérrez's time. The failure of development provided a particular sharpness to the term because it led to a different diagnosis of the Latin American situation.

When Latin America's poverty, political instability, and other social problems were diagnosed as "underdevelopment," then the logical antidote was "development." Under the influence of the Marshall Plan's success that rebuilt the crushed infrastructures of (West) Germany and Japan, and indeed made them into economic powers, investment into Latin America was intended to produce the same results. However, as these projects failed, leaving Latin American countries worse off than before, a new diagnosis began to emerge—dependence.[15] While the complexities of dependency theory cannot be elaborated fully here, let it suffice to note that while the antidote to underdevelopment was development, the antidote to dependence was liberation. From academicians, to political parties, grassroots movements, and guerrilla factions, the term "liberation" emerged as the leitmotif to express dissatisfaction with present circumstances and to give voice to the yearning for something better.

As Gutiérrez took up the task described in *Gaudium et spes*, he could not but carry out theological reflection on liberation. Indeed, as he arrived at a definition of the theological task as a "critical reflection on praxis in light of the word of God," the primary form of praxis on which he reflected critically was the participation of Christians in the struggles for liberation. To that end, Gutiérrez identifies "three reciprocally interpenetrating levels of meaning" of the term liberation that demonstrate the complexity of the term and its usefulness in signifying what Christians mean by salvation.[16] Two important consequences flow from this move. The first is that, unlike some other liberation theologians, Gutiérrez does not assume "liberation" and "salvation" as two different concepts that need to be related somehow.[17] For him, liberation, seen in its fullest depths, expresses what Christians mean by salvation, provided that the term is understood in all of its complexity. Second, though Gutiérrez identifies the three levels of meaning, with three corresponding modes of knowledge, these important distinctions ultimately are meant to emphasize the unity of a single process.[18] "One [level of meaning] is not present without the others, but they are distinct: they are all part of a single, all-encompassing salvific process, but they are to be found at different levels."[19]

A first level of meaning for liberation exists within the socioeconomic realm, where liberation refers to freedom from conditions of dehumanizing deprivation, exclusion, and repressive violence (what will be termed material poverty). This first sense of liberation corresponds primarily to a "scientific" knowledge that can properly investigate the complex causes of material poverty and propose possibilities for liberative action. It can mean conflict because, at this level, liberation means contending with those structures at the basis of these conditions and struggling against those forces that hinder human fulfillment. Yet, the material-scientific emphasis in this level of meaning for liberation should not obscure a concurrent theological conviction: that the conditions of poverty against which people struggle are a violation of God's will for human flourishing. A Christian must understand the struggle for socioeconomic liberation as part, and only part, of the salvific promise of God.

The significance of the term liberation is not exhausted by the socioeconomic level of meaning, but also includes what Gutiérrez terms a "utopian-historical" level of meaning.[20] This refers to a sense of liberation as the freedom that results when human beings assume responsibility for their own destiny. If the socioeconomic level of meaning focuses on the striving for the conditions that make possible human surviving, this level deals with its thriving. It corresponds to a philosophical kind of knowing, a creativity and self-realization that mark a dynamic and nuanced anthropology. It is a utopian thinking that envisions history's end as the creation of new humanity in a new society of solidarity. If liberation theology connotes to some a reductionist emphasis on overcoming material need, then Gutiérrez's articulation of this level of meaning to liberation fills out the picture of human (personal and social) fulfillment and, theologically places this historical development of humanity within the ambit of the work of God's Spirit.[21]

The third level of meaning for liberation is explicitly theological; that is, it speaks of liberation from sin. The only source of this liberation, which can be called redemption, is God's gratuitous love through Christ. Corresponding to the knowledge that comes through faith, liberation at this level of meaning is the love of God that heals human selfishness. It is liberation from sin that is personal and social. For Gutiérrez, the primary knowledge Christians have of this liberation is found in the words and deeds of Jesus Christ, who preached and manifested the reign of God in human history. This kingdom or reign of God represents the fullness of liberation from sin, and it must be recognized as a gift. The tensive, interpenetrating way that the process of human liberation and the realization of God's reign are described by Gutiérrez speaks to how liberation expresses the insight at the heart of integral salvation. As Gutiérrez writes,

> The growth of the kingdom is a process which occurs historically in liberation. . . . Without liberating historical events, there would be no growth of the kingdom. But the process of liberation will not have conquered the very roots of human oppression and exploitation without the coming of the kingdom, which is above all a gift. Moreover, we can say that the historical, political liberating event is the growth of the kingdom and is a salvific event; but it is not the coming of the kingdom, not all of salvation.[22]

Church as Sacrament of Liberation

Gutiérrez describes salvation as integral not just at the level of concept, but in the church's pastoral practice and self-understanding. This means that the church's view of salvation is integral with the manner that it identifies and carries out its mission in the world. Precisely because theology is a second moment to the church's praxis, Gutiérrez maps the developments in Roman Catholic soteriology by locating the salvation question within pastoral models of the church.[23] He identifies three previous models, "Christendom," "New Christendom," and the "Distinction of Planes," whose respective weaknesses in formulating salvation stem from a concomitant misconception of the proper presence of the church in the world. Ultimately, in light of the complexity of liberation presented to the church today, Gutiérrez envisions the church as the mediator of that very communion between God and humans and among themselves that is integral salvation. The journey to this vision can be seen in the important corrections that refined each church model, a trajectory culminating in those changes articulated by the Second Vatican Council and in a prophetic model that emerges in a theology of liberation.

Beginning with the medieval notion of "Christendom," Gutiérrez identifies a perspective in which the church is viewed as the sole vehicle of salvation, and consequently, it must intervene directly in the affairs of the world. This view, elsewhere identified as "political Augustinianism," reflected the quantitative approach to the question of salvation that assumed the inability of those outside of the church to attain it.[24] This is no random selection on the part of Gutiérrez, for the Christendom mentality represents the form of Christianity that came in the colonization of the Americas. When Pope Alexander VI granted the petitions of the Catholic Kings of Spain and Portugal for the titles to lands in the New World in 1493, it was with the promise that the Iberian rulers would extend the dominion of the Catholic faith.

The transitions exemplified in the French revolution and more proximately in the Bolivarian revolutions of Latin America indicate a separation of Christendom's identification of faith and social identity. That shift to the "New Christendom" involved some affirmation of the world's "self-consistency," but one that still required the indirect help of the church. The New Christendom represented a step forward because it began to recognize the world as an autonomous sphere in which justice and human rights could be pursued.[25] However, Gutiérrez recognizes in this model the presence of an "ecclesiastical narcissism" in which the church remained the exclusive center of God's saving work, maintaining its political power. The New Christendom shared with its predecessor the attitude summed up in the phrase, "extra ecclesiam nulla salus."[26]

Out of the New Christendom came the developments that Gutiérrez names the "distinction of planes," a mentality that embodied the effects of the nineteenth and early-twentieth century neo-scholastic theology. In some ways, this model represented a development from the New Christendom in its assertion of the world's autonomy such that the church ceased to have aspirations as a directly political power. However, the effect of this distinction was to relegate the church's sphere of activity exclusively to "spiritual" matters. At most, the church could inspire others to work in the temporal sphere. Similarly, while in the distinction model there came to be an imagining of the possibility of salvation outside the boundaries of the church, that salvation was defined in a spiritual, post-historical manner. Ultimately, these dualisms latent in the "distinction of planes" model underwent crises that would make its continuing dominance impossible and open the path to a theology of liberation.

The ecclesiology of the Second Vatican Council represents a triumph to Gutiérrez because its retrieval of biblical themes and images for the church resulted in a sociality, a rediscovery of the communitarian dimension of the faith and ways to live it.[27] It also presupposed an "uncentering" of the church that must cease considering itself as the exclusive place of salvation and orient itself toward a new and radical service of people.[28] Two images stand out for Gutiérrez. The first comes from the words of Pope John XXIII's discourse one month prior to the opening of the Council, "As for the under-developed countries, the church is, and wishes to be, the church of all, and especially the church of the poor."[29] If the struggle for liberation is a crucial sign of the times, then the church that is true to its evangelical calling needs to be a church of and for the poor. Of the many illuminative images of the church proposed by the Council itself, Gutiérrez draws most heavily from *Lumen Gentium*'s description of the church as a sacrament, an image that complements that of the church of the poor and ties it most directly to the notion of salvation.[30]

The sacramentality of the church does not consist in a triumphal demarcation of its privilege over against the world; rather, its sacramentality is as the mediating presence of the communion between God and humans and among themselves that is salvation. As such, the church must be an effective sacrament that, in its external behavior and internal structure, is a place of integral liberation. Unlike the previous ecclesial models, as a sacrament of salvation-liberation, the church is not an end in itself but can only find meaning in its capacity to signify the reality of the reign of God—including a break with unjust social orders.

The integral understanding of the church deepens the interpretation of elements too often spiritualized. For example, Gutiérrez emphasizes the centrality of the Eucharist as that communion of Christians with one another and the Triune God that calls the church to cast its lot with the oppressed and the exploited in the struggle for a more just world. Therefore, the annunciation of the gospel, or evangelization, is a proclamation that the love of God is present in history, and thus, every human action can be understood in relation to Christ. This liberative hermeneutic that upholds traditional affirmations while deepening their meaning in light of integral salvation is the proper lens through which to understand the role of Jesus Christ.

Jesus of Liberation, Christ of Solidarity

Like other liberation theologians, Gutiérrez invokes the image of Jesus as liberator.[31] Too often though, critics have seized upon this designation to attack what they perceive as a reduction of the salvific work of Christ. While it is true that in his theology, Gutiérrez spends relatively little time developing a detailed Christology in the traditional sense, it does not mean that Christ is unimportant or that only Jesus's humanity is of consequence. To the contrary, Gutiérrez places Christ at the center of the salvific process. However, his treatment of Christ, as can be seen in the treatment of integral salvation and liberation, must be contextualized as a response to deficiencies in neo-scholastic approaches to Christology and as an articulation of the experience of Christian faith in modern Latin America. Gutiérrez's reflections on Jesus do not represent a dogmatic choice, the "Jesus of history" over the "Christ of faith," but rather, a recognition that the Jesus Christ revealed in the Scriptures is the one who grounds dogmatic belief, and as such, is the object of Christian worship and model for Christian behavior.

Gutiérrez's reflections on Jesus Christ are part of a significant shift from the Catholic Christology of the manuals, whose deductive approach focused on a dogmatic outline of the central Christological mysteries (incarnation, crucifixion, resurrection), and the Chalcedonic formulation of Christ's full humanity and divinity.[32] In this former line of thinking, Christology fell under the consideration of God as the redeemer, and so Christ's nature and his theologized role in terms of redemption (often under the triad of the offices: teacher, priest, and king) dictated the form and content of reflection. The effect was that the deductive, dualistic Christologies of this period worked from abstract principles and obscured the relationship of Jesus's ministry and preaching to the Christological dogmas. Though there were some intuitions in popular piety that worked to overcome this split, the tendency was still to lift up a savior who delivered one from suffering in this world for bliss in the next.[33] Informed by the biblical renewal of the twentieth century, Gutiérrez and others bring out the richness of the gospel portrayal of Jesus and its relation to salvation.

To claim Jesus as a liberator is not to deemphasize or reject Christological dogmas. To the contrary, Gutiérrez finds the Chalcedonic formula a key theological illustration of the differentiated unity that he ascribes to integral salvation. However, that unity is not coherent in the abstract consideration of the Christological mysteries. The leap from the incarnation to the crucifixion elides the words and deeds of Jesus that both elucidate the significance of incarnation and substantiate the meaning of crucifixion-resurrection. Thus, Gutiérrez gives voice to a thoroughly incarnational Christology, one that understands the incarnation not just as an effective act, but as that which grounds and models the communion of God with humanity in history.

If Rahner described Jesus as the *Ur-Sakrament* of God, then for Gutiérrez, Jesus Christ as liberator is the fullest realization of the salvific will of God. He is God become poor. He proclaims God's reign of justice. His ministry manifests that divine communion that is the hope of salvation. Furthermore, Jesus's preference for the poor and the opposition that his ministry generates reveal the historical and social character of sin. Jesus enters into conflicts and is killed for a message that touches upon all of the levels of meaning to the term liberation. Jesus's resurrection is the liberation of humanity from all sin, a true integral liberation.

As a result, the manner in which Gutiérrez treats the subject of Jesus Christ fortifies those in the struggle for justice and reveals that that struggle is not understood correctly unless it is seen in the wider spectrum of sin. In speaking about the "universality and totality" of Jesus's life and teaching, Gutiérrez notes how they "touch the very heart of political behavior, giving it its true dimension and depth. Misery and social injustice reveal 'a sinful situation,' a disintegration of fellowship and communion; by freeing us from sin, Jesus attacks the roots of an unjust order."[34] Ultimately, as James Nickoloff puts it, "In the midst of social liberation and the utopian project the light of Christian faith discloses the love of One whose self-gift alone makes the complete realization of human freedom possible."[35] Evoking the language of patristic theology, Gutiérrez sees Christ as the source of a new creation, one in which human beings are free to love as God loves. God becomes history in the person of Jesus, but not simply as a completed, effective act. For Gutiérrez, Jesus is the "future of our history."[36]

If there has been a development in Gutiérrez's thinking about Christ, it has been to deepen the notion of solidarity. Gaspar Martinez has noted how in Gutiérrez's later works the "Christ of *actio* is going to be more and more seen as the Christ of *passio*"; that is, Christ's action as liberator is complemented by a suffering Christ in radical solidarity with the poor.[37] It is a shift that highlights how Gutiérrez has forefronted the gratuitousness of God's love as both mystery and promise. It also links the previous themes considered here with perhaps Gutiérrez's single most important theological contribution—his elucidation and development of the "preferential option for the poor."

Preferential Option for the Poor

At its heart, the notion of the "preferential option for the poor" wrestles with a profound dilemma concerning the nature of poverty. On the one hand, those who suffer under and against poverty testify that it is dehumanizing and destructive. Despite this clear sense in which poverty is considered evil, there is also that long trajectory in the Jewish and Christian traditions that speaks of poverty in a positive light. From the Psalmist's exaltation of utter dependence on God, to Jesus's beatitudes, "blessed are the poor," and Francis of Assisi's marriage to "Lady Poverty," the condition of poverty has been used to indicate something desirable, even essential, in the life of the authentic believer. How does the Christian confront this dilemma?

In their 1968 conference in Medellín, the Latin American bishops delineate three meanings of poverty, and Gutiérrez has always affirmed this understanding in his work.[38] Specifically, poverty is distinguished as: (1) material poverty, (2) spiritual poverty, and (3) poverty as commitment.[39] Understanding these different senses of poverty clarifies the ambiguous treatment of the term in the tradition and grounds the preferential option for the poor as the spirituality that flows from Gutiérrez's theology of salvation.

Complex in its manifestations, material poverty is the deprivation of the conditions necessary for human survival and flourishing. Gutiérrez captures this material sense of poverty when he describes it as "death before one's time."[40] Since his earliest work, Gutiérrez has asserted this meaning. What has developed in Gutiérrez's thinking over the years is an expanding acknowledgment of the multiple causes and the various forms in which poverty manifests itself. Though in many ways latent in his thought from the beginning, the poverty and unjust treatment suffered by others because of gender, racial, or ethnic discrimination becomes more clearly acknowledged by Gutiérrez.[41] Whatever its cause or manifestation, the Christian cannot but agree with the Bible that material poverty is evil—it is a violation of God's will for human life and flourishing.

The analysis of material poverty yields two central insights of a critical and theological nature respectively. The first is that, as a complex phenomenon, poverty cannot be understood as stemming simply from a moral weakness or indolence on the part of the poor. Global poverty involves greater structural forces, and those who wish to address material poverty must confront that reality. Because this structural reality is complex, it requires a wide range of intellectual and analytical contributions. Much controversy surrounding liberation theology has centered precisely on this point as critics see an over-reliance on Marxist analysis.[42] Though Gutiérrez certainly evinces the influence of dependency-theory economics in his early writing, he has clarified on numerous occasions the important but relative role that the social sciences play in relation to theological thinking.[43]

Theologically, poverty cannot be reduced to merely an economic status, and thus, a problem strictly of secular governance and economic agency. Material poverty, and the dehumanizing conditions it indicates, must be evaluated by Christians as a violation of God's will for human flourishing, and therefore, an intrinsic part of Christian discipleship involves participating in the effort to liberate the victims of poverty. The great contribution in Gutiérrez's thought is how he is able to weave together the critical and theological insights regarding poverty while overcoming the dilemma over poverty's character.

While always clearly identifying material poverty as evil, Gutiérrez recognizes the powerful traditions behind speaking of poverty in a positive light. The key is how to lift up these traditions without having them obscure the scourge of material poverty that permeates the world today. Therefore, Gutiérrez turns to the notion of spiritual poverty as that attitude of availability that should characterize the faith of every believer. Biblically, spiritual poverty refers to utter dependence on God. The great sin identified by the Hebrew Bible is to forget spiritual poverty and to view oneself or another as a source of power, life, etc. Understood this way, spiritual poverty is completely distinct from material poverty. Every believer should seek spiritual poverty. Yet, this is not enough. Is there no connection between material and spiritual poverty? There is, and it is found in a third understanding of poverty extant in the tradition. It is a sense of poverty as commitment. This sense of poverty flows from spiritual poverty and manifests itself in acts of solidarity with those who suffer from material poverty, a dynamism that is captured by the phrase, "the preferential option for the poor."

Perhaps no other concept in Gutiérrez's work evokes more criticism than the term "preferential." Because it is often seen as a restriction of universality, the notion of preferential love has been understood by critics as antithetical to the Christian belief in God's universal and unconditional love. Yet, Gutiérrez views it as a reflection of biblical teaching. Citing the great reversals in many of Jesus's parables ("the last shall be first"), Gutiérrez understands preference not as exclusive but as indicating those who have a primacy in their need for human solidarity.[44] As the parable of the prodigal son illustrates, preferential love does not exclude others, but to the contrary, invites them into a communion born of solidarity.

Entering into this solidarity of preference for the poor is incumbent on the life of the disciple. So, to speak of a preferential "option" is not to speak of something optional in the Christian life, a choice a disciple may or may not make. Rather, it emphasizes opting as a daily commitment. Making an option for the poor is to opt for the God of the reign that Jesus proclaimed. It is to opt for a life in solidarity with those who suffer material poverty and in resistance to its causes. It is a response to the invitation for communion, with God and others, so that Gutiérrez says, "the poor themselves must make this decision as well."[45]

What is striking about Gutiérrez's treatment of the preferential option for the poor is that while the phrase sums up the fullness of the Christian disciple's call to conversion and life of discipleship, it does not remain in exclusively human terms. "The ultimate reason for a commitment to the poor and oppressed does not lie in the social analysis . . . as Christians, we base that commitment fundamentally on the God of our faith. It is a theocentric, prophetic option we make, one which strikes its roots deep in the gratuity of God's love and is demanded by that love."[46] Ultimately, or perhaps better, primally, the preferential option for the poor is God's option. It is a gratuitous option that often defies human reason, but it speaks to that very divine option for communion that is the hope for salvation.

Conclusion

Gustavo Gutiérrez has characterized a principal sign of our times as the "irruption of the poor."[47] This irruption consists in marginalized voices, those who have existed as non-persons, taking agency and making their presence felt. Gutiérrez's theology evinces that presence by articulating the gospel promise of salvation and seeing within it the fullness of human liberation. No more can Christian theology speak of a heavenly promise that ignores earthly suffering. The vision of salvation as the communion of human beings with God and each other overcomes dangerous dualisms that were part and parcel of the colonial, neo-scholastic theology dominant in the last century—and still latent in many ways. Though liberation theology might conjure up images of guerrillas and gun-belts, these caricatures do not do justice to Gutiérrez's elucidation of integral salvation, of liberation, the role of the Church and Jesus Christ, and the preferential option for the poor. It is a truly revolutionary vision, but one that calls for self-sacrificial love and rests ultimately in the gratuitous hands of God.

NOTES

1. Gustavo Gutiérrez, *A Theology of Liberation*, 2nd ed. (Maryknoll, NY: Orbis Books, 1971, 1986), 85, 91, 104 (hereafter cited as TL followed by page number).
2. TL, 11.
3. On the *nouvelle théologie*, see Jürgen Mettepenningen, *Nouvelle Théologie: Inheritor of Modernism, Precursor of Vatican II* (London and New York: T & T Clark, 2010).
4. See Juan Alfaro, *Lo natural y lo sobrenatural* (Madrid: Matriti, 1952).
5. Stephen Duffy, *The Horizon of Grace: Nature and Grace in Modern Catholic Thought* (Collegeville, MN: Liturgical Press, 1992).
6. TL, 83–86.
7. Gaspar Martinez, *Confronting the Mystery of God: Political, Liberation, and Public Theologies* (New York: Continuum, 2001).
8. Dean Brackley notes how Gutierrez's use of the verb, *convocar*, to speak of the universality of salvation, is overlooked. *Divine Revolution* (Maryknoll, NY: Orbis Books, 1996), 77. Cf. TL, 45.
9. For an enlightening comparison of Gutiérrez's view of history with Karl Rahner and Johann Metz, see Gaspar Martinez, *Confronting the Mystery of God*, 216–51.
10. In this respect, Gutiérrez is influenced by the biblical scholarship of Gerhard von Rad on the Pentateuchal traditions and the theme of salvation.
11. Commentators note that while TL uses language that seems to stress human efforts, Gutiérrez's later works demonstrate a deepened emphasis on the gratuity of God. See Gutiérrez, *We Drink From Our Own Wells* (Maryknoll, NY: Orbis Books, 1984), 109, and Gutiérrez, *On Job* (Maryknoll, NY: Orbis Books, 1987), 51.
12. Gutiérrez, "Saying and Showing to the Poor: 'God Loves You.'" in *In the Company of the Poor* (Maryknoll, NY: Orbis Books, 2013), 27–34.
13. *Gaudium et spes*, #1 in Walter M. Abbott, ed., *The Documents of Vatican II* (New York: America Press, 1966), 199–200.
14. *Gaudium et spes*, #4, *Documents*, 201.
15. Dependency theorists included André Gunder Frank and Fernando Henrique Cardoso. For a good summary, see Arthur McGovern, *Liberation Theology and Its Critics: Toward An Assessment* (Maryknoll, NY: Orbis Books, 1989), 125–29.
16. TL, 24.
17. See, for example, Clodovis Boff, *Theology and Praxis* (Maryknoll, NY: Orbis Books, 1987).
18. Here one sees the influence of Jacques Maritain's *Les degrés du savoir* (1932) that classifies knowledge as: scientific, utopian-philosophical, and the way of faith. In English, *Distinguish to Unite: Or, The Degrees of Knowledge* (London: Geoffrey Bles, 1959).
19. TL, 103.
20. Gutiérrez filters many sources when he invokes the language of utopia, including Paul Blanquart, Ernst Bloch, Karl Mannheim, Paulo Freire, and José Carlos Mariátegui. See Miguel Manzanera, *Teología y salvación-liberación en la obra de Gustavo Gutiérrez*, (Bilbao: Mensajero, 1978), 143–48.

21. This sanguine view of history's positive progression, characteristic of Gutiérrez's early work, is modified as he reflects more on the gratuitous mystery of God and the limitation of human efforts to comprehend and express it. Representative of this move are his books *On Job* and *Las Casas*.
22. TL, 104.
23. For example, see his discussion of these models in "Different Responses," chapter four of *A Theology of Liberation*.
24. On political Augustinianism, see Henri de Lubac, *Augustinianism and Modern Theology*, trans. Lancelot Sheppard (New York: Herder, 1969).
25. This relative autonomy is articulated well by Jacques Maritain, *True Humanism* (New York: Scribner's, 1938).
26. That is, "outside the Church, there is no salvation."
27. On sociality in Gutiérrez, see Brackley, *Divine Revolution*, 77ff.
28. TL, 143–44.
29. Words that have been echoed by Pope Francis, who shortly after being elected, stated, "Oh, now I would like a poor Church, and for the poor." [www.reuters.com] Last accessed August 9, 2014.
30. See *Lumen Gentium*, #9, *Documents*, 26.
31. E.g., Leonardo Boff, *Jesus Cristo Libertador* (Petrópolis: Editora Vozes, 1972), and Jon Sobrino, *Jesucristo liberador* (Madrid: Editorial Trotta, 1991).
32. For a helpful treatment of this biblically informed shift in twentieth-century Roman Catholic Christology, see Elizabeth Johnson, *Consider Jesus: Waves of Renewal in Christology* (New York: Crossroad Publishing, 1990).
33. In attempting to overcome these dualisms, Gutiérrez and other liberation theologians should be viewed not only as distinct from Marxist thought, but as directly critical of its formulation of religion as escapist or strictly ideological in function.
34. TL, 134.
35. James Nickoloff, "The Church and Human Liberation: The Ecclesiology of Gustavo Gutiérrez" (PhD dissertation, Graduate Theological Union, 1989), 267.
36. Gutiérrez, *The Power of the Poor in History* (Maryknoll, NY: Orbis Books, 1983), 12–16.
37. Martinez, *Confronting the Mystery of God*, 234.
38. Because he served as a consultant in the drafts of the documents, it is unclear whether Gutiérrez was influenced by CELAM or the opposite. At the very least, there is a close synergy in the formulation of these meanings.
39. Document on the Poverty of the Church, #4 in *The Church in the Present-Day Transformation of Latin America*.
40. A phrase Gutiérrez takes from a description of the fate of indigenous peoples in the Americas. See *The Power of the Poor in History*, 77.
41. This is a topic on which Latin American theologians have been in dialogue with U.S. black, feminist, and Latino/a theologians for some time. See Sergio Torres and John Eagleson, eds., *Theology in the Americas* (Maryknoll, NY: Orbis Books, 1976).

42. In addition to the Vatican "Instruction on Certain Aspects of Liberation Theology," see John Milbank, *Theology and Social Theory: Beyond Secular Reason* (London: Blackwell, 1990).
43. His best clarification can be found in *The Truth Shall Make You Free: Confrontations* (Maryknoll, NY: Orbis Books, 1990).
44. Late laborer [Mt 20: 1–16]; wedding banquet: invited/uninvited guests [Mt 22:2–20]; Beatitudes [Lk 6:20] poor (ptochoi), hungry (peinontes), weeping; Jesus: righteous/sinners [Mk 2:17]
45. Gutiérrez, "Option for the Poor," in Jon Sobrino and Ignacio Ellacuría, eds., *Mysterium Liberationis* (Maryknoll, NY: Orbis Books, 1989), 240.
46. Ibid.
47. Gutiérrez, "Option for the Poor," 235.

ABOUT THE CONTRIBUTORS

EDITOR

Justin S. Holcomb is Affiliate Professor of Christian Thought and Theology at Gordon-Conwell Theological Seminary. Previously, he taught at the University of Virginia. Justin is the author or editor of numerous books, including: *Christian Theologies of Scripture*, *Christian Theologies of Sacraments*, *Know the Heretics*, and *Know the Creeds and Councils*.

CONTRIBUTORS

John Behr is the Dean of St. Vladimir's Orthodox Theological Seminary and Professor of Patristics. His early work was on asceticism and anthropology, focusing on St. Irenaeus of Lyons and Clement of Alexandria. He is writing a series of books on "The Formation of Christian Theology," two volumes of which have already appeared: vol. 1, *The Way to Nicaea* and vol. 2, *The Nicene Faith*. On the basis of these two volumes, he published a synthetic work, *The Mystery of Christ: Life in Death*. This was followed by an edition and translation of the fragments of Diodore of Tarsus and Theodore of Mopsuestia, setting them in their historical and theological context. He also recently published a more poetic and meditative work entitled *Becoming Human: Theological Anthropology in Word and Image* and a full study of St. Irenaeus: *St. Irenaeus of Lyons: Identifying Christianity*. He is currently working on a new edition and translation of Origen's *On First Principles* and a study of the Gospel of St. John.

J. Todd Billings is Gordon H. Girod Research Professor of Reformed Theology at Western Theological Seminary in Holland, Michigan. He is the author of several books, including *The Word of God for the People of God*, *Union with Christ*, and *Calvin, Participation, and the Gift*, winner of a 2009 John Templeton Award for Theological Promise. He has written articles for *International Journal of Systematic Theology*, *Pro Ecclesia*, and *Theology Today*.

W. T. Dickens is Professor of Religious Studies and Director of the Franciscan Center for Catholic Studies at Siena College. He is the author of *Hans Urs von Balthasar's Theological Aesthetics: A Model for Post-Critical Biblical Interpretation* and, most recently, "The Uses of the Bible in Theology" in John Riches, ed., *New Cambridge History of the Bible: Volume IV: Modernity, Colonialism and their Successors*. He has published in *Christianity Today*, *Journal of Religious Ethics*, and *Heythrop Journal*.

Giles E. M. Gasper is a Senior Lecturer in Medieval History, in the Department of History, Durham University, UK. He is the author of *Anselm of Canterbury and His Theological Inheritance*, and has co-edited (with Ian Logan) *Anselm of Canterbury and His Legacy*. He has also published widely on medieval attitudes toward economy, material and spiritual, and has co-edited (with Svein Gullbekk) *Money and the Church in Medieval Europe, 1000–1200*. He also leads an international project on the scientific works of Robert Grosseteste: the Ordered Universe Project.

James R. Gordon is a Guest Professor of Biblical and Theological Studies and Philosophy at Wheaton College. He is the author of *The Holy One in Our Midst: An Essay on Christ's Flesh*. He has published essays in the *International Journal of Systematic Theology* and the *Heythrop Journal*.

Tom Greggs is Professor of Historical and Doctrinal Theology at the University of Aberdeen. His publications include *Barth, Origen, and Universal Salvation: Restoring Particularity*; *Theology against Religion: Constructive Dialogues with Bonhoeffer and Barth*; and *New Perspectives for Evangelical Theology*. He serves as editor of Brill's *Companions to Modern Theology Series* and Edinburgh University Press's *Critical History of Theology Series*.

Kerrie Hide is a theologian and spiritual director. She is the author of the award-winning *Gifted Origins to Graced Fulfilment: The Soteriology of Julian of Norwich*. She has written many articles on mystical theology, prayer, and spirituality, most recently, "Sacred Heart," "Silence Enflamed: John of the Cross and Prayer," and "Quiet Loving: The Prayer of Quiet in Teresa of Jesus." After eighteen years lecturing in the School of Theology at Australian Catholic University and nine years as a spiritual director at St. Mary's Towers, Douglas Park, she now continues to enjoy spiritual direction, retreat work, and writing.

David Hogg is Senior Pastor of Christ Baptist Church, Raleigh, North Carolina. Previously, he served as Associate Dean of Academic Affairs at Beeson Divinity School. He teaches church history and doctrine with a particular emphasis in medieval theology. In addition to his book, *Anselm of Canterbury: the Beauty of Theology*, Hogg has published works on medieval spirituality and various doctrines in historical perspective.

Frank A. James III is the President and Professor of Historical Theology at Biblical Theological Seminary in Hatfield, Pennsylvania. He formerly served as Provost and Professor of Historical Theology at Gordon-Conwell Theological Seminary and also served as President of Reformed Theological Seminary in Florida. He has published more than sixty academic articles and is the author or editor of numerous books, including: *Church History: From Pre-Reformation to the Present*; *Peter Martyr Vermigli and Predestination: The Augustinian Inheritance of an Italian Reformer*; co-editor with Heiko Oberman of *Via Augustini: Augustine in the Later Middle Ages, Renaissance and Reformation*; editor of *Peter Martyr Vermigli and the European Reformations: Semper Reformanda*; translator/editor of *Two Theological Loci: Predestination and Justification*; co-editor with Emidio Campi and Peter Opitz of *Petrus Martyr Vermigli: Humanismus, Republikanismus, Reformation*; and co-editor with Charles Hill of *The Glory of the Atonement*. He is one of the founding members of the *Reformation Commentary on Scripture*.

Michael Edward Lee is Associate Professor in the Department of Theology and the Latin American & Latino Studies Institute at Fordham University. He is the author of *Bearing the Weight of Salvation: The Soteriology of Ignacio Ellacuría* and editor of *Ignacio Ellacuría: Essays on History, Liberation, and Salvation*. His forthcoming book will examine the theological legacy of Archbishop Oscar Romero.

David Vincent Meconi, SJ, is Associate Professor of Historical Theology at Saint Louis University; he is also the editor of *Homiletic and Pastoral*

Review. He has published the *Annotated Confessions of Saint Augustine*; *The One Christ: St. Augustine's Theology of Deification*; co-edited (along with Eleonore Stump) the *Cambridge Companion to Augustine*; and *The Enemy Within: Augustine on Sin and Self-Sabotage*.

Thomas H. McCall is Professor of Biblical and Systematic Theology and Director of the Carl F. H. Henry Center for Theological Understanding at Trinity Evangelical Divinity School. He is the co-editor (with Michael C. Rea) of and a contributor to *Philosophical and Theological Essays on the Trinity* and the co-author (with Keith D. Stanglin) of *Jacob Arminius: Theologian of Grace*. He is also the author of *Which Trinity? Whose Monotheism? Philosophical and Systematic Theologians on the Metaphysics of Trinitarian Theology*, as well as *Forsaken: The Trinity and the Cross, and Why It Matters*, and he is a co-author of *Two Views on the Doctrine of the Trinity*. He has published articles in *Philosophia Christi*, the *Trinity Journal*, the *International Journal of Systematic Theology*, and the *Scottish Journal of Theology*, and he has contributed chapters to several edited volumes.

Donald S. Prudlo is Associate Professor of Ancient and Medieval History at Jacksonville State University in Alabama. He is the author of *The Martyred Inquisitor: The Life and Cult of Peter of Verona (†1252)*, *The Origin, Development, and Refinement of Medieval Religious Mendicancies*, and *Certain Sainthood: The Origins of Papal Infallibility in Canonization*, in addition to many articles and chapters on such topics as hagiography, scriptural theology, and Church history. He is currently writing on the history of the early Dominican Order.

Andrew Radde-Gallwitz is Assistant Professor for the Program of Liberal Studies at the University of Notre Dame. He has published two books on the Cappadocians and is finishing the "trilogy" with *Gregory of Nyssa on the Trinity and Christ*. His monograph *Basil of Caesarea, Gregory of Nyssa, and the Transformation of Divine Simplicity* received the Templeton Award for Theological Promise in 2011. With colleagues, he has published annotated translations of patristic texts: *St. Basil of Caesarea: Against Eunomius* with Mark DelCogliano and *Athanasius and Didymus: Works on the Spirit* with Mark DelCogliano and Lewis Ayres.

His articles have appeared in the *Journal of Theological Studies, Vigiliae Christianae*, and the *Journal of Early Christian Studies*. Currently, he is the series editor and a translator for the *Cambridge Edition of Early Christian Writings* and serves on the advisory board of the *Journal of Early Christian Studies*.

Ryan M. Reeves is Associate Professor of Historical Theology and Dean of the Jacksonville Campus of Gordon-Conwell Theological Seminary. He is the author of *Political Obedience and Resistance in Tudor England: 1528–1570* and *The Story of Creeds and Confessions*.

Thomas P. Scheck is Associate Professor of Theology at Ave Maria University. He is the author of *Origen and the History of Justification*; *Erasmus's Life of Origen*; and eight translations of writings of the Church Fathers, the most recent being St. Jerome's *Commentary on Isaiah*.

R. Jared Staudt is Assistant Professor of Theology and Catholic Studies and Director of the Catholic Studies Program at the University of Mary. He served as managing editor and co-editor of the journal *Nova et Vetera* and has written articles for *The Thomist, Nova et Vetera, Logos: A Journal of Catholic Thought and Culture*, and *Angelicum*.

Carl R. Trueman is the Paul Woolley Professor of Church History at Westminster Theological Seminary, Philadelphia. He is the author of *Luther's Legacy: Salvation and English Reformers, 1525–1556*; *John Owen: Reformed Catholic, Renaissance Man*; and numerous other books. He serves on the editorial board of the Reformed Historical Theology Series for Vandenhoeck and Ruprecht.

D. H. Williams is Professor of Religion in Patristics and Historical Theology at Baylor University. He has published numerous academic articles for English and Chinese readers, and is the author or editor of books, including: *Transformations in Biblical Literary Traditions: Incarnation, Narrative, and Ethics*: *Commentarium in Matthaeum* by Hilary of Poitiers. Complete English translation and annotation. Fathers of the Church series vol. 125; *Tradition, Scripture and Interpretation: A Sourcebook of the Ancient Church*; *Evangelicals and Tradition: The Formative*

Influence of the Early Church; *Retrieving the Tradition and Renewing Evangelicalism: A Primer for Suspicious Protestants*; and *Ambrose of Milan and the End of the Nicene Arian Conflicts*.

John Yocum has taught at Greyfriars, Oxford and Loyola School of Theology, Manila. He is the author of *Ecclesial Mediation in Karl Barth*, and co-editor of two volumes on Aquinas.

INDEX

Abelard, Peter, 118–119, 120, 121, 122; atonement, 118; disappointment over satisfaction model, 119; rejection of ransom theory, 119; doctrine of salvation, 119; sanctification and its outworking, 120; soteriology and self-improvement, 119; view of the atonement different than Anselm, 118

Acts 2:23, *44*; 2:36, *106*; 17:24, *263*

Anabaptists, 29, 186

Anselm of Canterbury, 4, 116–117, 121, 122, 124–142, 169; authority, 136–137; baptism, 135, 136; *Cur Deus Homo*, 117, 124, 126, 127, 128, 129, 130, 133, 135, 137, 169; devil, 133–135; divine-human relationship, 118; economy of salvation, 125, 134, 135, 137–138; filioque clause, 129; human depravity, 117; influence, 137–139; *Monologion*, 124, 128; obedience, 136; original sin, 131, 134, 135, 136; post-lapsarian, 129; *Proslogion*, 124, 127, 128, 133; rejection of ransom theory, 116; Scripture, 129–131; sin, 131–133; theology of salvation, 117, 118, 125, 128, 129, 131, 135, 138; traducianism, 129; Trinity, 128; view of the atonement, 118, 125, 135; view of incarnation, 125, 131, 135

antinomianism, 186, 188, 204

Apollinarianism, 96, 100, 110

Aquinas, Thomas, 4, 119–120, 121, 122, 143–159, 183, 192, 228, 336, 345; Christ's work of mediation between God and humanity, 151–154; Council of Lyons, 144; deification and merit, 147–150; effects of Christ's Passion, 144; free will and its role, 147; humanity of Christ, 151, 154; incarnation, 150, 151; justice and justification, 145–147, 154; justification, 119, 146, 148, 153; justification and affect on interior disposition, 119, 120, 154; justification and grace, 144, 145; justification as ongoing process, 120; justification as process of conversion, 147; love of God, 120; Paschal mystery and primary events of salvation, 151; salvation, 119, 120, 144, 149, 150; salvation and human cooperation, 153; salvation and the work of Christ's resurrection, 153; sin and grace, 120; source of salvation in Christ, 150–154; *Summa Contra Gentiles*, 144; *Summa Theologiae*, 144; two types of justice, 145–146

Aristotle, 103

Arminian, 253

Athanasius, 3, 4, 12, 13, 18, 19, 76, 125, 134; active reception, 79; Arians, 76; Christology, 87; Christ's death as sacrificial offering, 84; *Contra Gentes—De Incarnatione*, 76, 83, 84; Council of Nicaea, 76; creation, 77–79; descending of the Word, 84; *Discourses*, 76; divine dilemma; 82–85; divine descent, 82; first cause, 84; full divinity of the Son, 85; grace, 79; incarnation, 77, 82, 84, 86; Irenaeus, 77; ongoing spiritual conflict, 81; partitive exegesis, 86; perfection of the divine work, 89; *philanthropia*, 78;

369

Athanasius (*cont.*)
right objective, 81; role of Holy Spirit in salvific plan, 87; salvation, 82, 89; Scripture, 77; sin and its consequences, 80–81; union with God through the Son of God, 85–89

Augustine, 3, 13, 15, 19, 59, 116, 125, 134, 182, 183, 189, 196, 204, 210, 211, 215, 228, 264, 294; Christology, 68; *The City of God*, 59; communion with God, 65, 67; *Confessions*, 60, 63, 64, 68; Council of Chalcedon, 68; *De doctrina Christiana*, 60; *deification*, 61, 72–73; divided hearts, 64, 73; divine healing, 65–68; effect of salvation, 71; God's goodness, 66, 67; humanity's need of salvation, 60; human rebellion, 61, 63; incarnate Christ, 61, 73; incorporation of humans into Christ's body, 61; legacy of pride, 62; *The Literal Interpretation of Genesis*, 60; moral example of Christ, 70; nature of God's grace, 60; second emptying, 72; theology of salvation, 60, 61–65, 68, 73; theology of sin and grace, 216–217; transformation of the saved, 71–73; unification of natures, 69; whole Christ, 71

Balthasar, Hans Urs van, 5, 6, 124, 257, 304, 318, 322–324; "autonomy" as false freedom, 325; anonymous Christian, 338; atonement, 327–333, four areas of agreement with Rahner, 329; Christian life, 333–336; Christ's suffering at human hands, 331; *Communio*, 319; distaste for propositionalism, 322; co-redeemers through relationship with Christ, 335; divine abandonment, 333; doctrine of justification, 333; doctrine of sanctification, 333; Eastern Christian emphasis on the atonement, 330; Father's wrath, 331, 332; forgiveness in Christ, 333; God-forsakenness, 331; God's glory and salvific effect, 337–338; humans as apex of creation, 336; intersubjective encounters, 323; life after death as surpassing fulfillment of human race, 337; love of God versus love of neighbor, 336; Mary's archetypal faith, 335–336; mystical union, 331; neoscholasticism, 322; original sin and acceptance of Church's position, 326; personal relationship with Jesus of the faithful, 335; principle of divine immutability, 332; reconciliation, 337; salvation, 330, 337; self-transcendent dynamism, 322; sin, 324–326; solidarity in suffering of the Son, 337; supernatural existential, 322; *Theological Aesthetics*, 319

baptism, 135, 136, 182

Barth, Karl, 5, 6, 124, 256, 300–317, 339; atonement, 312; *Christian Life*, 311; *Church Dogmatics*, 300, 307, 308, 310, 311; creation and redemption as two points of one ellipse, 302; doctrine of God, 301, 302, 304; doctrine of election, 301, 305, 306; doctrine of reconciliation, 307–311, 312; doctrine of revelation, 301; election and the God of salvation: In Christ, 303–307, 312; Gospel as nature of election, 306; "in Christ," 303, 304, 312; justification, 307, 308; life of faith and the scope of salvation, 311–314; otherness of God, 301; predestination, 306; *Romerbrief*, 300; salvation, 307, 308, 311, 312, 314; sanctification, 309, 310; self-election of Jesus Christ, 302; soteriological existentialism, 303; soteriological objectivism, 312; soteriology, 306, 312; universalism, 313, 314

Basil of Caesarea, 4, 13, 18, 95, 98–102; *Against Eunomius*, 98; and Apollinarius, 100; and baptism, 101; and healing, 100; and Pelagianism, 102; and salvation, 98, 99, 101, 102; contrasts of

Christ's birth, 100; economic text, 98; *Homily on Humility*, 101; immanent and economic Trinities, 98; interchangeability of humanity and flesh, 99; mode of theology, 98; subsistence before the ages, 98; two perspectives on the Son of God, 98

Behr, John, 41, 363

Bernard of Clairvaux, 216

Billings, J. Todd, 208, 363

Bucer, Martin, 188, 210, 230

Calvin, John, 4, 5, 186, 187, 188, 208, 263, 264; adoption, 209, 210; atonement, 221; baptism and Calvin's theology, 210; departs from Augustine on justification, 217; doctrine of justification, 187, 209, 210, 212, 213, 215, 218, 219, 220, 221, 222; double grace, 187, 209, 212, 214, 215, 216, 217, 218, 220, 222; double grace and the Christian life, 217–219; divine nature, 221; engrafted into Christ, 210, 214; exegetical theologian, 209; expansion of theme through biblical exegesis, 212–216; inseparability of justification and sanctification, 215; *Institutes of the Christian Religion*, 208, 212, 213, 214, 216, 217, 218, 219, 221; mystical union, 220; Osiander controversy, 219–221; prayer and Spirit activation, 217; sacrifice of praise, 218; sanctification, 187, 213–214, 215, 218, 219, 220, 221, 222; shared view with Luther, Melanchthon on doctrine of justification, 212; sum of the gospel, 209, 222; theology of salvation, 208, 209, 215, 221, 222; Trinitarian, 209; theology of union with Christ, 209–211, 212, 214, 216, 217, 220, 221, 222; union with Christ in Calvin's early work, 210–211; union with Christ and Calvin's use of the church fathers, 216–217; view of Mass, 218; work of the Holy Spirit, 220

Cappadocians, 3, 4, 19, 95–112, 106, 110; and Apollinarianism, 96; baptism, 110; Cappadocian Fathers, 95; Christological dogma, 97; doctrinal polemic, 110; mystery of salvation, 96; salvation and Christ's humanity, 97; salvation as the overcoming of death, 96; soteriology, 97, 110

Catholic Reform (a.k.a., Catholic Counter-Reformation), 4, 5, 187–188; 225–247; baptism, 233, 238; confession, 233, 239; contesting the Reformation, 229–231; Council of Trent, 225, 226, 227, 232, 233, 235, 236, 237, 238, 241; Decree on Justification and its significance, 235, 236, 238; developing doctrine, 228–229; divine grace, 229; double justification, 188, 230, 234, 237; Erasmus, 229; extrinsic imputation, 232, 233; First Justification, 227, 233, 238; forensic justification, 230; free will of mankind, 229, 236, 238, 240; fundamental matters, 234–236; hierarchy, 226; imputed justice error, 233; Incarnation, 240, 244; Jansenism, 243; Jesuit order, 225; justification nature and content, 226, 231, 234, 236–238, 237, 239; justification and Catholic doctrine, 232–234; justification and the sacraments, 238–241; limited atonement, 236; Luther against, 229, 232; mediation, 226; nominalism, 228; Paschal mystery, 227, 240; Pelagianism, 229, 234, 235; predestination to evil, 236, 242; sacraments, 226, 227, 239; salvation, 226, 227, 228, 230, 231, 236, 241; salvation and justification as processes, 233; salvation as sanctification, 227, 237; sanctification, 237, 239, 244; scripture, 226; Second Justification, 231; Tridentine Council, 231–232, 241–243; voluntarism, 228; will of God for salvation, 236

Christology, 19
Christus Victor, 2
Clement of Rome, 23
Colossians 1:15, *43*; 1:18, *227*, *234*
Council of Trent, 5, 187, 225, 226, 227, 232, 233, 235, 236, 237, 238, 241, 252
Cyril of Alexandria, 216
Cyril of Jerusalem, 15, 16

deificatio, 19
deification, 2, 18, 61, 72–73
Deuteronomy 6:5, *273*; 7:9, *263*; 7:12, *263*; 11:26–28, *263*; 30:15, *263*
Devil, 115, 133; harrowing of Hell, 115
Dickens, W. T., 318, 364

Enlightenment, 252, 254
Ephesians 1:22–23, *234*; 1:23, *109*; 5, *336*; 5:27, *240*; 6:12, *14*
Erasmus, 201, 229
Eunomius, 16, 98, 110
Exodus 3:14, *171*
Ezekiel 33:11, *263*; 33:20, *263*; 44:9, *27*
Ezra 9:13–14, *263*

Faith and Science, war between, 252, 255
First Corinthians 2:2, *123*; 4:17, *101*; 5:9–11, *28*; 8:11, *263*; 10, *30*; 12:5–9, *68*; 13, *122*; 15, *46*, *108*; 15:21–22, *83*; 15:28, *109*; 15:36, *46*; 15:44, *46*, *46*; 15:45–46, *48*, *49*; 15:50, *48*
First John 2:1–2, *263*; 4:14, *263*
First Peter 1:4; *18*; 3:15, *130*; 3:18–20, *116*
First Thessalonians 4:1–7, *28*
First Timothy 2:3–4, *263*; 2:4, *236*; 2:6, *115*, *263*; 4:10, *263*; 6:15, *83*
fundamentalism, 256

Galatians 4:27, *54*; 5:6, *233*; 6:7–9, *28*
Gasper, Giles E. M., 124, 364
Genesis 1, *337*; 1:26, *55*; 1:26–27, *43*; 1:27, *62*; 1:31, *62*; 2:7, *49*; 3:5, *62*, *63*; 3:17, *263*; 4:7, *263*; 45:5, *8*, *44*

Gordon, James, 281, 364
Greggs, Tom, 300, 363
Gregory of Nazianzus, 4, 14, 16, 17, 19, 95, 110, 125, 134; and the incarnation of Christ, 102, 104; and salvation, 102, 104; Apollinarian controversy, 104; autobiographical Christology, 102; deifying humanity, 104; exchange, 103; mixture versus complete mixture, 102–103, 104; *Theological Orations*, 102, 104; sacrament of baptism, 104; Tree of Knowledge as contemplation, 103
Gregory of Nyssa, 4, 19, 95, 96, 133; *Catechetical Oration*, 107; Christology, 109; Christ's role in saving humanity, 106, 108; divine nature, 107; doctrine of perpetual progress, 109; Eunomius, 16; God's universal providence, 107; humanity's original state as perfection, 105; human nature, 107; incarnation, 107; like by like, 108; Logos and deception, 107; mixture, 106, 107; *On Virginity*, 105; *On the Making of Humanity*, 105; paschal transformation, 107; three themes about the eschaton, 109; universal salvation, 109; vision of salvation, 108
Gutiérrez, Gustavo, 5, 6, 258, 344–362; Christological mysteries, 354–355; Church as sacrament of liberation, 351–354; definition of salvation, 345, 351; "distinction of planes," 353; dualistic salvation, 346, 347, 348; "ecclesiastical narcissism," 352; efficacy of human action, 348; God's self-revelation, 346, 348; integral salvation, 346–348, 354; "irruption of the poor," 359; Jesus of liberation, Christ of solidarity, 354–356; Latin America, 345; liberation from sin, 351; liberation theology, 6, 258, 344, 345, 348–351; neo-scholastic thought versus Gutiérrez, 346, 353,

359; patristic theology, 356; "political Augustinianism," 352; Roman Catholic Church, 344, 352, 354; socioeconomic, 350; soteriology, 348, 355; *Theology of Liberation*, 344, 345; theology of salvation, 346, 347, 348, 350; salvific will of God, 355; three levels of meaning in liberation, 350–351; three meanings of poverty, 357–359; three models of soteriology, 352; unity in history, 348; universal call of humanity, 348; "utopian-historical," 350

Hebrews 2:9, 263; 2:10, *19*; 2:9, 14–15, *83*
Hide, Kerrie, 160, 364
Hogg, David, 115, 365
Holcomb, Justin S., 363

Irenaeus, 3, 13, 15, 16, 41, 115, 134; *Against the Heresies*, 41, 46; animation, 46, 47, 49, 50, 52; arc of the economy, 48, 49; baptism as regeneration, 53; beginning with Christ, the Savior, 41–45; Christ is first human, 51–55; Christ first shows life of God in human form, 43; *Demonstration of the Apostolic Preaching*, 41; economy, 44, 45, 52; finding of salvation, 51; generations, 46, 53; gospel as recapitulation of Scripture through the cross, 42; humanity subject to mortality, 52; inheritance, 48; pre-exist, 45; sign of Jonah, 49–51; task of theology, 44; type, 43, 45; vivification, 46, 47, 49, 52
Isaiah 25:8, *48*; 42–53, *164*; 42:5, *48*; 45:2, 263; 54:1, *53*; 57:16, *48*

James 2, *122*; 2:17, 26, *28*
James, Frank A., III, 181, 365
Job 36:5, 263
John 1:3–4, *46*; 1:29, 263; 3:17, 67, 263; 5:34–40, 263; 9:3, *54*; 12:47, 263; 14:6, 26; 15:5, 234; 19:5, 55

Julian of Norwich, 4, 120–123, 160–177; atonement, 164; be-closed, 169; beholding and seeing, 162–163; bliss, 169; Christogenesis, 167; Christophany, 163; illness experience, 160; knowledge that leads to love of God, 122; mysticism, 121; oneing through joy, 169–172; oneing through love, 167–169; prayer and beseeking, 173; revelations of God, 122; *Revelation of Love*, 160; salvific presence of Christ, 171, 174; showings, 162; soteriology, 121, 173; soteriology of oneing, 161–162, 163–174; suffering and salvation, 161, 164–167; three beholdings, 162; three revelations of the crucified Christ, 164–172; view of salvation, 122, 161, 162, 167

late medieval soteriologies, 182
Lee, Michael Edward, 344, 365
Liberalism, modern, 256
liberation theology, 6, 257, 258
Lombard, Peter, 137, 143
Luke 6:46, 28; 19:41, 263; 23:47, 26; 24:26–27, 42
Luther, Martin, 4, 5, 29, 182, 187, 188, 191–207, 210, 216, 251, 253; *Anfectungen*, 182, 183, 184, 189, 194; Antinomian Controversy, 203, 204; baptism and Luther's understanding of, 194–195, 199; Crucial Period of 1514–1520, 194; distinction with regard to perspicuity, 201; divine grace, 184; divine will, 193; doctrine of justification, 181, 183, 185, 188, 186, 193, 195, 198, 200, 202, 204, 211; error with Erasmus, 201; Heidelberg Disputation, 195, 196, 197, 198, 200; human will, 201; humility and development of, 195–204; imputation, 200; *Large Catechism*, 202; Law-Gospel dialectic, 202, 253; *Ninety Five Theses Against Indulgences*, 196; *pactum* idea, 193; *Small Catechism*, 202; theology of the cross, 197;

Luther, Martin (*cont.*)
theology of human impotence, 200; theology of salvation, 183, 192, 193, 199, 204; theology of sin and grace, 211; theses for debating theological and philosophical topics, 196; transubstantiation, 199; sanctification, 185; union with Christ, 211; *via moderna*, 192; whole Christ, 199; will of God, 201; wonderful exchange between Christian and Christ, 184

Mark 10:45, *115*; 16:15, *263*
Matthew 5:17, *28*; 5:20, *30*; 5:44–45, *25*; 7:24, *28*; 11:29, *26*; 20:28, *115*; 22:9, *263*; 24:13, *17*; 25:1–12, *27*
McCall, Thomas H., 261, 366
Meconi, David Vincent, 59, 365
Melanchthon, Philip, 185, 188, 200, 210, 211; doctrine of justification, 211; imputed righteousness, 185, 200, 211; sanctification, 211
Middle Ages, 4, 115; and soteriology, 122
Moral example, 2, 70
Moral Transformation, 2
Moravian theology, 253, 254

neo-scholasticism, 257, 319
Nicene Creed, 1, 330

oneing, 4, 161–162, 163–174
Origen, 3, 13, 14, 16, 22, 65, 108, 115; adoption, 31; *Commentary on Romans*, 17; conversion in three stages, 29; divine-human cooperation, 35; doctrine of salvation, 22, 29; faith and works, 28–32; final salvation, 25; grace of Christ, 25; Hexapla, 22; justification, 27, 31; moral transformation, 35; reconciliation, 31; salvation, 33–37; theory of original sin, 24; two justifications, 29; two kinds of faith, 29; unity and synthesis, 29; universal reconciliation,

32–33; work of the Incarnate Word, 24; works of the law, 33–37
original sin, 182, 189, 235, 266, 288, 294

Paschal mystery, 151, 227, 240
Pelagius, 182, 251, 288; denial of intrinsic grace, 228; emphasis of free will, 228
Penal Substitution, 2
Philippians 2:7, *69*; 2:12, *226*; 3:6, *42*
Pietism, 253, 254
Platonism, 24
Prudlo, Donald S., 225, 366
Protestantism: salvation from *anfectungen*, 182–187, two branches, 186
Proverbs 1:23, *263*; 1:44, *101*
Psalm 32:1–2, *29*; 71:19, *63*; 106:31, *33*; 145:9, *263*

Radde-Gallwitz, Andrew, 95, 366
Rahner, Karl, 5, 6, 257, 318, 320–322, 346, 355; anonymous Christian, 338–339; atonement, 327–333, four areas of agreement with Balthasar, 329; baptized Christian, 339; Christian life, 333–336; divine immutability, 332; doctrine of justification, 333; doctrine of sanctification, 333; Eucharist and other sacraments, 334; forgiveness in Christ, 333; *Foundations of Christian Faith*, 318; God-forsakenness, 328; humans as apex of creation, 336; life after death as surpassing fulfillment of human race, 337; nature of poverty, 356; neoscholasticism, 320, 321; personal relationship with Jesus of the faithful, 335; pre-apprehension, 321; preferential option for the poor, 356; "quasi-sacramental" event of Jesus, 239; reconciliation, 337; Resurrection, 328; salvation, 337, 338; salvific will of God, 328; self-delusion, 325; sin, 324–326; self-transcendence, 321, 324, 325, 327, 338; supernatural existential, 321, 337, 338; *Theological*

Investigations, 318; transcendental theology, 322, 338; view of death, 328
Ransom, 2, 115
reconciliation, 182, 284, 307–311, 312, 337
Reeves, Ryan, 251, 367
Reformation, 4, 181, 229–231; context of salvation, 181
regeneration, 182, 186, 268–273, 296
Revelation 5, *42*; 21:20, *240*
Romans 1:17, *196*; 2:6–10, *28*; 3:6, *67*; 3:9–18, *24*; 3:28, *33*; 4:5, *147*; 4:6–8, *30*; 4:7–8, *29*; 4:24–25, *35*; 5, *332*; 5:14, *41*, *43*; 5:18, *25*, *263*; 6, *214*; 6:3, *53*; 6:11, *35*; 8, *214*, *217*; 8:2, *33*; 8:17, *149*; 8:29, *215*; 9, *265*; 9:13, *66*; 10:9–10, *36*; 10:12, *263*; 11, *215*; 11:6, *33*; 14:12, *28*; 14:15, *263*

Salvation, 181, 252, 258, 259; and faith through repentance, 15–16; as a line, 16–18; as demonstration of God's omnipotence, 14–15; as divinization, 18; as sacramental process, 187–188; by grace, 189; fulfilled through baptism, 16; of exchange, 19; role in modern theology, 259; salvific mission of Jesus, 181
Satisfaction, 2, 119
Scheck, Thomas P., 22, 367
Schleiermacher, Friedrich, 5, 6, 253, 281–299; blessedness, 6; *Christian Faith*, 254, 282, 283, 285, 298; Christology, 293; Christ's and the corporate life of blessedness, 289–290; Christ's person and work, 291–296; consciousness of grace, 298; conversion, 296–297; corporate consciousness of sin, 288, 290; creation and sin for redemption, 290–291; doctrine of regeneration, 296; doctrine of salvation, 285, 298; doctrine of sanctification, 296, 297; doctrine of sin, 285, 288; empirical view of salvation, 284, 295; Fall of humanity, 288; Father of Modern Liberal Theology, 282; incarnation of Christ, 293; individual's experience of Christ's redemption, 296; justification, 297; liberal Enlightenment, 282; magical view of sin and salvation, 284, 295; mystical view of salvation, 283, 295; original and actual sin, 287–288, 289, 293; reconciliation, 284; redemption in Christ, 284, 289, 295; religious consciousness, 283; repentance and faith, 296; sin and God-consciousness, 285, 286–287, 290, 291, 292, 293, 294, 295, 297, 298; sin and self-consciousness, 285, 287; sin and salvation, 283–285; sin in light of redemption, 285; two distinct groups of actual sin, 289; unclouded blessedness, 295
Second Chronicles 15:1–2, 263
Second Corinthians 3:12–4:6, *42*; 5:10, *28*; 5:14, *83*, *263*
Second Peter 1:4, *148*; 2:1, *263*; 3:9, *263*
Second Vatican Council, 352, 353
Staudt, R. Jared, 143, 367
Synod of Dordt, 252

Theologies of Salvation, 1, 2; mapping of, 6; Patristic theologies, 3; unifying theme, 6
theosis, 18, 19
Titus 1:3, *83*
Trueman, Carl, 191, 367

Vermigli, 186, 210; justification, 186; regeneration, 186; sanctification, 186

Wesley, Charles, 11, 261, 267
Wesley, John, 5, 251, 261–280; baptism and new birth, 270; Calvinist soteriology and differences, 263; divine justice, 264; doctrine of assurance, 274; doctrine of irresistible grace, 262, 263; doctrine of justification, 261, 266–268, 271; doctrine of limited atonement, 262, 264; doctrine of original sin, 270;

Wesley, John (*cont.*)
doctrine of salvation, 261, 266; doctrine of sanctification, 262; doctrine of unconditional election, 262; entire sanctification, 273; evangelism and works of mercy and justice, 275; genuine Christians, 270; implications of the Gospel and the hope of glory, 275–277; Methodist Articles of Religion, 267; perseverance and assurance in the Christian life, 273–275; predestination and election, 262–266, against Reformed, 265; regeneration and sanctification, 268–273; regeneration as gate into process of sanctification, 272; salvation, 273, 276; sanctification of the Holy Spirit, 253, 266, 267, 268, 271, 272; theological framework of Wesley's soteriology, 262; theology, 253; two senses of election, 265; Zinzendorf and Wesley's rejection of instantaneous perfection, 270

Williams, D. H., 11, 367

Wisdom of Solomon, 80

Yocum, John, 76, 368

Zwingli, Ulrich, 187, 263